English and Celtic in Contact

Routledge Studies in Germanic Linguistics

SERIES EDITORS: EKKEHARD KÖNIG, *Free University Berlin, Germany*
JOHAN VAN DER AUWERA, *Antwerp University, Belgium*

English and Celtic in Contact

Markku Filppula, Juhani Klemola, and Heli Paulasto

Routledge
Taylor & Francis Group
New York   London

First published 2008
by Routledge
711 Third Avenue, New York, NY 10017

Simultaneously published in the UK
by Routledge
2 Park Square, Milton Park, Abingdon, Oxon OX14 4RN

Routledge is an imprint of the Taylor & Francis Group, an informa business

© 2008 Markku Filppula, Juhani Klemola, and Heli Paulasto

Typeset in Sabon by IBT Global.

Library of Congress Cataloging in Publication Data
Filppula, Markku.
English and Celtic in contact / by Markku Filppula, Juhani Klemola, and Heli Paulasto.
p. cm. -- (Routledge studies in Germanic linguistics)
Includes bibliographical references and index.
ISBN-13: 978-0-415-26602-4 (hardcover : acid-free paper)
ISBN-10: 0-415-26602-5 (hardcover : acid-free paper)
ISBN-13: 978-0-203-89500-9 (e-book)
ISBN-10: 0-203-89500-2 (e-book)
1. Celtic languages--Influence on English. 2. Languages in contact--Great Britain.
3. Sociolinguistics--Great Britain. 4. English language--Foreign elements--Celtic.
I. Klemola, Juhani. II. Paulasto, Heli. III. Title.

PE1582.C4F55 2008
422'.4916--dc22   2007051461

ISBN13: 978-0-415-26602-4 (hbk)
ISBN13: 978-0-203-89500-9 (ebk)
ISBN13: 978-0-415-63672-8 (pbk)

Contents

EPILOGUE
The Extent of Celtic Influences in English

List of Figures

List of Tables

List of Maps

Abbreviations

AAVE	African American Vernacular English
ACC	accusative
AI	Anglo-Irish
AmE	American English
Arm.	Armorican (Breton)
B.	Breton
BrE	British English
C.	Cornish
CamE	Cameroon English
CE	Celtic English
CUD	*A Concise Ulster Dictionary*
DAT	dative
DOST	*A Dictionary of the Older Scottish Tongue*
EDD	*The English Dialect Dictionary*
EI	embedded inversion
EngE	English English
EModE	Early Modern English
FEM	feminine
FF	focus fronting
G.	German
GPC	*Geiriadur Prifysgol Cymru* [Dictionary of the Welsh Language]
HE	Hiberno-English
HebE	Hebridean English
HVE	*A Handbook of Varieties of English*
ICE	*The International Corpus of English*
INF	infinitive
Ir.	Irish
IrE	Irish English
L.	Latin
LAE	*The Linguistic Atlas of England*
LAEME	*A Linguistic Atlas of Early Middle English*

LALME	*A Linguistic Atlas of Late Mediaeval English*
ME	Middle English
MED	*Middle English Dictionary*
MEG	*A Modern English Grammar*
M.Ir.	Middle Irish
Mn	Manx
ModE	Modern English
MW	Middle Welsh
MxE	Manx English
NfldE	Newfoundland English
NICTS	*Northern Ireland Corpus of Transcribed Speech*
NORM	non-mobile, older, rural male
NP	noun phrase
NIrE	northern Irish English
NSR	Northern Subject Rule
O	object
OE	Old English
OED	*The Oxford English Dictionary*
OEG	*Old English Grammar*
OF	Old French
OHG	Old High German
O.Ir.	Old Irish
OSaxon	Old Saxon
OW	Old Welsh
PF	progressive form
PL	plural
PP	prepositional phrase
PRO	pronoun
PT	particle
REL	relative (pronoun/particle)
REL-COMP	relative complementiser
RP	received pronunciation
S	subject
SAWD	*The Survey of Anglo-Welsh Dialects*
ScE	Scottish English
Sc.G.	Scottish Gaelic
SED	*The Survey of English Dialects*
SIrE	southern Irish English
SND	*The Scottish National Dictionary*
SSE	Standard Scottish English
StE	Standard English
TL	target language
TMA	tense-mood-aspect
UE	Ulster English

U.Sc.	Ulster Scots
V	verb
V2	verb-second (constraint)
VP	verb phrase
W.	Welsh
WE	Welsh English

Acknowledgments

A substantial part of the research reported in this book was carried out under the auspices of the research project entitled *English and Celtic in Contact*, which was financially supported by the Humanities and Social Sciences Section of the Academy of Finland for the years 2000–2002 (Academy Project no. 47424). The work was subsequently continued and completed within our follow-up project, also funded by the Academy of Finland, and entitled *Vernacular Universals vs. Contact-Induced Language Change* (2005–2008; Academy Project no. 210702). It is clear that a volume of this size—and, hopefully, of some depth, too—could not have been accomplished without the financial support from the Academy. Other institutions that have supported our work in many ways include, of course, our home universities in Joensuu and Tampere, and we also benefited from a cooperative agreement between our first project and the Research Unit for Variation and Change in English (*VARIENG*) at the University of Helsinki, where Juhani Klemola was able to work in the period 2000–2002. Of particular importance has been the scholarly and material support offered by the School of Celtic Studies at the Dublin Institute for Advanced Studies. Markku Filppula was given the opportunity to spend the academic year 2001–2002 there as Visiting Professor, and with the help of funding from the School he returned there for two other research and writing periods in 2005 and 2007. Apart from these periods, the School and its magnificent library have over the years provided us with a base for our research on several other occasions. We remain particularly grateful to the Director of the School, Prof. Fergus Kelly, and his successor as Director from 2005 to 2006, Prof. Liam Breatnach, as well as to the School Administrator, Mrs Eibhlín Nic Dhonncha, for generously allowing us to use the School's facilities during our stays in Dublin.

Other institutions that have supported our work in some way or another include *LANGNET*, the Finnish Graduate School in Language Studies, which provided funding for Heli Paulasto for the period 2000–2002; and *CREW*, the Centre for Research into the English Literature and Language of Wales at the Swansea University, where Heli Paulasto was able to access their archives of recordings from different dialects of Welsh English.

In the course of the last few years we have been greatly helped in various ways by a large number of colleagues. The project got to a most fruitful start through the *International Colloquium on Early Contacts between English and the Celtic Languages*, which our project group organised at the University of Joensuu Research Station in Mekrijärvi, Finland, 24–26 August, 2001. This Colloquium brought together a select group of scholars from different parts of the world, with each contributing to the general theme from various points of view: historical, general linguistic and typological, Celticist, and Anglicist. The volume arising from the Colloquium, *The Celtic Roots of English*, has proved to be an invaluable source of information and inspiration for us and, indeed, for anyone interested in the early history of the language contacts in Britain. We are greatly indebted to all of the participants at the Colloquium and especially those contributing papers to the Colloquium volume: Anders Ahlqvist, Andrew Breeze, Richard Coates, Nick Higham, Stephen Laker, Erich Poppe, Patricia Ronan, Peter Schrijver, Hildegard L.C. Tristram, Theo Vennemann, David L. White and Kalevi Wiik.

Nick Higham and Ray Hickey also deserve our best thanks for reading and commenting on earlier versions of some of the chapters in the present book. Anders Ahlqvist, Angelika Lutz, Hildegard L.C. Tristram and Theo Vennemann have likewise shared with us their wisdom on matters Celtic on numerous occasions over the years and provided food for our thoughts on the subject of language contacts and especially Celtic influence on the languages of western Europe. We have also greatly benefited from our close links with many colleagues working or associated with the School of Celtic Studies in Dublin. We remain particularly grateful to the late Proinsias Mac Cana; Mark Scowcroft, Roibeard Ó Maolalaigh, Malachy McKenna, and Brian Ó Curnáin.

The series of colloquia on *Celtic Englishes*, organised by Hildegard L.C. Tristram in Potsdam on four different occasions from 1997 onwards, has served as an important catalyst for our research, by helping us to exchange views with other scholars, too numerous to list here, from all over the world. Some of the best results from these discussions, we hope, have found an adequate expression in especially Part II of this book.

It is a well-known fact that what we call here the 'Celtic hypothesis' has yet to win the support of those scholars who are wont to think that Celtic influence on English has been minimal. This, indeed, is the traditional wisdom in this matter. In this context, we would like to thank those who have on various occasions wanted to exchange views with us, despite possible differences of opinion, thereby demonstrating their openness to new and unconventional approaches to prevailing views. We have particularly benefited from discussions with Michael Benskin, David Denison, Dieter Kastovsky and Peter Kitson.

We are greatly indebted to scholars and/or publishers who have kindly given us permission to use maps from their published works: Prof. Charles W.J. Withers for permission to reproduce three maps from his works; Prof.

Kenneth MacKinnon for permission to reproduce his linguistic map of Scotland; Professors John Aitchison and Harold Carter for permission to use their language map of Wales; Dr W.T.R. Pryce for the map on the mid-eighteenth-century language situation in Wales; Prof. Matthew Spriggs for the map on the retreat of the Cornish language; The Four Courts Press, Dublin, for the map of British river-names in Jackson (1953); Prof. Clive Upton and the University of Leeds for map M70 from *The Linguistic Atlas of England*; and Dr Michael Barry and the Society for Folklife Studies for the map showing the distribution of Celtic numerals in Northern England and Southern Scotland.

Finally, we would like to thank Ms Minna Korhonen for her indispensable help in compiling the bibliography and preparing the texts and the other materials for publication. Our publisher, Routledge, deserve special thanks for their patience in waiting for so long for this book to be completed. We can only hope that the years we have spent on it have resulted in a volume that makes the long wait worthwhile.

Joensuu and Tampere, November 2007
Markku Filppula   Juhani Klemola   Heli Paulasto

Introduction

Throughout its recorded history, the English language has been known to have absorbed linguistic influences of all kinds from other languages, such as Latin, Scandinavian and French, in particular. Indeed, it is this permeable nature of English that has often been put forward as a major factor explaining the spread of English all over the world and its present-day status as a *lingua franca*. Against this background, it seems remarkable that there is one group of languages which—as is commonly argued—has left virtually no traces in English, despite a close coexistence in the British Isles spanning for more than one and a half millennia. This group is, of course, the Insular Celtic languages, the present-day members of which are Welsh, Irish and Scottish Gaelic. Their 'resurrected' siblings Cornish and Manx Gaelic could arguably also be included in that number, although they no longer have the same status as living community languages.

The usual explanation for the impermeability of English against Celtic influences rests not so much on any linguistic properties of English or Celtic but on sociopolitical and cultural factors surrounding the relationships between the English and the Celtic populations, starting from the Anglo-Saxon conquest of Britain in the mid-fifth century onwards and extending up to the present day. The Celts have throughout the history of their encounters with the English and their ancestors, Anglo-Saxons, been the underdogs from a political, military and also cultural point of view, and it is this hegemony of the English which is commonly believed to have blocked any significant linguistic influences from the Celtic languages upon English. The small number of Celtic loanwords in English is usually cited as definitive proof of this; the conquering nation has never, as the argument goes, had any practical need to borrow words from the language of the conquered.

Why, then, investigate Celtic influences in English, when several generations of scholars have painstakingly proved that, apart from those few loanwords, the Celtic languages have not left any marks in English? First of all, fresh archaeological and historical evidence is now available about the relationships of the Celts and the Anglo-Saxons in the first few centuries following the arrival of the Anglo-Saxons which sheds new light on the relative positions of these populations, population movements, and especially on the vexed question of the fate of the British Celtic population in the aftermath of the Anglo-Saxon settlement. Rather than being exterminated by the Anglo-Saxons, as the 'clean sweep' theory has maintained, the Celtic-speaking population continued to live side by side with their new rulers in many areas and, after a period of extensive bilingualism, were gradually absorbed into them both linguistically and culturally. This is also supported by the latest population genetic studies, which point to a significant degree of continuity of the indigenous Celtic-speaking population even in the southern parts of England. Taken together, all this evidence has repercussions on the question of the linguistic outcomes of the Celtic–English contacts.

Secondly, the standard arguments about the lack of evidence for Celtic contacts rest on grounds which cannot be sustained in the light of our present-day knowledge about language contacts and their typical outcomes globally. The nature of contact influences has been found to vary depending on the type of sociohistorical conditions in a given contact situation. Thus, in conditions of language shift, such as those which have characterised many parts of the British Isles for centuries, contact influences can be expected to be found in the domains of phonology and syntax rather than lexicon. Efforts to brush aside the Celtic substratum on the basis of lexical evidence only are therefore seriously misguided. We believe that it is time to reinterpret the available evidence by putting it in a cross-linguistic perspective and availing of the recent advances in the general theory of language contacts, language typology and areal linguistics.

Thirdly, there is also new evidence about the history and later stages of both English and the Celtic languages which can be brought to bear on this issue and which was not there when the early twentieth-century philologists formulated their views. Fourthly, it is often forgotten that the prevailing view on the paucity of Celtic influences in English has never been accepted by all of the scholars working on historical and linguistic contacts between English and Celtic. From very early on, there have been dissident voices, which have not, however, received the attention they would have deserved but which merit to be re-heard now. Indeed, there is reason to believe that the traditional views on the nature and outcomes of the English–Celtic contacts have at least partially been inspired by other than purely linguistic agendas. We are here referring to an ideological stand known as 'Anglo-Saxonism', which—as will be shown below—has informed the views of many influential scholars writing on these issues. It is true that extreme views have also been expressed on the part of those who have defended the 'Celtic hypothesis'. 'Substrato-maniacs' or 'Celto-maniacs' are the terms which have sometimes been used for representatives of this position by those who want to deny any Celtic influences in English. The existence of these kinds of extremist views is yet another factor which underlines the need for a new, open discussion on the exact nature of the English–Celtic contacts.

The book has been divided into two major parts, the first of which examines the earliest, i.e. mediaeval, contacts and their historical background.

The discussion focuses on a number of syntactic, phonological and also lexical features which can be considered to have a Celtic substratal origin or which are hard to explain without assuming at least some kind of Celtic connection. The second part is devoted to similar Celtic influences in the modern age, which means essentially the emergence of the so-called Celtic Englishes, i.e. Celtic-influenced varieties of English, in the formerly or presently Celtic-speaking areas in Wales, Scotland, Ireland and the Isle of Man. Although the sociohistorical settings of the modern contacts are different in some respects from those in the mediaeval periods, the linguistic outcomes are rather similar. Indeed, the Celtic substratal influences that we can now witness in the various 'Celtic Englishes' provide indirect support for similar effects in varieties of mediaeval English. Finally, in the Epilogue, we return to the ongoing debate on the extent of Celtic influences in English across the centuries and seek to provide answers and conclusions drawing on the discussion in the first two parts of the book.

Finally, a note on the division of labour between the authors. Each of us has contributed to this book not only on the basis of his/her areas of expertise but by reading through and commenting on the draft chapters prepared by one or the other of the co-authors. In that sense we share the responsibility for the contents of this book, including possible errors and other shortcomings.

Part I
Early Celtic Influences in English

1 The Historical Background to the Early Contacts

1.1 THE ARRIVAL OF THE ANGLO-SAXONS AND THE CONQUEST OF BRITAIN

The mid-fifth century AD has come to be cited as the crucial date which marks the beginning of a new era in the relationship between the Insular Celts and the Anglo-Saxons. The last Roman legions had left Britain in the early part of the fifth century, leaving behind a country which was characterised by confusion and lack of a strong administrative centre. Although there is evidence for some amount of contacts between the Celts (i.e. Britons) and the Anglo-Saxons even before the mid-fifth century (see, e.g. Jackson 1953: 197; Higham 1994: 118–145), historical tradition has it that it was in 449 that the first major Anglo-Saxon force, led by Hengest and Horsa, set foot in Britain. Though first invited by the Britons as allies against foreign raiders such as the 'Picts' of Scotland and the 'Scots' (i.e. the Irish), they soon embarked on a series of rebellions against their hosts, which eventually led to an almost wholesale conquest of Britain within the next couple of centuries. As Jackson (1953: 199) writes, our main source of information here is the historical account by the British monk Gildas, who according to Jackson wrote his *De excidio et conquestu Britanniae* sometime in the first half of the sixth century. Sims-Williams (1983: 3–5) points out some caveats in this dating, including the doubtful authority of the *Annales Cambriae*, on which it mainly rests. He is himself content to settle for a fairly broad dating in the sixth century, at a period earlier than the first reference to Gildas by Columbanus ca 600, and later than the fifth century "because of Gildas's vagueness about the known history of the early part of that century" (*op. cit.*, 5). However, a somewhat earlier date is proposed by Higham (1994: 141), who places the composition of *De excidio* within the late fifth century, that is, around fifty years after the *adventus Saxonum*. Although little is known about Gildas's person or even where he wrote his work, there is evidence which suggests that he was based somewhere in central southern England (Higham 1994: 111–113; see, however, Sims-Williams 1983 for a more sceptical view). Other important near-contemporary sources are the two Gallic Chronicles of 452 and 511 (see Higham 1992: 69). Well-known, though significantly later, sources are the *Historia Ecclesiastica Gentis Anglorum* from the early eighth century, written by the Anglo-Saxon monk Beda Venerabilis (the Venerable Bede), and somewhat later still, the *Anglo-Saxon Chronicle*, which was compiled by several authors working in different places at different times, with the earliest versions dating from the ninth century.

While the first hostilities between the Britons and the Anglo-Saxons were relatively widespread and extended even to the western parts of Britain, they did not lead to permanent settlements by the latter except in some eastern parts of the country. Furthermore, after their initial setbacks, the Britons were able to fight back the invading Anglo-Saxon armies and even secure peace for some decades during the latter half of the fifth century. Gildas names Ambrosius Aurelianus, a British aristocrat probably of Roman extraction, as the person who was alone able to rally the Britons behind him to battle off the Saxon armies:

> After a time, when the cruel plunderers had gone home, God gave strength to the survivors. Wretched people fled to them from all directions, as eagerly as bees to the beehive when a storm threatens, and begged whole-heartedly, 'burdening heaven with unnumbered prayers', that they should not be altogether destroyed. Their leader was Ambrosius Aurelianus, a gentleman who, perhaps alone of the Romans, had survived the shock of this notable storm: certainly his parents, who had worn the purple, were slain in it. His descendants in our day have become greatly inferior to their grandfather's excellence. Under him our people regained their strength, and challenged the victors to battle. The Lord assented, and the battle went their way.
>
> From then on victory went now to our countrymen, now to their enemies: so that in this people the Lord could make trial (as he tends to) of his latter-day Israel to see whether it loves him or not. This lasted right up till the year of the siege of Badon Hill, pretty well the last defeat of the villains, and certainly not the least. That was the year of my birth; as I know, one month of the forty-fourth year since then has already passed.

> (Winterbottom 1978: 28)

After a short-lived truce, the situation changed rapidly along with new invasions by the Saxons along the Thames valley and from the southern coast, starting already at the beginning of the sixth century. As Jackson (1953: 203–206) writes, relying here on the evidence from the Anglo-Saxon Chronicle, the second half of the sixth century witnessed great expansion of the Anglo-Saxon kingdom of Wessex, formed in the first half of the sixth century by the Saxon chiefs Cerdic and Cynric. By around 600, Wessex reached as far west as the River Severn, and further south, to the forest of Selwood on the borders of Wiltshire and Somerset. This meant that the Britons of Wales were cut off from the Britons of the south-west of Britain, leading eventually to the separation and division of the (Late) British dialects into Welsh and Cornish, respectively. After a brief respite of some fifty years, the kingdom of Wessex pushed further west, first conquering the remaining parts of Somerset, Devon and possibly parts of Dorset (although, as Jackson points out, the Chronicle has nothing to say about Dorset at this period), with the conquest of Devon being completed in the early decades of the eighth century. Cornwall remained in British hands for another hundred years, and according to Jackson (1953: 206) retained some form of independence, though probably sharing the power with the Anglo-Saxons in the final stages, up until the time of Athelstan, who was king of England from 925 to 939. Wakelin (1975: 67) provides a more detailed account of the Saxon settlements in Cornwall in 1086 on the basis of the Domesday Book. From this survey of tenure and population as well as the place-names recorded in it, Wakelin concludes that the north-east and south-east of Cornwall were firmly Anglo-Saxon by this time, with its nomenclature being mostly English; to the south and west of these areas, by contrast, the majority of the place-names and settlements were still Cornish (Wakelin 1975: 65f.). Yet, combining the evidence from Domesday Book and other sources, such as the Bodmin Gospels, written in the early tenth century, leads Wakelin to conclude that by 1086 the whole of Cornwall had already been brought under the rule of an Anglo-Saxon minority (Wakelin 1975: 67).

In the north of Britain, the Anglo-Saxon conquest proceeded similarly along major waterways such as the Trent and the Humber. Settlements in the north and the Midlands led to the establishment of the Anglian kingdoms of Lindsey and Mercia, respectively. The latter was rather weak at first, as Jackson (1953: 207) writes, and did not become a powerful kingdom until the second quarter of the seventh century. Under their king Penda (d. 655 AD), Mercia conquered large areas both from their West Saxon cousins in the south and the Welsh in the west. Jackson refers here to the often-expressed view according to which the Mercians also managed to reach the sea in the north and thus break the land connection between the Welsh and the Britons of the North. He does not, however, find any solid evidence to substantiate this claim; even the victory at the battle of Chester in 613 or 616 was won by the Northumbrians, not by the Mercians (Jackson 1953: 210–211). In any case, the Anglo-Saxon advances to the north proved to have significant consequences for the later development of the Celtic languages, as it meant an areal separation of the Welsh and Cumbric dialects of Late British.

The western expansion of Mercia under Penda and his followers also led to the establishment of the borderline between Wales and England around such landmarks as the River Wye in the south and the boundary earthwork known as Wat's Dyke, running from the River Dee to near the town of Oswestry. This, as Jackson remarks, probably marked the western border of Mercia about the middle of the seventh century (1953: 211). Somewhat later, Wat's Dyke was followed by another earthwork called Offa's Dyke, raised by king Offa of Mercia in the late eight century. Its southern end was at the mouth of the River Wye, from which it ran via Hereford and Shrewsbury northwards, finishing near Wrexham. According to Jackson (1953: 211), Offa's Dyke consolidated the borderline situation which had already been established for more than a hundred years earlier.

In the far north, the earliest Germanic settlements recorded in the Anglo-Saxon Chronicle were those under king Ælle, who reigned over the kingdom of Deira in the late sixth century. However, on the basis of some archaeological evidence Jackson dates the beginning of the Anglo-Saxon settlements to a period about a hundred years earlier, in areas of Yorkshire and in the city of York itself, which has one of the earliest Anglo-Saxon cemeteries in the whole country (Jackson 1953: 211–212). Jackson also refers to Hunter Blair (1947), who has sought to prove that the earliest Saxon settlements go back to the late Roman period and were in fact the result of a conscious Roman policy aimed at building an efficient defence against the continual raids of the Picts and Scots from the north. Whether Hunter Blair's account fully matches the archaeological evidence remains open to question, as Jackson notes (*op.cit.*, 212, fn.).[1] In any case, there seems to be little doubt about the early presence of the Anglo-Saxons in the northern parts of the country.

Further north from Deira the Anglian invaders formed the kingdom of Bernicia, with Bamburgh as its centre. This seems to have taken place a little later than the founding of Deira. At the end of the sixth century, these two northern kingdoms were joined together by king Æthelfrith (593–617), giving rise to the powerful kingdom of Northumbria. Under Æthelfrith and his successor Edwin (617–633) Northumbria was able to greatly expand its area and eventually held the overlordship over the whole of England except Kent. During this period, the south-eastern parts of Scotland were also brought under Anglian rule, and by the middle of the seventh century, as Jackson writes, "the whole of south-east Scotland from the Forth to the Cheviots east of the watershed between Clyde and Tweed, Liddel and Tyne, was in English possession" (1953: 214). By contrast, it is less certain when the areas west of the Pennines were conquered by the Anglo-Saxons. Jackson treats with some scepticism views expressed by Ekwall and Stenton, according to which the occupation of large parts of Lancashire, Westmorland and Cumberland happened as early as the time of Æthelfrith, some parts of Lancashire even earlier, as Ekwall had suggested on the basis of a number of English place-names. Basing his own account on evidence discussed by Myres and Hunter Blair, among others, Jackson concludes that the process of occupation must have started about the middle of the seventh century but that the areas in question were not in English hands until the last quarter of that century (Jackson 1953: 217). He goes on to note that this was not by any means a final arrangement, as the British kingdom of Strathclyde continued to have a strong presence in the south-west of Scotland and was early in the tenth century able to recapture Cumberland, which was not won back by the English until 1092.

Summing up the advance of the Anglo-Saxon occupation, Jackson (1953) shows on the basis of river-name and other evidence how the Anglo-Saxon invasions proceeded in a wave-like process from the south and east towards the west and north (see Map 1.1 from Jackson 1953: 220).

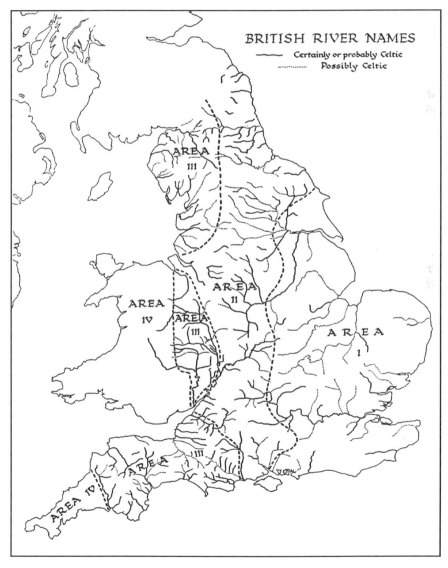

Map 1.1 Four stages of the Anglo-Saxon occupation of England, based on evidence from Brittonic river-names (from Jackson 1953: 220). Reproduced by permission of The Four Courts Press, Dublin.

In *Area I*, as Jackson explains, Brittonic river-names are rare, and they are mainly those of large or medium-sized rivers, e.g. the Trent, the Thames, the Thame, and the Darent.[2] Combining this evidence with other types of historical evidence leads Jackson to conclude that this area corresponds more or less with the extent of the first English settlements down to about the first half of the sixth century (*op.cit.*, 221–222). In *Area II*, by contrast, Brittonic river-names are much more common, and the number of those with a certain Celtic origin is greater than in *Area I*. In settlement terms, this area reflects the advancement of the Anglo-Saxon occupation by the second half of the sixth century in the south and the first half of the seventh in the north (*op.cit.*, 222). *Area III*, then, covers in the north those areas of present-day Cumberland, Westmorland and Lancashire which lie west of the dotted line; in the Welsh border areas parts of Shropshire, Worcestershire, Herefordshire and Gloucestershire; and finally, in the south, all areas in the south-west of England between the line and the River Tamar. As can be expected, the proportions of Brittonic river-names are at their largest in these areas, and they also include names of minor rivers, even streams. *Area III* represents the third and final stage of the Anglo-Saxon conquest, as Jackson points out; in the north this means the middle and third quarter of the seventh century, the middle and second half of the seventh century on the Welsh Marches, and the middle of the seventh to the earlier part of the eighth century in the south-west of England (*op.cit.*, 222–223). Finally, *Area IV* is left blank on the map, as it consists of much of present-day Wales (including Monmouthshire and parts of Herefordshire) and Cornwall, which remained Celtic-speaking until at least the Norman Conquest and was therefore overwhelmingly Brittonic in its nomenclature, too (*op.cit.*, 223). The same applies to Strathclyde in the north-west of England and south-west of Scotland, and the western and northern parts of Scotland.

Widely accepted as Jackson's account of the advancement of the Anglo-Saxon conquest is, more recent scholarship has pointed out the need to supplement the evidence obtainable from river-names with other types of linguistic and other evidence. Thus, Coates (2000a: 10) stresses the need to consider names of inhabited places and other geographical features as a useful source of evidence for the survival of Brittonic speech in different parts of England in the post-Conquest centuries. This is a topic to which we turn next. Place-name and toponymic evidence will be further discussed in Chapter 2, section 2.4, which also deals with other lexical influences from Celtic.

1.2   WHAT HAPPENED TO THE CELTS?

The question of the survival of Britons in the areas conquered by the Anglo-Saxon invaders has preoccupied the minds of several generations of scholars, be they historians, archaeologists, or historical linguists. The traditional view on the nature and impact of the Anglo-Saxon settlement, first formulated by nineteenth-century historians, holds that the Anglo-Saxon intruders drove out or exterminated the native British and Romano-British population and usurped all their lands and property. As a consequence of this massive 'ethnic cleansing', it was believed, the English people are of virtually pure Germanic extraction, with no admixture of native British elements. This view, which could be called 'Germanist' (see, e.g. Higham 1992: 1–16), was canonised in such influential textbooks as Freeman (1870) and reasserted in the following century in Stenton (1943) and Myres (1986), for example. In fact, it remained a practically unquestioned doctrine among historians and archaeologists at least until the second half of the twentieth century.

The Germanist view of the English settlement, like so much of other scholarly work in nineteenth-century Victorian England, was inspired by an ideological myth known as 'Anglo-Saxonism'; other terms used for the phenomenon are 'Teutonism' and 'Gothicism'.[3] In Frantzen and Niles's (1997: 1) words, Anglo-Saxonism can be defined as "the process through which a self-conscious national and racial identity first came into being among the early peoples of the region that we now call England and how, over time, through both scholarly and popular promptings, that identity was transformed into an originary myth available to a wide variety of political and social interests". As an example of the Anglo-Saxonist approach to the nature of the Anglo-Saxon conquest, we may quote the following extract from the *Select Charters* by William Stubbs, an influential nineteenth-century historian:

[the] . . . inhabitants [of Britain] were enervated and demoralized by long dependence, wasted by successive pestilences, worn out by the attacks of half-savage neighbours and by their own suicidal wars; whose vast forests and unreclaimed marsh-lands afforded to the newcomers a comparatively easy conquest, and the means of reproducing at liberty on new ground the institutions under which they had lived at home.

This new race was the main stock of our forefathers: sharing the primaeval German pride of purity of extraction . . . and strictly careful of the distinction between themselves and the tolerated remnant of their predecessors . . .

Our whole internal history testifies unmistakably to our inheritance of Teutonic institutions from the first immigrant.

(Stubbs 1870: 1–3, quoted in Higham 1992: 3)

Influential though the Germanist view on the Anglo-Saxon conquest and the fate of the Celtic population is even today, it has by no means gone unchallenged in historical or archaeological scholarship. Indeed, there is now widespread consensus among historians that it is no longer tenable. Already in her O'Donnell Lecture entitled "The British or Celtic Part in the Population of England", published in 1963 (see Chadwick 1963), the historian Nora Chadwick provides a critical discussion of the evidence from Gildas and, on the basis of some contemporary continental sources and the archaeological and place-name evidence, concludes that

> the Anglo-Saxon Occupation of England was a gradual process which involved no change of population on any large scale, nor is this any necessary corollary of the fact that a change of language took place here, as in Brittany, where a similar change of language was the result of an extensive colonization and peaceful penetration, but without any evidence of displacement of the original population. We have seen that the occupation of England by the Angles, Saxons, and Frisians appears to be an element in the widespread expansion of peoples among the countries bordering the shores of north-western Europe during the closing years of the Roman period. This is the conclusion to be drawn from contemporary continental notices, such as that of Procopius, supported by the later statement of the monk of Fulda, by the text of the *De Excidio*, and by the archaeology and place-name evidence.

(Chadwick 1963: 146–147)

Another factor which according to Chadwick may have led to misunderstandings about the fate of the British population after the arrival of the Anglo-Saxons is the different patterns in settlements between Saxons and Britons. Unlike the latter, who were scattered in small communities in the open country, the Saxons preferred to live in concentrated villages, from which they ruled over the surrounding areas. They generally adopted new sites for their villages and gave them new Anglo-Saxon names. Thus, the fact that there are heavy concentrations of Anglo-Saxon place-names in certain parts of the country does not in itself prove that the Celtic population would have disappeared altogether (Chadwick 1963: 116). Chadwick makes no secret of her own position when she writes:

> ... although I firmly believe myself that the predominant element in the population of England is Celtic, I am aware that proof is not possible, and therefore I may not be able to persuade you to the belief which I hold.

(Chadwick 1963: 111)

Despite the obvious problems in providing conclusive evidence, the line of argumentation suggested by Chadwick has in the last decade or so received support from other researchers dissatisfied with the traditional Germanist account. Thus, Laing and Laing (1990) scrutinise a wide range of evidence comprising finds from archaeological sites, the technology used to produce pottery and other household objects, different kinds of artistic objects and designs, place-names, personal names, population estimates, and the earliest historical records. On the basis of all this they conclude, on the one hand, that "[t]here is no evidence whatsoever for the widespread massacre of the Romano-British population in either towns or countryside" (Laing and Laing 1990: 69); and on the other, that "the overwhelming evidence is for a peaceful and nearly wholesale assimilation of Romano-British and Anglo-Saxon cultures which, eventually by the seventh century took on the umbrella term of 'Saxon' or 'English' " (*op.cit.*, 95).

In a similar vein, Higham (1992) argues that the Anglo-Saxon settlement could not possibly have taken the form of a mass migration followed by large-scale 'ethnic cleansing', as had been assumed by scholars advocating the Germanist view. This is because the Germanic immigrants formed only a small proportion of the population of the country; they were a minority formed by warrior tribes, who eventually took over the existing Romano-British social and economic structure. The estimates of the numbers of Anglo-Saxon immigrants over a period of about a hundred years vary from Higham's (1992: 225) figure of some 10,000, to Härke's (2003: 21) 200,000. Given a Romano-British population of about one million in the mid-fifth century in the later settlement areas of the Anglo-Saxons (as estimated by Härke 2003), the immigrant:native ratio must have been of the order of 1:5 at best. In other words, the immigrants remained a clear minority in that period. This estimate must be considered a very cautious one in the light of some other studies which place the ratio at 1:20 or even as low as 1:50 (see, e.g. Laing and Laing 1990: 84). In any case, as both Higham (1992) and Härke (2003) argue, instead of wholesale extermination there must have occurred a process of acculturation through which the majority of the native British population gradually adopted the Anglo-Saxon language and customs.

So, far from being extinguished as a race, the majority of the Celtic population of Britain remained in place and continued to live as part of the crossbred Celtic-Anglo-Saxon community, which had adopted the Anglo-Saxon language, religion and material culture (Higham 1992: 234). Of course, the proportional numbers of the Celtic and the Anglo-Saxon populations differed greatly from one area to another. For instance, Jackson (1963) has shown on the basis of evidence of place-names that, in the north of England, "a fairly considerable number of people of British race and language" survived the Anglo-Saxon invasion, especially in some parts of Northumbria (*op.cit.*, 83). In northern Cumberland, then, there was an influx of Britons from Strathclyde in the tenth century, which meant a reintroduction of the Cumbric language there. Indeed, Cumbric may have survived there as late as the beginning of the twelfth century (Jackson 1963: 82). Similarly, the Britons retained a stronger presence in the western parts of England than in the east or south-east, in particular. Davies (1997: 5) points out that up until the twelfth century Welsh was the dominant language in areas extending in the east well beyond Offa's Dyke, in present-day western Shropshire and Herefordshire. Writing a little earlier than Davies, Gelling (1992) also discusses the survival of the British people in the West Midlands. She presents linguistic evidence for a significant amount of British place-names and toponyms in the five counties of Warwickshire, Staffordshire, Cheshire, Shropshire, and Herefordshire. Apart from river-names, which—as Gelling notes—have the highest rate of survival in circumstances where one language supersedes another, these include names of mountains and conspicuous hills, as well as those for forests, hybrids and yet others which are easily explicable in Welsh but meaningless in English (Gelling 1992: 54f.). She concludes that in most of the West Midlands, Welsh speech did not disappear until the end of the ninth century; in some areas, such as the Archenfield district of Herefordshire, Welsh continued to be used "throughout the Anglo-Saxon period" (Gelling 1992: 70).

How long the processes of the acculturation and assimilation of the Celts took is hard to define on the basis of the existing evidence. Härke (2003: 23) mentions some archaeological data obtained from burial sites which give some indications of the period of assimilation: thus, by the seventh century, men buried with weapons (i.e. Anglo-Saxons) had the same stature averages as those without (i.e. the Britons), whereas earlier skeletal data indicate a clear separation of the two groups. He also points out that the last textual sources in which Britons are specifically mentioned as distinct from the Anglo-Saxons date from the eighth century. To this he adds that Britons are no longer referred to in the legislative documents written in King Alfred's time, i.e. in the ninth century. This seems to indicate that, at least for legal purposes, the two parts of the population of Wessex had become indistinguishable by about that time (Härke 2003: 23). This does not mean, however, that the ethnic division would necessarily have ceased to exist, at least in some more remote areas.

Population genetic studies offer an intriguing corollary perspective on the question of the survival of the Britons and the proportional numbers of the Celtic and Anglo-Saxon populations in post-Roman Britain. The early population genetic studies of the 1960s and 1970s, based on the distribution of the ABO and the Rh blood groups, are summarised by Potts (1976), who argues that although the genetic evidence supports the 'clean sweep' or 'ethnic cleansing' theories of the nineteenth-century English historians in the case of the south-eastern counties of Cambridgeshire and Norfolk, "further west the genetic evidence suggests that there was a substantial survival of the pre-English inhabitants, while further north the genetic contribution of the Anglo-Saxons must have been almost negligible" (Potts 1976: 248). The conclusion that Potts draws on the basis of the genetic blood group evidence agrees to a remarkable degree with the results of the recent historical, archaeological, and place-name evidence we have discussed above:

If, for example, the percentage of gene p before the Anglo-Saxon settlement varied from 26 per cent in the south and east, as in northern France today, down to 23 per cent in the west and north, as in people of north Welsh descent today, and if the Anglo-Saxons and Danes averaged 29 per cent gene p, then the Celtic survival must range from almost negligible in Norfolk to about one-third in Essex and Kent, the Thames Valley and the lower Severn region and to two-thirds in Dorset and Somerset. In the north midlands and the East Riding it may have averaged about one-half of the ancestors of the present population, while in the rest of Yorkshire and Lancashire it must be even greater; in Durham and the Lakes about three quarters of the ancestors of the present population must have been there in the Roman times. In northern Northumberland, the nuclear region of Bernicia, the proportion of Anglo-Saxon ancestors must be even smaller, perhaps one-tenth, although in the Tyne valley it may be somewhat higher.

(Potts 1976: 248–249)

Since the 1990s, the focus of population genetic studies has shifted away from blood group analysis to molecular genetics. The development in the field has been very rapid, and the results have proved so fruitful for the study of population history and archaeology that a new discipline, 'archaeogenetics', has been born (for a discussion, see Renfrew & Boyle [eds] 2000, and Renfrew 2001). As can perhaps be expected in a fast developing field of study, the results of archaeogenetic studies are not always uniform. Thus, Weale *et al.* (2002) argue that their analysis of Y chromosome variation in a population sample of 313 males from seven English and Welsh towns offers evidence to support the thesis of Anglo-Saxon mass migration from continental Europe.[4] However, Capelli *et al.* (2003) present a comparable analysis of Y chromosome variation based on a considerably larger sample of 1772 males from 25 small urban locations in the British Isles and Ireland. Capelli *et al.* (2003: 981–982) argue that quantitative analysis of the data strongly suggests that nothing like complete population replacement has taken place anywhere in the British Isles. Furthermore, they point out that, while their data show considerable continental introgression in the central-eastern part of England, data from southern England provide evidence for significant continuity of the indigenous population, indeed, to the extent that "southern England [. . .] appears to be predominantly indigenous and, by some analyses, no more influenced by the continental invaders than is mainland Scotland" (*op.cit.*, 982). Capelli *et al.* (2003: 983) argue that their method, with nearly two thousand geographically structured samples, provides more reliable evidence than studies based on what they call "typical sampling schemes" (i.e. studies using samples from a strictly limited number of often metropolitan locations).

Striking confirmation of Capelli *et al.*'s results can be found in the results of the Oxford Genetic Atlas Project. This project, led by Professor Bryan

Sykes, set out to collect and analyse both matrilinear mithocondrial DNA and patrilinear Y-chromosome samples of over ten thousand volunteers from all over Britain and Ireland. The results of the ten-year project, reported in Sykes (2006), offer compelling evidence in support of the survival of the Celtic-speaking population in Britain and Ireland:

> Overall, the genetic structure of the Isles is stubbornly Celtic, if by that we mean descent from people who were here before the Romans and who spoke a Celtic language. We are an ancient people, and though the Isles have been the target of invasion and settlement from abroad ever since Julius Caesar first stepped on to the shingle shores of Kent, these have barely scratched the topsoil of our deep-rooted ancestry. However we may feel about ourselves and about each other, we are genetically rooted in a Celtic past. The Irish, the Welsh and the Scots know this, but the English sometimes think otherwise. But, just a little way beneath the surface, the strands of ancestry weave us all together as the children of a common past.
>
> (Sykes 2006: 287)

The results of Sykes and Capelli *et al.* agree well with those of the earlier genetic studies based on haematological evidence; taken together, these genetic studies offer significant support for the thesis that, at least outside central-eastern England, Anglo-Saxon immigration did not result in any large-scale population replacement.

1.3   THE CELTIC–ENGLISH INTERFACE IN THE LATE MIDDLE AGES

By the late Middle Ages English had established itself as the language of the vast majority of the population in England and was encroaching on the position of its Celtic rivals in Wales, Cornwall and Scotland. Ireland, too, became a battle zone between the two languages a few centuries later. In this section we give a brief description of the main phases in the advance of English into these areas.

In some parts of Wales, English has been the spoken language since the early Middle Ages. Thus, Williams (1935: 242) writes that the eastern Radnorshire plain in Mid-Wales was largely English in speech as early as the eighth century AD. Southern Pembroke, the Gower peninsula, and the eastern edges of the border area were also among the Welsh regions to experience early anglicisation. Not only were they located within the territories of the Anglo-Norman Marcher Lords, but in the early twelfth century, Henry I authorised groups of English and Flemish colonists to settle in South Pembroke and the Gower in order to secure the conquest (Davies 1993: 114).

Although these little pockets of English did not expand much over the centuries, they managed to resist the pressures from the surrounding Welsh language areas remarkably well. Being isolated, their dialects remained distinct from other South Welsh English dialects far into the twentieth century (see, e.g. Penhallurick 1994). Similarly, the Flemish settlements in Pembroke and south-west Wales managed to hold on to their language until relatively late, up until the beginning of the thirteenth century (Davies 1997: 5). However, as was already noted by Ellis (1882: 176), Flemish is unlikely to have left any significant mark in the English dialects of the area, as it was very similar to West Saxon at the time of the colonisation.

The boundaries which were set by the early twelfth century between *Pura Wallia*, the Welsh kingdoms in the north and west, and *Marchia Wallie*, the territories of the Anglo-Norman lords in the east and south of Wales, also mark the establishment of Welsh culture regions, the so-called Outer and Inner Wales, most clearly indicated today by the incidence of spoken Welsh (Pryce 1978). The dominance of English in Outer Wales is, however, a late development: Williams (1985: 65) observes that the mediaeval March developed into an original, culturally complex hybrid society, but that the bulk of the population remained consistently Welsh in speech and culture. Intermingling of cultures and languages took place to a limited extent. The whole period from the coming of the Normans until the end of the mediaeval period and up until the late eighteenth century was characterised by a clear-cut separation of languages, with a marked geographical distribution and an almost imperceptible percolation of English among the peasants from the east.

The subjugation and death of Llywelyn ap Gruffudd (Llywelyn II), the last indigenous prince of Wales, in 1282, marked the next turning point in the history of Wales (John Davies 1993: 158–161). The English finally gained political power in Wales, and during the following centuries, they established walled and fortified towns along the border and the northern coast to protect their interests. The division between the English gentry and the Welsh peasantry was heightened further, as English gradually replaced French and Latin as the language of law and administration. The Welsh-speaking gentry began to feel that a fluent command of English was increasingly essential for them (Janet Davies 1993: 19–22). The next significant step on the road to anglicisation of Wales took place when, at the beginning of the modern period, England took a firmer grip of Wales by bringing the local Welsh nobles under the authority of the English King. The formal annexation was carried out through the Acts of Union in 1536 and 1543. The effects of these upon the language situation in Wales and the subsequent developments will be discussed in Chapter 3.

In Cornwall, the retreat of the Cornish language became almost inevitable, once the ancient spatial link between Cornish and Welsh (i.e., descendants of the earlier Brythonic language) had been severed and the country was subjugated by the invading Saxons. Spriggs (2003: 242) provides a cartographic illustration depicting the main stages in the withdrawal of the Cornish language towards the western end of the peninsula (see Map 1.2).[5]

As Map 1.2 indicates, English had advanced into areas west of the River Tamar by the year 1000, and steadily continued to encroach on the Cornish-speaking areas in the following centuries. By 1600, the Cornish language survived only in the western half of the peninsula, and by 1750, it had already retreated to the westernmost tip of it. Given the smallness of the Cornish-speaking populations, it was only a matter of time before the pressure of English became too overwhelming for Cornish to survive (see Chapter 3, section 3.5).

As in Wales and Cornwall, English started to make inroads into the Celtic-speaking areas of Scotland very early on. According to McClure (1994: 24), the Angles obtained a permanent foothold in some south-eastern parts of Lowland Scotland as early as the latter half of the sixth century. Having defeated the British kingdom of Rheged ca 590, followed by a similar victory over the Scots of Dal Riada in 604, the Angles established their Germanic language in areas which had earlier been dominated by Celtic language and

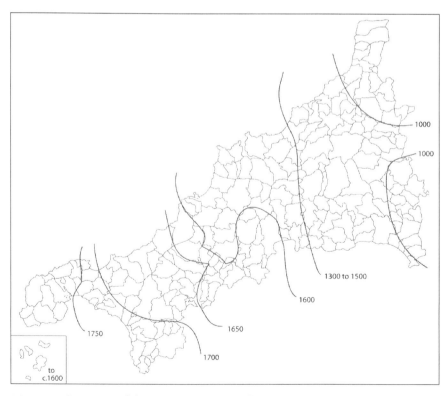

Map 1.2 The retreat of the Cornish language (from Spriggs 2003: 242). Reproduced by permission of the author.

culture. The Anglian advance did not come to a halt until about a hundred years later, in 685, when the Picts defeated them in the battle of Nechtansmere (McClure 1994: 24). In the following centuries, the linguistic boundary between Celtic and Anglian English was gradually pushed north-westwards, and by the end of the mediaeval period it was close to the so-called Highland Line, a linguistic boundary which cuts across Scotland from around present-day Glasgow in the south-west to an area east of Inverness in the north-east and up to the northern coast of Scotland. The wave-like nature of the spread of English and retreat of Gaelic over the centuries can be seen on Map 1.3 from Withers (1979: 51).

Yet, in his analysis of the factors leading to the decline of Gaelic, Withers (1984: 27) emphasises that it is the processes behind this decline rather than the dates or extent of shift that are better known to us. As some of the major factors he lists the increased status and prestige of English as compared with Gaelic, the extension of the feudal system, the role of the burghs (see below), and a gradual political estrangement between the Lowlanders and the Highlanders. Later on, various administrative measures were introduced to consolidate the position of English at the expense of Gaelic (*ibid.*).

Illustrative of the main trend of development as Map 1.3 is, it does not do full justice to the complexity of the linguistic scene in mediaeval Scotland. As Davies (1997: 7) writes, Scotland was a real 'melting pot' for different languages, especially in the twelfth and thirteenth centuries: apart from Gaelic and English, with their many varieties, there were still speakers of the ancient Brythonic (Cumbric) language and of Scandinavian languages in some western areas, and French was also introduced into Scotland by the Norman settlers. Yet Gaelic remained the first language of at least half of the population in this period, as is pointed out by McClure (1994: 29). It was not until the fourteenth century that this complexity was significantly reduced, when (a form of) English emerged as the prevailing language, especially of business and commerce, the main centres of which were the numerous new towns, 'burghs', founded by the Norman settlers (McClure 1994: 28–29; Davies 1997: 8). It was the Lowland English of the burghs which from the thirteenth century onwards gradually evolved into a variety distinct from the English(es) of England, viz. Scots or *Scottis*, as it was first called, as opposed to *Inglis*. In the fifteenth and sixteenth centuries, as McClure (1994: 32) writes, Scots gained the status of the language of government and administration in Scotland and also became a vehicle for a flourishing national literature.

As compared with Wales or Scotland, it took considerably longer for English to make its entry into Ireland. The year 1169 is usually mentioned as the first date for the introduction of English into Ireland, although it is likely that some contacts between English speakers and the Irish Gaels had taken place even earlier (see, e.g. Kallen 1994). In any case, the arrival of the Anglo-Normans, the then rulers of England, marked the beginning of the history of English in Ireland, and led to the establishment of English and

THE DECLINE OF GAELIC AS A WAVE PROCESS : 1020–1961

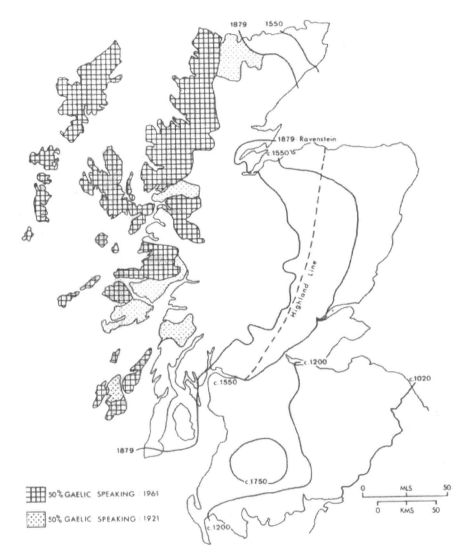

Map 1.3 The decline of Gaelic as a wave process: 1020–1961 (from Withers 1979: 51). Reproduced by permission of Professor C.W.J. Withers and The Association for Scottish Literary Studies.

Norman French (which was the language of the Anglo-Norman nobility) as vernacular languages spoken in Ireland alongside the indigenous Irish. Latin was yet another language besides Irish and French with which English had to compete for the next couple of centuries. Latin and French were in fact long used as the languages of administration and education in Ireland as well as in England and Wales, while English was the language used by the majority of the common soldiers who had come to Ireland under the leadership of their Anglo-Norman lords.

Despite the fact that the Anglo-Normans soon managed to take over nearly all of the province of Leinster and parts of Munster and Ulster, it was not long after their first arrival that Norman French began to decline and, within a relatively short space of time, the Norman population became gaelicised in their language and customs (Bliss 1979: 12). English, which was the language of the tenants of the Norman lords, at first gained some ground during the thirteenth century, but the pressure of Irish pushed it, too, into a steady decline in the following centuries. That the English language was indeed under growing pressure in the fourteenth and fifteenth centuries is also shown by the various administrative measures introduced by the English rulers to halt the process of gaelicisation. The best-known of these are the so-called Statutes of Kilkenny, which were originally written in Norman French and passed by a Parliament held in Kilkenny in 1366. These statutes sought to turn the tide by imposing heavy penalties on those who were found using Irish. They, as well as other similar measures, turned out to be of no effect, and Irish continued to encroach upon the positions of English not only in rural areas but also in towns, including even Dublin (Bliss 1979: 13). Thus it was Irish which emerged victorious from this first round of battle with English and the other languages spoken in mediaeval Ireland. There is some contemporary historical evidence which shows that the English speakers in mediaeval Ireland were almost entirely assimilated to the Irish language and culture, and that by 1600 English survived only in some of the major towns like Dublin and the eastern coastal regions around Dublin, known as the English Pale, and in few scattered rural areas in the south-east of Ireland (see, e.g. Bliss 1979). On the other hand, other similar evidence has been adduced to suggest some degree of continuity between mediaeval and modern Irish English (for further discussion, see, esp. Kallen 1994, 1997a; Filppula 1999).

2 The Linguistic Outcomes of the Early Contacts

2.1 INTRODUCTION

The historical and other evidence discussed in the previous chapter shows that in many parts of Britain conditions favourable to bilingualism existed for a considerable period of time after the first arrival of the Anglo-Saxons. Thus, Jackson (1953: 245) considers it likely that there was a bilingual stage, when the Britons were able to speak both Anglo-Saxon and British; on the other hand, the Anglo-Saxons probably had no particular need to learn the language of those whom they had conquered. However, as in conditions of extensive bilingualism generally, one could expect linguistic influences to seep through from one language to the other. In the British context, it is most likely that English (Anglo-Saxon) exercised a strong influence on Brythonic but, at the same time, transfer of Celtic features to English must also have taken place, especially in the speech of the rapidly increasing numbers of Brythonic speakers acquiring and shifting to the language of their rulers. The mechanisms of transfer and linguistic contact effects must have been very much like those which can be witnessed in the later contacts between English and the Celtic languages in Wales, Ireland or Scotland. These include, quite centrally, 'interlingual identifications' of the type discussed by Weinreich (1953); through these, speakers acquiring a new language seek both categorial and structural equivalence relations, or as the case may be, dissimilarities, between their native language and the new 'target language'. In conditions of a fairly rapid language shift, accompanied by lack of adequate language instruction, in particular, this kind of process can be expected to lead to transfer of many features of the phonology and syntax (rather than of lexicon) of the indigenous language to the new language. Writing on the global experience from similar situations, Thomason and Kaufman (1988) explain this phenomenon as follows:

> [I]f shift occurs rapidly, and if the shifting group is so large numerically that the TL [target language] model is not fully available to all its members, then imperfect learning is a probability, and the

learners' errors are more likely to spread *throughout the TL speech community*.

(Thomason and Kaufman 1988: 47; our emphasis)

As regards the Celtic contact effects in English, a well-known difficulty lies in identifying and documenting transfer effects in the extant early English texts, especially those from the Old English (OE) period. The dearth of such evidence explains the prevailing view of Anglicists, according to which Celtic languages have had hardly any influence upon English. It has been argued that, because of the political and social hegemony of the Anglo-Saxons, the linguistic influences went rather one-sidedly from English to Celtic, and whatever impact the Celts had on the English language was restricted to a handful of loanwords such as *bard*, *crag*, *glen*, and *whiskey*, to which can be added a number of place-names and river-names such as *London*, *York*, *Avon*, and *Thames*. The standard 'textbook' view on this matter is succinctly expressed by Pyles and Algeo (1993) as follows:

> We should not expect to find many [Celtic loanwords in English], for the British Celts were a subject people, and a conquering people are un-likely to adopt many words from those whom they have supplanted.

(Pyles and Algeo 1993: 292)

The statement by Pyles and Algeo is but one in the long series of similar ones found in both textbooks and even in scholarly pieces of research. An essentially similar account is given by Strang (1970) in her influential book on the history of English. According to her, "the extensive influence of Celtic can only be traced in place-names" (1970: 391). In another context, she notes that "[t]he poverty of the Celtic contribution to English vocabulary even in this area, and at a time when Celtic cultural influence was enormous, is very remarkable" (1970: 374). Looming large behind this position is the Danish philologist Otto Jespersen, whose authoritative statement dating back to the early years of the twentieth century can be said to have laid the basis for almost all of the subsequent treatments of this subject. Jespersen characterises the role of the Celtic languages in the development of English as follows:

> We now see why so few Celtic words were taken over into English. There was nothing to induce the ruling classes to learn the language of the inferior natives; it could never be fashionable for them to show an acquaintance with that despised tongue by using now and then a Celtic word. On the other hand the Celt would have to learn the language of his masters, and learn it well; he could not think of addressing his supe-riors in his own unintelligible gibberish, and if the first generation did

not learn good English, the second or third would, while the influence they themselves exercised on English would be infinitesimal.

(Jespersen 1905: 39)

It must be noted, however, that the views expressed by Jespersen and other like-minded scholars are mainly based on the small number of Celtic loanwords attested in English. An important role in consolidating this view has been played by Förster's study of the Celtic elements in OE vocabulary (Förster 1921), which has thereafter informed the opinions of most other writers on the subject. Apart from numerous Celtic-origin personal and family names, patronyms, names of occupations, place-names and river-names, Förster acknowledges only about a dozen relatively certain common-noun loans from Welsh, Cornish or Breton (i.e. words of Old British origin) and even fewer from Old Irish. The former are mostly terms used for animals or everyday household items such as OE *assa* 'ass' (G. *Esel*), borrowed from Old British *as(s)in* (itself from Latin *asinus*), and OE *bin(n)* 'basket' (G. *Korb*), ModE *bin* (G. *Behälter*). The latter group of loanwords are ones transmitted into OE through the influence of the early Irish missionaries and are therefore ecclesiastical in nature, e.g. OE *cros(s)* 'cross', from Old Irish *cross*; OE *cursian* 'curse', from O.Ir. *cūrsagim, cūrsaim* 'I reprove' (G. *Ich tadele, züchtige*). (For further discussion of Förster's lists, see section 2.4.)

A different perspective on the whole problem is opened by a growing number of scholars who have pointed out that the very nature of the contact situation in the period at issue was such that large-scale lexical influences were not even to be expected. Thus, Dal (1952) notes that the influence of the language of the conquered people would have been more manifest in the syntax of the language of the new *Herrenvolk* than in its lexicon for the simple reason that the conquered people had to learn the language of the conquerors, and in doing so, would most probably have retained some of the syntactic characteristics of their native language (Dal 1952: 114–115). Dal also provides a plausible explanation for the fact that only few of the syntactic loans are in evidence in OE texts: any Celticisms in the syntax of OE would have been labelled as vulgarisms and would therefore have had no place in the written standard of the Anglo-Saxon period. Regardless of this, they could well have lived on as features of the colloquial language (Dal 1952: 113).

Dal's account follows the line of argumentation found in some earlier and more or less contemporaneous works by Wolfgang Keller (Keller 1925), Walther Preusler (see, e.g. Preusler 1956) and Gerard J. Visser (Visser 1955). Dal's point about the limitations imposed by the OE prescriptive tradition on the evidence available from that period is also in line with the account of Tolkien (1963), who similarly notes the lack of "transcripts of village-talk" in the OE period, and who goes on to state that "[f]or any glimpse of what was going on beneath the cultivated surface we must wait until the Old English period of letters is over" (Tolkien 1963: 28).

Scholars who have questioned the 'mainstream' view on the extent of Celtic influences in English have put forward evidence suggesting transfer effects in several areas of English grammar. Keller (1925), who is perhaps the first to highlight the role of syntax rather than lexicon as the main area where Celtic contact effects can be expected, focuses on two features. The first is the OE distinction between the (reconstructed) *es-* and *bheu*-forms of the 'substantive' verb 'be', which Keller takes to be Celtic in origin. This distinction corresponds exactly to the Cymric one and has no parallels in the other Germanic languages. Tolkien (1963) is another author who discusses the *b*-forms of the OE substantive verb 'be' in the light of possible contact influence from Welsh. The second feature discussed by Keller is the OE gerund or 'verbal noun' construction, which according to him gave rise to the 'progressive form' *to be (a) doing*, as it is found in early Middle English (ME) and later in Modern English (ModE). This, as Keller argues, has a close parallel in the Cymric construction consisting of the substantive verb 'be' + preposition *yn* + verbal noun (e.g. *mae yn dysgu* '[he] is learning'; cf. section 2.2.5.1). He also draws attention to the fact that the English progressive form is not found in the other Germanic languages, except for the Low German dialect of Westfalish and also Dutch folk-speech, which, however, are structurally different from the English construction in that they involve the infinitive instead of the verbal noun.

The Celtic background of the English progressive is also the subject of much of the more recent research, starting with Preusler (1956), who wrote most of his works in the period before and after World War II. Others pursuing the same line of inquiry include the Norwegian scholars Dal (1952) and Braaten (1967), who have in the most recent research been followed by Tristram (1999a, 1999b), Mittendorf and Poppe (2000), Poppe (2003), Ronan (2003), and Filppula (2003). It is but one sign of the rapidly growing interest in this matter that the three last-mentioned were all published in the same volume, entitled *The Celtic Englishes III* (see Tristram 2003).

A third syntactic feature of English which has received a great deal of attention in the literature is the so-called DO-periphrasis. Apparently first raised by Preusler, the possible Celtic origin of this feature of English has continued to be a subject of debate ever since, with Poussa (1990), Tristram (1999b), and van der Auwera and Genee (2002) being some of the most recent contributors to the Celtic hypothesis on this matter. It seems that, despite the rather negative initial response to Preusler's (and also to Poussa's) view on this matter, the possible Celtic background to DO-periphrasis is now being seriously re-examined.

Other syntactic features of English which have been suggested as being possibly derived from Celtic languages include the so-called cleft construction or clefting for short; a predilection for analytically formed prepositional and phrasal verbs; relative clauses with 'stranded' prepositions and the 'zero'

relatives (also known as 'contact clauses'); reflexivisation; the 'internal possessor' construction; the group genitive; and certain patterns of subject–verb
concord, usually grouped together under the label of the 'Northern Subject Rule' or the 'Subject Type Constraint'. It is noteworthy that the bulk
of these already appeared in Preusler's list of Celtic-derived features, while
some have later been added and discussed by Tristram (1999a), in particular,
but also by other scholars, as examples of analytic typological or other features that are shared by Welsh and English, raising thus the question about
their origins. Some of the features mentioned here will be discussed in detail
in section 2.2 (see below for criteria for choosing them).

Contact effects have also been argued to have taken place in English
phonology and morphology, although the evidence is here less direct and
therefore thinner than in syntax. Tolkien (1963) mentions *i*-mutation as a
feature of OE which could have a Celtic connection, but he does not pursue
the matter in any detail, possibly because of problems of dating and some
details of the changes. Yet he points out that the English changes are "closely
paralleled by the changes which in Welsh grammar are usually called 'affection'" (1963: 32). Another phonological feature discussed by Tolkien is
the preservation in English of *þ* and *w*, a development which sets English
apart from most other Germanic languages and could be of Celtic (Welsh)
origin. Among the few other writers who have discussed possible Celtic
influences in English phonology or morphology are Kastovsky (1994), who
points out that the erosion and eventual levelling of inflectional endings in
OE may well have been due to contact with the surviving Celtic population; Hickey (1995), who suggests certain lenition phenomena and various
'low-level' phonological and prosodic phenomena as areas which may plausibly derive from Celtic; Schrijver (1999), who examines the contact background of front rounded vowels in different dialects of OE; and Tristram
(1999a), who mentions retroflex *r* and the sonorisation of initial spirants
in the south-western dialects of English as features which might be due to
early substratal influences. Like Kastovsky (1994) and Hickey (1995), but
in more explicit terms, Tristram (1999a) ascribes the attrition of declension
and conjugation in English to substratal and/or adstratal contact influences.
She underlines the nature and importance of the early Celtic–English contact situation for the kind of typological shift—or 'disruption' even—that
the Celtic languages and English have experienced through the centuries,
starting most probably before the end of the first millennium and continuing up to the present day. Both language groups have shed a large part of
their morphological inflections and gradually moved from predominantly
synthetic constructions to analytic ones. These changes will be examined in
greater detail in section 2.3.

Finally, before moving to a detailed discussion of some of the features
mentioned above, it has to be noted that even the lexical loans from Celtic
languages to English are considerably more numerous than is traditionally
assumed. Gillies (1994: 165) speaks of a certain tradition of "under-reporting

of Celtic loans" in the field of English lexicography, which he puts down to either lack of knowledge about the possible Celtic sources or to ideological bias. At any rate, the number of recognised Celtic loanwords is likely to rise to much higher figures than hitherto acknowledged. This is especially true of many regional dialects of English, but also of earlier varieties of literary language. In recent years, a major contribution to the study of Celtic vocabulary in OE and ME has been made by Andrew Breeze, who has proposed Celtic origins for numerous words that have hitherto not been recognised as borrowings from Celtic languages (see, e.g. 1994, 1997). In most cases these are words whose origins have for long been unclear or in dispute. Similar efforts in the study of place-names have been carried out by Margaret Gelling (see Gelling 1992), Richard Coates (see, e.g. Coates 2000b), and Andrew Breeze (see, e.g. Coates and Breeze 2000). The present authors have also carried out extensive searches for hitherto unrecognised lexical items which can plausibly be derived from Celtic sources. These and the other lexical loans will be discussed in detail in section 2.4.

Our criteria for selecting the features to be discussed more thoroughly below are as follows. First, we have chosen to focus on those features for which, all kinds of evidence considered, the 'case' for Celtic influence on English seems the strongest. A second, auxiliary, criterion is the degree of attention that a given feature has attracted in historical-linguistic scholarship; it is reasonable to assume that the more attention a feature receives, the more possibilities it offers for a contact-linguistic investigation. A third criterion, then, is a linguistic one, viz. the degree of similarity or dissimilarity between English and the other Germanic languages, on one hand, and between English and the Celtic languages, on the other. Both dimensions are important here, and in this regard we follow the methodological approach advocated, e.g., by Vennemann (2000), who writes:

> [W]henever a variety of English spoken in a Celtic country deviates substantially from standard varieties, a good deal of the differences can be traced to similar properties of the regional Celtic, and that whenever English deviates from the other Germanic languages, chances are that the differences (or at least a goodly portion of the differences) can be traced to similar properties of Insular Celtic.

> (Vennemann 2000: 406)

Of course, we make no claim of being able to prove Celtic influence 'beyond any reasonable doubt', even though there are cases which can be persuasively argued to be Celtic in origin. For some others—it has to be said from the outset—it seems impossible to find conclusive evidence for Celtic influence; for yet others, we believe that the case for Celtic influence is not (yet) convincing enough. Yet for both of the latter types, too, a detailed discussion is called for because of the attention they have received in the literature. It is our hope that providing as much of indirect or circumstantial evidence as possible we can at least increase the probabilities for the Celtic hypothesis to be either vindicated or refuted.

2.2   GRAMMAR

2.2.1   The Internal vs. External Possessor Constructions

Constructions used to express the relationships between items possessed and their possessor do not at first glance belong to the 'core grammar' of languages. Yet, recent typological research has shown that there are interesting divisions between languages in this respect and ones which may have far-reaching implications for their historical and other connections, including possible linguistic contact effects. In this section we will discuss the distinction between the so-called internal vs. external possessor constructions in English and the Celtic languages and their historical background.

Briefly, internal possession denotes constructions in which the possessor assumes the form of a possessive pronoun, e.g. *He's got a nasty wound on **his** head*. In the case of external possession, the definite article occurs in lieu of a possessive pronoun, e.g. *He's got a nasty wound on **the** head* (both examples from Mitchell 1985: §§ 303–310). In ModE, there is a strong preference for the internal possessor construction, despite its optionality in some cases and the use of the external type as the only or preferred alternative in some others (as in *He looked her in **the** eyes*). In earlier English, by contrast, the external type was the prevailing one, but starting already in the OE period, a change has gradually taken place from external to internal possessor constructions. Of particular interest here is the question of why this change has taken place in English but not in (most) other Germanic languages.

2.2.1.1   *The Change from External to Internal Possessor Constructions in English*

We begin with Ahlgren's (1946) account of the development of the possessor constructions in earlier English. On the basis of a detailed study he concludes that, already in OE, there was a gradual increase in the use of the possessive pronouns and concomitant loss of constructions based on the so-called dativus sympatheticus. The latter is exemplified by (1) from the Anglo-Saxon Chronicle, while the innovative internal possessor type occurs in (2), taken from the Blickling Homilies (both examples from Ahlgren 1946):

(1)   *Him* het se cyng *þa eagan* ut adon. (Anglo-Saxon Chronicle
       1096; cited in Ahlgren 1946: 197)
       Him/Dat ordered that king the eyes out put
       'The king ordered his eyes to be put out.'

(2)   Hie hine sona genamon and *his* eagan ut-astungon. (Blickling
      Hom. p. 229; cited in Ahlgren 1946: 197)
      They him soon captured and his eyes stuck out
      'They soon captured him and stuck out his eyes.'

Ahlgren's findings are confirmed by Mitchell's (1985: §§ 303–310)
description of 'nouns of possession', i.e. "nouns denoting parts of the body,
mental faculties, articles of clothing and other personal belongings". Before
explaining the situation in earlier English, however, Mitchell outlines the
ModE system as follows: ModE may have either a possessive or a definite
article when the possessor is the subject of the clause, e.g. *He's got a nasty*
wound on his/the head; the article is preferred when the possessor is not
subject of the clause but is otherwise specified, as in *She hit him a savage*
blow on the head/She hit him on the head (where *him* is historically accusative or dative); the possessive is essential in sentences like *There was a*
nasty look in his eye/A grimace of pain passed over his face (Mitchell 1985:
§ 303).

On the question of the patterns used in earlier English, Mitchell first
notes that the modern patterns were "well established in OE" but that
the situation was "more complicated". He cites examples from OE texts,
some of which have the 'dative of possession' or 'dativus sympatheticus'
(i.e. external possessor patterns), while others have possessives (i.e. internal
possessive patterns). As he points out, the dative of possession is most commonly found in OE with pronouns, but it is also used with numerals and
nouns (*op.cit.*, §§ 306, 307). In poetry, the most common patterns are those
without demonstrative or possessive, i.e. predominantly external possessive
constructions. He finds further support for his observations in the work of
Klaeber (1929), who notes the same patterns (see Mitchell 1985: § 309),
and particularly, in that of Ahlgren (1946).[1] Mitchell summarises, and evidently concurs with, Ahlgren's findings on the pattern of development in
OE, although he does not comment on Ahlgren's suggestion about possible
foreign influence (Mitchell 1985: § 310):

> The 'dativus sympatheticus' becomes less frequent and the possessive
> more common throughout the OE period, though (as one would ex-
> pect from the MnE fluctuations) the latter never completely supersedes
> the demonstrative; see further §§338–9. Among the factors called in by
> Ahlgren to account for this change are the levelling of the dative and
> accusative (pp. 14 and 202–2); fluctuation in the use of the dative and
> accusative, either with OE verbs which take both cases, e.g. *belgan* and
> *fylgan* (pp. 203–6) or under foreign influence (pp. 206–10); and the
> preference for the possessive in the Latin of the Vulgate and the Fathers,
> which (he argues) led to the disuse of the dative in direct translations
> and in works based on Latin sources (pp. 210–16).

What Ahlgren means by 'foreign influence' in this connection relates, first, to the influence exerted by the Danes on especially the northern OE dialects, in which confusion between the dative and the accusative forms is first attested (see Ahlgren 1946: 206 ff.). According to Ahlgren, this confusion ran parallel with the disappearance of the 'dativus sympatheticus' and its gradual replacement by the possessive adjective (*op.cit.*, 210). A second source of foreign influence was the formal Latin used in the Bible and the Lives of the Saints; this, as Ahlgren notes relying on Löfstedt's (1928–1933) study of historical Latin syntax, favoured the possessive adjective over the 'dativus sympatheticus', which was generally used to depict the usage of 'vulgar' speakers. According to Ahlgren, the Latin usage is reflected in OE translations from Latin; in these, the possessive adjective is the preferred choice (Ahlgren 1946: 211). The possibility of Celtic influence is not discussed by Ahlgren.

Leaving the question of contact influences aside for a while, there seems to be wide consensus about the general decline of the external possessor construction in earlier English. Thus, Mustanoja (1960: 98) gives the following account of the decline of the sympathetic dative construction: "This construction, common in OE (e.g., *feoll him to fotum;—seo cwen het þæm cyninge þæt heafod of aceorfan;—him com to gemynde þæt*), is comparatively infrequent in ME and loses ground steadily".

In more recent research, this is confirmed by Vennemann (2002a), who cites some early attestations of the internal possessor construction in OE. As regards the factors causing this change, Vennemann seeks to refute the view that the loss of the external possessor construction in English could be explained as a consequence of the loss of case distinctions (see below).

The change from external to internal possessors receives further support from our own searches through the ME section of the *Helsinki Corpus*. The nouns searched included *foot*, *hand* and *head* (in their many variant forms). We found only a handful of instances of external possessor patterns involving the use of the definite article, and almost all of these occurred in the first subperiod (1150–1250).

2.2.1.2   *Possible Explanations for the Rise of the Internal Possessor Construction in English*

It is customary in historical linguistics to look first into the possibility of language-internal factors. In this case, the task is far from straightforward. Indeed, Visser (1963–1973: § 697) arrives at the conclusion that it is "difficult to find a proper explanation [based on language-internal factors]". Ahlgren (1946), as noted above, offers an explanation according to which the change at hand resulted from a confusion between, and eventual collapse of, the dative and the accusative forms in English, starting in the OE period and possibly promoted by Danish influence. This process, he argues, also entailed the disappearance of the 'dativus sympatheticus' and its gradual replacement by the possessive adjective (Ahlgren 1946: 206–210).

Persuasive as it seems at first glance, Ahlgren's account is fraught with problems. The evidence from other Germanic languages, especially the Scandinavian languages and Dutch,[2] makes it rather doubtful whether the collapse of the OE dative and accusative case forms could be the crucial explanatory factor. Besides Vennemann (2002a), this point is made by McWhorter (2002), who writes:

> But this surely cannot serve as an explanation for the loss of external possessor marking when Dutch and Scandinavian have experienced the same collapse of dative and accusative and yet retain the feature. It is also germane that even a language that does retain the dative/accusative contrast robustly, Icelandic, has nevertheless shed dative-marked external possessives in favor of marking them with the locative. Obviously collapse of case marking was not a causal factor in English (cf. Haspelmath 1999: 125).
>
> (McWhorter 2002: 226)

Another possible explanation based on language-internal factors would be to regard the loss of external possessors and replacement by internal possessors as a 'natural' development in languages, requiring no external trigger. This hypothesis is considered but rejected by Vennemann (2001, 2002a) for two reasons:

(i) If the change were so natural, we would expect other European languages to have undergone it, too; but they have not.
(ii) If the change were so natural, we would expect external possessors to be rare in the languages of the world; but they are not: External possessors are widespread in all parts of the globe. (Vennemann 2002a: 227)

Since the language-internal explanations do not seem to give satisfactory answers, we can next turn to language contacts as the possible source of the change in the possessor patterns in English. As mentioned above, Ahlgren (1946) discusses two types of foreign influence on the development of the possessor constructions:

(i) the influence exerted by the Danish element on especially the northern OE dialects, in which confusion between the dative and the accusative forms is first attested;
(ii) the influence of the formal Latin used in the Bible and the Lives of the Saints, which favoured the possessive adjective over the 'dativus sympatheticus'. (Ahlgren 1946: 206–211)

The main factor speaking against Danish or other Scandinavian influences is that these languages retain external possessors, despite the collapse of dative/accusative case-marking (cf. Vennemann 2002a: 228). Latin influence also turns out to be improbable because French and other Romance languages preserve external possessors, despite the heavy influence from Latin throughout their histories (cf. Vennemann 2002a: 228; McWhorter 2002: 226). The same argument can be wielded against influence from French or other Romance languages (cf. McWhorter 2002: 226). This leaves us with the possibility of Celtic influence, to which we now turn.

2.2.1.3 The Possibility of Celtic Contact Influences

Pokorny (1927: 252) is perhaps the first to draw attention to the Irish and Welsh tendency to use possessive pronouns instead of the definite article in reference to body parts, items of clothing, household items, and physical or mental states of a person. As examples, he cites the following sentences from the Old Irish text *Y Táin*: *benaid a chend de* 'he cut his head off' (*Y Táin*, p. 454); *Tíscaid a ētach de* 'he undressed himself' (lit. 'he took off his clothes'; *Y Táin*, p. 747). Pokorny further notes that, among the sixty-one examples of phrases given under the noun *lám* 'hand' in Windisch's dictionary of Old Irish, only four are without the possessive (1927: 252). According to him, the same tendency is found in Welsh and is, in fact, even more striking there than in Irish. While in Modern Irish one can also use the definite article, as in *Do bhaineamar dínn na bróga* 'we took off our shoes' (lit. '. . . the shoes'), Welsh would insist on the possessive pronoun in the same position: *Mi a dinnais fy esgidiau* 'I took off my shoes' (Pokorny 1927: 253). In this respect, Welsh behaves like English, and English, in turn, differs from the other Germanic languages or French. Pokorny's conclusion is that the English usage derives from the Celtic substratum, which in turn owes this tendency to pre-Indo-European: "Ich zweifle daher nicht, daß der englische Brauch auf das keltische Substrat zurückgeht, der wiederum in diesem Falle voridg. beeinflußt ist"[3] (Pokorny 1927: 253).

Pokorny finds further support for his substratum account from the English dialects of Scotland, which according to him also often exhibit the same feature, in agreement with Gaelic (Pokorny 1927: 253). The earlier pre-Indo-European influence, then, is supported by his observation that the possessive pattern is used in Old Egyptian in the same contexts as in the Celtic languages (*ibid.*).

In modern research, this commonality between the Celtic languages and English is discussed, e.g. by Tristram (1999a: 24–25) and Vennemann (2000, 2002a). Both authors underline the special position of English among the Germanic languages in that it favours internal possessor constructions instead of the external ones. On the question of possible contact influences which could account for this feature of English, Tristram writes, "In its history, English underwent a typological change from the external to the internal [possessor] construction, possibly due to linguistic contact with Brythonic/Welsh" (Tristram 1999a: 25).

The Celtic hypothesis receives significant support from the areal-typological survey by König and Haspelmath (1998), who are able to establish that the external possessor construction constitutes a characteristic feature of most European languages, so much so that it can be considered one of the 'European areal features' defining a European Sprachbund (see also Haspelmath 1998: 228). More specifically, their survey shows that the external possessor construction is lacking only in Welsh, Breton, English, Dutch, Hungarian, and Turkish. In English, however, and also in Dutch, it is still preserved in certain contexts as a relic feature. Thus English, though it is by far the best known European language, turns out to be the most 'atypical' European language with regard to this particular feature (König and Haspelmath 1998: 587–588).

König and Haspelmath (1998) also establish a typological correlation between the existence in a language of the external possessor construction and 'implicit possessors'. The latter term refers to those cases in which the possessor, though not explicitly specified, is implied by the context. Thus, Slavic, Romance and Germanic languages (except again English and Dutch), all of which use external possessors, also typically have implicit possessors. By contrast, English, Welsh and Breton (and also Turkish and Hungarian) have only internal and 'explicit possessors'. König and Haspelmath (1998: 579) provide the following illustration of the types of contexts which in Welsh, Breton and English generally require an explicit possessor. As can be seen, the possessor is in all of these the subject and the thing possessed the object of the clause.

(3)   *Welsh*:
      Y mae 'r   plant wedi codi *eu* llaw.
      PT sont ART enfants après lever leur main
      'Les enfants ont levé la main.'

(4)   *Breton*:
      Bremañ   e savom   *hor* gar   dehou.
      maintenant PT soulever:1PL notre jambe droite
      'Nous levons maintenant la jambe droite.'

(5)   *English*:
      She opened her eyes. (*She opened the eyes.)
      'Elle ouvrit les yeux.'
      (König and Haspelmath 1998: 579)

According to König and Haspelmath (1998), one of the factors influencing the convergent development of the external vs. internal possessor constructions in English and the Celtic languages has been the gradual disappearance from both language groups of the dative of possession or sympathetic dative constructions. On the Germanic side, they believe, this process has gone hand in hand with the loss of the dative case in English, Dutch and continental Scandinavian. The Celtic languages have also lost the dative case and external possessor patterns relying on it. Thus, one can find examples of the 'datif sympathique' in Old Irish, but even there it had a completely marginal role; in present-day Celtic languages, it does not exist at all (König and Haspelmath 1998: 583). König and Haspelmath note, however, the present-day Irish locative construction ('possesseur externe à l'adessif' in their terminology) involving the preposition *ag* 'at'. Examples of this are:

(6) Bhí an lámh ar crith aige.
     était la main sur trembler à lui
     'La main lui tremblait.'

(7) Tá an srón ag cur fola aige.
     est le nez à semant de.sang à.lui
     'Le nez lui saigne.'
     (König and Haspelmath 1998: 561)

König and Haspelmath draw further comparisons between Irish, Scandinavian languages, and Modern Greek, all of which have lost the old external possessor construction but developed a new one in which the possessor is expressed by means of a locative prepositional phrase (König and Haspelmath 1998: 588). The Swedish pattern is illustrated in (8):

(8) Någon   bröt armen på honom.
     quelqu'un cassa le:bras sur lui
     'Quelqu'un lui a cassé le bras.'
     (König and Haspelmath 1998: 559)

2.2.1.4 *Some Problems with the Celtic Hypothesis*

Turning now back to the Celtic languages and their possible role in shaping the English usage, a first complicating factor is the prominence of the external rather than the internal possessor constructions in at least some Celtic languages and the fluctuating usage in both Welsh and Irish. Thus, Proinsias Mac Cana (personal communication) points out that Irish, in particular, favours, and has favoured of old, the external possessor pattern, i.e. use of the definite article to modify the object or thing possessed. There is some support for this in the rather scant literature on the subject. Thus, writing on Irish, Ó Searcaigh (1950) notes that "[t]he article is often substituted for a possessive adjective" and gives examples such as those in (9)–(11):

(9) Goidé mar atá *an* bhean 's *an* chlann.
'How are your wife and family?' (Cf. Anglo-Irish "How is the wife?")

(10) Deir an doctúir go bhfuil *an* croidhe lag aige.
'The doctor says his heart is weak.'

(11) Tá *an* chos ag cur orm i gcomhnuidhe.
'My foot is still causing me pain.'
(Ó Searcaigh 1950: 242–243)

In Welsh, the situation is more complicated. Modern Welsh can be characterised as being "exclusively internal" (Alan Thomas, personal communication), hence, different from Irish in this respect. In earlier Welsh, a certain amount of variation seems to have occurred, although the internal possessor construction was the preferred one. For instance, in his *Grammar of Middle Welsh* Evans (1964) writes that

[s]ometimes the article is apparently used for a possessive personal pronoun: *Ac yna y kymerth y vorvynn santes y kythreul gyr guallt y penn* 'And then the maiden saint caught the demon by the hair of his head' B ix. 331.7, *Ac yna ny byd idaw dim a dotto yn y geneu* 'And then he will not have anything that he may put in his mouth' ii. 16. 15, *Or trewir dyn ar y pen* 'If a person be struck on his head' L1B 56. 29.

(Evans 1964: 25)

Notice, however, that the *y* in the examples above could also represent the third person singular masc. of the prefixed pronoun; in that case, however, lenition of the following consonant would normally occur, but this is not always indicated in MW orthography, as Evans points out (Evans 1964: 25). He also refers to Ó Searcaigh's (1950) observations on the Irish usage and the same kind of variation phenomena there.

Further evidence of fluctuating usage in certain contexts in Welsh, too, is provided by Morris-Jones (1931), who notes that nouns like *enaid* 'life, soul', *einioes* 'life(time)', *corff* 'body', *calon* 'heart', *pen* 'head, end' "may take the article instead of a prefixed genitive pronoun", e.g.:

(12) A ydyw'r *pen* yn well?
'Is your head better?' (Morris-Jones 1931: 7)

Names of close relations form another context in which the definite article often occurs (*op.cit.*, 7). Morris-Jones adds a comparative remark on French, Spanish, Italian, and German as languages in which the pattern with the article (i.e. external possession) is "the usual construction" (*ibid.*).

Despite the observed variation in Welsh usage, Havers's (1911: 250–251) examples of internal possessors in Middle Welsh (MW) texts, cited in Vennemann (2002a: 217), support the view that the internal possessor was the prevailing one in earlier Welsh:

(13) llad   y   ben
      he-cut-off his head
      'He cut off his head.'

(14) ae vedru   yn y   lygat
      and-he thrust into his eye
      'And he thrust into his eye.'

(15) pwy a tynnawd   *dy* lygat
      who that tore-out your eye
      'Who is it that tore out your eye?'

Vennemann (2001) offers the following explanation for the difference between Irish and the other Celtic languages:

> In Modern Irish the construction type with a locative prepositional phrase has been further developed into an external possessor construction similar to the type illustrated above [. . .] for Modern Scandinavian Germanic. In view of the observation that innovations in the affected possessor construction tend to be contact phenomena, it appears likely that the Irish development occurred under Scandinavian influence in the Viking period.
>
> (Vennemann 2001: 362)

Although the internal differences among the Celtic languages can be explained by Scandinavian influence on Irish, as Vennemann suggests, there remain some other problems with the Celtic hypothesis. Thus, McWhorter (2002) argues against Celtic influence on the English possessor patterns on the grounds that there are scarcely any other traces of Celtic influence in English, especially in its syntax and lexicon; likewise, the timing of Celtic influences is problematical. Instead, McWhorter favours Scandinavian influence on English. According to him, it could have been transmitted through two mechanisms operative in language contact situations in general, viz. *trigger weakening* and general *'trimming' of overspecified and complex features*. External possessors could have belonged to the latter group:

> In many cases, already in Old English features were ripe for marginalization in a contact situation, because they occurred only variably. This

is the case with inherent reflexives, *external possessors*, directional adverbs, the *be*-perfect, the *become* passive, V2, and indefinite *man*.

(McWhorter 2002: 262; our emphasis)

McWhorter's account gives rise to the following counterarguments:

(i)   the 'standard' view on small amounts of Celtic influence in English syntax, phonology and lexicon has been contested in some recent research, see, e.g. Tristram (1999a); Filppula, Klemola and Pitkänen (2002) and the articles/references there;
(ii) the timing of Celtic influences can be explained by the prescriptive and conservative influence of the West Saxon literary tradition, see, e.g. Dal (1952), Tolkien (1963);
(iii) it remains unexplained why the earlier external possessors developed in English into internal possessors and not to the Scandinavian type of locative external possessors; cf. 'Celtic Englishes' such as Irish English which have locative external possessors due to influence from Irish;
(iv) Scandinavian languages retain the external possessor construction, albeit in a different form.

On the other hand, McWhorter's contact-based account lends indirect support for Vennemann's theory of Scandinavian influence on Irish, which has developed a similar construction type with a locative prepositional phrase.

2.2.1.5   Conclusion

To conclude, there are grounds for arguing that English and the Celtic languages, especially Welsh (and Breton), differentiate themselves from the other Indo-European languages in the ways they express the possessor–possessed relationships. Unlike the latter, they rely almost exclusively on internal possessor constructions and, in the course of their histories, seem to have shed all but few remnants of the earlier external possessor constructions. The fact that this process appears to have taken place in the Celtic languages earlier than in English leaves room for a contact explanation, especially because English has come to be very 'un-Germanic' in favouring the internal possessor constructions. It is this same feature which makes the other suggested sources, including language-internal factors, unlikely. It is true that the observed differences between Irish and Welsh weaken the case for Common Celtic influence on English. Yet it is quite plausible that the Welsh usages which rely on the internal possessor construction have triggered and promoted the change from external to internal patterns in English. This explanation does not exclude the possibility of mutually reinforcing adstratal influences in the subsequent centuries, which may then have led to the uniqueness of these two languages (alongside Breton and also Irish to some extent) among Indo-European languages.

In this case, the dating of the change does not constitute a problem either, as in English the change from external to internal possessor constructions starts off as a gradual one in the OE period and continues into the ME period, being thus in line with some of the other syntactic changes affecting English in those periods. Whether the internal possessor construction is ultimately of Semitic origin and carried on from there into Celtic languages and English as a 'transitive' contact phenomenon, as Vennemann argues (2000), is another matter which we cannot pursue here.

2.2.2   The Old English Distinction between the *es- and *bheu-forms of the Verb 'be'

While most of the grammatical features we have chosen for discussion in this book are ones which have survived into present-day English in some form or another, the feature at issue here is a putative early structural loan, which disappeared from the language as early as the beginning of the ME period. Keller (1925) is, to our knowledge, the first to pay attention to the OE distinction between the *es- and *bheu-forms of the verb 'be' and its possible Celtic background. He notes that the OE forms based on the reconstructed root *bheu* and their meanings 'is always/generally' or 'will be' are closely paralleled by the corresponding Celtic and especially Cymric forms. He further points out that, although *partially* similar parallels are found in other Germanic dialects, none of these have developed a full present tense paradigm for both roots with clearly distinct meanings. Keller concludes that this feature was introduced into English by the early Britons trying to acquire English: "[D]ie altenglischen Formen und Funktionen der Wurzel *bheu*, die den anderen germanischen Dialekten fremd sind, entstanden im Munde und im Denken von englisch sprechenden Briten"⁴ (Keller 1925: 60).

Keller's account has gone largely unnoticed amongst Anglicists, possibly because he wrote in German. For example, for all his thoroughness, Mitchell (1985) does not consider the possibility of contact influence at all in his discussion of the OE verbs *beon* and *wesan*, their meanings and their treatment in the literature. He first refutes Jost's (1909) distinction between 'konkret' (*wesan*) and 'abstrakt' (*beon*); the latter was according to Jost limited to 'future' and 'abstract' sentences, the former to 'concrete' ones (1985: §§ 651–664). Mitchell goes on to refer to Visser's treatment (in Visser 1963–1973 ii: § 723), where Visser suggests that futurity is also present in 'generic' and 'gnomic statements' using *beon*. Next, Mitchell (1985: § 659) turns to Mustanoja (1960: 583), according to whom the main function of *wesan* was to express 'a state prevailing generally or at the time of speaking', that of *beon* 'future or iterative activity'. Finally, Mitchell (1985:

§ 659) quotes Campbell (1959), for whom *beon* expresses: (a) an invariable fact; (b) the future; and (c) iterative extension into the future (OEG § 768). Mitchell concludes his survey as follows (§ 664):

> Since exceptions like these exist at all periods, one may perhaps wonder whether there were ever any firm rules and despair at establishing them. [. . .] [T]he departure from what 'rules' did exist was a gradual movement, part of the continuing process of change. That this should be so is scarcely surprising in light of the general confusion of forms in ME described in *OED*, s.v. *be v.*; of Mustanoja's statement (p. 583) that '*traces* of this old use of the *b*-forms to express futurity occur in early ME and *to some extent* even later in the period' [my italics]; and of the subsequent disappearance of even these traces.

Despite differences of terminology, the majority of the scholarly opinion seems to agree that the *b*-forms had the two basic meanings of generic/iterative and future activity (as, indeed, described by Keller). It also seems clear, as Mustanoja has shown, that these uses of the *b*-forms do not survive much beyond early ME.

Turning back to the possible Celtic connection of the feature at hand, it is quite remarkable that very few Anglicists seem to have explored it at all.[5] For example, in his grammar of Old English Campbell discusses the OE indicative forms *eom* 'I am', *bēo* 'I shall be', together with their dialectal distribution (see Campbell 1959: § 768). He lists the present indicative plural forms *biðon/bioðon* as some of the major Mercian forms but does not comment on their background (*op.cit.*, 350).

A notable exception is, as the Celticist (sic!) David Greene (1966: 136) points out, the Anglo-Saxon scholar J.R.R. Tolkien, who in his O'Donnell lecture entitled *English and Welsh* (see Tolkien 1963) discusses the parallelism between the OE and the Welsh paradigms for the verb 'be' as one of his prime examples of probable linguistic contact between the two languages. Like Keller (whose work is not, incidentally, referred to in Tolkien's lecture), Tolkien pays attention to the distinction both languages make between what he terms the 'actual present' and the 'consuetudinal present'/'future', each expressed by a different set of forms (the latter relying on forms beginning with *b*- both in OE and Welsh). Tolkien, too, makes a special mention of the uniqueness of the OE system among Germanic languages. Besides the similarities in the forms and functions of the OE and Welsh 'be' verbs, he notes the difficulty of explaining the short vowel in the OE 3sg. form *bið* as a regular development from earlier Germanic, while there is no such problem if the corresponding Welsh form *bydd* (from earlier **bið*) is considered (Tolkien 1963: 30–32).

Tolkien weighs the possibility of 'accidental' similarity and the possible role of analogy as an explanatory factor, but concludes that

[i]t will still remain notable, none the less, that this preservation occurred in Britain and in a point in which the usage of the native language [i.e. Welsh] agreed. It will be a morphological parallel to the
phonetic agreement, noted above, seen in the English preservation of
þ and *w*.

As yet another factor suggesting Celtic influence on the OE paradigms,
Tolkien mentions the Northumbrian OE plural consuetudinal form *biðun/
bioðun*. He considers this to be an innovation developed on British soil and
refers to its "unnecessary invention" and "wholly anomalous" method of
formation from the point of view of English morphology (1963: 32). By
contrast, Welsh *byddant* offers itself as a parallel and as a possible source of
this feature (*ibid.*).

The earlier Welsh parallel to the OE distinction is clear, which becomes
evident from the paradigm that Morris-Jones (1913: 346) gives for the
mediaeval (Middle) Welsh consuetudinal present and future of the verb 'to
be' (note that the forms marked with † are obsolete in Modern Welsh; where
the Modern form or spelling differs is given in brackets):

    1. byðaf, † byðif,   1. byðwn
    2. byðy (byddi)   2. byðwch
    3. byð   3. byðant
    Cons. bit (bid)   † byðhawnt, † bint
    Fut. † bi, † byðhawt, † biawt
    Impers. (byddys, byddir)

A similar account, albeit with a slightly different orthographic notation,
is given in Strachan (1909: 98, § 152):

    1. bydaf   bydwn
    2. bydy   bydwch
    3. byd   bydant

The existence of the Welsh parallel and the uniqueness of OE amongst
Germanic languages with respect to this feature make it more than likely
that the OE distinction between the **es-* and **bheu*-forms of the verb 'be'
is a result of early linguistic contacts between the Britons and the Anglo-
Saxons.

2.2.3   The Northern Subject Rule

The Standard English subject–verb agreement pattern, where the inflectional marker -*s* is only attached to third person singular forms, is a badly
mutilated survivor of an earlier, considerably richer Germanic agreement

pattern. Thus it is not surprising that in regional dialects of English at least three alternative patterns have evolved. A typical agreement pattern in some traditional dialects in the south-west of England and East Anglia, as exemplified in (16), has done away with the inflectional marker -*s* altogether (cf. Wakelin 1977: 119–120),

(16) I/you/he/she/it/we/you/they *read*

whereas in some southern/south-western dialects the inflectional marker -*s* has been generalised over the whole paradigm, as in (17).

(17) I/you/he/she/it/we/you/they *reads*

The third variant of the subject–verb agreement paradigm, the so-called Northern Subject Rule, is employed in many traditional northern and North Midlands dialects. In these varieties the presence of the inflectional marker -*s* depends on the nature and position of the subject, as in the following examples from Ihalainen (1994: 221):

(18) They *peel* them and *boils* them.

(19) Birds *sings*.

The name 'the Northern Subject Rule' (NSR) for this construction type was coined by Ossi Ihalainen (1994: 221).[6] The NSR states essentially that in the present tense, the verb takes the -*s* ending in all persons, singular and plural, unless it is adjacent to a personal pronoun subject (except for the third person singular, where the -*s* ending is used regardless of the type and proximity of the subject NP). Thus in *They peel them*, where the subject is an adjacent personal pronoun, no ending is used, whereas in *Birds sings*, where the subject is a full noun phrase, or in *They peel them and boils them*, where the subject of *boils* is not adjacent to the verb, the inflectional ending -*s* is used. In this section we will discuss the geographical distribution and history of the NSR and suggest that the occurrence of this agreement pattern in northern dialects of English is due to Brythonic substratal influence.

2.2.3.1   *The Geographical Distribution and History of the Northern Subject Rule*

James Murray, in his *Dialect of the Southern Counties of Scotland* (1873), is one of the first scholars to draw attention to the peculiar agreement pattern in the dialects of Scotland and northern England. Murray (1873: 211–212) states that

[i]n the PRESENT TENSE, aa *leyke*, wey *leyke*, yee *leyke*, thay *leyke*, are only used when the verb is accompanied by its proper pronoun; when the subject is a noun, adjective, interrogative or relative pronoun, or when the verb and subject are separated by a clause, the verb takes the termination -*s* in all persons. [. . .] Such expressions as "the men *syts*" are not vulgar corruptions, but strictly grammatical in the Northern dialect.

Slightly later, Joseph Wright in his *English Dialect Grammar* (1905: 296) presents a relatively detailed description of the geographical distribution of the NSR construction in late nineteenth-century English dialects:

§ 435. Present: In Sh. & Or.I. Sc. Irel. n.Cy [north country] and most of the north-midland dialects all persons, singular and plural, take **s**, **z**, or **ǝz** when not immediately preceded or followed by their proper pronoun; that is when the subject is a noun, an interrogative or relative pronoun, or when the verb and subject are separated by a clause. [. . .] When the verb is immediately preceded or followed by its proper pronoun, the first pers. sing. and the whole of the plural gen. have no special endings in the above dialects, except occasionally in parts of Yks. Lan. and Lin.

The evidence to be found in *The Survey of English Dialects (SED)* analysed in Klemola (2000) presents a roughly similar geographical distribution of the NSR construction in traditional mid-twentieth-century dialects of English English; the *SED* data discussed in Klemola (2000: 331–335) indicate that the NSR was, at the time the *SED* fieldwork was conducted, in use in the pre-1974 counties of Northumberland, Cumberland, Durham and Westmorland, and to some extent in Lancashire, Yorkshire, Lincolnshire, Derbyshire and Nottinghamshire. In other words, the geographical distribution of the construction seems to have remained stable over the roughly one hundred-year period from Wright to the *SED*.

Turning to the earlier history of the NSR, Mustanoja (1960: 481–482) briefly mentions the NSR type agreement pattern as a feature of northern ME and Middle Scots, and furthermore, points out that the rule is generally followed in these northern varieties of ME and that "the exceptions to this rule are mostly due to the requirements of the metre or to southern influence". As far as the geographical distribution of the NSR is concerned, McIntosh (1989) shows that in late ME at least, subject–verb agreement followed the NSR in the area north of a line which runs across England roughly from Chester to the Wash. McIntosh (1989: 117) gives the following paradigm for the fully northern late ME subject–verb agreement system (which observes the NSR, or 'the personal pronoun rule', to use McIntosh's terminology):

	(i) subject not a personal pronoun in contact with verb	(ii) personal pronoun subject in contact with verb
3 sg	-es	-es
1,2,3 pl	-es	-e, -ø; in the south of the N area, often -en

McIntosh (1989: 117–118, 120) also mentions an interesting "mixed lect" paradigm which was used in an area immediately to the south of the Chester–Wash line, in the Fens and parts of Cambridgeshire and Northamptonshire. This mixed lect, while making use of the endings current in the Midlands paradigm, -eth and -en, still follows the NSR in its use of these endings. The paradigm McIntosh (1989: 120) gives for this mixed lect has the form:

	(i) subject not a personal pronoun in contact with verb	(ii) personal pronoun subject in contact with verb
3 sg	-eth	-eth
1,2,3 pl	-eth	-en (-e, -ø)

Unfortunately, very few texts written in northern dialects have survived from the early ME period, and the texts that have survived are too short to give any reliable picture of the agreement system in northern dialects at the time. But the evidence from late ME texts would seem to indicate that the NSR was already fully established at the time during the fourteenth century when northern ME texts become more common. It is probably this that led Murray (1873: 212) to argue that the NSR-type agreement pattern predates the first written records of northern ME: "before the date of the earliest Northern writings of the thirteenth century, the form without the -s had been extended to all cases in which the verb was accompanied by its proper pronoun, whether before or after it, leaving the full form in -s to be used with other nominatives only". This provides us a *terminus ante quem* for the introduction of the NSR in the northern varieties of ME; how long the construction may have been in use in spoken language before its first attestation in written documents must unfortunately remain an unanswerable question.

2.2.3.2   The Origins of the Northern Subject Rule

Although the NSR construction was already described by such eminent nineteenth-century philologists as James Murray and Joseph Wright, it was not until Otto Jespersen that any explanations for the origin of this type of an agreement pattern were offered. Jespersen (MEG VI: § 3.2) considers the NSR a development of an OE agreement pattern (cf. Campbell 1959: § 730):

> In OE a difference is made in the plural, according as the verb precedes *we* or *ge* or not (*binde we, binde ge,* but *we bindaþ, ge bindaþ*). This is the germ of the more radical difference now carried through consistently in the Scottish dialect, where the *s* is only added when the vb is not accompanied with its proper pronoun, but in that case it is used in all persons.

King (1997), after citing Macafee's (1992–1993: 21) statement that "it is unclear how this double system of concord arose", proceeds to explain the rise of the NSR construction in essentially similar terms as Jespersen. She refers to Campbell's (1959: § 730) discussion of the OE usage where the plural endings *-aþ, -on, -en* can be reduced to *-e* when the pronouns *we* or *ge* follow the verb, and concludes:

> As a result of this reduction, verb forms with this <e> (presumably representing schwa) would cease to be distinctive for person in the present tense or for mood, since both singular and plural in the subjunctive would become identical in <e>. [. . .] Where loss of person markings in verbs is concerned, in both Old and Middle English periods (especially for the latter in the North), the forms of most of the personal pronouns were distinct enough from each other to supply any 'missing' information on person.
>
> (King 1997: 176–177)

The attempts to explain the NSR as a system-internal development in northern dialects of ME have not managed to give a satisfactory explanation for the agreement pattern that is governed simultaneously by the type of the subject NP (lexical noun vs. pronoun) and its proximity to the verb. The possibility of an external, contact-induced explanation for the construction was already hinted at by Eric Hamp (1975–1976) in an addendum to an article that focused on the lack of NP–VP concord in British Celtic:

> Angus McIntosh points out to me in conversation that Northern English, in earlier documents and in some surviving dialects, requires 3sg. verb with a noun subject (*horses runs*) but plural with a pronoun (*þai run*) provided no expression intervenes; therefore, with a relative, *þai þat runs*. This looks for all the world like an independent witness from Cumbrian or Strathclyde substratum syntax.
>
> (Hamp 1975–1976: 73)

From a typological point of view, agreement systems of the type exemplified by the NSR appear to be extremely rare. In general, this type of agreement seems to be found in verb-initial languages. Thus Vennemann (2001), citing Lipiński (1997: 491 f.) for Arabic and Jenni (1981: § 6.3.2) for Hebrew, points out that similar agreement patterns are found in Semitic languages;[7] White (2002: 158) adds Tagalog to the list. However, the closest parallel, both structurally and geographically, to the construction type is found in the Brythonic languages—Welsh, Cornish and Breton (cf. Evans 1971: 49). In his grammar of Modern Welsh, King (1993: 137) states that "3rd pers. pl. forms are only used when the corresponding pronoun **nhw** *they* is explicitly stated. In all other cases where the subject is 3rd pers. pl., the 3rd pers. sing. form must be used" (cf. also Evans 1971: 42). The examples King gives are:

(20) *Maen nhw*'n dysgu Cymraeg   [pl. verb]
They are learning Welsh

(21) *Mae* Kev a Gina yn dysgu Cymraeg   [sing. verb]
Kev and Gina are learning Welsh

(22) *Gân nhw* ailwneud y gwaith 'ma yfory   [pl. verb]
They can redo this work tomorrow

(23) *Geith* y myfyrwyr ailwneud y gwaith 'ma yfory   [sing. verb]
The students can redo this work tomorrow

Furthermore, a third person singular form of the verb is used in relative clauses, where the (plural) relative is the subject (Evans 1971: 43).

In Modern Welsh, in other words, the third person singular form of the verb is used when the subject is a full noun phrase in plural. With an adjacent pronominal subject, or when there is no overt subject, third person plural agreement is used. The paradigm for Modern Welsh is thus:

1. maent   [they] are
2. maent hwy   they are
3. mae 'r bechgyn   the boys are

where 1. (no overt subject) and 2. (adjacent personal pronoun subject) are grouped together as against 3. (full noun phrase subject). This system, although it is not identical with the NSR paradigm, where 1. and 3. are grouped together as against 2., is still remarkably similar to the northern English agreement pattern.

There is some disagreement about the antiquity of this agreement pattern in written Welsh (cf. Evans 1971; Greene 1971; Jackson 1973–1974; Hamp 1975–1976). Evans (1971), however, is convinced that this agreement pattern has always been a feature of spoken Welsh: "on the basis of what evidence is available, it appears safe to conclude that lack of concord was the normal practice in spoken Welsh from the very beginning" (Evans 1971: 50). Furthermore, Evans (1971: 49) points out that similar agreement patterns are also found in Cornish and Breton, and suggests tentatively that "the three languages could have inherited lack of concord from the parent British", in other words, that the agreement pattern dates back to the sixth century or earlier (cf. also Lewis and Pedersen 1961: 269; Jackson 1973–1974: 2–3).

Isaac (2003a: 53–57) argues against the possibility of contact-induced change as an explanation for the NSR, opting instead for a system-internal explanation:

> [T]he prehistory and history of the NSR can be formulated entirely in terms of the phonological, morphosyntactic and lexical development of English itself, without reference to Celtic languages of any variety. And since it can be so formulated, it must be so formulated.
>
> (Isaac 2003a: 57)

Isaac's explanation for the rise of the NSR runs as follows:

(i)　As a consequence of the levelling of unstressed vowels, the third person singular and plural endings in the present tense of verbs in OE (*-(e)þ* and *-aþ*) fell together in ME, resulting in identical forms for the singular and the plural (Northern *-(e)s*).

(ii)　In ME, the unstressed forms of third person singular and plural forms of the personal pronoun fell together in *ha*.

The NSR then, according to Isaac (2003a: 56–57), arises during the ME period in northern dialects as a disambiguation strategy: with nominal subjects a distinction between singular and plural can still be made (*the man bindes* vs. *the men bindes*), but with unstressed pronominal subjects the distinction is lost, resulting in identical forms for the singular and the plural (*ha bindes* vs. *ha bindes*). The ambiguity was then, according to Isaac, resolved "by transferring the plural ending of the subjunctive and preterite to the present indicative, producing *ha bindes* vs. *ha binde* (*binden, bind*)" (*ibid*.). Thus, Isaac argues, the NSR can—and, according to him, therefore also must—be explained through the 'natural', internal history of the English language.

Though Isaac's explanation may at first sight seem attractive, it is not without its problems. First of all, Isaac's explanation only supplies an answer to the subject-type constraint (full NP vs. pronominal) of the NSR; it does not address the question of adjacency at all. Secondly, and perhaps more importantly, Isaac's explanation relies crucially on the coalescence of the unstressed third person singular and plural forms of the personal pronoun in ME. However, he fails to notice that the unstressed *ha* forms in early ME have only been attested in (south-west) Midlands and southern documents (cf. *OED Online* s.vv. *hi, hy; he; heo*; see also Gericke and Greul 1934). Crucially for the NSR, unstressed *ha* forms are not attested in northern ME, where, already in the earliest surviving ME documents, descendants of Scandinavian *th*-forms are used instead, as Lass also observes: "Northern Middle English dialects generally show a full Scandinavian paradigm from earliest times, with descendants of *þeir, þeirra, þeim*" (Lass 1992: 120). In other words, Isaac's explanation for the motivation of the NSR relies on an assumption that is arguably no less speculative than the explanation that seeks to explain the NSR through Brythonic substratum influence.

2.2.3.3   Conclusion

By examining data ranging from ME documents representing northern dialects to the *SED* data representing nineteenth and twentieth century traditional dialects, we have shown that the NSR both displays a clear and relatively stable geographic distribution in the north of England and has been a feature of these northern dialects at least from the late ME period onwards (and probably earlier). Typological comparison shows that the closest parallels to this rare type of subject–verb agreement pattern are to be found in Brythonic languages, where a fairly similar agreement pattern is found from at least the sixth century onwards. This prompts the question of the possibility of the NSR manifesting substratum influence from the Brythonic language of the Britons in the north of England. In the light of what is known about the early settlement in the north of England, the possibility of such substratum influence is plausible. Further evidence for this possibility is offered by the data on traditional enumeration from parts of the north of England, which may represent a survival from the Brythonic language spoken by the Britons in the north (cf. section 2.2.8.3). Although it cannot be argued that these three different strands of evidence would conclusively show that such interference through language shift has taken place, there is sufficient evidence to argue that contact between English and a Brythonic language spoken in the north of England is a credible explanatory factor for the rise of the NSR.

2.2.4   Periphrastic DO

The use of the periphrastic auxiliary verb DO is one of the most prominent characteristics of ModE verb syntax.[8] It is also a feature that sets English apart from not only the other Germanic languages, but also Standard Average European, as Denison (1993: 255) remarks. Thus it is not surprising that the question of the origins of periphrastic DO has been one of the central problems in English historical linguistics, and that there is a wide diversity of opinions on this matter.[9] The earliest attestations of the periphrastic DO construction are found in affirmative declarative sentences in thirteenth-century south-western ME, as in example (24) (from Denison 1993: 264):

> (24)   c1300(?C1225) *Horn* 1057
> His sclauyn   he dude dun   legge
> His pilgrim's cloak he did   down lay
> 'He laid down his pilgrim's cloak.'

In negative declaratives (25) and questions (26) periphrastic DO is found slightly later, from the end of the fourteenth century onwards (examples [25] and [26] from Denison 1993: 265):

> (25)   c1460(?c1400) *Beryn* 557
> that were   grete vnry3te, | To aventour oppon a man þat
> that would-be great wrong | to venture   against a man that
> with hym did nat fi3te.
> with one did not fight

> (26)   c1380 *Firumb.(1)* (Ashm) 3889
> How dost þow, harlot, þyn erand   bede?
> How do   you   rascal   your message deliver
> 'What kind of message are you delivering, rascal?'

During the following centuries the system of auxiliary verbs slowly developed towards its present shape, so that by the early eighteenth-century periphrastic DO had become firmly established in negatives, questions and in emphatic contexts. In affirmative declarative contexts, however, the use of periphrastic DO began to decline during the latter half of the sixteenth century, and by about 1700 periphrastic DO in affirmative declaratives had practically disappeared from what was becoming Standard English. Unstressed periphrastic DO in affirmative declarative statements has, however, survived in some south-western dialects of English, as exemplified in (27) and (28) below (from Klemola 1994: 33):

> (27)   When they do meet they do always fight. (31 So6; Stogursey, Somerset)

> (28)   If I did do it I did always stand 'em first. (32 W6; Netheravon, Wiltshire)

In this section we will approach the question of the origins of periphrastic DO from the vantage point of the dialectal distribution of unstressed periphrastic DO in affirmative statements in English dialects. We begin with a survey of the geographical distribution of unstressed periphrastic DO in affirmative statements. The starting-point for the discussion is the distribution of DO in traditional dialects of present-day English. The present-day dialectological facts are then projected backwards in time in an argument that the geographical distribution of DO during earlier historical stages of English can to some extent be inferred from the mid-twentieth-century starting-point. The dialectological survey is followed by a discussion of the origins of periphrastic DO, concentrating on the causative hypothesis, mainly associated with Ellegård (1953), and on the Celtic hypothesis. The implications that the geographical distribution of periphrastic DO may have for the Celtic hypothesis are also addressed. Finally, we will evaluate the likelihood of substratal influences from Brythonic languages in the light of the evidence discussed.

2.2.4.1   The Geographical Distribution of Periphrastic DO in English Dialects

The use of unstressed periphrastic DO in affirmative declarative sentences is a well-known, almost stereotypical feature of the south-western dialects of English English. However, even the relatively recent discussions of south-western dialects offer surprisingly conflicting descriptions of the geographical distribution of the construction. Thus, for example, Wakelin (1977: 120–121) claims that the use of periphrastic DO is a very isolated feature found in some south-western localities, possibly a remnant of a single, larger area (cf. also Wakelin 1983: 8; 1984a: 83). Rogers (1979: 39), on the other hand, has argued that the use of DO-periphrasis is more widespread in the south-west of England. Klemola (1996) presents an attempt to determine the geographical distribution of periphrastic DO in the traditional dialects of England on the basis of all the available evidence.[10]

Map 2.1 presents the geographical distribution of unstressed periphrastic DO in affirmative statements in the traditional dialects of England towards the middle of the twentieth century. The map is drawn on the basis of an extensive survey of both the published *SED* materials (Orton *et al.*: 1962–1971) and the unpublished material collected in the *SED* fieldworker notebooks.[11] The focal area of periphrastic DO usage in English dialects, as shown on Map 2.1, is in the West Wiltshire-East Somerset area. The round shape of the isogloss on Map 2.1 would seem to indicate that, historically, periphrastic DO was an innovation that took place somewhere in the focal area of West Wiltshire and East Somerset and spread from there. Indeed, in the light of historical documents this seems to be the case, as Ellegård (1953: 47) confirms: "Our findings also make it probable that periphrastic *do* really originated in the West (or rather, South-West)".

But what about the geographical distribution of periphrastic DO before the mid-twentieth century and the *SED* evidence? Although the use of unstressed periphrastic DO in affirmative declarative sentences is mentioned as a characteristic feature of south-western dialects already in many

Map 2.1 The geographical distribution of unstressed periphrastic DO in affirmative statements in the traditional dialects of England and Wales in the mid-twentieth century (from Klemola 1996: 64).

nineteenth-century dialect descriptions, these early dialect studies, as a rule, are not very helpful when one tries to determine the geographical distribution of DO-periphrasis in any detail. Thus, for example, Joseph Wright states in his *English Dialect Grammar* (1905: 297) that "the periphrastic form *I do love*, &c. for *I love*, &c. is in gen[eral] use in the south-western dialects", but does not give any more detailed indication of the geographical boundaries of the use of DO-periphrasis. The use of periphrastic DO is also mentioned in many other nineteenth-century south-western dialect descriptions: Cornwall (Jago 1882: 57), Dorset (Barnes 1886: 23), Gloucester (Robertson 1890: 37), and Somerset (Elworthy 1877: 49–51). There is, however, one nineteenth-century dialect survey which offers us a very detailed picture of the geographical distribution of the use of periphrastic DO in mid- to late nineteenth-century England. This is Alexander Ellis's monumental study, *On Early English Pronunciation. Part V: The Existing Phonology of English Dialects Compared with that of West Saxon Speech* (Ellis 1889). Although Ellis does not explicitly discuss the geographical boundaries of the use of periphrastic DO, it is still possible to reconstruct in some detail the area where the construction was used on the basis of the comments scattered over the ca 1300 pages of Ellis's dialect survey.[12] Map 2.2, drawn on the

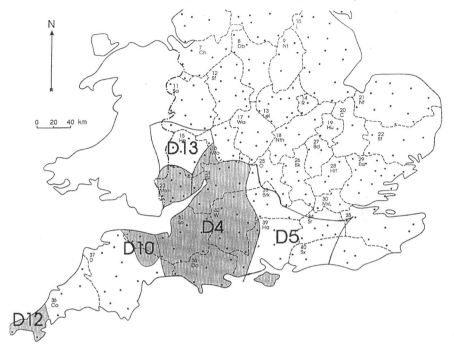

Map 2.2 The geographical distribution of unstressed periphrastic DO in affirmative statements in the rural dialects of England in the mid-nineteenth century on the basis of Ellis (1889) (from Klemola 1996: 26).

basis of the remarks found in Ellis (1889), represents as accurate a picture of the geographical distribution of periphrastic DO in the mid- to late nineteenth century as we can ever hope to obtain.

When Maps 2.1 and 2.2 are compared, it becomes immediately clear that there is a remarkably good fit between the geographical distribution of periphrastic DO, as described by Ellis (Map 2.2), and the distribution that can be inferred from the *SED* data collected in the 1950s, about a hundred years after Ellis (Map 2.1). Ellis's study is based on material that was collected during the time period 1868–1881 (Ellis 1889: xviii–xix). Ellis does not state explicitly how old his dialect informants were on average but, judging from the description of the interview method of his principal fieldworker, Thomas Hallam, we may safely assume that the informants whose speech Ellis analysed were typical NORMs (non-mobile, older, rural males), probably over sixty years old (for the term NORM, see Chambers and Trudgill 1998: 29–30).[13]

One of the assumptions behind the apparent-time method in the sociolinguistic study of linguistic change is that "each generation acquires its basic motor-controlled vernacular and its evaluative norms between the ages four and seventeen" (Downes 1984: 198). This means, for example,

that the basic vernacular speech of those who were sixty years old at
around 2000 would have been acquired during a roughly ten-year period
between the years 1945 and 1955, and that their vernacular speech can
therefore be taken as representative of the speech patterns that were in use
at that time.[14] Applying the above-mentioned basic assumption behind the
apparent-time method to Ellis's survey (and assuming that Ellis's dialect
informants were 60+ years old on average), we can infer that Ellis (1889)
reflects the situation during the first quarter of the nineteenth century. The
SED data displayed on Map 2.1, on the other hand, also based on data
collected from NORM informants, were collected during the 1950s, and
can thus be taken to reflect the situation during the last decades of the nineteenth century. In other words, the close match between Map 2.2, based on
Ellis (1889), and Map 2.1, based on the *SED*, together with the backwards
projection principle of the apparent-time method, warrants the conclusion
that the *SED* data probably reflect fairly accurately the dialectal distribution of periphrastic DO as far back in time as the first decades of the nineteenth century.

There are no reliable, systematic descriptions of English folk-speech that
could take us further back in time than the first decades of the nineteenth
century. However, as Ihalainen (1994) has argued, English (traditional)
dialect areas and characteristics on the whole have been remarkably stable
and in many cases well-established for centuries. This prompts the question
whether it is possible that the *SED* distribution of periphrastic DO, as shown
on Map 2.1, could indeed provide us with a fairly good indication of the
dialectal distribution of unstressed periphrastic DO even before the early
nineteenth century. Some evidence pointing in this direction can be found
in the surviving written documents from the ME and Early Modern English
(EModE) periods. Alvar Ellegård arrives at the following conclusion about
the geographical distribution of periphrastic DO in ME and EModE:

> The origin of the do-construction, according to my argument in Part I,
> has to be sought in the Central and Western parts of the South, from
> where it spread eastwards and northwards. All through the 15th cen-
> tury it is absent in prose works from the North, and is rare in the East.
> In the 16th and 17th centuries the do-form continues to be used much
> less often in the North than elsewhere.
>
> (Ellegård 1953: 164)

Ellegård's work is probably still the most detailed and reliable historical study on the origin and development of periphrastic DO. It is based on
an extensive and well-documented corpus of ME and EModE texts. Thus
Ellegård's conclusions about the dialectal distribution of periphrastic DO
can be considered reliable. A similar conclusion on the dialectal distribution
of periphrastic DO is found in Mustanoja's *Middle English Syntax*:

The earliest prose instances of periphrastic *do* date from c 1400, but the construction remains uncommon down to the end of the 15th century, being rarer in the East than in the West. The Paston Letters contain few instances of periphrastic *do*. In Caxton's early works it is much less frequent than in his later products. It is not found in the prose written in the North during the 15th century, and it remains comparatively rare in the northern prose works of the 16th and 17th centuries.

(Mustanoja 1960: 603–604)

There is also strong evidence to indicate that periphrastic DO was not used in Middle Scots during the fifteenth and sixteenth centuries. In her study based on the extensive *Helsinki Corpus of Older Scots* (1450–1700), Meurman-Solin (1993: 248) found that periphrastic DO is introduced into Scots prose as late as the latter half of the sixteenth century. She further argues that the form shows signs of having been introduced into Scots through the influence of southern English (presumably the London standard). As early Scots was very heavily influenced by the northern varieties of English, the fact that periphrastic DO seems not to have been an indigenous feature of early varieties of Scots lends further support to the claim that the construction is a southern borrowing rather than an original feature of the northern vernacular varieties of ME and EModE. In other words, it appears that periphrastic DO is a south-western innovation, and that the later introduction of DO to the northern vernacular varieties (in questions, negative, etc.) took place through the influence of the evolving standard variety of English as a *change from above*, to use the terminology introduced by Labov (see, e.g. Labov 1994: 78).[15]

To sum up the discussion on the geographical distribution of periphrastic DO: we have argued above that the mid-twentieth-century distribution of periphrastic DO in affirmative declarative sentences in traditional dialects of English, as shown on Map 2.1, can be used as the basis for a backwards projection of the distribution of this construction in earlier historical periods. The evidence found in Ellis (1889) and earlier, EModE and late ME written documents supports the argument that periphrastic DO was originally a feature of the south-western dialects of ME, and only later diffused to other vernacular dialects as a consequence of the growing influence of the southern standard from the seventeenth century onwards.

2.2.4.2   Origins of Periphrastic DO

2.2.4.2.1   Causative Hypothesis
According to the widely accepted theory mainly associated with Ellegård (1953), the periphrastic DO construction in English developed from an earlier, causative, use of the verb DO. In a nutshell, Ellegård's argument runs as follows: in late OE/early ME, a construction consisting of causative DO +

NP + infinitive came to be widely used in the east and south-east of England. This construction is exemplified by (29) (from Denison 1993: 257):

> (29) c1155 *Peterb.Chron.* 1140.22
>   Þe biscop of Wincestre ... dide   heom cumen   þider.
>   the bishop of Winchester ... caused them come (INF) thither
>   'The bishop of Winchester ... had them come there.'

The 'DO + NP + infinitive' construction had a variant, where the subject of the infinitive was not expressed ('DO + infinitive'), as in example (30), from Denison (1993: 257):

> (30) a1225(c1200) *Vices and V.(1)* 25.10
>   Ðis hali mihte ðe   dieð   ilieuen ðat ...
>   this holy virtue that causes believe that ...
>   'This holy virtue which causes one to believe that ...'

According to Ellegård (1953: 28–33; 118–119), the periphrastic DO construction then arose as a result of a reinterpretation[16] of such equivocal 'DO + infinitive' constructions that could be interpreted either as causative or as purely periphrastic constructions where DO was interpreted as a semantically empty auxiliary. The equivocal construction is exemplified in (31) (from Denison 1993: 278).

> (31) ?a1400(a1338) Mannyng, *Chron.Pt.2* 97.22
>   Henry ... I þe walles did   doun felle, þe tours   bette he doun.
>   Henry ... I the walls   'did' down fell the towers beat he down
>   'Henry ... felled the walls, he beat down the towers.'

As Denison (1993: 278) states, "*Did felle* [...] could be interpreted either as *did* 'caused' + *felle* 'to fell/be felled' or as *did* 'past tense' + *felle* 'cause to fell/be felled'". The interpretation of DO as a purely periphrastic auxiliary in these equivocal contexts then led to the rise of periphrastic DO in general.

One of the major problems for Ellegård's causative theory is that periphrastic DO first shows up in the south-western dialects of early ME, where the causative use of DO was very rare. Ellegård states the problem as follows:

> The very frequent use of *do x*—periphrastic and equivocal—in late 13th century south-western verse texts thus remains a problem. If it is not a development of an earlier widespread use of causative *do* in these dialects, how is this construction to be explained?

> (Ellegård 1953: 55)

Ellegård (1953: 119–148) also discusses a number of alternative explanations for the rise of the periphrastic DO construction. One of the alternative explanations that avoids the problem of virtual non-occurrence of causative DO in south-western dialects in the early ME period is that periphrastic DO in English arose as a result of Celtic substratum influence. This is the topic that we turn to next.

2.2.4.2.2 *The Celtic Hypothesis*

A number of scholars have argued that the origin of periphrastic DO in English crucially involves language contact and Celtic substratum influence.[17] As Garrett (1998: 285) points out in his otherwise very critical account of the Celtic hypothesis, "a point in favour of this view is that all three British Celtic languages have a construction formed with 'do' and a verbal noun".[18]

Walther Preusler (1938, 1956) was one of the earliest scholars to make explicit the claim that periphrastic DO in English is due to Celtic influence. Preusler (1938: 182; 1956: 334–335) argues that since in Welsh a construction with a verb corresponding to periphrastic DO is attested before the late thirteenth century, which is the period when Preusler considers periphrastic DO to have appeared in English, one must assume that it was the Welsh language that influenced English. Furthermore, Preusler (1938: 182) points out the fact that unstressed periphrastic DO has survived in the south-western dialects of English as an archaism and that it is significant that this archaic feature has survived just in the area where Welsh and Cornish influence must have been strongest.

Despite the problems that the occurrence of the periphrastic DO in the south-west causes for the causative theory of the origin of DO, Ellegård is reluctant to concede the possibility of Welsh influence:

> In spite of the fact that my investigation tends to show that English periphrastic *do* originated in the South West, which would seem to lend some support to Preusler's thesis, I do not think that it is acceptable. To establish a genetical connection between parallell [*sic*] expressions in two languages it is not enough to show that the expression exists in both languages, and is found earlier in one than in the other. We need more circumstantial evidence as well.
>
> In this case it is relevant to ask the following questions. First: is there any evidence that Welsh influence was especially strong in the 13th century, the time when the periphrasis is first found in English? Celtic influence is generally believed to have been fairly insignificant in English, and I do not see any reason why it should have been stronger in the 13th century than during all the previous centuries that the races had been in contact.

(Ellegård 1953: 119)

Ellegård, however, is characteristically careful not to completely rule out the possibility of Celtic influence:

> It would be rash, however, to exclude the possibility of Celtic influence altogether. A more detailed study of conditions in Welsh and Cornish in the 13th century may reveal facts that have a bearing on the problem. Until that is done—and I am in no position to do it—Welsh influence can only be referred to as a possible contributory factor to the rise of periphrastic *do* in English.
>
> (Ellegård 1953: 120)

One of Ellegård's main objections to Celtic influence has to do with timing: he argues that there is no reason to assume that Welsh influence on English could have been a significant factor at the time when the first instances of periphrastic DO are attested in south-western dialects during the thirteenth century (1953: 119). However, it is not necessary to assume that the possible Welsh influence must be concurrent with the first attestations of the construction in written documents. It is not implausible to assume that there may be a time delay of even several centuries between contact influence and the first attestation of that influence in written documents, as for example Dal (1952: 348–349) has plausibly argued in her discussion of the origins of the English progressive construction.

A further factor supporting the possibility of Brythonic influence on the rise of periphrastic DO in English is the geographical distribution of DO, both in the light of the dialectal evidence discussed above and the evidence from the first attestations that Ellegård discusses. The possible significance of the West Wiltshire/East Somerset focal area of periphrastic DO usage (cf. Map 2.1 above) is especially interesting in the light of the recent findings of Richard Coates. Coates (2002: 60–63) argues that a body of place-name evidence from north-West Wiltshire "suggests the late persistence of Brittonic in the north-west," and that it may be inferred "with some confidence that there was a small area of Brittonic culture persisting [in north-west Wiltshire] into the seventh century, of a type denser than that represented by the general rather high background level of Brittonic place-names in Wiltshire".

The existence of periphrastic *tun/doen* in southern German and some Dutch dialects (cf. Eroms 1998; van der Horst 1998; van der Auwera and Genee 2002: 286–288) may be considered a problem for the hypothesis that the rise of the English periphrastic DO is due to Celtic substratum influence originating somewhere in the south-west of England. Preusler (1938: 182–183) does not consider this to be a problem, however: he points out that it is probable that strong Celtic substratum influence is also present in southern German dialects. Peter Schrijver (personal communication) also points out that the possibility of Celtic influence in southern German and Coastal Dutch dialects should not be ruled out. Furthermore, Schrijver (1999) has argued that it can be established "on independent grounds that along the Dutch and Belgian coast up north into Frisia Celtic survived well into the first millennium and influenced local Germanic".

2.2.4.3　Conclusion

In the discussion above we have argued that the geographical distribution of unstressed periphrastic DO in English has been stable over long periods of time: the distribution of the construction in the traditional dialects of the twentieth century still reflects relatively accurately the distribution of the periphrastic DO construction in the EModE period and probably even beyond that time period. Thus the dialectal distribution of unstressed periphrastic DO accords well with Ellegård (1953), who argued that periphrastic DO originated in south-western dialects of ME some time during the early ME period. Furthermore, we have argued that the geographical distribution of periphrastic DO supports the conclusion that Celtic, especially Brythonic, contact influence must be taken into account as a likely contributory factor when explaining the origin of periphrastic DO in English.

Thus we concur with van der Auwera and Genee's (2002: 302) cautious conclusion: although it is unlikely that there will ever be sufficient direct evidence to prove any one theory on the origins of English periphrastic DO, there is enough evidence to conclude that Brythonic influence is one of the factors that must be taken into account in any discussion on the origins of English periphrastic DO.

2.2.5　The Progressive (or -*ing*) Form

The so-called progressive form (PF) is one of the most often mentioned features of English grammar which may have its origins in the Celtic languages. It is also one for which several competing explanations have been offered in the literature, ranging from the Celtic to the Classical and Romance languages, to universal features of language acquisition in contact conditions, and to possible *Sprachbund* developments in the languages spoken in the British Isles. As such, it presents the historical linguist with particularly complex problems. Before embarking on a detailed discussion on the subject, it should be noted that the term 'progressive form' is here used as a convenient and familiar enough cover term and is not meant to be tied to any single semantic notion such as 'progressivity' or 'processivity'. Indeed, in much of the previous research the more neutral term 'expanded form' is used, in recognition of the fact that this form can have different meanings.

We begin with a survey of some pioneering works on the possible Celtic background of the English PF. This will be followed by a similar survey of how the Celtic hypothesis has been received in the literature. From there the discussion moves on to a detailed examination of some of the most important *pros* and *cons* in the light of the most recent research conducted by us and other scholars.

2.2.5.1   Pioneering Works on the Celtic Hypothesis

Some of the earliest and most influential studies exploring the Celtic connection of the English PF are Keller (1925), Dal (1952), Preusler (1956), Wagner (1959), and Braaten (1967). Van Hamel (1912) should also be mentioned as a pioneering study and as a source of inspiration for subsequent research, although he focuses on the influence of Irish on what he calls the 'Anglo-Irish' dialect of English, i.e. Irish English or 'Hiberno-English'.

Keller's article marks, as he himself puts it, "den Anfang einer Erklärung typisch englischer syntaktischer Eigentümlichkeiten aus dem Keltischen" [the beginning of an explanation of some typical syntactic features of English in terms of Celtic influence] (1925: 66). Keller discusses two such features, the first of which is the OE *is/bið* distinction (see section 2.2.2 for discussion), while the second is the English gerund or verbal noun construction. For some reason or other, his views on the rise of the English gerund and the PF are much better known and more often quoted in later research than those on the OE verb 'be'. According to Keller, the use of the verbal noun as the predicate of the verb 'be' gradually led to the emergence of the so-called PF during the ME period. This construction, as Keller argues, was modelled on the parallel Cymric one consisting of the 'substantive' verb 'be' + (preposition) *yn* + verbal noun (e.g. *mae yn dysgu* '[he] is learning').[19] As a further factor speaking for Celtic influence on the English PF Keller observes that the English PF *to be (a) doing* has no parallels in the other Germanic languages, except for the Low German dialect of Westfalish and Dutch folk-speech, which, however, rely on the infinitive instead of the verbal noun or the *-ing* form. As already noted above, Keller dates the rise of the PF to the ME period; according to him, the verbal noun construction, or rather, the PF in its more or less present-day form, does not become established in English until the fourteenth century (Keller 1925: 60, 64). In this respect, there is a clear chronological difference between the emergence of the OE *is/bið* distinction, which is already found in OE literary sources, and the rise of the PF in ME. However, Keller offers no comment on this.

Writing both before and after World War II, Walther Preusler (our source here Preusler 1956) follows on Keller's footsteps, and generally speaking, concurs with Keller's account. As new evidence speaking for Celtic influence on the English PF, he mentions the early attestation of the verbal noun construction in northern English and Scottish dialects and also draws attention to the strong preservation of this construction in Scottish English even today. According to him, this regional distribution pattern undermines the plausibility of the rival explanations based on either independent development (the stand adopted, e.g. in Curme 1912), French influence (Einenkel 1914), or Latin/Greek influence (Mossé 1938).

Dal (1952) continues the line of inquiry opened by Keller and Preusler. Like Keller, Dal notes the verbal noun characteristics shared by the English PF and the Celtic periphrastic constructions, and the unique nature of the English construction among Germanic languages. However, unlike Keller, who posits a rather late date for the development of the English PF, Dal traces its origins much further back, arguing that the verbal noun already emerged as a grammatical category in the OE period under the influence of the Celtic periphrastic constructions. According to her, the OE 'verbal abstract' ending -*ung*/-*ing* had been used in especially some northern OE texts as a verbal noun, preceded by the verb *be*, and also governed by a preposition; in other words, in periphrastic constructions which resemble the progressive form. As an illustration, Dal cites the sentence *cwæð sum hālig biscop, þa he wæs on sāwlunga* '. . . when he was on the point of expiring' from an early Mercian text (*Old English Martyrology* 124.21; cited in Dal 1952: 37). Although there are differing views on the progressive interpretation of this example (see Braaten 1967: 176 for discussion), Dal takes it to indicate that already in OE the -*ung*/-*ing*-form had started to encroach on the territory of the present participle, realised by -*ande*/-*ende*, and was in fact beginning to merge with it, especially in texts written in northern areas which were not so strongly dominated by the West-Saxon literary tradition (see the discussion below).

Writing much later, Braaten (1967) follows up the line of argumentation put forward in the previous research and especially in that by Dal. Like Dal, he argues that, when the English PF (or 'continuous tense', as he calls it) began to develop, it was based on the type *wæs on sāwlunga* rather than the type **wæs sāwlende*. He emphasises, however, that the 'progressive' meaning of the OE construction could hardly have been as precise as that of the present-day PF (Braaten 1967: 176). In conclusion, Braaten provides a summary of the most important factors which according to him show that the ModE PF could not have developed out of the OE present participle construction and cannot be properly explained without assuming some degree of Celtic influence:

(i)   Modern English continuous tenses are clearly durative, while the OE phrase could be used to replace either a durative or a perfective verb— probably for dramatic effect.

(ii) The Modern English -*ing* participle (originally a verbal abstract) is different in nature from the OE -*ende* participle.

(iii) In other Germanic languages, the construction *be* + present participle never developed into anything like continuous tense.

(iv) The similarity between Modern English continuous tenses and corresponding constructions in Cymric is too striking to be purely coincidental.

(v)   Continuous tenses tend to be used more in bilingual or formerly Celtic-speaking areas than in other parts of the country. (Braaten 1967: 180)

Let us next see what kinds of response the above views have prompted among the scholarly community.

2.2.5.2   Reception of the Celtic Hypothesis among Anglicists and Celticists

Generally speaking, the response to the Celtic hypothesis among Anglicists and even Celticists has remained rather negative, or at best, 'non-committal' or 'qualified'. As an example of the former approach, one could mention Mossé (1938). Having surveyed the various parallels in the Celtic languages and their possible influence on the English PF, he arrives at the following overall conclusion:

> [T]outes ces locutions s'expliquent fort bien du point de vue de l'anglais, sans qu'il soit nécessaire de recourir à l'hypothèse d'une influence extérieure. L'analogie des tours celtiques et anglais est donc, à notre avis, une simple coïncidence.[20]

(Mossé 1938 II: § 105)

Mossé also makes it clear that, if we were to assume any influence from Celtic on this (or any other feature) of English, it would have had to manifest itself in OE. According to him, no such influence can be detected, which in turn is explained by the social inferiority of the British Celts, preventing linguistic contact influences (Mossé, *op.cit.*, § 105).

Nickel (1966) is more sympathetic than Mossé to the possibility of Celtic influence but, like Mossé, he does not find any evidence for it in OE. For him, the Cymric parallel consisting of the copula followed by the verbal noun could at best have indirectly promoted the rise of English constructions involving imperfective aspect. As regards ME, Nickel does not altogether exclude the possibility of some degree of contact influence on the emergence of the ME gerundial construction. Yet, in his view Celtic influence can only have provided a mere reinforcement of a tendency already existing in English (Nickel 1966: 299–300). This position seems to be shared by many other writers on this subject—if, indeed, they consider the possibility of Celtic influence in the first place (see below). Mustanoja's (1960) work on ME syntax is a major exception. Having discussed Latin and Old French influences—which he considers probable—Mustanoja devotes some attention to the possibility of Celtic influence on the English PF. He refers here to the views of some of the major proponents of the Celtic hypothesis, including van Hamel (1912), Keller (1925), Preusler (1938), and Dal (1952), agreeing with them that the frequent use of the PF in *modern* dialects of English spoken in Wales, Ireland and Scotland "suggests considerable Celtic influence on present-day English in these particular areas" (1960: 590). However, the small amounts of data from both OE and ME, as well as from mediaeval varieties of Irish and Welsh, do not according to him allow any conclusions on the question of early Celtic influence on English. This does not mean that such influences could not have been possible, as can be inferred from his concluding statement where he seems to distance himself from the Anglo-Saxonist 'ethnic cleansing' theory and at least leaves open the possibility of Celtic substratal influences:

> There might be something to say for Keller's (p. 66) and Miss Dal's assertions (pp. 115 and 116) that the ancient Britons were not exterminated but became amalgamated with the Germanic invaders and assumed their language while retaining some syntactical peculiarities of their ancient native tongue, but such statements remain necessarily hypothetical for lack of documentary evidence.

> (Mustanoja 1960: 590)

Next, there is the 'non-committal' position, represented by, e.g. Denison (1993). Although he surveys the existing accounts of the rise of the English PF, including those advocating Celtic origin, he does not want to commit himself to any conclusive judgment on the issue of Celtic influence, apart from stating that much of the evidence for Celtic contact effects is "largely circumstantial" and the argument "speculative" (Denison 1993: 402). Finally, at the other extreme are those studies which do not even mention the possibility of Celtic influence. These include some of the earliest works (see, e.g. Curme 1912) but, rather surprisingly, some recent ones, too (see, e.g. Mitchell 1985; Traugott 1992).

To sum up so far, the majority of Anglicists seem to favour accounts which either consider the emergence of the PF chiefly as an independent development in English (though possibly reinforced by the Latin model) or, alternatively, look to similar constructions in Latin, Greek or French as the principal source of the PF. Some of the most eminent exponents of the 'Independent Growth Hypothesis' are George O. Curme (see Curme 1912) and Gerhard Nickel (see Nickel 1966); others subscribing to this stand include F. Th. Visser (see Visser 1963–1973) and Bruce Mitchell (see Mitchell 1985). External influences are emphasised, for example, in the works of Otto Jespersen (see, e.g., Jespersen, MEG IV: §§ 12.1(2)–12.1(3)) and Ferdinand Mossé (see Mossé 1938). For them the most likely model for the OE progressive is to be found in Latin. Another supporter of foreign influence is Eugen Einenkel (see Einenkel 1914), who traces the origins of the English PF to a Romance (French) source.

While surprisingly few Anglicists give serious attention to the Celtic hypothesis, it is perhaps more understandable that very few scholars on the Celticist side have touched on the similarities between the Celtic and the English periphrastic progressive constructions and their possible common roots. Wagner (1959) must be mentioned as one of the first who explicitly discusses these commonalities in terms of some kind of contact effects. According to him, the rise of the English PF marks a typological change from the Anglo-Saxon and Germanic verbal system and has to be seen in the context of parallel developments in the Celtic languages. Indeed, he considers these developments to have led to the emergence of a typically British verbal type, where the term 'British' embraces both the Celtic languages and English (Wagner 1959: 150–151).

Wagner's view, which can be regarded as a forerunner of present-day 'areal linguistics', has become an object of fresh interest in recent years, among both Anglicists or general linguists and Celticists (see, e.g. Tristram 1999a; Filppula 2001; Vennemann 2001; Mittendorf and Poppe 2000; Poppe 2003). While Tristram is content to note the possible connection between the rise of the English PF and its parallels in Welsh, pending more detailed work on it (Tristram 1999a: 23), Vennemann is convinced that the former cannot be explained without assuming influence from the parallel Welsh constructions (Vennemann 2001: 355). Filppula (2001) considers Celtic substratum influence likely but wants to keep open the possibility that the PF and its Celtic parallels are, as suggested by Wagner, a result of adstratal developments shared by English and the Celtic languages.

Yet, by far the most thorough treatments of the subject on the Celticist side are those provided by Mittendorf and Poppe (2000), Poppe (2002) and Poppe (2003), who examine the putative Celtic and especially MW parallels to the English PF against the background of their syntactic and functional features. They conclude that there are "striking formal similarities between the Insular Celtic and English periphrastic constructions" and, even more importantly, establish that "striking similarities also exist between their functional ranges in the medieval languages" (Mittendorf and Poppe 2000: 139). This last statement refers to the uses of the periphrastic constructions to express not only processivity, the basic function of the periphrastic constructions, but also what these authors call 'expressivity' or 'foregrounding' in narrative discourse and 'habituality'. Poppe (2002) elaborates on the possibility of semantic influence from Celtic and suggests that, if there was any such influence, it would stem from the imperfective meaning inherent to the Celtic progressive construction (see also below). In his 2003 article, Poppe goes on to investigate in some detail the oft-mentioned putative parallels in Germanic dialects and also discusses the progressive constructions in Greek, Latin and Romance languages. Although the results of these three studies generally point to at least some degree of Celtic contact influences, the authors formulate their conclusions in rather cautious terms. Thus, Mittendorf and Poppe conclude that their study of the parallelisms between Welsh and English "adds another, new perspective to the problem"—i.e. one focusing on Celtic substrate influence on the English PF (Mittendorf and Poppe 2000: 139). Poppe (2003) considers language contact to be a possible explanation for the rise of the English progressive, given the formal and functional parallels between English and the Celtic languages and the coexistence of the Celtic and English populations in the British Isles over a long period of time. However, he adds that it is not a necessary explanation because of the various types of more or less similar progressive constructions in many other Germanic languages or dialects (2003: 84).

2.2.5.3   *Pros and Cons in the Light of Recent Research*

In this section we will discuss some of the principal factors adduced for or against the Celtic hypothesis. While the focus will be on the findings of recent research, the results of earlier work will also be considered, as they have in many ways defined the agenda for subsequent research on this vexed subject.

To begin with, the formal and functional parallels between the Celtic and the English constructions seem beyond any doubt and constitute one of the strongest factors speaking for Celtic influence on the English PF. As already noted above, this parallelism has been confirmed by several studies, both earlier (such as Keller 1925; Dal 1952) and recent (Mittendorf and Poppe 2000; Ronan 2003). Apart from the shared structural features and similarities in their functional range (see, esp. Mittendorf and Poppe 2000 quoted above), the semantics of both the Celtic constructions and the English PF centres around the notion of imperfectivity, which, as is suggested by Poppe (2002: 260), may have Insular Celtic as its primary source: "In the light of the discussion above of the values of Insular Celtic expanded forms, any semantic influence on English expanded forms from Insular Celtic would probably be along the lines of imperfectivity".

Poppe goes even so far as to suggest that this influence may have been of a long-standing and continual nature and may also have involved the later influence of the so-called Celtic Englishes on (Standard) English:

> [O]ne may also want to consider the possibility of long-term reinforcing influence of Brythonic/Celtic Englishes on English, and more specifically the possibility of a continual direct or indirect influence of Celtic imperfect progressives on the development of the English progressive.

> (Poppe 2002: 261)

Most of those who adopt a critical attitude towards Celtic influences on the English PF mention the dating of these influences as one of the major counterarguments against the Celtic hypothesis. Thus, Nickel (1966) concludes that the Cymric parallel construction can only have been relevant to the emergence of the ME gerundial construction, not the OE one. As regards the latter, the Cymric parallel could at best have indirectly promoted the rise of English constructions involving imperfective aspect. He also finds support for his view in the work of scholars defending the Celtic hypothesis, arguing that even the staunchest supporters of the Celtic hypothesis generally date the Celtic influences to the ME period (Nickel 1966: 300). He refers here specifically to Keller (1925), who does not include the PF among those features which could have been influenced by Brythonic in the OE period. As already mentioned, it is true that Keller accepts the rather late emergence of the verbal noun construction in fourteenth-century English texts. However, many other supporters of the Celtic hypothesis prefer to date the contact effects back to as early as the OE period, although they may not be so directly visible because of the stifling influence of the Anglo-Saxon literary tradition, which would have banned the use of the PF as a 'vulgar' feature. Thus, Dal (1952) considers the roots of the English PF to go back to OE and explains its late surfacing in texts as a result of 'delayed' contact effects:

> Das Hauptargument für unsere Auffassung der Sache ist aber, daß wir wegen der historischen und sozialen Verhältnisse keine reiche Verwendung von syntaktischen Keltizismen in der altengl. Literatur erwarten *können*. Die Kelten waren das unterdrückte Volk, ihre Syntax, soweit sie in englischer Sprache zum Ausdruck kam, trug das Gepräge von Vulgarismus, der von der gepflegten Literatursprache vermieden werden mußte. Es ist gewiß keine Seltenheit, daß Konstruktionen der vulgären und alltäglichen Sprache Jahrhunderte lang leben können, ohne in der Schriftsprache zu erscheinen.[21]

(Dal 1952: 113)

Dal's view on the delayed impact of everyday speech on the written language is by no means novel or restricted to those supporting the Celtic hypothesis. In the field of Anglo-Saxon studies, an essentially similar account is given, e.g. by Tolkien (1963), who notes the lack of "transcripts of village-talk" in the OE period, and goes on to state that "[f]or any glimpse of what was going on beneath the cultivated surface we must wait until the Old English period of letters is over" (Tolkien 1963: 28). The idea of 'delayed' contact effects has found further support in the recent work by, e.g. Hickey (1995) and Vennemann (2002a). It is also of some interest to note that Denison (1993), who is generally rather reserved about the role of the Celtic substratum, considers the delayed appearance in written texts of the alleged Celtic influence "plausible" (Denison 1993: 402).

Acceptance of the early dating of the PF also depends on the interpretation of the patterns of variation between the OE periphrastic present participle and verbal noun constructions and on the whole question of the genesis of the ModE PF. As is well known, there is as yet no general agreement on this last question, the major sticking-point being the exact historical relationship between the OE periphrastic forms and the ME and ModE PF with the -*ing* form of verbs. Some have argued for (more or less) direct continuity between the OE *be* + present participle construction (see, e.g. Curme 1912; Mossé 1938; Nickel 1966; Mitchell 1985) and assumed a rather complex—and it seems to us—unnecessarily laboured chain of phonetic changes in trying to explain the transition from the suffix *-inde/-ande* to *-ing*. In present-day and also in some of the earlier scholarship, an alternative view based on some kind of convergent development or merger between the two OE constructions appears to have gained ground. This is the position adopted, e.g. by Jespersen (MEG IV: § 12.1(7)) and Visser (1963–1973 III: § 1852–1860), and it is also supported by Dal (1952), one of the main exponents of the Celtic hypothesis. Dal (1952) discusses patterns of variation and functional interchangeability between *-inde/-ende* and *-ung/-ing* forms especially in some OE texts of Midland and northern provenance. She singles out four contexts in which the present participle and the construction consisting of preposition + the *-ung/-ing* form occur alongside each other with the same meaning:

(i) in appositional participial position, e.g. *spræc wēpende: spræc on wēpinge*;
(ii) as predicate with verbs of motion and stance (*Ruhe*), e.g. *cōm rīdende: cōm on rīdinge*;
(iii) as predicate with *bēon*, e.g. *wæs feohtende: wæs on feohtinge*;
(iv) as predicate of an object with verbs of perception and feeling, e.g. *geseah hine rīdende: geseah hine on rīdinge*. (Dal 1952: 101–102)

In Dal's view, these phenomena indicate that already in OE the *-ung/-ing*-form had started to encroach on the territory of the present participle and was in fact beginning to be confused with it especially in texts written in areas which were not so clearly dominated by the West-Saxon literary tradition. The main impetus for this development was according to Dal given by the Celtic periphrastic constructions, which thus explains the unique nature and course of development of the English progressive among Germanic languages. In recent research, the role of the Celtic substratum is in very clear terms acknowledged by Vennemann (2001), who writes:

> In my view the essential English innovation consists in the victory of the Celtic-motivated verbal noun construction (suffix *-ung/-ing*) over the Anglo-Saxon present participle construction (suffix *-inde/-ande*), where even the frequent use of the latter may have been provoked by attempts to integrate the Celtic aspect into English.

> (Vennemann 2001: 355)

A Linguistic Atlas of Late Mediaeval English (*LALME*) does not, unfortunately, shed much light on the question at hand because of the considerable amount of variation in the '*-ing(-)/-yng(e)*' types as against the '*-and(-)*' types. The maps showing the distribution of these two types indicate a certain tendency for the former to be the preferred choice in the southern as well as the Midland areas extending to the Welsh border, whereas there is more variation between these two forms and a noticeable bias towards -*and* in especially the east Midland areas (see Dot Maps 345 & 346 in *LALME*, Vol. I, p. 391). The predominance of the -*and/-ind/-end* etc. forms in these as well as the northern areas does not mean, however, that the merger between the two forms would not have been under way in these dialects, too, as is demonstrated by Mossé (1938 II: §§ 129–175; cited in Denison 1993: 403).

Let us next turn to areal and typological factors. As already mentioned, several writers (Keller, Dal, Wagner, etc.) have noted the uniqueness of the English and Celtic progressive constructions among western European languages. To these could be added Pokorny (1959), who draws attention to the non-Indo-European nature of the Insular Celtic tense-aspect system and its use of the structure 'be' + Preposition + Verbal Noun as 'progressive forms'. This is echoed in Wagner's (1959) aforementioned areal view of a typically 'British verbal type', which covers both the Celtic languages and English and, as regards the latter, marks a clear departure from the Germanic system. Pokorny's and Wagner's views have recently been taken up by Vennemann (2001), who extends the discussion to the 'Atlantic', i.e. Semitic, influences on the Celtic languages, and *via* them, upon English. Vennemann also discusses some other phenomena which distinguish English and Celtic from most other European languages and which according to him lend further support to the Semitic hypothesis. One of these, viz. the 'internal possession construction', was discussed in section 2.2.1.

Typological factors, albeit from a slightly different perspective, are in the focus of recent discussions by Hickey (1995) and Tristram (1999a). Both authors note the typological shift which the Celtic languages and English have undergone during their recorded histories. In both language groups there has been a noticeable drift from synthetic constructions to analytic ones, including such periphrastic constructions as are at issue here. What makes Celtic influence on English likely is the fact that in the Celtic languages this tendency set in earlier than in English and is by now more advanced especially in Welsh as compared with English. Changes towards analytical structures are particularly manifest in the declension of nouns, though not nearly so much in verbal morphology. Both Hickey and Tristram consider the contacts between English and the Celtic languages to have been instrumental in triggering the shift towards analytical structures in early English.

The uniqueness of the English PF among Germanic languages cannot be ascertained without considering some alleged parallels in other Germanic languages or dialects. Thus, Mac Eoin (1993) observes a similar progressive construction in Icelandic, which, as he argues, cannot be due to Celtic influence. However, Poppe (2003: 70–71) points out that according to some studies as many as 30 to 40 per cent of the first inhabitants of Iceland were Gaelic, which makes the Icelandic situation much more complicated than

Mac Eoin had assumed. On his part, Poppe surveys a number of periphrastic progressive constructions attested in some German dialects. He concludes that various German(ic) dialects have in the course of their history at least "experimented" with periphrastic progressive constructions, but with very few exceptions (such as the Rhineland dialect of German), they have not been fully grammaticalised in them. English thus remains the only Germanic language in which the periphrastic progressive is based on the merger of the formerly distinct participial and prepositional progressives (Poppe 2003: 75–76). Furthermore, Keller (1925), Vennemann (2001), and Filppula (2003) have pointed out a formal difference between the English and Celtic PF, on one hand, and those found in Germanic dialects, on the other: the latter are formed with the nominalised infinitive (as in *er ist am lesen* lit. 'he is at-the read') and not with the verbal noun type structure as in English. How important this difference is for the matter at hand remains debatable, but the use of the verbal noun in English may well be explained, as Vennemann (2001: 356) remarks, by the simple fact that Insular Celtic has no infinitive.

Yet another controversial problem is the nature and extent of influences from other than Celtic languages. Thus, Jespersen (MEG IV: § 12.1(3)) observes that the progressive in OE was more common in translations from Latin than in original OE texts; this he takes as proof of Latin influence on the OE translators, and hence, on the English PF. Another exponent of the 'Latin Hypothesis', as we might call it, is Mossé (1938), who states that Latin influence on OE was mainly transmitted through the practice of providing interlinear glosses or translations of Latin constructions which had no structural parallels in OE. These included, among others, the verb ESSE followed by the present (or the past) participle, as in *erat docens* 'was teaching' (Mossé 1938 I: § 156; see also Nickel 1966: 268). This could then be translated into English by the OE auxiliaries *beon/wesan* 'be' followed by the present participle. As a further factor supporting Latin influence Mossé mentions the relative infrequency of the PF in OE poetical texts (Mossé 1938 I: § 156).

The Latin Hypothesis has been contested especially by Nickel (1966). First, he points out the tendency of OE texts to have periphrastic constructions consisting of a verb followed by a noun even in translations of simple Latin verbs (Nickel 1966: 391–392). A second factor speaking against Latin influence is his observation that the PF occurs even in OE untranslated texts, and what is more, mostly in contexts which Nickel characterises as 'vivid descriptions', whereas texts written in more formal style make less use of it (*op.cit.*, 390).

Apart from Latin (and Greek), Romance influence has also been adduced as an explanation of the rise of the English PF. This position is represented especially by Einenkel (1914) but also by Visser (1963–1973). According to the former, the French gerundial-participle construction involving the suffix *-ant* provided the crucial stimulus for the English gerund (and the PF).

Einenkel's account was specifically aimed at refuting Curme's (1912) view, which looked to purely native origins for the English gerund. However, as noted by Dal (1952: 31), Einenkel's account fails to explain why the English PF eventually came to be based on the *-ing* form and not on the OE present participial forms ending in *-ende/-ande*, which would have been the expected development, given the formal similarity with the French form. However, this old participial ending did not survive but was replaced by *-ing* in the ME period, that is, in the very period in which French influence could have been expected to have been strongest. Visser (1963–1973), who generally speaking considers the PF to be an indigenous development, allows for the possibility of selective influence from French; he considers the French model to be particularly relevant for those ME *-ing* constructions which were preceded by the preposition *in*, emulating thus the French pattern *en chantant* 'in/while singing' (Visser 1963–1973 III: §1859).

Finally, any attempt at explaining the rise of the PF in English has to reckon with the possibility of a universal or 'natural' development, and hence, something that is independent from that of the parallel Celtic construction. As Vennemann (2001) notes, this is a line of argumentation adopted, e.g. in Bybee (1985), who seeks to demonstrate that the PF in English as well as in other languages is "a universally available verbal category belonging to the wider range of 'continuous' or 'imperfective' aspect, which would have 'originated in English independently of its existence in Insular Celtic'" (Bybee 1985: 141–146; cited in Vennemann 2001: 355).

However, as Vennemann rightly argues, the 'universalist' account runs into problems in trying to explain why English (and some continental Germanic dialects on the North Sea littoral) should be the only Germanic language that has undergone this development (*ibid.*).

2.2.5.4   *Conclusion*

The foregoing discussion has made it clear that there is no simple answer to the question of the nature and extent of Celtic influences on the English PF. Rather than trying to discover some new evidence which would help to settle this issue—indeed, such evidence is unlikely to be found—we have been content to survey and critically re-examine the existing evidence with a view to establishing as many indisputable facts as possible. On the basis of our investigation, the following emerge as established facts that can be used to support the Celtic hypothesis (see also Filppula 2003):

(i) Of all the suggested parallels to the English PF, the Celtic (Brythonic) ones are clearly the closest, and hence, the most plausible ones, whether one thinks of the OE periphrastic constructions or those established in the ME and modern periods, involving the *-ing* form of verbs. This fact has not been given due weight in some of the earlier work on this subject.

(ii)   The chronological precedence of the Celtic constructions is beyond any reasonable doubt, which also enhances the probability of contact influence from Celtic on English.

(iii) The sociohistorical circumstances of the Celtic–English interface cannot have constituted an obstacle to Celtic substratum influences in the area of grammar, as has traditionally been argued especially on the basis of the paucity of lexical borrowings from Celtic languages. On the contrary, recent research (and some of the earlier, too) has shown that the language shift situation in the centuries following the settlement of the Germanic tribes in Britain was most conducive to such influences. Again, this aspect has been ignored or not properly understood in some of the research which has tried to play down the role of Celtic influence in the history of English.

(iv)   The Celtic–English contacts in the modern period have resulted in a similar tendency for some regional varieties of English to make extensive use of the PF, which lends indirect support to the Celtic hypothesis with regard to early English.

(v)   The typological shift of English towards analytical structures, which it shares with its Celtic neighbours, increases the likelihood of Celtic influences on English grammar in general, and on the development of the PF, in particular.

The problem of the late emergence of the PF in English should not be exaggerated. It is quite probable that the PF was already there in the OE period as a feature of spoken, and perhaps 'non-standard', language and only made its way into written language with a certain delay, once the Norman Conquest had brought about a major change in the linguistic situation and brought the era of the Anglo-Saxon literary tradition to an end. Where, in our view, the Celtic influence on the English PF is most manifest is in the way in which the English PF has evolved through a merger of originally distinct participial and verbal noun constructions. As has been noted before on several occasions, this is a development which has no parallel in the other Germanic languages. However, the typological and areal considerations discussed above would seem to make it difficult to exclude the possibility of two-way, adstratal, influences between Celtic and English especially from the late medieval period onwards. It should be borne in mind that the periphrastic progressive was not fully grammaticalised even in the Celtic languages of the earliest period but has advanced steadily at the expense of the synthetic forms. Given the long-standing coexistence and contacts between the two language groups in the British Isles, adstratal influences may well have sped up the drift towards analytic (including periphrastic) constructions in both the Celtic language group and English. The 'experiments' with periphrastic progressives of various types which have been attested in some other Germanic languages or dialects may also have contributed to such developments. Finally, the geographical distribution of the PF in later and even present-day varieties of English is yet another factor which may shed further light on the issue of the origins of the English PF, but the discussion of these matters will be deferred to Chapter 4, section 4.3.

2.2.6   The Cleft Construction

Like the progressive construction discussed in the previous section, the cleft construction or 'clefting' for short is a robust feature of the Celtic Englishes (see the discussion in 4.2 below) and may therefore be of some interest from the point of view of the earliest contacts between English and the Celtic languages, too. Another indication of possible contact effects is the rather late emergence of the cleft construction in English, as compared with its Celtic counterparts. We will begin with a brief survey of the history of clefting in English. This will be followed by a discussion of parallel constructions in the Celtic languages. Other European languages will also be considered with a view to establishing whether this construction type constitutes an areal feature shared by languages spoken in a wider area than the British Isles. Finally, the *pros* and *cons* of the Celtic hypothesis with respect to this feature will be assessed in the light of the available evidence.

2.2.6.1   *The History of the Cleft Construction in English*

We start off with Mitchell (1985: § 1486), who states that there are no examples in OE of sentences with anticipatory *it* such as ModE *It's food that I want*. As Mitchell explains, this is because OE achieves the same effect by simply putting the element to be emphasised into initial position without clefting. He does, however, note Visser's (1963–1973: § 63) examples with *þæt* as the introductory pronoun in cleft-type constructions but does evidently not consider them similar to those introduced by OE *hit* 'it'. By contrast, Visser (1963–1973), whose paradigmatic example here is 'It is father who did it', lists examples of cleft constructions from OE onwards, noting that in OE introductory *hit* is sometimes omitted or, in some cases, replaced by *þæt* (1963–1973: § 63). The OE uses are illustrated in (32) and (33).

> (32)   Gast is se þe geliffæst (O.E. Gosp., John VI, 63; cited in Visser 1963–1973: § 63).

> (33)   þæt wæs on þone monandæg . . . þæt Godwine mid his scipum to suðgeweorce becom (O.E. Chron. an. 1052; cited in Visser 1963–1973: § 63).

Visser provides more examples from ME and later texts, indicating thus the gradually increasing use of the cleft construction over the centuries. As regards ModE, Visser also discusses and exemplifies the use of clefts in 'popular' Anglo-Irish where, as he puts it, they occur "with exceedingly great frequency, even the verbal elements in the sentence are given prominence in this way" (*op.cit.*, § 64).

Turning back to the early roots, Traugott (1992) is another writer seeking to date the emergence of the cleft construction. While acknowledging Mitchell's negative stand on the existence of *hit*-clefting in OE, she draws attention to Visser's examples with anticipatory *þæt*. However, she stops short of passing judgment on whether they should be considered similar to the structures introduced by anticipatory *it* (Traugott 1992: 280). The main part of her discussion of OE word order focuses on what she calls 'topicalised' (i.e., fronted) NPs, which served the same contrastive purpose as topicalised NPs (or clefts) in present-day English but with an even stronger effect (*op.cit.*, 281).

The most thorough treatment of clefts in OE and ME is Ball (1991), who presents a detailed analysis of more or less 'cleft-like' constructions and their frequencies in these periods. Her discussion confirms that the cleft construction, however defined, is an innovation in OE and that its frequencies remain very small in that period. In line with Mitchell (1985), she finds no *hit*-clefts which would perfectly match the stereotypical ModE *it*-cleft with 'specificational' reading, sometimes termed the 'stressed-focus *it*-cleft' (with a 'dummy' subject) in the linguistic literature (Ball 1991: 45). She does, however, note one possible exception, which according to her could be considered an instance of clefting. This is the example cited, but discarded, by Mitchell (1985: § 2135) from Ælfric:

> (34) þa cwædon þa geleafullan,
> 'Nis hit na Petrus þæt þær cnucað, ac is his ængel.'
> not-is it-**n.** not Peter-**m.** REL-**n.** there knocks but is his angel-**m.**
> 'Then the faithful said: It isn't Peter who is knocking there, but his angel.'
> (ÆCHom I.517-18.1; here cited from Ball 1991: 39–40)

Mitchell takes *hit* and not the focused noun, as in true clefts, to be the antecedent of the relative pronoun and therefore rejects this as an example of a cleft sentence (Mitchell 1985: § 2135; Ball 1991: 39–40). In Ball's analysis, the closest parallel to the ModE specificational clefts is the construction NP BEON REL-CLAUSE, as in the following example she cites from Visser (1963–1973: 49):

> (35) . . . min fæder is þe me wuldrað
> my   father is that me glorifies
> (Jn 8.54: . . . est Pater meus, qui glorificat me . . .)
> 'It is my father that glorifies me' (Jn 8.54)
> (ÆCHom ii. 234.3; cited in Visser 1963–1973: 49)

Unlike Visser, who treats (35) as a *hit*-cleft, with *hit* omitted, Ball is inclined to consider it a pseudo-cleft, although she acknowledges that it could also be analysed as a *hit*-cleft (Ball 1991: 27–28). The same pattern also occurs with non-inverted word order, as in the following example from Ælfric's *Lives of Saints*:

(36)   Nis seo orþung þe we ut blawaþ. and in ateoð
       not-is the breath that we out blow and in take
       oþþe ure sawul ac is seo lyft . . .
       or our soul but is the air
       'What we blow out and draw in isn't our breath, or soul; it is air'
                       —or—
       'It is not our breath, or soul, that we blow out and draw in, but
       air . . .'
       (ÆLS 1.214.3; cited in Ball 1991: 27)

Whether cleft or pseudo-cleft, Ball stresses that the construction NP BEON REL-CLAUSE is rare in OE and, in her data, occurs only in translations of a Latin headless relative. However, she notes that Ælfric avoids it in some cases even in translations and uses a simple sentence instead of the Latin-type construction. Her conclusion is that "in Late West Saxon, at least, NP/PRO BEON REL-CLAUSE was not the preferred construction for marking focus and open proposition" (1991: 52).

Another possible cleft construction discussed by Ball is the pattern PRO HIT/ÞÆT BEON REL-CLAUSE, i.e. a structure involving a topicalised pronoun followed by *hit* or *þæt*, as in the following example cited by Ball from Skeat (1890):

(37)   . . . and axodon hine hwæðer he hit wære þe   heora
       and   asked   him whether he it   were REL-COMP their
       cempena lareow geo   wæs. he þa oðsoc þæt he hit nære.
       soldiers' teacher formerly was   he then denied that he it not-were
       '. . . and asked him whether *it were he who formerly was the
       teacher of their soldiers*; he then denied that it was he.'
       (LS 8 (Eustace) 272; cited from Skeat 1890 in Ball 1991: 41)

As in the case of (35), Ball treats (37) and other similar examples as pseudo-clefts rather than *it*-clefts. In any case, as she notes, this pattern is also rare and relatively late (*op.cit.*, 41).

A further important observation made by Ball is the complete lack of pronoun-focus *hit*-clefts in OE; these are not attested until the early thirteenth century (Ball 1991: 45). 'Informative-presupposition' *hit*-clefts (in which the relative clause represents new rather than given information) do not emerge until late ME, although one can find earlier examples such as

(38), which could be considered predecessors of ModE adverbial/PP-focus *it*-clefts (Ball 1991: 45):

> (38) ##her swutelað on þison gewrite hu Æðelred kyning geuðe þ
>   Æþerices cwyde æt Boccinge standan moste. hit wæs manegon
>   earon ær Æðeric forðferde þ ðam kincge wæs gesæd þ he wære
>   on þam unræde þ man sceolde on Eastsexon Swegen underfon
>   ða he ærest þyder mid flotan com . . .
>   'It is shown here in this document how King Ethelred granted
>   that the will of Æthelric of Bocking should stand.
>   It was many years before Æthelric died that the King was told
>   that he [= Æ.] was concerned in the treacherous plan that
>   Swegn should be received in Essex when first he came there
>   with a fleet . . .' (W 16(2); cited from Whitelock 1930: 45 in Ball
>   1991: 45)

To complete the picture for OE and ME, Ball notes that clefts with sen-
tential focus emerge even later than pronoun-focus clefts, i.e. in the late ME
period (*op.cit.*, 46). Thus, we can conclude from the above discussion that,
despite the sporadic occurrence of all sorts of cleft-like constructions in OE
and ME texts, clefting seems to have been rather rare even as late as the late
ME and EModE periods. After then, cleft constructions become more frequent and both functionally and syntactically more versatile (see, esp. Ball
1991: 509 ff.). In these respects, Ball's findings confirm those of the earlier
writers quoted above and accord with the views of many others writing on
the emergence of the English cleft construction. For example, Strang (1970:
211) concludes that the 'empty' use of *it* (and *there* in 'existential' clauses)
is not established as a regular pattern until the fifteenth century. Görlach
(1991: 108) concurs with this and states that "[a]lternative means of topi-
calization, such as passive transformations or cleft constructions, were possible in EModE, but used more rarely". In a similar vein, Traugott (1972:
161) underlines the role of word order arrangements without clefting as the
principal means through which emphasis was expressed up to, and even
including, the EModE period when the word order system eventually began
to stabilise around the present-day patterns.

2.2.6.2   *Parallel Constructions in Celtic and Other European languages*

Clefting is a robust feature of all Celtic languages. In his comparative description of Celtic languages, Gregor (1980) points out that, while the sentence
normally starts with the verb, this word order "is frequently disturbed by
another characteristic", viz., "[a]n aptitude and fondness for emphatic
expression" (1980: 146–147). He further explains that, for emphasis, the
subject, object or other part of the sentence is put first, and the whole

sentence is cast in the form of a relative clause, with the fronted constituent felt as being dependent on an "understood 'It is'" (1980: 147). Thus, a sentence like *(It is) the woman (who) came* is rendered by the following constructions in Irish (Ir.), Scottish Gaelic (Sc.G.), Cornish (C.), Breton (B.) and Welsh (W.), respectively:

(39) Ir.: (Is é) an bhean a thainig.

(40) Sc.G.: Is a'boirannach a thàinig.

(41) C.: An venen a dheth.

(42) B.: Ar wreg a zeuas.

(43) W.: Y wraig sydd wedi dod.

(Examples from Gregor 1980: 147)

The bracketing in (39) shows that the cleft construction—or 'copula construction', as it is usually called in the Celtic grammatical tradition—need not have an overtly expressed introductory phrase in Irish. Indeed, it is often omitted because of the stressless nature of the copula, a feature which goes back to as early as Old Irish (see Thurneysen 1946: 494). Scottish Gaelic, by contrast, prefers the full form with the copula even today (see, e.g. Gillies 1993: 209–212; Lamb 2001: 87–91).[22] In present-day Cornish, Breton and Welsh the sentence always starts directly with the fronted item (for further details of differences between the Celtic languages, see Gregor 1980; Ball 1993 and the descriptions of each of the Celtic languages therein). A further well-known characteristic of clefting in these languages is its syntactic freedom: even the verb can be emphasised, as is seen in (44)–(46) from Irish, Welsh and Cornish, respectively:[23]

(44) Ir.: (Is) ag leigheamh atá sé 'Reading he is' (lit. (it is) reading that he is).

(45) W.: Darllen y mae ef.

(46) C.: Ow redya yma ef.

(Gregor 1980: 148)

Clefting is not an innovation in the Celtic languages as it is in English. In his description of Irish syntax, Mac Eoin (1993: 137) states that clefting is "a very common construction [. . .] at all periods". Thurneysen (1946: 492–494) cites examples like *is hé día as éola indium-sa* 'it is God who is knowing in me' from the mid-eighth century Würzburg Glosses, and similar constructions are found in the somewhat later Milan Glosses. Further documentation is provided by Pedersen (1913: § 538), who discusses early Irish cleft constructions under the heading of 'relative clauses' (G. *Relativsätze*). Ahlqvist (1977) notes that clefting has been attested in Irish earlier than in any other Western European language. He also raises the possibility that the cleft construction in these languages is ultimately of Celtic origin.

Although our sources for Old Welsh are much scantier than those for Old Irish, there is no question that clefting has been a characteristic feature of the Brythonic branch of Celtic from very early on. Thus, Pedersen (1913: § 547) writes that both Irish and British (i.e. the ancestor of Welsh) use what he calls 'relative inversion' (G. *Umschreibung*) for the purposes of emphasis:

Soll ein betontes Wort des Nachdruckes wegen an der Spitze des Satzes stehen, so tritt eine **relative Umschreibung** ein: das hervorzuhebende Wort wird Prädikatsnomen der (oft nicht ausgredrückten) Kopula und Beziehungswort eines Relativsatzes, der die eigentliche Aussage enthält.[24]

(Pedersen 1913: § 547; emphasis original)

Pedersen goes on to state that in Irish the division of the sentence into two parts is particularly clear, whereas in British it is less noticeable because the copula is mostly omitted and the degree of emphasis on the fronted item is often very small. Indeed, with fronted subjects and objects it is only the presence of (the relative particle) *a* before the verb which reveals the relative structure of the sentence, e.g. *Mc. seith meib a oed idaw* 'sieben Söhne waren ihm' [lit. seven sons REL were to-him, i.e. 'he had seven sons'] (*Mabinogion/The Red Book of Hergest*, 193; cited in Pedersen 1913: § 547). Tristram (2002a: 132) cites even earlier examples of clefting from the tenth-century prose work entitled the *Computus Fragment*, e.g. *is did ciman ha c(e)i* (Comp. 2) 'it is a full day that thou wilt get', *Is Aries isid in arcimeir [.e.]* (Comp. 9) 'It is Aries that is opposite [e]'.[25]

Further documentation of the early occurrences of clefts in the Brythonic branch is provided by Evans (1964), who gives examples of what he terms 'the mixed [word] order' in a number of MW texts, the earliest of which date from the eleventh century. For instance, in *The White Book Mabinogion* (from ca 1050–1100) there are sentences like *ys mi a'e heirch* 'it is I who seek her' (479.29), and in another early text, *Ymddiddan Myrddin a Thaliesin* (from before 1100), examples like *Oed maelgun a uelun in imuan* 'It was Maelgwn that I could see fighting' (57.5) (Evans 1964: 140–141). As Evans notes, the copula, which still occurs in these examples, was eventually dropped before the word or phrase to be emphasised, leading to the Modern Welsh constructions without the copula, as exemplified above (Evans 1964: 141; see also Watkins 1993: 336–337).

Apart from the Celtic languages, clefting is a well-known characteristic of French syntax. Unlike the Celtic copula constructions, French has an introductory 'dummy' pronoun (*ce*) similar to the English *it*. The similarities between the English and the French constructions raise the question of possible contact influence from French especially in the post-Conquest centuries. Indeed, Ball (1991) finds that, in late ME texts, cleft constructions with pronoun foci (e.g. *It is he/she that . . .*) are "particularly evident in translations from French" (Ball 1991: 231). However, her comparison with Hatcher's (1948: 1076) chronology for the French clefts with pronoun foci (see Ball 1991: 280) shows that, despite similar developments, French influence is hardly likely because of the earlier attestation of the English pronoun-foci clefts. In Ball's words, '[t]he two languages are moving along the same lines, but English appears to have had a head start of at least a century. We can, therefore, dismiss the possibility of French influence' (Ball 1991: 280).

Ball also discusses the possible influence of French on Adv/PP-focus *it*-clefts, the first clear examples of which do not occur until the late fourteenth century in more literary English works, i.e. in a period which witnessed the greatest influx of French loanwords. Ball notes, relying again on Hatcher's (1948) study, that the French PP-focus *ce*-cleft is also late and infrequent, and could therefore hardly have provided the source for similar English clefts. She leaves this question open "pending more precise information about the history of the French cleft" (Ball 1991: 461–462).

Latin parallels to OE clefts have already been referred to in connection with the construction NP BEON REL-CLAUSE, which, as Ball (1991) has found, occurs only in translations of Latin headless relatives. On the other hand, the rarity of this pattern in OE, combined with Ball's observations that Ælfric and other OE authors sometimes seem to avoid it in their translations of Latin texts (see Ball 1991: 52 for examples), casts some doubt on the likelihood of any significant Latin influence on English clefts. Ahlqvist (2002), relying on Löfstedt's (1966) findings, also points out a possible Latin parallel to English clefts but notes that the Latin construction does not involve the introductory pronoun, and furthermore, it appears to be quite rare.

Northern Germanic languages such as Swedish also belong to languages which have cleft constructions in their syntactic repertoire. Ahlqvist (2002) refers to a study by Beckman (1934), who dates the first occurrence of clefting in Swedish to the fourteenth-century poem *Erikskrönikan*. In Modern Swedish, as Ahlqvist points out, the cleft construction is quite common (see Ahlqvist 2002 for examples), whereas it is not at all so prominent in German. These observations receive some quantitative support from a study by Ball, whose comparison between the translations of the Gospels in several languages showed that, where ModE, French and Danish used *it/ce/det*-clefts, Modern German mostly opted for a simple sentence without clefting (Ball 1990; our source here Ball 1991: 81). Another writer commenting on the contrast between English and German in their levels of use of clefting is Wehr (2001: 272), according to whom this feature is 'unidiomatic' in German or in any case rare in the spoken language. On the other hand, Wehr stresses the difference between English, on the one hand, and French and the Celtic languages, on the other: in the latter two groups, clefting is an (almost) obligatory means of expressing prominence, whereas in English and also German, Italian or even Latin, emphasis can also be conveyed by prosodic means alone, with clefting being an optional feature (Wehr 2001: 255).

Many linguists have wanted to see a connection between rigidity of word order and clefting and to explain the spread of the cleft construction as a reflex of increasing constraints on word order arrangements. However, Ball (1991) is an exception here. In her view, the relationship between rigidity of word order and increasing frequencies of clefts from the EModE period onwards "is unlikely to be straightforward" (1991: 497), because, as she puts it, "alternatives involving movement have long since disappeared" (*op. cit.*, 518). As more probable factors explaining the spread of clefts in later English she singles out the invention of printing, the rise of literacy, and the development of the written language; parallel developments in French and Scandinavian languages are also potentially relevant (*ibid.*). Persuasive as Ball's arguments are, from a wider cross-linguistic perspective it is hard to ignore the fact that clefting is a particularly robust feature of languages that have rigid word order systems. Thus, Ahlqvist (2002) considers clefting to be a particularly suitable means of expressing emphasis in strict VSO languages such as the Celtic languages. Writing much earlier, Jespersen (1937: 86) also seeks to establish a more general connection between rigid word order and clefting (which also provides a plausible explanation for the observed differences among Germanic languages):

> In some, though not in all cases, this construction may be considered one of the means by which the disadvantages of having a comparatively rigid grammatical word-order (SVO) can be obviated. This explains why it is that similar constructions are not found, or are not used extensively, in languages in which the word-order is considerably less rigid than in English, French, or the Scandinavian languages, thus German, Spanish and Slavic.

It should be noted that clefting is by no means restricted to Indo-European or even European languages. Ahlqvist (2002) notes its presence in Finnish, where it is, however, probably due to Swedish influence. Outside Europe, it is found, e.g. in Maori (see Ahlqvist 2002) and some African languages (see, e.g. Holm 1988: 212; Sebba 1997: 187–188). Interestingly, it is also a feature of several English-based creoles, which adds yet another, 'universalist', perspective to the matter at hand (Sebba 1997: 187–188).

2.2.6.3   *Possibility of Celtic Substratum Influence on English and Other Western European Languages*

Very few scholars have so far ventured to suggest that the English cleft construction could have a Celtic connection. The lack of 'hard' evidence for substratal influences may well be one factor here, but it may equally reflect the generally negative attitude of 'mainstream' Anglicists towards the idea of Celtic substratum influences. However, as mentioned above, the Old Irish scholar Anders Ahlqvist (1977) has suggested that the cleft construction in Western European languages could ultimately derive from Celtic where it has been attested earlier than in any other of these languages. Interestingly, similar ideas had been expressed in some of the earlier Celtological literature, especially by Heinrich Wagner. In his discussion on what he calls *mise en relief*, Wagner first notes the identical nature of this syntactic phenomenon in Celtic languages and Berber languages. He then goes on to suggest that there is a clear "geolinguistic connection" (*ein sprachgeographischer Zusammenhang*) between the French *mise en relief* construction, i.e. *c'est*-clefting, and its Insular Celtic parallels (Wagner 1959: 173 ff.). He does not comment on the rise of the English cleft construction in this connection but draws attention to the frequent use of clefts in Hiberno-English, which according to him depends on the corresponding Irish usage. He also wants to refute the view that seeks to explain the emergence of cleft constructions in languages as a 'psychologically' natural phenomenon, which can be predicted to occur in a wide range of languages. In a characteristically insightful way, which has only many decades later found a theoretically sophisticated expression in the concept of 'grammaticalisation', Wagner remarks:

> Es kommt aber nicht darauf an, ob in einer Sprache eine Konstruktion vorkommt oder nicht, sondern inwiefern sie als grammatische Kategorie ausgebildet ist oder nicht, und welchen syntaktischen Umfang diese Kategorie, sofern sie lebendig ist, besitzt.[26]

> (Wagner 1959: 173)

In Celtic languages and in French, as Wagner continues, the *mise en relief* construction is firmly embedded in the grammatical system and is closely connected with other systems which include, for example, question formation in these languages (Wagner 1959: 174).

Wehr (2001), who also explores the areal-linguistic dimension of clefting, suggests that the Celtic languages and French (and also Portuguese, which makes extensive use of clefting) belong to a 'Western Atlantic *Sprachbund*'. These languages share other features as well, most notably what Wehr describes as *Swächung des Einzelwortes* ('weakening of the individual word'), a tendency which involves several phonological processes such as sandhi phenomena, *enchaînement* ('chaining'), *liaison*, elision and fusion.

It is this loss of autonomy of the individual word which according to Wehr lies behind the prominent status of clefting in these languages; in other languages such as English, which preserve the possibility of 'word accent', clefting is not a necessary device for expressing emphasis.

From an even earlier chronological perspective on cross-linguistic influences, Hamp (1973: 231) hints at the possible Gaulish impact on French clefting:

> [W]hile modern French cleft sentences look strongly like a Gaulish syntax and word-order (hypothetical, since we really have almost no Gaulish discourses) imposed on Latin morphology in creolized phonetics, the rules for que follow generally those of late Latin and of Europe.

Another scholar drawing attention to the possible Gaulish substratum in French is Lambert (1994). He notes the similarity between the French formula *c'est . . . qui (que)* and the Irish *is é a rinne é* 'c'est lui qui l'a fait', and writes: "On s'est demandé si la formule française était due à un substrat celtique: jusque ici aucun texte gaulois n'en a apporté le témoignage"[27] (Lambert 1994: 68).

Unfortunately, as both Hamp and Lambert point out, the question of Gaulish influence on French clefting cannot be solved in the absence of sufficient data from Gaulish. Yet, there seems to be an increasing amount of evidence from Gaulish inscriptions suggesting that this language made at least some use of clefting and fronting ('topicalisation') devices, although scholars are not agreed on the interpretation of some of the forms found in the extant inscriptions (for discussion, see, e.g. Evans 1990: 168). Perhaps the most thorough analyses of the Gaulish sentence from this perspective have been put forward by John T. Koch (see, e.g. Koch 1985). On the basis of the so-called Chamalières tablet discovered in 1971 and some other inscriptions, he seeks to identify cleft sentences in continental Celtic and concludes that Gaulish must have had clefting and topicalisation patterns which were constrained 'movements' leaving the main structures of the sentence unaffected (Koch 1985: 34).[28] Some scholars have gone so far as to suggest that the syntax of Gaulish, and more generally, of Gallo-Brittonic was 'topic-prominent' rather than 'subject-prominent', which would explain the centrality of clefting (and other types of fronting) in even the later phases of this language group, including the parent language of Welsh (see Evans 1990: 169–172 and especially his reference to the work by James Fife).[29]

Turning now back to English, German (2003), who relies on Ball's (1991) findings on the relatively late attestation of clefts in ME, suggests "a possible French adstratal or even a Celtic substratal origin" for the English cleft construction. Of these two potential sources, French influence on ME was already suggested in an early study by Leon Kellner (1892), as noted by

Ball (1991: 14), who does not consider it likely because of the chronological precedence of at least some types of English clefts (see the discussion above). German, however, draws attention to the possible significance of the fact that the English cleft construction bears a closer resemblance to the corresponding Brythonic construction than the French one: *c'est* normally remains in the present tense (in standard French); it also shows singular or plural concord. In English, by contrast, the verb is either *is* or *was* (cf. MW *ys/oed*), and it remains in the singular.[30] There is also a difference in the behaviour of pronouns following the copula: it is in the nominative in ME and in Brythonic, but in the accusative in French. As yet another factor which may indirectly support Celtic influence even on English clefting, German discusses the case of Breton French. According to his observations, this variety makes more extensive use of *c'est*-clefting than does standard French, and even allows structures like *c'est aller qu'il fait* (lit. It is go he does) or *c'est à travailler avec son père qu'il est*, which echo the Celtic patterns and are also closely reminiscent of the types of structures found in Hiberno-English. German's hypothesis is that these structures are the result of an unconscious semantic reconstruction and structural blending of the French and Breton patterns in the minds of bilingual speakers (2003: 401–402). Breton French may, indeed, be compared in this respect with Hiberno-English or Hebridean English in which clefting also abounds as a result of the influence from the Celtic substrata (see the discussion in 4.2 below). What also enhances the value of Breton French as a useful point of comparison is the fact that this variety displays another syntactic feature familiar from the Celtic Englishes, viz. periphrastic DO, realised by the verb *faire* 'do'. Writing on the possible Celtic background of periphrastic DO in various European languages, van der Auwera and Genee (2002) cite Trépos's discussion of the periphrastic use of *faire* in Breton French (or 'Franco-Breton', as van der Auwera and Genee call it). According to Trépos, the use of *faire* in this function is "un *bretonnisme* que l'on entend souvent dans la bouche des bretonnants parlant français; c'est parce que le français n'a pas d'équivalent"[31] (Trépos 1980: 274; cited in van der Auwera and Genee 2002: 299).

Finally, Tristram (1999a) approaches the question of substratal or other influences on English clefts from the point of view of the typological convergence of English and the Celtic languages. She lists clefting as one of the features which in her view are the result of the "typological disruption" which affected these languages when they came into contact with each other some 1,500 years ago, and which has caused them to converge on a number of syntactic and other features, including the attrition of declension and conjugation, attrition of gender and adjectival inflection, word order, aspect, etc. (for further discussion, see Tristram 1999a). As regards clefting, Tristram notes its frequent use in Welsh, Irish, and Irish English. She also points out that in Welsh even a verb can be 'topicalised' by means of clefting, whereas Standard English clefting is 'less advanced' in this respect (1999a: 22).

2.2.6.4   Conclusion

The foregoing discussion has brought to light some evidence which strongly suggests at least some degree of Celtic influence on English clefts. This includes:

(i)   later attestation of cleft constructions in English as compared with Celtic languages;

(ii)   robustness of clefting in even the earliest stages of the Celtic languages, probably going back to continental Celtic (Gaulish), although the data from Gaulish are not uncontroversial enough to ascertain the exact status of clefting at that stage; in any case, there is little doubt that the cleft construction was part of the grammar of those speakers of late British who first came into contact with the Anglo-Saxon settlers;

(iii)   syntactic similarities especially between the earliest types of clefts in English and their Celtic parallels (the types *min fæder is þe me wuldraö, Nis seo orþung þe we ut blawaþ* and '*Nis hit na Petrus þæt þær cnucaö . . .*', as discussed above); these similarities also extend to certain types of questions;

(iv)   prominent role of cleft constructions in present-day (and earlier) Celtic-influenced varieties of English, which may have, as in the case of some other syntactic features such as the 'expanded form' of verbs, promoted the use of clefting in standard varieties of English, too. One could add to this the equally prominent role of clefting in Breton French, as compared with standard French.

Yet, possible influence from other sources cannot be excluded on the basis of the existing evidence. Thus, there remains the possibility of some kind of an areal-linguistic connection between languages spoken in the (north-)western parts of Europe, along the Atlantic coast, as suggested by Wehr (2001). If clefting is indeed an areal feature, this would entail some degree of historical and linguistic contacts between the languages sharing this feature (and possibly others, too). While it may not be so easy to document such connections between, say, Portuguese and English or Swedish, it is more than likely that there is some kind of a 'geolinguistic connection' between the English cleft construction and French *c'est*-clefting, as suggested by Wagner (1959) and, more recently, by German (2003). That may well have involved mutually reinforcing influences, despite the claim by Ball (1991) that the cleft constructions of these two languages have emerged independently of each other. The Latin model cannot be completely ruled out either; its influence would, however, be mainly limited to the OE period and to certain types of clefting (the type *min fæder is þe me wuldraö*), which can, on the other hand, also be argued to reproduce the corresponding Celtic patterns.

Finally, it is hard to ignore the role of general typological considerations: the oft-mentioned cross-linguistic connection between rigidity of word order and clefting may have promoted the rise of clefting in English, once the syntactic patterns had been established. This process may have been set in motion by the kind of 'typological disruption' discussed by Tristram (1999a), leaving again room for external causation and influence from the Celtic languages.

2.2.7   Relative Clause Structures

This section deals with various kinds of relative clause structures which have, or have been argued to have, close parallels in the Celtic languages. The first of these is the zero relative construction or 'contact-clause', as it is also often called. Closely associated with zero relatives are two other, partially overlapping, phenomena, viz. 'resumptive pronouns' and 'preposition stranding'. Jespersen (MEG III: § 4.3.2), who was the first to use the term 'contact-clause', defines the phenomenon as follows:

> By the side of clauses with *that*, *who*, and *which* we have from early times relative clauses without any connective word—**contact-clauses** as we may term them—which have always been very frequent in colloquial English, but which were also persecuted by scholars.

Resumptive pronouns are pronominal and anaphoric reflexes of the antecedent in the subordinate clause, e.g. in *That's the chap that **his** uncle was drowned*, recorded from Welsh English (see Parry 1979: 146 and the discussion below). Preposition stranding, then, occurs in prepositional relative clauses where the preposition can be left 'hanging' or 'stranded' at the end of the relative clause, e.g. . . . *the rock we sat down on* . . . (cited in Isaac 2003a: 47). As in this example, the relative element is often suppressed, especially in speech.

Although Jespersen does not consider the possible Celtic origins of the contact-clause or the two other features illustrated above, they have been the subject of many other debates, as will be seen below. Before that, however, the historical background and major stages of development of the contact-clause and the two other associated structures need to be examined in some detail. This will be followed by a discussion of the Celtic parallels and the likelihood of substratal influences from the latter.

2.2.7.1   *The History of the Contact-Clause in English*

Visser (1963–1973: § 18) discusses the contact-clause under the heading of '*apo koinou*' constructions, his paradigmatic example being *I have an uncle is a myghty erle*. He states that these occurred in OE but were "not frequent". In ME and EModE, by contrast, "its frequency is considerable"; in later ModE it becomes "archaic" and "dies out" in present-day English (1963–1973: § 18). In a later section (§ 21), Visser notes the frequent use of *apo koinou* constructions in present-day dialectal English, especially Anglo-Irish. As far as traditional dialects of EngE are concerned, Visser's observations are confirmed by Wright (1905), who notes omission of both object and subject relatives ('the objective case' and 'the nominative' in Wright's terminology) in sentences like *I know a man will do for you* (Wright 1905: 280).

To return to the general history, Traugott (1992) speaks of the 'absence of a relative marker' but also refers to the term 'contact-clause' (see also Traugott 1972: 157–158 for an earlier discussion of the same phenomenon). She concurs with Visser, considering this type to be "relatively rare in OE". Nonetheless, Traugott regards it as a native construction because of its appearance in the earliest poetry and even in translations of Latin texts where the original has an overt relativiser (1992: 228). She illustrates the latter type of context with the following OE example:

> (47)   & sægdon him ða uundra dyde se hælend
>   and told   them those wonders did that Saviour (*JnG* (Li) 11.46)
>   [Lat. 'et dixerunt eis *quae* fecit iesus']
>   (Traugott 1992: 228)

Traugott further notes that the contact-clause is "usually found in relative clauses with predicates such as *hatan* 'to call, name', *wesan* 'to be', *belifan* 'to remain', *nyllan* 'to not want', verbs that are either stative or are used statively in the constructions under discussion" (*ibid.*). What are also of particular interest in this connection are her observations on the occasional use of resumptive pronouns in OE writing (1992: 229). These are seemingly repetitious pronominal reflexes of the antecedent in the subordinate relative clause and occur almost always with the relativiser *þe*, but also occasionally with *þæt*. In example (48), the relativised NP is in an accusative form:

> (48)   ... & ic gehwam wille þærto tæcan þe hiene (ACC)
>   and I whomever   shall thereto direct PT him
>   his   lyst   ma   to   witanne
>   of-it would-please more to   know
>   'and I shall direct anyone to it who would like to know more
>   about it'
>   (*Or* 3 3.102.22; cited in Traugott 1992: 229)

In (49), then, the relativised NP is a dative:

> (49)   Swa bið eac þam   treowum þe him (DAT) gecynde biþ
>   So   is also to-those trees   PT to-them   natural is
>   up heah to standanne
>   up high to stand
>   'so it is also with trees to which it is natural to stand up straight'
>   (*Bo* 25.57.20; cited in Traugott 1992: 229)

An example of a genitive NP is given in (50):

(50) Se   wæs Karles sunu þe Æþelwulf West Seaxna cyning
That was Charles' son PT Æþelwulf West Saxons' king
his dohtor hæfde him   to cuene
his daughter had for-himself as queen
'he was the son of Charles whose daughter was the queen of
Æthelwulf, King of the West Saxons'
(*Chron A* (Plummer) 885.18; cited in Traugott 1992: 206)

Stranded prepositions also occur in OE relative clauses introduced by *þe*
or *þæt*; an example of the latter can be seen in (51):

(51) þurh   þa   halgo rode (FEM ACC) þet Crist   wæs on þrowod
through that holy cross   that Christ was on tortured
(*Chron E* (Plummer) 963.63; cited in Traugott 1992: 227)

Before continuing the discussion, it is useful to bear in mind that the
status of OE relatives is not always clear. Traugott (1992) draws attention
to frequent ambiguities between 'true' relative clauses, i.e. dependent structures, on the one hand, and independent, appositional clauses involving
demonstrative pronouns in subject position, on the other. As Traugott notes,
neither punctuation nor word order can provide us with definite guidelines
here; it is only when the putative relative clause is embedded in the middle
of the matrix clause that we can speak of certain cases of relativisation (*op.
cit.*, 225). This of course adds to the problems faced by language historians
in their efforts to make cross-linguistic comparisons.

Both the contact-clause and resumptive pronouns continue to be used
in ME. Mustanoja (1960: 205) comments on the more frequent deletion of
subject-relative as compared with object-relative in ME texts; this he considers to indicate a later development of the latter type of deletion phenomenon. He also pays attention to the more common use of the contact-clause
in poetry than in prose (*ibid.*). Fischer (1992) confirms Mustanoja's observations on the commonness of zero relatives in subject position and cites the
following examples from early and late ME texts, respectively:

(52) Adam ben king and eue quuen / Of all ðe ðinge [Ø] in werlde
ben.
'Adam and Eve are king and queen of all the things [that] are in
the world'
(*Gen. & Ex.* 296–297; cited in Fischer 1992: 306)

(53) . . . I know no knyght in this contrey [Ø] is able to macche hym.
(Malory Wks (Add.59678) 377.35–36; cited in Fischer 1992:
306)

Writing on cleft sentences with deletion of relative, Ball (1991: 298) also concurs with Mustanoja's account and finds several illustrative examples of clefts with subject-deletion in late ME texts, including the ones in (54) and (55):

(54) c1330 Arth. & M.(A) 1957: þus telleþ þe letters blak / *It was Merlin wiþ hem spak.*
'This is what the black letters say: It was Merlin with them spoke.'
(Cited in Ball 1991: 298)

(55) c1450 Mkempe 69.22: [concerning M.'s 'cryings'] For summe seyd *it was a wikkyd spiryt vexid him* sum seyd it was a sekenes; sum seyd sche had dronkyn to mech wyn . . .
'For some said it was a wicked spirit vexed her; some said it was a sickness; some said she had drunk too much wine . . .'
(Cited in Ball 1991: 298)

Ball also finds zero relatives to be even more common in existential sentences than in clefts. She cites several instances from late ME texts, all but one of them involving subject-deletion.[32] The following are from Gower and Malory:

(56) c1393 Gower CA 4.3556: So stille that *ther was noman / It herde* . . .
'So still that there was no man heard it . . .'
(Cited in Ball 1991: 299)

(57) 1485 Malory M. d'A.(Cx) 420.40: In the meane whyle came in a good olde man . . . and *there was no knyght knewe from whens he came.*
'In the meanwhile, a good old man came in . . . and there was no knight knew where he came from.'
(Cited in Ball 1991: 299)

As in OE, resumptive pronouns occur in ME almost always in relative clauses introduced by the indeclinable relative particle *þe*, which is later replaced by *þat* (Fischer 1992: 309). As Fischer states, their primary function is to express oblique case, especially the genitive, as in the following example:

(58) Ther-ynne wonyþ a wyȝt, þat wrong is *his* name, . . .
'There lives a creature whose name is wrong'
(*Ppl.C* (Hnt 143) i, 59; cited in Fischer 1992: 309)

A resumptive pronoun can also appear in other syntactic positions, e.g. in the accusative:

(59) ... it was þat ilk cok, / þat petre herd *him* crau, ...
       (*Cursor* (Vesp) 15995–6; cited in Fischer 1992: 309)

It was not until the WH-pronouns, which were capable of indicating case, had developed that resumptive pronouns gradually disappeared from standard language; they were no longer needed to fill a 'systemic gap', as Fischer concludes (1992: 309).

Also writing on the developments in ME, Hamp (1975: 298) distinguishes three major changes in English relative clause patterns over the late ME period. He describes them as follows:

  (i)   Important changes surfaced between the fourteenth century and 1550.
  (ii) *Rel* came to be frequently an invariant neuter in surface form [i.e. *þæt*].
  (iii) Deletion of *Rel* changed by 1550 prevailingly from that of the subject (under certain restrictions) to that of the object.

Hamp further suggests that "the later facts of English deletion may be put in strikingly direct relation with certain configurations of Medieval Welsh surface structure" (*op.cit.*, 299). He refers to Bever and Langendoen (1972), who according to Hamp "cannot explain why German, unlike English, cannot delete *Rel*; nor why OHG and OSaxon could" (Hamp 1975: 299). He himself explains deletions in the latter two by "rules inherited from Germanic grammar", but the later English deletions by Welsh influence.

This brings us suitably to the Celtic, and especially Welsh, parallels to the contact-clause. These will be the topic of the next section.

2.2.7.2   *Parallels in Welsh and Other Celtic Languages*

In both earlier and present-day Welsh, deletion of the relative pronoun is very common. As Evans (1964: 60) states, a relative pronoun is present only in affirmative clauses, where it functions as subject or as object of the relative clause. Even in these, the pronoun may be omitted before *oed* 'was', as in *e gvyr oed en e grogi* 'the men [who] were hanging him' (*op.cit.*, 61). In negative clauses, no form of the relative pronoun is used, and the same holds for a number of other contexts, such as before compound verbs containing certain prefixes or where the verb is preceded by certain negative or pre-verbal particles (*op.cit.*, 61–63). In the Welsh grammatical tradition, these kinds of clauses are called 'proper relative clauses', as opposed to 'improper relative clauses', which express a genitival or an adverbial relationship (either with or without a preposition), or in which the relative element is a nominal predicate (Evans 1964: 60, 64). The improper relative clauses have no relative pronoun, but the verb is preceded by the particles *yt, y(d), ry/yr* (affirmative), *ny(t), na(t)* (negative). As Evans points out, these particles gradually came to be felt as what he terms 'relative conjunctions' (*op.cit.*, 64). Improper relative clauses involve what we have above labelled as resumptive pronouns. In a genitival clause, this is a possessive pronoun, as in Evans's example *y brenhin y kiglef . . . y glot a'e volyant* 'the king whose fame and renown I have heard of' (lit. '. . . I have heard of his fame and renown'). In adverbial prepositional clauses, the resumptive pronoun or element consists of a conjugated form of the preposition, as in *y coedyd y foassant vdunt* 'the woods to which they fled' (lit. '. . . they fled to them') (see Evans 1964: 65–67).[33]

A further feature of Welsh relative clauses is the phonological process of lenition, which is in fact shared by the relative clauses of the other Brythonic languages, as Thurneysen (1946: 323) points out. Lenition occurs where the antecedent is the subject or object of the relative clause and where the verb of the relative clause is preceded by a leniting particle *a* (*op.cit.*, 323). In Old Irish, as Thurneysen writes, lenition is obligatory in subject relative clauses but optional in object clauses (*op.cit.*, 314). What makes lenition important in this connection is the fact that it is, as Hamp (1975: 300) points out, closely associated with the deletion of the relative element or particle. This has become a prominent feature of what Hamp calls Welsh 'object syntax', leading to a close phonetic similarity between the lenited object noun and the lenited verb with the deleted relative particle *a*. To a bilingual Welsh–English speaker, "suppression of an overt *Rel* segment had a strong linkage with non-subject syntax", thus explaining why *Rel* deletion is a regular feature of object relative clauses (*op.cit.*, 300). Hamp further notes the frequent occurrence of *Rel* deletion in Anglo-Irish, citing Synge's writings as evidence of this feature (referred to by Bever and Langendoen, too, as Hamp points out). In Hamp's view, the Anglo-Irish usage can be explained by influence from Irish, which behaves similarly to Welsh in this respect (*op.cit.*, 301, fn. 4).

An essentially similar account, albeit in more traditional terms, of the Welsh relative clauses and omission of the relative element is given by Rowland (1876), who states that "the relative pronoun is very often omitted" (1876: 263). Rowland also discusses and illustrates the use of resumptive pronouns and the conditions for their use:

> When the relative is under government of a preposition, the preposition is sometimes placed before the relative, sometimes after the verb of the clause in the form of a pronominal preposition. The latter is by far the more elegant and idiomatic construction.
>
> (Rowland 1876: 262)

Rowland's examples of both types of construction are

Y cyfaill at yr hwn yr anfonais lythyr, the friend, to whom I sent a letter.

Y cyfaill, yr hwn yr anfonais lythyr ato, the friend, whom I sent a letter to.

(Rowland 1876: 262)

Rowland notes that, when the omitted relative is governed by a preposition, the preposition stands after the verb in the form of a pronominal preposition, as in the following examples (see *op.cit.*, 263):

Y wlad y daethost allan *o honi*. ['The country that you came from (*lit.* out of) (it).'] Y dydd y'm ganed *ynddo*. ['The day that I was born (in it).'] Yn y cyfyngder trallodus y'n dygwyd *iddo*. ['In the grievous distress that we were brought (in)to (it).']

On the basis of even a brief and simplified description such as the one given above, it should be evident that the relative clause systems of the Celtic languages, especially those of Welsh, could have provided the model for the English contact-clauses. It is therefore not surprising that the possibility of early Celtic influence on this aspect of English syntax should have attracted the attention of scholars. Given some of the formal differences, such as the lenition phenomenon and the existence of pronominal prepositions in Welsh but not in English, it is equally unsurprising that controversies should exist even in this area, as we will see in the next section.

2.2.7.3   *Possibility of Contact Influences*

Zero relatives have been argued to have a Celtic background, e.g. by Preusler (1956: 337–338). Relying on Jespersen (MEG III: § 7.1.2) and Kellner (1892/1905: § 111), he notes the rapid increase in the use of zero relatives in English from the thirteenth century onwards. However, contrary to the position adopted by Jespersen, Preusler rejects the possibility of Scandinavian influence, because the same developments take place in Scandinavian languages at about the same time as in English and, hence, too late to have triggered the same process in English. What according to Preusler suggests Celtic influence is the fact that, in Celtic (Welsh), relative deletion can occur regardless of whether the antecedent is in the nominative or accusative. This is the situation in earlier English, too, whereas in ModE nominative relative deletion is much more restricted. This feature of Celtic explains, as Preusler argues, the earlier English developments, which, as in the case of the progressive form discussed in section 2.2.5, were largely due to the transfer effects in the speech of English-speaking Britons:

Die kymrischen relativsätze haben [. . .] oft keinen relativum, sondern werden durch bestimmte verbformen gekennzeichnet. Im munde englisch

sprechender briten konnte sich also leicht der sog. contact-clause ein-
stellen, der im heutigen Englisch so beliebt ist [. . .][34]

(Preusler 1956: 337)

Preusler's substratum account of English zero relatives has in recent
research been taken up by Tristram (1999a), who discusses them briefly
under two headings: 'hanging prepositions' (by which she refers to the phenomenon better known as 'preposition stranding') and 'zero relatives'. As
regards the latter, Tristram is content to point out the possibility of relative
deletion in both English and Welsh, although, following Preusler (1956),
she notes the difference between the two insofar as deletion of subject relatives is concerned. Tristram's discussion of preposition stranding is equally
brief: referring to Preusler (*op.cit.*) and Molyneux (1987), she outlines the
systems of preposition stranding in English relative *that*-clauses and compares these with Welsh where, in contradistinction to English, the stranded
element is a prepositional pronoun inflected for gender and number and
therefore stressed. Unfortunately, Tristram does not pursue the matter of
possible contact influences beyond these observations.

Taking issue with Tristram's suggestions, Isaac (2003a) completely rejects
the possibility of contact influences with respect to preposition stranding
in English. His main objection is that "there is no preposition stranding
in Celtic", and that the English constructions with stranded prepositions
"could not be more foreign to Celtic syntax". He contrasts Welsh examples
such as . . . *y garreg eisteddon ni arni* . . . (lit. the rock$_i$ sat.1PL we on-her$_i$)
'. . . the rock we sat down on . . .' with English ones such as . . . *the rock we
sat down on* . . ., arguing that they represent two very different syntactic
types. In order for the Celtic pattern to have provided the model for the English clauses the latter should now be realised by a construction such as . . .
the rock$_i$ we sat down on it$_i$ . . . But since this is not the case, and since structures of the last-mentioned type are alien to English syntax, Isaac concludes
that the English relatives with stranded prepositions provide "no evidence of
linguistic contact between English and Celtic" (2003a: 48).

While Isaac's argument is convincing insofar as present-day Standard
English is concerned, it completely overlooks the possible reflexes of the
Celtic patterns of relatives in the earlier stages of English and in nonstandard varieties of English. As mentioned above, the OE indeclinable relative
þe (and occasionally *þæt*) allowed the use of a resumptive pronoun in the
relative clause to avoid ambiguity, a usage which continued into ME, as is
confirmed by Mustanoja (1960), Fischer (1992), and the other authors cited
above.

It should also be noted that dialectal varieties of English have been found
to make frequent use of resumptive pronouns that are clearly reminiscent of
the Celtic (Welsh) 'improper relative clauses', which also involve resumptive
pronouns as was shown above. Thus, the *Survey of Anglo-Welsh Dialects*

records examples such as *That's the chap that his uncle was drowned* (questionnaire item IX.9.8) at two locations in Dyfed/Cardiganshire (see Parry 1979: 146). Commenting on this usage, Parry (*ibid.*) compares it with Welsh constructions of the type *Dyma'r dyn y canodd ei fab yn y côr*, literally 'This is the man that his son sang in the choir'. What adds further weight to the possibility of contact influences is the fact that similar phenomena occur in Irish English and also Scottish English. The following examples are cited in Filppula (1999) and (Miller 1993), respectively (Miller's term for resumptive pronouns is 'shadow pronouns'):

(60) And there was a holy well . . . is a holy well there where the people go . . . on pilgrimage *to it*, [. . .] (Example from Co. Kerry, Ireland; cited in Filppula 1999: 186)

(61) . . . the spikes that you stick in the ground and throw rings *over them* . . . (Scottish English; cited in Miller 1993: 111)

Filppula (1999) also finds similar structures in the contact-English spoken in the Hebrides, witness (62). He refers to Gillies's (1993: 184–185) account of similar relative structures in Scottish Gaelic, exemplified in (63):[35]

(62) And I hope many's a good bottle you will serve and have a dram *out of it*. (SA 1969/157/B/Tiree: D.S.; cited in Filppula 1999: 193)

(63) am fear a bha mi a' bruidhinn ris
'the man to whom I was talking' (lit. 'the man who I was talking to him'). (Gillies 1993: 184)

These examples indicate a certain degree of grammaticalisation of this kind of relative syntax at least in the modern dialects spoken in or near the Celtic-speaking areas (see further discussion of these in Chapter 4, section 4.2).[36] It is therefore not at all unreasonable to assume, contrary to what Isaac (2003a) maintains, that similar constructions could have emerged in the earliest contact situations, leading eventually to relative structures in which the pronoun was suppressed in the same way as in Standard English relative clauses with stranded prepositions.[37]

Another critic of Tristram's—and especially Preusler's—account is Poppe (2006), who provides a detailed discussion of both Welsh relative clauses and their Germanic counterparts. Starting off with the alleged Celtic influence on contact-clauses, Poppe emphasises the role of lenition as a formal marker of subordination even in those cases in which the relative marker *a* has been elided. This he takes to be a crucial distinguishing feature between the English contact-clause and the Celtic relatives and something which in his view would have worked against transfer in a contact situation. From a general contact-linguistic point of view, however, it is hard to see how a phonological feature like this (although syntactically conditioned) could have precluded syntactic contact effects which could be assumed to have been more dependent on the overt presence—or absence, as in this case—of the relative element itself. Besides, being simplificatory in nature, deletion of the relative pronoun would accord well with what usually happens in contact situations.

Other, potentially more serious, objections raised by Poppe concern the date of emergence of the contact-clause in English and the existence of 'pan-Germanic' parallels to it. As for the former question, Poppe suggests that "the decisive phase of interference [from Welsh] would postdate probably at least 1200". Here he evidently thinks of the relatively late dating of the elision of relative markers in mediaeval Welsh. However, it is not at all clear that this happened at such a late date in Welsh; on the contrary, from the literature on MW one can gather that relative deletion was by that stage an established feature of at least the spoken varieties, if not of the written language, and hence, could well have been present even in the earlier stages (see, e.g. the discussion in Evans 1964). Also, the 'improper' relative clauses with resumptive pronouns probably date back to Old Welsh, as Isaac (2003b: 93) writes. It is true, as Poppe remarks, that Preusler as well as Keller (1925) assume a rather late emergence of 'Celticisms' in English syntax, but in this case at least, the 'symptoms' of contact, albeit rather infrequent, are to be found in OE already. Why this case should be so different from, e.g. the rise of the progressive form in English (see the discussion in 2.2.5 above), may well be explained by what Poppe has to say about the existence of the Germanic roots of the contact-clause.

Citing Ebert (1978), Poppe first notes that 'asyndetic relative clauses' (which is the term used by Ebert here) are a rare feature of both the oldest stages of English and of Scandinavian languages but become more frequent in their later histories. He then turns to other treatments of this subject and finds further support for the Germanic origins especially in the work of Dekeyser (1986). According to the latter, the subject contact-clause (but not the non-subject ones for which Dekeyser proposes a different origin) arose in OE and can be seen as "an offshoot of a much wider phenomenon inherent to all the 'primitive' Germanic dialects", which he describes as "the Old Germanic asyndetic parataxis without an overt subject" (Dekeyser 1986: 112–113; cited in Poppe 2006: 197). Dekeyser further states that this feature was later lost in German and Dutch, but was grammaticalised in English and the Scandinavian languages. As regards the origin of the non-subject contact-clause, which according to Dekeyser was "extremely rare" in OE, his suggestion is that it was due to "the introduction of a new relativization strategy with a deletable *that* and fixed word-order" (1986: 109, 115; cited in Poppe 2006: 197). Dekeyser does not, however, comment on the possible factors affecting the rise of this new strategy, apart from stating that it coalesces with the introduction of *that* as a relative marker and also with the stabilising of the SVO word order in EModE (1986: 114). In our view, it is quite plausible to assume that the syntax of the Welsh 'improper relative clauses' has promoted the development of non-subject contact-clauses in English, as was suggested by Hamp (1975). Poppe (2006), however, does not follow this line of reasoning; besides Ebert and Dekeyser, he refers to Gärtner's (1981) study of asyndetic relative clauses in Old High German and their later history, which, as Poppe argues, provide further evidence of early Germanic parallels to the English contact-clauses.

2.2.7.4   *Conclusion*

The above discussion has shown that the Celtic and English relative constructions are not so different as Isaac (2003a), in particular, has argued. Despite some obvious formal dissimilarities between Celtic and present-day Standard English, the evidence from the earlier and nonstandard varieties shows that parallel structures have existed, and still exist to some degree. This leaves room for a contact-based explanation, especially with regard to structures involving resumptive pronouns, which were a feature of earlier English but are now mainly (though not exclusively) found in dialectal varieties spoken in the formerly Celtic-speaking areas. The case for contact, it has to be admitted, would not be nearly so strong, if one were to consider only preposition stranding in the ModE sense, i.e. without resumptive pronouns.

As regards the early Germanic parallels discussed by Dekeyser (1986) and Poppe (2006), in particular, the situation is much the same as with the OE relative clauses: a lot depends here, too, on how the putative early Germanic relative structures are interpreted. Are they dependent clauses, and thus, 'genuine' instances of relative structures, or independent clauses, juxtaposed to each other in asyndetic parataxis? If the former is the case, it would explain why the contact-clause appears as early as in OE. Yet, what would remain unexplained on this account is the gradual increase of this type of relative clause in later English, as opposed to German or Dutch, which lose it over time—not to mention the extension of the contact-clause to non-subject relatives in ME. Even under this scenario, then, English undergoes a clear typological change which distances it from its Germanic neighbours, and given that there are other similar divergent developments (cf. the discussion on some of the other syntactic features in this chapter), we are brought back to the question of Celtic influence as a factor promoting such change. Needless to say that, if the latter alternative holds (viz. that the alleged Germanic parallels are not to be considered relative structures on a par with those found in OE or Celtic), then that would further enhance the probability of early Celtic influence on the English contact-clause.

2.2.8 Other Grammatical Features with Possible Celtic Origins

In this section we discuss a number of syntactic features which have either received very little or no attention in the literature on English–Celtic contacts, or for which the evidence for contact origins remains tenuous. The first of these represents once again a development that is shared between English and Brythonic Celtic but is not found in the other Germanic languages. The remaining features are grammatical constructions that have survived into the modern period but are restricted to some very conservative dialects of English.

2.2.8.1 *The Development of the* Self-*forms as Intensifiers and Reflexives*

Self-forms in ModE are used for two purposes: first, they function as reflexive pronouns or reflexive anaphors to mark co-reference, e.g. between the subject and object of a sentence (as in *John hurt himself very badly*); secondly, they are used as intensifiers to assign prominence to some constituent of a sentence (as in *John himself was very badly hurt*). Though not so obvious at first sight, ModE is unique amongst Germanic languages with respect to the uses of these forms and also different from OE, which followed the Germanic pattern. This in itself suffices to raise the question of possible external influence on English, and indeed, such suggestions have been made in the literature. Thus, Vezzosi (2005a, 2005b) discusses the parallel development of the intensifying *self*-forms in English and in Brythonic languages (Welsh and Breton), suggesting that the English forms are modelled on the latter on the basis of their typological characteristics and the clear chronological precedence of the Brythonic forms.

According to Vezzosi (2005a: 228), the ModE uses of the *self*-forms differ from the other Germanic languages in two major respects: first, ModE uses the same forms for both the intensifier function and for reflexive anaphora, unlike the other Germanic languages, which have two different forms for these functions (e.g. the German intensifier *selbst* vs. the reflexive series *mich/dich/sich/*etc.). Secondly, ModE has its own *self*-form for each person (*myself, yourself, him-/herself*, etc.), whereas the other Germanic languages have a special reflexive form only for the third person (e.g. G. *sich*); for the other persons objective forms of the 'ordinary' personal pronouns must be used. As Vezzosi (2005b: 176) points out, this latter feature makes English rather unique even from a wider cross-linguistic perspective and—what is of particular interest to us in this connection—is shared only by the Celtic languages and Creoles.

As said above, the situation was different in OE, which still retained the Germanic system—as does Frisian, the closest cognate language of English, even at the present day, as Vezzosi points out (2005a: 228). In his description of the OE system of reflexives, Mitchell (1985: § 265) writes that "[t]he personal pronoun serves as a reflexive, either alone or emphasized by *self*, which is usually declined to agree with the pronoun in number, gender, and case".

This means that the reflexive pronoun system and the intensifier *self* were formally distinct in OE, with the latter being mainly used to emphasise or to avoid ambiguity. On the other hand, Mitchell emphasises the role of the context in disambiguating between reflexive and non-reflexive uses of, e.g. *hine* and *hine selfne* in OE texts (1985: § 276). However, he accepts the view that *self* was not in OE a reflexive marker but was used to emphasise (1985: § 475). In any case, the dual function of the *self*-forms as intensifiers and reflexive markers does not get established until the ME period (Visser 1963–1973: § 438; Vezzosi 2005a: 228).

Vezzosi surveys several of the earlier suggestions as to how the language changed to give way, first, to the gradually increasing use of the *self*-forms in ME as both intensifiers and co-reference markers, and then to the establishing of these in their ModE functions in EModE. Among these is Keenan's (1996) proposal, according to which the *self*-forms are the result of a reanalysis of sequences consisting of a 'pleonastic reflexive' (see Mitchell 1985: § 271) and the intensifier *self* as one unit. Vezzosi questions Keenan's account on the grounds that it does not explain why the *self*-forms replaced the old Germanic system of OE; why the *self*-forms came to be used for all persons; and why these changes occurred in the ME period and not before (2005a: 229–230). Another suggestion discussed by Vezzosi is that put forward by van Gelderen (2000), who argues that the *self*-forms emerged as a result of two interacting processes or factors: a reanalysis of *self* as a noun and the differing 'pronominal' or 'deictic force' of the personal pronouns. The former accounts for the emergence of the so-called nominal series of reflexives, consisting of the possessive pronominal forms + *self* (*myself, yourself,* etc.). The latter, in turn, explains why the *self*-form is first attested with the third person, which has greater deictic force than the first or second person pronouns, thus preventing its anaphoric use; being 'weaker' and therefore less liable to cause problems for the identification of the intended referent, the first and second person pronouns better allow themselves to be used anaphorically. Vezzosi's response to van Gelderen's analysis is that the third person pronoun has a deictic force in all old Indo-European languages by its nature and that already in OE there are cases of *himself* used as an intensifier without a pronominal focus. She also sees no motivation for an adjective to change into a noun and especially into one which has such severe distributional constraints as *self* has (2005a: 230).

A third proposal dealt with by Vezzosi comes from König and Siemund (2000), who claim that, from a cross-linguistic perspective, intensifiers can undergo semantic change into reflexive anaphors. Such a change has according to these authors taken place in Rheto-Romance and Brazilian Portuguese. Vezzosi counters this argument by noting that it does not explain why *himself* first appears as an intensifier and only later as a reflexive anaphor (Vezzosi 2005a: 230–231). On the other hand, in an earlier context (see

Vezzosi 2003), Vezzosi herself considered the possibility of explaining the rise of the reflexive anaphor *himself* in the light of the kind of grammaticalisation theory represented by König and Siemund (2000). On this account, reflexive anaphors first arise to solve possible referential ambiguities by adding the intensifier *self* to the simple pronoun; after a while, the old usage without the intensifier gives way to the *self*-form as the primary disambiguating strategy and eventually gets completely lost, except in certain well-defined contexts (such as after prepositions where the two strategies can still be used interchangeably).

What the grammaticalisation hypothesis leaves unexplained according to Vezzosi is, first, why the grammaticalisation of *self*-forms does not follow the expected course of development, starting with anaphors in object position, which are in greatest need of disambiguation, and proceeding only after that to prepositional phrases. Vezzosi cites evidence from OE texts to show that *self*-forms appear in prepositional object position as early as in direct object position (2005a: 233). Secondly, this account cannot explain why the Germanic-type monomorphemic intensifier was replaced by the kind of *self*-forms that English now has, or why they were extended to all persons as reflexive markers, unlike in the other Germanic languages (2005a: 233).

Vezzosi's conclusion is that the Celtic hypothesis offers the best explanation for the special features of the English *self*-forms and the observed differences between English and the other Germanic languages. The parallelism between the English and the Celtic systems is, indeed, very close: in both MW and Middle Breton the intensifier is composed of a pronoun in the genitive case followed by *hun/an* 'one; self'. Vezzosi (2005a: 237) cites examples of *e hun* 'himself' from various MW and Middle Breton sources to illustrate the Celtic contexts of use, which—as she points out—are very similar to those of the *self*-forms in ME. A further factor speaking for Celtic influence on the rise of the *self*-forms is the areal distribution of *himself* in the ME period: on the basis of the evidence from the *Helsinki Corpus* and the *Linguistic Atlas of Early Middle English*, Vezzosi is able to show that *himself* as reflexive anaphor occurs more frequently in West Midland texts than in those from other parts of England (Vezzosi 2005a: 239). As yet another piece of evidence she mentions the word *oneself*, which also has a counterpart in all Insular Celtic languages (*an-unan* 'oneself'). Attested relatively late, this word has previously been explained as an analogical extension of the *self*-forms to the 'impersonal pronoun'. For Vezzosi, however, the Celtic counterpart is a more plausible source, given the general parallelism between the systems of these languages (2005a: 239).

The case of the *self*-forms is an interesting addition to the list of those features that set English apart from its Germanic sisters and at the same time link it with its Celtic neighbours. It underlines the importance of typological and areal comparisons, which in this case, too, have helped to shed new light on the extent of foreign and especially Celtic influences on English.

2.2.8.2   *Comparative* nor

The use of *nor* and its variants *na, no, ne, nai, nag* instead of *than* in comparative clauses is well attested in Scots and English from the fourteenth century onwards. This *nor* construction is also widely used in dialects, especially in the north of England. The origin of the *nor* construction in English is obscure, with a number of competing explanations. In this section we will first discuss the geographical distribution of the *nor* construction and then move on to review a number of attempts to explain its origin in English. Finally we will focus on one of the etymologies suggested, namely the possibility that the *nor* construction in English shows traces of Celtic, and especially Brythonic influence.

The Distribution of nor

The use of *nor* (*na, no, ne, nai, nag*) in comparative clauses is illustrated by the following examples from the third edition of the *Oxford English Dictionary* (*OED3*):

(64)   That na man . . haif ma personis with him na may suffice . . till his estate (1424 Acts Parl. Scotl. (1814) II 3/2)

(65)   Odere tythynges cannot I tell yow no thes for soothe but be here sey. (?1438 *Let.* in *Wilts. Archaeol. & Nat. Hist. Soc.* (1879) 18 12)

(66)   Here [sc. a serpent's] venyme is more greuous by day ne [L. *quam*] by nighte. (a1398 J. Trevisa tr. Bartholomaeus Anglicus *De Proprietatibus Rerum* (BL Add.) f. 268)

(67)   Ye schall here myche more in thys pertys nor I can at Brytys. (1479 R. Cely *Let.* 14 June in *Cely Lett.* (1975) 52)

The construction is very common in the *Helsinki Corpus of Older Scots*, especially from the period SC2 (1500–1570) onwards, as the following examples from the Corpus illustrate:

(68)   and ȝe sal be compellit to laubir the naikyt feildis vitht ȝour auen handis to there proffet. ȝe sal nocht alanerly be iniurit be euil vordis bot als ȝe sal be violently strykkyn in ȝour bodeis, quharfor ȝe sal lyf in mair thirlage ***nor*** brutal bestis quhilkis ar thirlit of nature. (SC1 AR/NI PAM COMPL 73)

(69)   A nucle kow will give mor milk in the day ***nor*** a forrow kow will doe. The mor milk a kow gives shoe is ever the leaner in the flesh. So a nucle kow is leaner ***nor*** a forrow kow, or a forrow

kow is leaner *nor* a yeild or Shamloh kow. (SC3 EX HANDO SKENE 69)

Indeed, in written texts, comparative *nor* and its variants seem to be predominantly a feature that is found in Scottish texts. The variant *nor* receives a characterisation 'chiefly *Sc., Irish English, U.S. regional,* and *Eng. regional*' in the *OED3* (s.v. *nor*), while the other variants are listed as predominantly Scottish in distribution (*no,* 'chiefly *Sc. Obs*'; *na,* '*Sc. and Eng. regional (north-west.)*'). The variants ending in a vowel (*na, no, ne*) have been attested slightly earlier, during the fourteenth/fifteenth centuries in written texts, than the *nor* variant, as confirmed by *A Dictionary of the Older Scottish Tongue (DOST)* (s.v. *nor*): "Ultimately superseding *na* conjunction but of later origin, all the apparent early instances being from recensions of the sixteenth century; at first only before vowels?" The date of first attestation during the ME period is also confirmed by Bruce Mitchell in his *Old English Syntax* (§ 3255): "the first use of these words [i.e. *ne* and *na*], and of *nor,* for 'than' are recorded in the period c. 1375–1400 [. . .] I have found no OE examples".

In spoken dialects, comparative *nor* appears to have a predominantly Scottish and northern English distribution. Murray (1873) confirms that *nor* was in general use in nineteenth-century Lowland Scottish dialects: "*Than,* after the Comparative Degree, is expressed indifferently by several words: 1. By *nor,* perhaps the commonest form still in use, as well as with the writers of the Middle period. [. . .] The older form of *nor* was *na*" (Murray 1873: 169).

The English Dialect Dictionary (EDD) states that *nor* after comparatives is "in gen.[eral] *dial.* use"; the English data recorded under the *EDD* entry for *nor* indicate that the form was in use in most of England, with the exception of the south-eastern counties of Sussex, Kent, Essex, Middlesex, Buckinghamshire, Hertfordshire, Essex, Northamptonshire and Cambridgeshire. In the *SED Basic Material* data from the mid-twentieth century, the distribution of comparative *nor* can be mapped on the basis of the answers to question VI.12.4 (Map 2.3); the distribution is predominantly northern, with some additional examples from the central Midlands.

To summarise the geographical distribution of comparative *nor*: in historical written documents comparative *nor* and its variants seem to be predominantly a Scottish feature; in spoken dialects it is found outside Scotland especially in the northern dialects of English, although it may have earlier had a more widespread distribution also in the south of England.

The Origin of Comparative *nor*

The *OED* and the *DOST* agree in considering the origin of the *nor* construction to be obscure or uncertain. There have been a number of attempts to find an etymology for the construction, however. Holthausen (1913: 339–340) argues that a construction of the type 'He is older nor I' simply

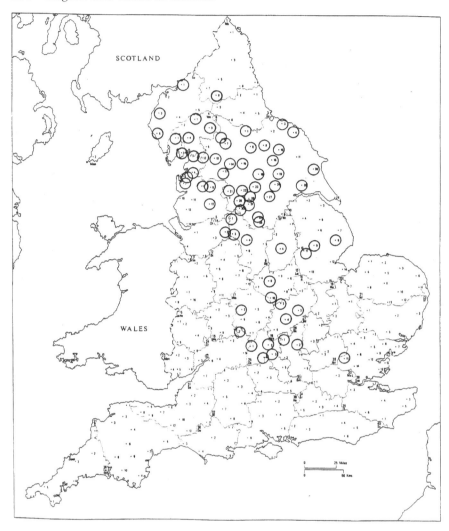

Map 2.3 Comparative *nor* in the *SED Basic Material* (VI.12.4).

represents the combination of the two propositions 'he is older, and not I' through the loss of what Holthausen calls a "syntactic pause" and consequent shift of stress.

Small (1924) is a thorough study of the semantics and syntax of the comparative particle in English. Though the focus of his study is naturally on the origin and development of the *than* forms, Small also touches on the origins of comparative *nor*. He considers the rise of the *nor* construction in ME rather difficult to explain, but offers phonetic reduction and consequent reanalysis as a possibility:

As to how such a form could arise in English without any apparent historical basis, it is probable that the slurring of *than* (e.g. *He is taller 'n his brother*) coupled with the adversative element that is felt in comparison favored some such adversative particle as light-stressed *ne* or *na*.

(Small 1924: 40)

André Joly (1967) seeks for an explanation in another direction. He argues that the OE comparative particle *þonne* must be analysed as consisting of two parts, instrumental *þon* and the negative particle *ne*:

[S]ince, as it has been suggested above, *þonne* cannot reasonably be derived from the temporal adverb (*þonne*), but must be related to the instrumental *þon*, one can only infer that the OE comparative particle has to be analysed as *þon + ne*, i.e. the instrumental to which is added a significant element whose presence is phonetically marked. My assumption is that this significant element is no other than the *negative particle*.

(Joly 1967: 17)

Joly then argues that the comparative constructions with *nor* and its variants that are attested from the fourteenth century onwards only serve to confirm his theory that the OE comparative particle must be analysed as *þon + ne*. According to Joly, comparative *nor* and its variants were already latent in the OE period, only to surface during the fourteenth century.

Joly's explanation has not been universally accepted. Bruce Mitchell discusses Joly's theory in his *Old English Syntax* and concludes his devastating review of Joly (1967) as follows:

I know of no evidence for his [Joly's] (1967, p.21) assertion that 'OE generally seems to have favoured the use of negation with the comparative conjunction' beyond the circular one that it is true if Joly's claim that *þonne = þon + ne* is true.

(Mitchell 1985: § 3207)

To conclude the discussion so far, it seems fair to say that the origin of the comparative *nor* has not been explained satisfactorily within the Anglicist tradition. Thus, it is not surprising that some scholars have turned to the Celtic languages, and especially Welsh, for an explanation. One of the first scholars to notice the Celtic parallels was Jamieson (1808) who, in his entry for comparative *nor* in the *Etymological Dictionary of the Scottish Language*, draws attention to the "C[ambro-Britannic] Gael[ic] Ir[ish] *na*". A similar observation is also made by Davies (1883), who explicitly links comparative *nor* in English with the corresponding Old Welsh comparative particle. The Welsh parallel is indeed quite interesting. According to Evans (1964: 43), *no(c)* is used as a comparative particle already in MW: "An adjective in the comparative is followed by *no(c)* 'than': *y neb a vei uch noc ef* 'the one who would be above him', *mwy a wneuthum i no thydi* 'more did I do than thou' ". According to the *Geiriadur Prifysgol Cymru* [A Dictionary of the Welsh Language], the first attestation of the comparative particle *no(c)* can be found in the thirteenth-century *Black Book of Carmarthen*. In other words, comparative *no(c)/na(c)* in Welsh pre-dates the English construction and is therefore a potential model for the English construction from the chronological perspective, as well. Stephen Laker (n.d.: 18–20; cf. now also Laker [forthcoming]) has argued that the Welsh comparative particle *no(c)* dates back to the Old Welsh period, possibly to the sixth century. The conclusion Laker (n.d.: 23) draws from his detailed study of the history of the negative comparative particle is that Welsh substrate influence offers the most plausible explanation for the rise of comparative *nor* construction in ME.[38]

2.2.8.3   The Cumbric Score

As an additional example of a grammatical subsystem which presents possible evidence for a Brythonic substratum in regional varieties of English, we will in this section review some of the literature on the so-called sheep-scoring numerals, reported from many locations in the north of England, mainly during the nineteenth century. The existence of traditional enumeration systems clearly derived from a Brythonic language (most probably Cumbric) in many locations in the north of England is relatively well documented (see, e.g. Ellis 1879; Witty 1927; Jackson 1955; Barry 1967, 1969; Wakelin 1977: 127–128; Price 1984: 150–152).[39] The first recorded example of these numerals in England dates from 1745, and the majority of the 100 or so recorded examples of the numerals were published before 1880 (Barry 1967: 25, 1969: 76). The distribution of the recorded examples in the north of England is given in Map 2.4.[40]

These counting systems are often referred to as 'sheep-counting numerals', though as Barry (1969: 75) points out, the use of these numerals—in most of the reported cases—seems to have been connected with knitting, children's games or nursery rhymes rather than counting sheep. Price (2000: 123) prefers the term 'Cumbric score', following Jackson (1955: 88), who offers the following characterisation of them:

> [T]he old Cumbric numerals [which] have survived very extraordinarily to modern times among the Pennine shepherds of Cumberland and the West Riding, for the purpose of counting sheep [. . .] a garbled version of something which must have been identical with the numerals in Welsh.

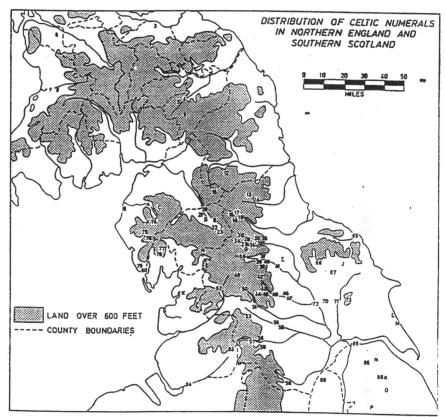

Map 2.4 The distribution of Celtic numerals in Northern England and Southern Scotland (from Barry 1969: 77). Reproduced by permission of the author and of the Society for Folklife Studies. Each number on the map refers to a location where a specimen has been recorded.

Barry (1967: 27) gives the following example from Millom, Furness, as an example of the sheep scoring numerals:

(70)   aina peina para pedera pump
       ithy mithy owera lavera dig
       aina-dig peina-dig para-dig
       pedera-dig bumfit
       aina-lumfit peina-bumfit
       para-lumfit pedera-bumfit giggy

Barry (*ibid.*) also lists the corresponding Modern Welsh numerals for comparison:

(71) un dau tri pedwar pump
chwech saith wyth naw deg
un-ar-ddeg deuddeg tri-ar-ddeg
pedwar-ar-ddeg pymtheg un-ar-bymtheg
dau-ar-bymtheg deunaw pedwar-ar-bymtheg ugain

The following versions of the Cumbric score (from Barry 1969) offer an indication of the variation that exists between specimens of the counting system found in different localities in the north. The specimens also show the existence of rhyming pairs and alliteration, an indication of the fact that the counting system has mainly survived in children's games and in nursery rhymes:

	Welsh	Borrowdale (Cumb.)	Kirkby Stephen (Westmorland)	High Furness (Lancs)	Nidderdale (W. Yorks)
1	un	yan	yan	yan	yain
2	dau	tyan	tahn	taen	tain
3	tri	tethera	teddera	tedderte	eddero
4	pedwar	methera	meddera	medderte	peddero
5	pump	pimp	pimp	pimp	pitts
6	chwech	sethera	settera	haata	tayter
7	saith	ethera	littera	slaata	layter
8	wyth	hevera	hovera	owra	overo
9	naw	devera	dovera	dowra	covero
10	deg	dick	dick	dick	dix
15	pymtheg	bumfit	bumfit	mimph	bumfit
20	ugain	giggot	jiggot	gigget	jiggit

There appears to be no doubt about the linguistic affinities of these numerals, as Barry (1969: 87) states:

The evidence of origin presented by the numerals themselves is conclusive in associating them with the Welsh branch of the Brythonic division of the Celtic languages, on account of the structure of the numerals 11 to 20, where Welsh has 1 on 10, 2/10, 3 on 10, 4 on 10 for 11, 12, 13, 14 and 5/10 for 15, and then proceeds 1 on 15 (really 1 on 5/10), 2 on 15, (2 x 9 = 18), and 4 on 15, for 16, 17, (18), 19, whereas all other

Celtic languages, Brythonic and Goidelic, have 1, 2, 3, 4, 5, 6, 7, 8, 9/10 for the teens.

Price (2000: 124) concurs with this: "that they are in some way connected with the Welsh numerals cannot reasonably be doubted". Price draws attention especially to those forms that seem unaffected by the tendency to group the numbers in alliterative pairs: "namely 'five', 'ten', 'fifteen' and perhaps 'twenty': *pimp* is exactly the Welsh *pump* (-u- being pronounced 'i'), and *dick* and *bumfit* are too close to Welsh *deg* and *pymtheg* (the first syllable of which is pronounced 'pum') for the resemblance to be purely fortuitous". Price also draws attention to the pattern in numerals 11 to 20 that Barry refers to in the quotation above.

Less is known about how these numerals came to be used in the North Country. Barry (1969: 78–87) summarises in detail the three theories put forth to explain the origin of these numerals in Northern England: (a) survival, (b) importation from Scotland and (c) importation from Wales. Of these three the survival theory, according to which the numerals represent a survival from the Brythonic language spoken in the area before the Anglo-Saxon invasions, was in vogue during the nineteenth century, until it was abandoned in favour of one or the other of the importation theories (Barry 1969: 78–79). However, there is no substantial evidence in favour of any one of these theories, and as Barry (1969: 79) notes,

> the swing towards a theory of importation may well now have become more dogmatic than the available evidence can justify and indeed this has found support principally because of the difficulties of the survival theory rather than on account of any positive information which has been put forward.

The geographical distribution of the Brythonic numerals in northern English has obvious parallels with some of the other linguistic features we have discussed, such as the distribution of the NSR. It also agrees well with what is known about the chronology and density of the Anglo-Saxon settlement in the north of England. Thus, it seems plausible that the Cumbric score does indeed represent a survival from the Brythonic language earlier spoken in the area.

2.2.8.4   *Pronoun Exchange and Other Related Phenomena*

Our focus in this section is on the so-called Pronoun Exchange construction in the traditional southwestern and West Midlands dialects of English English. The term 'Pronoun Exchange' refers to the use of the subjective case form of personal pronouns in non-subject positions, as in example (72), and the concomitant use of the objective case form in subject position, as in example (73):[41]

(72) So farmer # Salisbury say + . . . come to *we*, "Want some grass
      cut up there?" (So11: Somerset, Horsington)

(73) Sam Paul were hauling hay, from out here in uh one of them
      grounds. # This side of the lane were good, tother were bad. *Him*
      comed up this way, see, a couple of times by a load of hay. (So13:
      Somerset, Merriott)

Pronoun Exchange is often mentioned as a typical feature of south-western and West Midlands dialects, but the details of how it operates in these
dialects are still rather poorly understood.

In addition to Pronoun Exchange, we will also discuss two other characteristic features of pronoun morphosyntax in the south-western dialects of
English English: the use of *en* /ən/ as the oblique form of the third person
singular masculine pronoun, exemplified in (74), where *en* refers to cider-
cheese, and gender in third person singular pronouns, exemplified in (75),
where *he/him* refers to a brick:

(74) Then you'd press *en* down again, you see, and let *en* bide for two
      days. Well, press *en* down. Keep on pressing *en*. And then you
      uh # take *en* out and give *en* to the cows out in the field. (So3:
      Somerset, Wedmore)

(75) I know what we'll do. # We'll get a brick, and chuck *him* up in
      the air, and if *he* do come down, we got to # go to work, and
      if *he* stop up there," he said "we got to have a day off". (So1:
      Somerset, Weston)

We will begin this section with a discussion of Pronoun Exchange and its
geographical distribution and origins in English dialects, arguing that this
area of pronoun syntax has been affected by contacts with Welsh and Cornish. We will then move on to discuss the third person singular masculine
pronoun *en* /ən/, concentrating on its geographical distribution and ana-
logue in Cornish. Finally, we will briefly discuss the gender system in south-
western personal pronouns and the possibility of adstratal convergence in
the development of the gender systems in south-western dialects of English
and the surrounding Brythonic languages.

Pronoun Exchange
Wakelin (1977: 114–115) characterises Pronoun Exchange in the following
terms:

In dialect, it is frequently possible for the personal pronouns to 'exchange' their subjective and objective roles, but the conditions under
which these exchanges occur are contextually restricted, the objective

form being used for the subject when the pronoun is unemphatic, and, conversely, the subject form being used as the emphatic form of the object.

Wakelin's characterisation of Pronoun Exchange has been repeated in many subsequent discussions of south-western dialects, but, as we will argue below, his claim that the phenomenon is linked with the expression of emphasis, is debatable.

The following examples from the *SED* tape-recordings show Pronoun Exchange operating practically throughout the paradigm of personal pronouns in the south-western dialects. In examples (76) to (80) we find the subjective form used in object position:

(76) # Back over here, my old uncle, he brung *I* up. My father died when I were about a fortnight old. # And Uncle [/] Uncle [\] Charle + . . . well, that was my old uncle, he brought *I* up. (Do1: Dorset, Sixpenny Handley)

(77) They got hold of her. # Out bolts another, and uh # my mate were up on the top there with a gun. He shot + . . . bowled *she* over. That were more vixen than the + . . . no dog in there. Aye. So we had *they*. (Do1: Dorset, Sixpenny Handley)

(78) Well, when a mole come on to *he*, usually through one of them there # wires. Then he # had that muzzle in front of en. I soon get *he* rid. # Or # those already knock *he* out, see. (Do2: Dorset, Ansty)

(79) # So farmer # Salisbury say + . . . come to *we*, +" Want some grass cut up there. (So11: Somerset, Horsington)

(80) # Oh, well, if I know, I've [/] I've [\] almost fo- +/. SS> <OS They didn't use to say much to *they*. Didn't they just pull 'em round? OS> (D2: Devon, Swimbridge)

The converse, use of the objective form in subject position is exemplified in (81) to (84):

(81) Well, # *her* couldn't go on with the farming, *her* sold out. And my uncle took it on. (D6: Devon, South Zeal)

(82) *Him* can't # sort of go down in it like they used to. If you can make out that. But if their udders and that were washed down clean. AP> <SE Hmm. SE> <AP They uh [/] they [\] were right. AP> (So13: Somerset, Merriott)

(83) Because # *us* used + . . . *Us* didn't have no # [/] *us* didn't have no
[\] stores or nothing of that then in they days. *Us* used to # bake
down under the + . . .
(D9: Devon, Widecombe in the Moor)

(84) *Them* got to be looked after, see. Well, if *them* gets aught older,
them'll let it in.
(Gl1: Gloucestershire, Deerhurst)

As examples (76) to (84) show, Pronoun Exchange operates across the
whole paradigm of personal pronouns. The only exceptions to this are (a)
the first person singular where, while the subjective form is found in non-
subject positions, as in example (76), no examples can be found of the converse, *i.e.* the objective form in subject position; and (b) the 2nd person,
singular and plural, where case syncretism is widespread, as in Standard
English. However, in those dialects where the 2nd person singular *thou/
thee* forms have survived, it is possible to find the objective *thee* form also
in subject position.

It has often been claimed that the use of Pronoun Exchange is linked
with the expression of emphasis (see, e.g. Barnes 1886: 19; Wakelin 1977:
114–115; Edwards 1993: 229–230). Wakelin (1977: 114–115) states that
the objective form is used in subject position when the pronoun is unemphatic and, conversely, that the subjective form is used as the emphatic
form of the object. Wakelin does not state explicitly what he means by the
'emphatic form', but the examples found in the *SED* tape-recordings would
seem to indicate that, at least if emphasis is understood to include the use
of contrastive stress, Wakelin's explanation does not work: subjective forms
in non-subject positions do not necessarily receive contrastive stress. In fact,
we have so far not been able to identify any clear grammatical factors governing the use of Pronoun Exchange. The only thing that can be said with
any degree of certainty is that the emphasis explanation does not work.
This, in fact, is also the conclusion that Ihalainen (1985: 160) arrives at:
"Unfortunately, at this stage, no more can be safely said about nominative
objects other than that they are by no means restricted to emphatic contexts
and that they appear to be quite frequent in uninhibited speech". Shorrocks
(1992: 439), in his detailed discussion of case assignment in dialectal pronoun morphosyntax, reaches a similar conclusion:

> In the answers to all of the questions considered here, and to other, it
> is difficult to discern a clear overall pattern across the south-western
> counties, let alone across the southern counties as a whole. Certainly the
> picture is more complex than scholars have generally suggested.

Although we are not in a position to offer any clear-cut answers to the
problem of the possible grammatical constrains that govern the use of

Pronoun Exchange, we believe that we can offer a novel interpretation of the possible origins of the phenomenon through a careful analysis of the geographical distribution of Pronoun Exchange in south-western and West Midlands dialects. The mapping of the distribution of Pronoun Exchange given below in Map 2.5 is based on the answers to 15 *SED Basic Material* items.[42] *SED* questions VI.14.14 and IX.8.2 and the relevant types of answer found in the *SED Basic Material* illustrate the kind of data Map 2.5 is based on:

VI.14.14
You say of a woman who rules her husband: . . . . **She wears the breeches.**

- Her wear(s) the breeches
- Her wear(s) the trousers
- Her weareth the trousers
- Her ought to wear the breeches
- Her's got the breeches on

IX.8.2
Jack wants to have Tommy's ball and says to him, not: Keep it!, but: . . . . **Give it me!**

- Give it I
- Give it to I
- Give it back to I
- Give en to I

Map 2.5 is drawn on the basis of the answers to the 15 *SED Basic Material Questionnaire* items. The striking feature of Map 2.5 is that it divides England up vertically into a western area where examples of what, at first sight, looks like Pronoun Exchange are found, and an eastern area where no examples of Pronoun Exchange can be found in the *SED Basic Materials*. This is somewhat unexpected, given that the 'normal' orientation of dialect isoglosses in England tends to be horizontal, with isoglosses dividing the country up into southern and northern dialect areas rather than eastern and western ones.

Map 2.5, however, is somewhat misleading in that we have there lumped together the examples where the objective form is used in subject position with the examples where the subjective form is used in non-subject positions. This is not an entirely appropriate way to present the data, since it may hide interesting variation in the geographical distribution of the subjective form used in non-subject positions, as opposed to the distribution of the objective form used in subject position. Therefore we decided to remap the data into two separate maps, one for the cases where the objective form is used in subject position (Map 2.6)[43] and the other for the examples where the subjective form is used in non-subject positions (Map 2.7).[44]

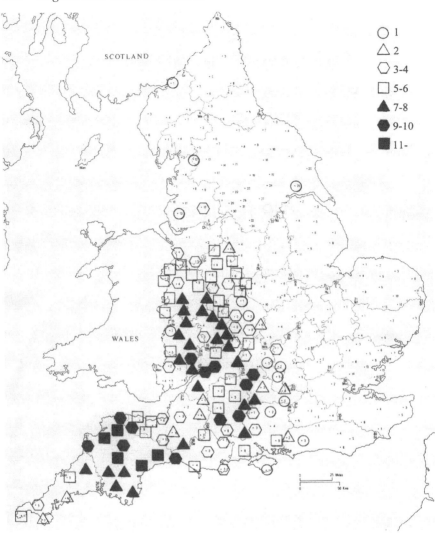

Map 2.5 The geographical distribution of Pronoun Exchange in English dialects (drawn on the basis of the answers to the 15 *SED Basic Material Questionnaire* items listed in endnote 42).

Maps 2.6 and 2.7 reveal a surprising asymmetry in the distribution of the two 'exchanges' that, taken together, are understood to constitute the Pronoun Exchange construction. The use of the objective form in subject position (Map 2.6) is, on the basis of the *SED* data, widespread in south-western and West Midlands dialects, with two core areas, one in Devon and the other in Herefordshire and parts of Gloucestershire, Worcestershire and Shropshire. The converse, however, the use of the subjective form in

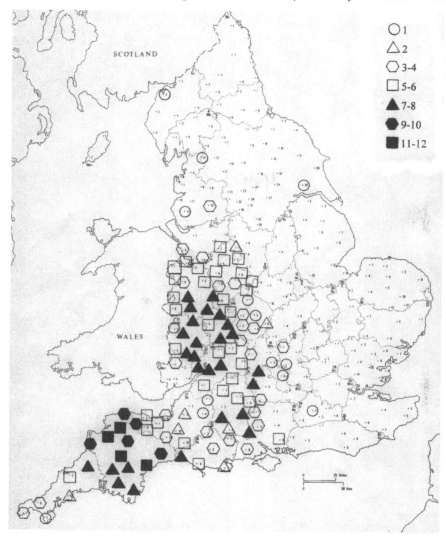

Map 2.6 The geographical distribution of the objective form of the personal pronoun used in subject position in English dialects (drawn on the basis of the answers to 12 *SED Basic Material Questionnaire* items listed in endnote 43).

non-subject positions (Map 2.7), has a much more restricted geographical distribution in the *SED* data: it is mainly found in an area which consists of parts of Somerset, Wiltshire, Dorset, Hampshire, Berkshire and Gloucestershire. But the most interesting feature of the distribution is that subjective forms in non-subject positions are not found at all in the core areas of the use of the objective form in the subject position, i.e. in Devon and Herefordshire, Worcestershire and Shropshire.

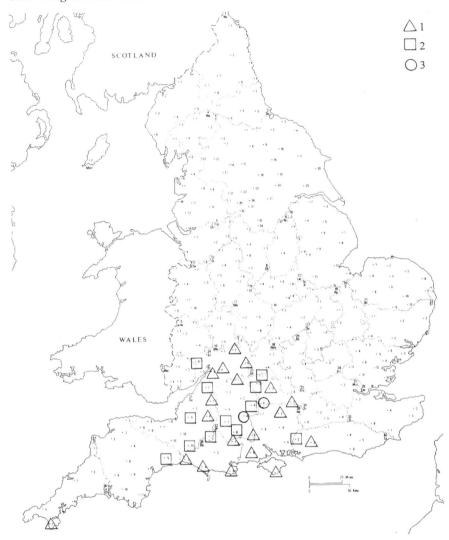

Map 2.7 The geographical distribution of the subjective form of the personal pronoun used in non-subject position in English dialects (drawn on the basis of the answers to 3 *SED Basic Material Questionnaire* items listed in endnote 44).

How can we explain this asymmetry in geographical distributions? The obvious explanation is that anything resembling Pronoun Exchange—at least in the *SED* data that this discussion is based on—in fact only operates in a relatively small geographical area in parts of Somerset, Wiltshire, Dorset, Hampshire, Berkshire and Gloucestershire, i.e. in the area where we find examples both of the use of the objective form in subject position and the use of the subjective form in non-subject positions on Maps 2.6 and 2.7. In

Devon and the West Midlands, on the other hand, we do not find Pronoun
Exchange at all. What we do find in these areas, however, is widespread
syncretism of the subjective and objective cases in personal pronouns. For
Devon, this case syncretism was in fact already noticed by Martin Harris in
his PhD thesis. Harris (1967: 70) characterises the system of personal pronouns in South Zeal, Devonshire, as follows:

> The most important feature of the system [of personal pronouns in
> South Zeal, Devonshire] is thus that, except for the first person singular,
> there is no subject:object opposition in stressed positions and only a
> limited subject:object opposition in unstressed positions.

Harris (1967: 70)

Harris (1967: 67) presents a paradigm for the distribution of personal
pronouns in South Zeal, reproduced here as Table 2.1. This table shows
clearly the almost complete syncretism of subjective and objective case
forms in stressed positions and the very definite move in a similar direction
in unstressed positions in Devonshire dialect.

Table 2.1 Morphology of the personal pronouns (South Zeal, Devonshire)
(from Harris 1967: 67).

	Stressed		Unstressed	
	Subject	*Non-Subject*	*Subject*	*Non-Subject*
1st person singular	/aj/	/miː/	/aj/	/miː/
2nd person singular and plural	/jy/	/jy/	/jy/ /jə/ /iː/	/iː/
3rd person singular (concrete, non-female)	/iː/	/iː/	/iː/	/n/ /ɪm/
3rd person singular (female)	/ər/	/ər/	/r/	/r/
3rd person singular (abstract)	Not found	/ɪt/	/ɪt/ /t/	/ɪt/ /(ə)t/
1st person plural	/əs/	/əs/	/əs/	/əs/
3rd person plural	/ðej/	/ðej/	/ðej/ /əm/	/əm/

There is a close match between the core areas of the use of the objective form in subject position (and, in effect, case syncretism) on Map 2.6 and Jackson's Area III (see Jackson 1953: 220), where "Brittonic river names are especially common, including often those of mere streams, and the proportion of certainly Celtic names is highest of all" (Jackson 1953: 222). This, together with the fact that case inflections and the distinction between nominative and accusative forms in pronouns have disappeared from the Brythonic languages, Welsh and Cornish (Lewis and Pedersen 1961: 162; 203–215), raises the possibility that contacts with the speakers of these Brythonic languages have played a role in the evolution of the pronoun system in the dialects of Devon and the West Midlands. Whether the possible contacts could have led to adstratal convergence with bi-directional linguistic interference in these areas (cf. Tristram 1999a) is a question that cannot be answered here. We do believe, however, that the data discussed here have shown that the possibility of contact influence in the case of the development of the pronoun systems in the dialects of Devon and parts of West Midlands should not be ruled out.

Third Person Singular en /ən/

In the south-western dialects of English English, the third person singular personal pronoun has an oblique form *en* /ən/, which is unique to this dialect area. As examples (85) and (86) show, *en* can refer both to inanimate referents (*chimney*) and human ones.[45]

(85) I said, +" Well, I'm on the six to two next week. # I'll come home one day and sweep the chimney. "+ Said, +" How art going to sweep *en*? "+ I said, +" I'll sweep *en* same as we used to up in the country up the Kimbers. "+
(So1: Somerset, Weston)

(86) # Sep Smith or Peg Smith. One of the two. Anybody could fling a stone further than him, they'd give him a sovereign. Nobody couldn't beat *en*.
(So1: Somerset, Weston)

As Britton (1994: 16) observes: "Murray in *OED* s.v. *hin, hine* derived this variant form from <hine> /xine/, the Old English accusative form of the masculine pronoun, and this etymology has been accepted in all subsequent references to the history of <'en>". Britton challenges the etymology offered by Murray, and argues instead that the <'en> form in southern and south-western dialects of English descends from <him> as a result of a phonological change under reduced stress. Britton (1994: 18) dates this change—primarily on the basis of lack of earlier textual evidence—to "roughly the first hundred years of the early Modern English period", i.e. to the sixteenth century.

While not arguing against either Murray's or Britton's etymology for *en*, we would like to open up a further dimension to the question of the possible origins of the south-western dialectal *en* 'him, it'. First of all, a few observations on the geographical distribution of *en* in English dialects. Map 2.8 (*LAE* M70), reproduced here from the *Linguistic Atlas of England* (*LAE*) (Orton, Sanderson and Widdowson 1978), indicates that *en* is a south-western/southern feature, not found in the West Midlands dialects. This is also corroborated by the *SED* tape-recordings data. Map 2.9 presents the

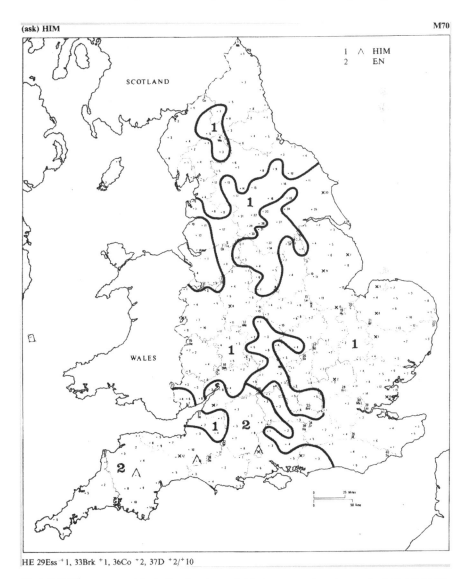

Map 2.8 The geographical distribution of third person singular *en* /ən/ (*LAE* M70; Orton, Sanderson and Widdowson 1978). Reproduced by permission of the University of Leeds.

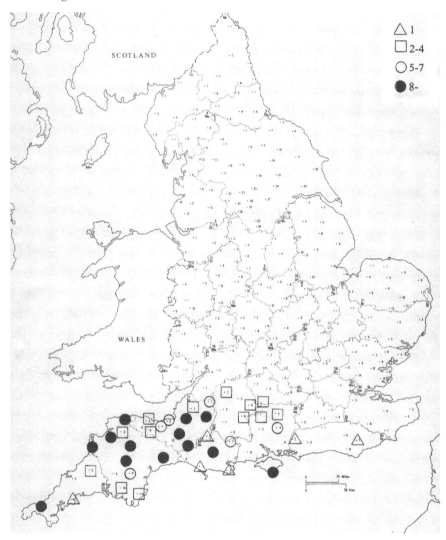

Map 2.9 The geographical distribution of third person singular *en* /ən/ in the *SED* tape-recordings.

distribution of *en* in the spontaneous conversational *SED* tape-recordings, and shows a similar geographical distribution, comprising Devon, Dorset, Somerset, and parts of Cornwall, Wiltshire and Hampshire.

The significance of the geographical distribution of *en* is linked to the fact that the infixed form of the third person singular masculine pronoun <n> in Cornish (and <en, hen> in Breton; see Lewis and Pedersen 1961: 209, 212) is practically identical in form with the south-western third person singular *en* /ən/, whereas the corresponding MW forms are *'e*, *'y*, and *'s* (Evans 1964:

55). Jenner (1904: 99) gives as an example of the Cornish third person singular masculine pronoun '*n*: *mî a'n pes* 'I pray him', and comments (*ibid.*): "This form is commonly used in the earlier MSS. It represents an accusative *en* or *hen* which still exists in Breton".

Whether Murray is correct in arguing that the south-western dialectal /ən/ derives directly from OE *hine*, or Britton is correct in arguing that it is a later south-western innovation that arose *via* a phonological change from *him*, the fact remains that the *en* /ən/ form is, and as far as we can tell, always has been a dialectal form restricted to the south-western dialects of English English. This dialectal distribution prompts the question: why is this innovation restricted to south-western dialects of English English and not found elsewhere in England? While it would be unwarranted to argue that the south-western *en* /ən/ represents substratal influence from Cornish, the formal and functional similarities between the Cornish <'n> and the south-western dialectal *en* /ən/ do warrant the consideration that the Cornish pronoun has acted as a reinforcing influence in the development of the south-western dialectal form. Contacts between speakers of Cornish and the adjacent English dialects would go some way towards explaining why the *en* /ən/ pronoun has the geographical distribution in the south-west of England that it has.

Gender System in South-Western Personal Pronouns
As Tristram (1999a: 21) notes, the tripartite inflectional grammatical gender distinction (masculine, feminine and neuter) was lost both in Welsh and in English. Grammatical gender in Welsh (and in Brythonic languages in general) developed in the historic period into a two-way system, masculine and feminine (Lewis and Pedersen 1961: 159), whereas in English the gender system developed into a three-way system of natural gender, only marked in some third person pronouns and WH-pronouns.

In traditional south-western dialects of English English, however, the gender system differs fundamentally from the Standard English three-way system of natural gender. William Barnes (1886) characterises the nineteenth-century Dorset gender system as follows:

> Whereas Dorset men are laughed at for what is taken as their misuse of pronouns, yet the pronouns of true Dorset, are fitted to one of the finest outplannings of speech that I have found.
>
> In Dorset-speech, things are offmarked into two classes:
>
> 1. Full shapen things, or things to which the Almighty or man has given a shape for an end; as a tree, or a tool: and such things may be called the Personal Class: as they have pronouns that belong to man.
>
> 2. Unshapen quantities of stuff, or stuff not shapen up into a form fitted to an end: as water or dust: and the class of such things may be called the Impersonal Class, and have other pronouns than those of the personal class.

(Barnes 1886:17)

Elworthy's (1877) treatment of gender in nineteenth-century West Somerset dialect indicates that a similar gender system was operative also in Somerset:

> The use of the pronoun of the third person resembles that of the demonstrative adjective, with respect to the class of noun for which it is substituted. Every class or definite noun, i.e. the name of a thing or object which has a shape of its own, whether alive or dead, is either masculine or feminine, but nearly always the former; indeed, the feminine pronouns may be taken as used only with respect to persons. [. . .] Sometimes even for a woman the pronoun *he* is used; [. . .] *It* is simply an impersonal or abstract pronoun, used to express either an action or a noun of the undefined sort, as cloth in the quantity, water, snow, air, etc.

> (Elworthy 1877: 32–33)

It thus seems that, while Standard English developed a natural gender marking system which shows a three-way distinction between masculine, feminine and neuter in third person singular pronouns (and a two-way distinction between HUMAN and NON-HUMAN in WH-pronouns), the south-western dialects came to have a two-way system where the basic division is between COUNT and MASS nouns. In subject position, COUNT nouns select the third person singular pronoun *he* (with the exception of female humans that select the *she*-form), and MASS nouns select the *it*-form of the third person pronoun; in non-subject-positions, count nouns select *en* or *(h)er*, while MASS nouns select *it*.[46]

The exact details of the geographical distribution of the gender marking system in the south-west remain to be worked out, but it seems to be limited to the south-western dialects of England. Again, this raises the question: why in the south-west and not elsewhere? Our admittedly somewhat tentative suggestion is that the evolving two-way system of grammatical gender in the adjacent Brythonic languages, Cornish and Welsh, may have played a role in the south-western reanalysis of the gender system.[47]

2.3   PHONOLOGY

On the whole, very little has been written on contact effects in the phonological domain. This can be taken to mean that scholars do not see any significant phonological changes in OE or in later stages of English which could have derived through contacts with the Celtic languages (see, e.g. Laker 2002: 192 and the references there). However, it is not always changes or innovations in a language that are due to contact; preservation of a feature can be equally symptomatic of contact, albeit less visible. One good candidate for such a case is the presence of interdental fricatives in English and Welsh/Brythonic. Observed and commented on in an early work by Edwards (1844/2000), this feature has since attracted the attention of many scholars. We may begin here with the OE scholar J.R.R. Tolkien, who in his O'Donnell lecture (see Tolkien 1963) discusses the preservation of /θ/ and /ð/ in English. He notes that English remains conservative in this respect from a general Germanic point of view: no other Germanic dialect preserves them both; /θ/ is preserved only in Icelandic.[48] This raises the question of possible contact influence, which Tolkien puts as follows:

> It may at least be noted that Welsh also makes abundant use of these two sounds. It is a natural question to ask; how did these two languages, the long-settled British and the new-come English, affect one another, if at all; and what at any rate were their relations?

> (Tolkien 1963: 20)

More lately, the question of interdental fricatives and contact influence is taken up by Tristram (2002b), who considers preservation of the interdental fricatives in English and Welsh as a "remarkable" fact from a typological point of view. Indeed, she goes on to suggest that it is one of the phonological features defining a 'linguistic area' of Britain and Ireland, which means that the presence of this feature in these languages is due to some degree of contact between these languages. This account is given some plausibility because of the markedness of interdental fricatives from a cross-linguistic perspective.[49] However, it is strongly opposed by Isaac (2003a), according to whom Tristram's suggestion ignores the principle of differentiating between archaisms and innovations. Isaac seeks to show that dental fricatives do not constitute an innovation in either the Germanic or the Celtic languages and cannot therefore be considered symptoms of earlier contact between the two language groups. What according to him are diagnostic features of contact are 'shared innovations', not 'shared archaisms' (Isaac 2003a: 53). And the English preservation of dental fricatives is of the latter type, as Isaac argues, on the grounds that the continental Germanic languages have in the course of their history lost this feature.

While Isaac is right in claiming that the preservation of this feature in English is an archaic feature in a Germanic perspective, he overlooks the possibility of 'conserving' contact influence or externally motivated retention. As Thomason and Kaufman (1988: 58, 242) show, it often happens in language contact situations that certain features are preserved or even reinforced because of a close parallel in the other language(s) participating in the contact situation (cf. also the 'reinforcement principles' proposed by Siegel 1999). Thus, the presence of dental fricatives in Welsh and in most of the other Celtic languages in the earliest periods of the interface could well explain the preservation of the same feature in English, as opposed to its

Germanic sisters, which began to lose these sounds at quite an early stage (Icelandic being a notable exception). This, incidentally, seems to be what Tolkien had in mind, although he did not elaborate on his observations in contact-linguistic terms. It sounds persuasive to say, as Isaac does, that preservation of a feature in a language is not so 'significant' as the replacement of a feature through an innovative change (Isaac 2003a: 53). On closer inspection, however, one should perhaps distinguish between 'significance' and 'salience'. As compared with innovations, preserved features are surely less salient but that does not mean that they could not prove significant, e.g. from the point of view of the future typological development of the language; witness the divergent paths taken by the Germanic languages, for example. Neither does it mean that language contact could not have played a role—direct or indirect, as in the case at hand—in the retention process (see Tristram 2002b: 262 for a similar argument).

Another question of possible phonological influence raised by Tolkien concerns OE *i*-mutation or *Umlaut*, which he puts forward as a possible reflex of the corresponding phonological changes in Welsh. Although Tolkien acknowledges "differences in detail and in chronology in the two languages", he points out that the English changes are "closely paralleled by the changes which in Welsh grammar are usually called 'affection'" (Tolkien 1963: 32).[50] Scholars trying to account for these changes are also faced with similar problems, as Tolkien notes; to these belongs the question of the role played by anticipation, vowel harmony and epenthesis. Although he does not pursue the matter any further, he is confident that "the study of them together throws light on both" (*ibid.*). He does, however, point out the importance of place-names borrowed by the English in Britain for the dating of *i*-mutation in OE and in Welsh. Referring in a footnote to Förster's dating in *Der Flussname Themse* (Förster 1941), Tolkien expresses as his own view that the process of *i*-mutation started in pre-invasion times and is not peculiar to the English dialect of Germanic (Tolkien 1963: 33, fn. 1).

Tolkien's discussion of *i*-mutation and its Welsh parallels has not, to the best of our knowledge, been followed up in later research, probably because of the problems of dating (acknowledged by Tolkien himself, as noted above), and also because of the cross-linguistic generality of this type of change.[51]

As further areas of possible substratal transfer in phonology, we should mention 'low-level' influences as discussed by Hickey (1995). The term 'low-level' refers here to such non-distinctive sound phenomena as allophonic realisations, phonetic reductions and mergers. In British Celtic, as Hickey notes, these phenomena entailed, most notably, the weakening or 'lenition' of consonants in voiced and intervocalic environments and vowel reduction in unstressed syllables. He suggests that contacts between the British Celts and the Anglo-Saxons may well have at least accelerated (possibly already existing) similar tendencies in the allophony of OE and thus contributed to the phonetic weakening and eventual loss of unstressed syllables in that language, too (Hickey 1995: 109). Though not part of the conventional wisdom in Anglicist scholarship, the scenario put forward by Hickey receives indirect support from some studies of the early continental contacts between Celtic and its neighbouring languages: Hickey refers here to Martinet's (1952) suggestion that the lenition found in Western Romance is due to influence from continental Celtic, which exhibited the same feature (Hickey 1995: 111).[52]

Hickey also discusses the question of the Germanic initial stress accent and its possible continental Celtic origin. Here, however, he does not endorse the view expressed by, e.g. Salmons (1984), who maintains that accent shift, and more specifically, initial fixed accent would be typical of contact situations and would have characterised the Germanic–Celtic interface in the early stages of their contacts (Hickey 1995: 96–97). Initial stress, or rather, "unambiguous signs" of it, as Hickey puts it, are present in Celtic, Germanic and Italic "from the very beginning", although scholars are not agreed on their source (*op.cit.*, 99–100). All in all, Hickey concludes that the putative phonological parallels between continental Celtic and Germanic "are accidental if they occur at all" (Hickey 1995: 98).

This does not, however, exclude the possibility of Celtic low-level influences on English in Britain. On the contrary, Hickey asserts that "there would seem to be no *a priori* objection to postulating an influence of the speech habits of the British Celts on the Germanic invaders cum settlers" (*op.cit.*, 110). This line of reasoning is supported by facts about the development of the Celtic languages in the early periods, which show loss of especially intervocalic consonants and vowel reduction in unstressed syllables, which in turn lead to morphological analyticity (*op.cit.*, 111–112). Hickey further emphasises that these changes need not affect the system of the language at the time at which they enter but may lead to far-reaching changes, which he describes as 'delayed effect contact':

> One can think of delayed effect contact as setting a ball rolling which gains more and more momentum and may eventually lead to a restructuring of the grammar as was clearly the case in Celtic. In the case of English this is the switch from synthetic to analytic which was rendered necessary with the progressive weakening of inflectional endings and verb prefixes—something which did not occur in German to anything like a similar extent.
>
> (Hickey 1995: 115)

Tristram (1999a) puts forward a very similar account based on the idea of restructuring and concomitant typological change, which affected both Celtic and English. Although she first states that she has found "no transfer features on the phonological or the lexical level" [from Celtic languages in English], she argues that "the very vital contribution of the speakers of the

Brythonic languages to the creation of the English language lay in triggering the (initial) typological change from a predominantly synthetic language to a predominantly analytical language" (Tristram 1999a: 30).

Writing also on the typological differences between English and German morphophonology and their causes, Kastovsky (1994) raises the possibility of Celtic contact influence. According to him, the advanced reduction of final and medial syllables in OE dialects as compared with Old High German could well be due to the contact situation and the concomitant modification of the speech rhythm, leading to a greater intensity of initial stress in the former. He considers this line of reasoning to be supported by the fact that the Northumbrian dialects of OE exhibit more reduction than the southern ones and at a time before Scandinavian influence could be expected to appear in texts (Kastovsky 1994: 149 f.).

Finally, although it seems hard to pin down any specific and 'clear' contact effects in the phonological domain, new discoveries may, and are indeed made, as evidenced by the recent work of Peter Schrijver and Stephen Laker. Schrijver (1999) argues that there are a number of common developments in the vowel systems of what he labels 'North Sea Germanic' (Old English, Old Frisian and Old Coastal Dutch) that can plausibly be explained as "adaptations of the PGm. [Proto-Germanic] vowel system to the system of British Celtic or a closely related Celtic dialect on the Continent around the fifth to ninth centuries A.D." (Schrijver 1999: 33). Schrijver singles out the lack of long *$\bar{a}$ and the presence of phonemic front round vowels as the most striking correspondences between his reconstructed North Sea Germanic vowel system and the contemporaneous Brythonic vowel system. He argues that bilingualism is the most obvious way to explain these similarities:

> Speakers of a British type of Celtic came into close contact with powerful immigrants who spoke Germanic, as a result of which they themselves adopted Germanic speech. In doing so, however, they retained the phonological distinctions of their first language, British Celtic, a procedure that is well attested in second language acquisition in general.[53]

(Schrijver 1999: 28)

Laker (2002) adduces persuasive evidence for an early British Celtic substratum in the northern (especially Northumbrian) varieties of OE. While most of the present-day southern dialects of English preserve the plosive consonant cluster *kw-* inherited from OE in words like *quick* (< OE *cwicu*), some conservative northern dialects have *hw-* or *w-* in the same position, as is shown by the *SED* data (see Orton *et al.* 1978: Ph. 212; quoted here from Laker 2002: 184). As Laker points out, it is generally assumed that initial *hw-* or *w-* in these dialects must have been preceded by spirantisation of the original combination *kw-* to *χw-*, which then yields *hw-* through aspiration and a further change to *w-* in some northern dialects in the modern period. On the basis of the geographical distribution of χw- in ME, it has been suggested that this feature of the northern dialects is a result of Scandinavian influence (see, e.g. Lutz 1988; Dietz 1989; both cited in Laker 2002: 185–186).

Laker argues, however, that this account is unable to explain the spirantisation involved in this change, because the feature at issue is not restricted to the northern dialects but is also attested in several early twentieth-century southern dialects, which cannot be expected to show much, if indeed any, Scandinavian influence. Instead, the change at hand can be explained in terms of early influence from British Celtic. Laker's explanation rests on the existence in British Celtic of χw-, but not of the *kw-* or *hw-* clusters which probably were part of the OE consonant inventory. Thus, in the process of the Celtic speakers shifting to OE, χw- would have been the closest cluster to substitute for the two new, but phonetically sufficiently similar *kw-* or *hw-* clusters. This line of reasoning is indirectly supported by the behaviour of later English loanwords adopted into Welsh, which display the same spirantisation in the same kind of contexts (for some examples, see Laker 2002: 194). Though not yet vindicated by more detailed research into the matter, Laker's results are telling proof of the possible gaps in our existing knowledge about the extent of phonological contacts between Celtic and English.

2.4   LEXIS

According to Thomason and Kaufman (1988), the appropriate method for examining a possible contact situation requires that we pay attention to different subsystems of the languages in contact:

> The appropriate methodology, then, requires examination of a contact situation as a forest rather than as a collection of isolated trees. In order to support a claim that feature x arose in language A under the influence of language B, we need to show that features a, b, c, y, z—at least some of which belong to a subsystem different from the one x belongs to—also arose in A under the influence of B.

> (Thomason and Kaufman 1988: 61)

To bring in evidence from another subsystem, this section deals with the question of lexical interference from the Celtic languages. We will begin with a short survey of studies on the Celtic impact on place-names and personal names in England. This will be followed by a review of lexical borrowings from the Celtic languages into English.

2.4.1   Onomastics

2.4.1.1   *Place-Name Evidence*

As Richard Coates (2002, 2004) has recently argued, the number of Brittonic place-names in English is larger than has traditionally been acknowledged by place-name scholars, but all in all it remains rather moderate, at least in the south and the east of England. Coates (2004) points out further that the distribution of the Brittonic place-names "suggests a more persistent survival of cohesive groups of Brittonic-speakers in a limited number of areas".

Indeed, in some parts of the country place-name evidence would seem to point towards a relatively late survival of Brittonic speech. Thus, for example, Jackson (1963) discusses the place-name evidence from Cumbria and Northumberland, and argues that the evidence, especially "the exceptionally high proportion of British village names", warrants the conclusion that "a fairly considerable number of people of British race and language did survive the conquest, especially in some parts of Northumbria" (1963: 83). Jackson also presents evidence indicating that the Cumbric language may have survived in northern Cumberland "as late as the beginning of the twelfth century" (1963: 84). As far as the West Midlands area is concerned, Gelling (1992) puts forward linguistic evidence for a significant amount of British place-names and toponyms in the five counties of Warwickshire, Staffordshire, Cheshire, Shropshire and Herefordshire. She concludes that in most of the West Midlands, Welsh speech did not disappear until the end of the ninth century; in some areas, such as the Archenfield district of Herefordshire, Welsh continued to be used "throughout the Anglo-Saxon period". Indeed she claims that "large areas of the country must have been wholly or partly Welsh-speaking up to and beyond the Norman Conquest" (Gelling 1992: 70). Gelling distinguishes between nine categories of lexical material suggesting continuity of Welsh speech in the West Midlands:

  (i) items which preserve or incorporate recorded Romano-British toponyms;
 (ii) names of rivers;
(iii) names of mountains and conspicuous hills;
 (iv) names of forests;
  (v) names which do not fit into any of the above mentioned categories but which are easily explicable in Welsh but meaningless in English;
 (vi) hybrids, with one element in Welsh and one in English;
(vii) English names which refer to Welshmen;
(viii) names containing *ecles* 'church' or 'Christian community';
 (ix) names containing OE loanwords from Latin.

Coates (2000b: 112) draws attention to an area "roughly centred on the upper valley of the Bristol Avon", where the place-name evidence suggests relatively late survival of a Brittonic-speaking population. Coates (*op.cit.*,

115) argues that there is a considerable body of both phonological and structural place-name evidence that makes it "possible to mount a fairly substantial case that Brittonic of a relatively late type was spoken in an ill-defined area centred on north-west Wiltshire". The phonological evidence consists of the borrowing of Brittonic [μ] as OE [v] instead of the more general [m] in place-names such as *Cheverell* and *Keevil*. Coates (*op.cit.*, 113) points out that this sound change took place during the seventh century and that the existence of names such as *Cheverell* thus suggests "that Brittonic was still spoken here in the seventh century by people capable of influencing the linguistic behaviour of the West-Saxon overlord class and its administrators". The structural evidence Coates adduces for the case consists of compound names of the modern Brittonic type, where the specifier follows the head ('head-initial compound names'), such as *Chittoe* and *Penselwood*.[54]

The survival of a late variety of Brittonic in this area has an interesting parallel in the area of English dialect grammar, pointed out by Klemola (2002). Klemola draws attention to the fact that the area in north-west Wiltshire identified by Coates as an area of relatively late Brittonic survival coincides surprisingly well with the heartland of DO-support in affirmative sentences in traditional southwestern dialects and the area where Ellegård (1953) locates the origin of DO in English (on this issue, see section 2.2.4).

The general issue of the place-name evidence for Celtic survival in England is discussed in a recent book by Coates and Breeze (2000), who present a number of "etymological studies on a range of names of rivers, other landscape features and inhabited sites" and a gazetteer of over 900 place-names presented as "reasonably-claimed examples of Brittonic and Goidelic names in England". One of the aims of Coates and Breeze is to show that the number of Celtic place-names in England is greater than has generally been assumed:

> Our main aim, in summary, is to show that the number of Celtic names of England is greater than is accepted at present, and to promote enquiry into other problematic names on the presumption that a credible Celtic etymology may emerge. We hope to persuade others that our view about the extent of the Celtic contribution to English place-naming is correct by our attention to evidence and by the soundness of our science. We do not expect or intend to overturn the apple-cart, and certainly have no deeply radical claims to make about the survival of Celtic speech in pockets in various parts of England.
>
> (Coates and Breeze 2000: 11–12)

2.4.1.2 *Personal Names*

Förster (1921: 177) and Jackson (1953: 244) have shown that a large number of personal names in Anglo-Saxon are of British origin.[55] Förster (1921:

174–177) lists the following as examples of Irish and British men's names found—mixed with English names—in the ninth-century document *Liber vitae Dunelmensis* (ed. J. Stevenson, Surtees Soc. 1841), listing members of a Northumbrian brotherhood, probably at Lindisfarne: **Irish**; *Abniar, Adamnan, Bressal Brōn, Crīnoc, Cuna, Cunen, Demma, Dengus, Fergus, Fīnan, Faelfi, Fladgus, Mucca, Ultan*; **British**; *Adda, Arthan, Cada, Clyduinin, Coloduc, Cundigeorn, Hiudu, Penda, Pobbidi, Rī-uuala, Rī-uualch, Tūda, Ūnust.*

The name of *Cædmon*, the ox-herd who, according to Bede, became "England's first Christian poet", is the Primitive Welsh **Caduann* (Jackson 1953: 244). As Clark (1992: 463) notes, "despite his English cultural identity, Cædmon might, as an ox-herd, be supposed descended from an enslaved people". British names, however, were not restricted to lower social strata only. This is witnessed by a number of British names in the genealogies of the royal families of Wessex and Lindsey, e.g. *Cerdic* (cf. Myres 1986: 146–150; Clark 1992: 463), *Ceawlin, Ceadda, Ceadwalla* (Clark 1992: 463), *Caedbaed* (Myres 1986: 140–141). The fact that a relatively large number of early Anglo-Saxon nobility had British names has not escaped the attention of scholars: Jackson (1953: 244) points out that the existence of such names implies considerable intermarriage and fusion between the Anglo-Saxons and the British, and can consequently also be taken as an indicator of "some degree of bilingualism". Cecily Clark (1992: 463) is somewhat more guarded in her estimate when she concludes that "[a]ssuming any such names necessarily indicate British blood would go well beyond the evidence; but their adoption by English royalty must mean respect for Celtic traditions". And more recently, David Crystal (2004: 33) has considered the existence of the British names for Anglo-Saxon noblemen as one of the "great puzzles in the history of the language".

2.4.2   Lexical Borrowings

According to the widely held and generally accepted view, Celtic languages have—perhaps surprisingly—not really left their mark on the vocabulary of the English language at all. Förster (1921) presented what Coates (2007: 177) calls "a canonical list" of early Brittonic lexical loans into OE. That list consisted of 15 words, only 4 of which, *binn* 'manger', *brocc* 'badger', and *cumb* 'valley' and *luh* 'sea; pool' are, according to Coates (*ibid.*), still generally accepted. In a relatively recent survey, Kastovsky (1992: 318–320) lists 6 true Brythonic borrowings into OE: *binn, bannoc, gafeluc, dunn, broc, assen*, and a further 3 items from the glosses to the Lindisfarne gospels: *bratt, carr* and *luh*. Indeed, the observed paucity of early loans from Brittonic is often brought up as a decisive argument against the possibility of the types of structural transfer we have discussed above: the possibility of any structural interference is ruled out as impossible on the basis of the almost complete lack of lexical influence from the Celtic languages.[56] A recent article by John McWhorter (2002), where he discusses a number of structural characteristics of English that seem to imply external causation, offers a good example of a statement along these lines:[57]

> The first problem is that we would expect that a structural impact so profound would be accompanied by a robust lexical one. Yet the Celtic contribution to the English lexicon, beyond place names, two now defunct items incorporated on the continent before the Germanic settlement of England, and seven mostly defunct ones introduced by Christianizing missionaries from Ireland, is so small that Kastovsky (1992: 318–319) requires barely half a page to list the fourteen, most now obsolete. To be sure, Thomason and Kaufman (1988: 116–118) note that lexical loans amidst shift-based interference are often not as numerous as in cases of one language borrowing from another. However, the glaring paucity of Celtic loans in English surpasses even the degree Thomason and Kaufman refer to, suggesting that it is appropriate to question whether any interference in fact took place.
>
> (McWhorter 2002: 252)

It is noteworthy that the statements about the small number of Celtic loans in English practically always make reference to Förster's canonical list of early Brittonic loans into OE. This can be misleading; when later, ME and EModE loans, are taken into account, the number of Celtic loans in English becomes considerably larger. It is also important to bear in mind that the time-lag between adopting a loanword and its first attestation in written texts may be several centuries, as is shown by Burnley's (1992: 418–419) discussion of the lexical legacy of Scandinavian in ME, and Pödör's (1995–1996: 187) survey of Scottish Gaelic loanwords in Lowland Scots. Furthermore, when we consider non-literary registers, such as dialect vocabulary, the number of Celtic loans in English becomes even larger (for discussion of these, see below).

A number of scholars, many of them Celticists, have argued that the question of Celtic loanwords in English is not as clear-cut as is generally assumed. Thus William Gillies, in a Colloquium on Mediaeval Dialectology held in 1994, argued that

> [a] further parallel exists, in the form of under-reporting of Celtic loanwords in the English lexicographical tradition. This is a case that needs to be argued patiently and in detail, since the field has in the past been tarnished by sub-scientific and 'lunatic fringe' interventions. Nevertheless it is clear to me that, for a mixture of reasons (primarily ignorance and ideological bias) there are words and phrases which could be added to the list of recognized Celtic loans in English, but which currently appear as 'of uncertain origin' or similar.
>
> (Gillies 1994: 165)

Anders Ahlqvist (1988) has presented a similar argument in an article where he proposes a Celtic etymology for two English words, viz. *jilt* and *twig*, while Andrew Breeze has suggested a considerable number of Celtic loans in both OE and ME in an extensive series of articles published over the last 20 years or so. In addition to confirming earlier findings, Breeze has pointed out new loanwords in greater numbers than in any of the lists offered so far. Many of these are words the origins of which have so far been unclear or in dispute. They include items like OE *deor* 'brave', *trum* 'strong', *truma* 'host', *cursung* 'curse', *gafeluc* 'javelin', *stær* 'history', *syrce* 'coat of mail'; ME *clog(ge)* 'block, wooden shoe', *cokkunge* 'striving', *tirven* 'to flay', *warroke* 'hunchback', and many more (see, e.g. Breeze 1993a, 1993b, 1997). According to Breeze (2002), there are at least seven types of Celtic loanwords in English: (1) Brittonic words in OE; (2) Irish words in OE; (3) Welsh words in ME; (4) Irish words in ME; (5) Welsh words in EModE; (6) Irish words in the same; and (7) Scottish Gaelic words in the same. On the basis of these findings it is quite evident that Celtic loans in OE and ME are commoner than is generally believed, and more such discoveries can be expected to be made.

Our own searches through the *Middle English Dictionary* (*MED*) and the second edition of the *Oxford English Dictionary* (*OED2*) show that a considerable number of Celtic loanwords can be found in English in the ME and the ModE periods. The *MED* contains 89 words which are considered by the compilers of the dictionary as demonstrably or probably of Celtic origin, 6 of them originating in the OE period.[58] A search of the etymologies in the *OED2*, on the other hand, produced over 520 lexical items which are unquestionably Celtic. Although the majority are found in regional varieties of English and are not recorded in the *OED* until in the ModE period, there are nevertheless 59 items the first appearances of which are dated prior to the year 1500, with 11 of them appearing before 1200.

When considering lexical influences from the Celtic languages in regional varieties of British English, we can expect to find more examples of loans. We only need to mention Dolan's (1998) *Dictionary of Hiberno-English* as evidence of the considerable lexical input of Irish to the development of Hiberno-English. The lexical impact of the Celtic languages on Celtic varieties of English will be discussed further in Chapter 4, section 4.4, but what about early Celtic loans in local dialects of English English? Wolfgang Meid (1990) has suggested that a possible reason for the small number of loanwords in the southern and south-eastern parts of England in the Anglo-Saxon period could be that the British population in these parts of the country used Latin to such an extent that their Brythonic vocabulary was not transferred into English. Meid suggests, however, that the situation in the north and the west was probably different, and that in these parts of the country some Celtic loans may have survived, at least in the local dialects.[59] Meid's argument has not always been considered convincing, but we would like to suggest that some support for it can be found, albeit from a much later period, in a detailed study of eighteenth- and nineteenth-century dialect vocabulary in the north and west of England.

John Davies published in the 1880s a series of articles in the *Archeologia Cambrensis* (Davies 1882–1883, 1884, 1885). In these articles Davies presents lists of over 1500 dialect words from Lancashire, Cheshire, Cumberland, Westmorland, Yorkshire, Northamptonshire and Leicestershire, and for each of these words he suggests a Celtic etymology. As far as we know, Davies's list has never received systematic critical attention, and such a study is obviously also beyond the scope of our discussion here.[60] However, in the following we have chosen a small number of items from Davies's list, items that are plausible candidates for Celtic loans in northern and western dialects of English English. Most of the words discussed below are not listed at all in the *OED2*, but they are all found in the *EDD*, with an indication of a northern and/or western English provenance:

Bullin: the *EDD* entry for *bullin* begins as follows:

BULLIN, *sb*. *Obs*. Shr. A receptacle for 'bottoms' of yarn.

OED2 has no entry for *bullin*, but in Davies (1884) s.v. *bullin* we find the following:

Bullin, a receptacle for bottoms of yarn, like a beehive, made of straw (S.).[61]

Davies goes on to give the Welsh *bwlan* (*būlan*) 'a round vessel made of straw, to hold corn' as the source for the Shropshire dialect word. *Geiriadur Prifysgol Cymru* (*GPC*), under s.v. *bwlan, bylan*, lists the meaning 'budget, vessel made of straw to hold corn and wool, & c., fig. squat person' as the putative source of the Shropshire *bullin*.

(Work-)bracco: *EDD* lists the following three meanings for this word:

1. *adj*. Fond of work; industrious; intent upon one's work.
2. *Obs*. Unwilling to work.
3. *Sb*. The power and will to work.

According to the *EDD*, the word has a fairly wide geographical distribution mainly in western and northern dialects: *bracco* is reported from Lancashire, Cheshire, Staffordshire, Derbyshire, Northamptonshire, Warwickshire, Worcestershire, Shropshire and Oxfordshire, but also from Essex and America. The *OED2* lists *bracco* as a variant form of *work-brittle*, with a meaning similar to the one given in the *EDD*, and suggests that "the second element appears to be <u>BRITTLE</u> *a*. ['Liable to break, easily broken; fragile, breakable; friable'], but the sense-development is obscure". Davies (1884), again, gives the meaning of *bracco* as "diligent, gen. with work, as *work-bracco* or *braccon*; not stinting with his work," and compares the word to

"Welsh *brac*, lavish, open, free". *GPC* s.v. *brac* lists the following meanings for the term: 'ready, free, generous, prompt, glib, open; light (of soil)'.

Caukum: this dialect word meaning 'a practical joke, a foolish frolic' is given a Cheshire provenance in the *EDD*. The word is not found in the *OED2*. Davies (1884), however, includes the word, with a meaning identical to the one found in the *EDD*. Davies compares the word to "W. *coeg*, for *coec*, vain, foolish, pert; *coegyn*, a vain, saucy fellow; Corn. *coc*, vain, foolish; W. *coegio*, to deceive, make a fool of; Arm. *gogea*, to deceive, to rally".

And in the *GPC* s.v. *coeg*, we find the following meanings 'vain, empty, false, deceitful, mean, evil, good-for-nothing; arrogant, scornful, sarcastic' with first attestations of the word in the thirteenth century.

Claud: The *EDD* lists the word *claud* as a North Country dialect word, with the meaning 'a ditch or fence'. The word is not listed in the *OED2*. Davies (1884), however, includes *claud* in his list, and suggests the following as the source of the word in North Country dialects: "W. *clawdd*; O.W. *claud* (Ir. Gloss., 59), a ditch, trench, embankment, fence; Ir. *cladh*, a dike, an embankment". *GPC* s.v. *clawdd* gives the following meanings: 'soil thrown up in digging a pit or trench, mound, wall made of earth, dyke, earthwork, bulwark; boundary; hedge, fence'. Furthermore, the *GPC* compares the word with Cornish *kledh*, *cleath* and Breton *kleuz*, and derives the term from Celtic **klādo*.

Goggy: in the *EDD*, we find the following under *goggy*:

GOGGY, *sb. Obs.* n.Cy. Yks. Lan. A child's name for an egg.

Again, the word is not listed in the *OED2*, whereas it is included in Davies (1882), where the word is compared to "W. *cocwy*, a matured egg; Ir. *gug*, an egg". Davies also adds the following note to the entry on *goggy*: "These Celtic child-words, of which there is a considerable number, are a proof of intermarriage between the two races". The *GPC* lists *cwcwy, cocwy, cucwy* meaning 'egg, matured or perfect egg; egg-shell; shell' with first attestations from the thirteenth century.

The five dialect words discussed above present just a tiny sample of the words listed in Davies (1882–1883, 1884, 1885). By mentioning Davies's studies in this connection, we are not so much making any claims of new discoveries, but rather wish to draw scholars' attention to these extensive lists of putative Celtic loans in English dialect vocabulary from the north and west of England. Davies's lists would surely merit a close scrutiny; potentially, such a study could have a profound effect on our views about the role of Celtic loans in English (dialect) lexicon.

2.4.3   Conclusion

To conclude, there is relatively extensive place-name evidence that suggests that in some parts of England, especially in the north, in the West Midlands and in the south-west, considerable pockets of British speakers survived for centuries after the Anglo-Saxon conquest. Jackson (1963) has argued that there is evidence for a Cumbric-speaking population surviving in Northumberland until the early twelfth century; Gelling (1992) presents place-name and toponymic evidence that leads her to conclude that the Welsh language survived in most of the West Midlands until the end of the ninth century, and in some areas "throughout the Anglo-Saxon period"; and, most recently, Coates and Breeze (2000) have shown that a concentration of Brythonic place-names showing evidence of post-600 borrowing exists in north-west Wiltshire, which implies the existence of a late Brythonic-speaking population in that area.

As far as general vocabulary goes, it seems beyond dispute that the Brythonic impact on OE vocabulary was minimal; only a handful of borrowings have been convincingly identified from the OE period. However, there is growing evidence pointing towards the conclusion that the number of borrowings during the ME and EModE periods is greater than has generally been assumed. This raises the question of the possible extent of time-lag between a borrowing and its first attestation in written records, especially in the case of registers which would have been considered inferior to the written variety. As Pödör (1995–1996: 187) has shown in the case of Scottish Gaelic loanwords in Lowland Scots, the gap between borrowing and first attestation may be several centuries long. This, taken together with the so far largely unexplored issue of Celtic borrowings in regional dialect vocabulary, indicates that the amount of lexical borrowing from the Celtic languages is not quite so minimal as has been assumed in many previous works.

2.5   CONCLUSION

In this section, we are content to present a short summary of the various kinds of evidence discussed in Part I. As will become evident from the discussions in Part II and the following Epilogue, the issue of the nature and extent of Celtic influences in English needs to be seen against the whole history of the contacts between these languages, including those taking place in the later periods. Therefore, we defer passing our final judgment on the issue at hand to the Epilogue.

Our discussion of the demographic and historical evidence has shown that, first of all, the demographic and sociohistorical circumstances surrounding the *adventus Saxonum* were such that linguistic contact influences were not just possible but inevitable. The earlier held view that the vast majority of the indigenous Celtic population were either extirpated or driven away from their settlement areas has turned out to be untenable in the light of the most recent evidence. Secondly, and following on from the first point, there was in all likelihood a period of extensive bilingualism for a considerable length of time after the *adventus*. Thirdly, during this period of bilingualism, the Britons shifted to English and were gradually assimilated to the Anglo-Saxon population both culturally and linguistically. Fourthly, the rate of language shift varied from one area to another: this process was first completed in the east and south of England, but much later in the other areas.

To turn next to the linguistic evidence, a central place in our argumentation is occupied by two types of evidence which, we believe, have not been sufficiently considered in most of the previous works, viz. contact-linguistic and areal-typological evidence for Celtic influence on English. The wide range of linguistic features discussed in Chapter 2 shows that Celtic influences are not confined to just one or two features, but appear to have affected several 'core' areas of English grammar and morphophonology. What is more, our discussion of features such as the *b*-paradigm of the OE verb 'be', the progressive form and the cleft sentence strongly suggests that the Celtic impact on English grammar is already visible in OE, contrary to the widely held view that it does not manifest itself until much later (see also the recent work by Angelika Lutz [Lutz, forthcoming], who arrives at a similar conclusion).

Lexical influence from Celtic remains limited, not because of lack of contacts between the two populations, but because of the nature of the contact situation: in conditions of large-scale language shift, such influences are not even expected. Therefore, the numbers of Celtic loanwords do not constitute significant counterevidence to influences in other domains of language.

Finally, what also emerges from our discussion as something that needs to be reassessed is the very notion of 'contact influence': it is important to bear in mind that it does not pertain to just direct borrowing but may also involve convergent, adstratal, developments. These, in turn, are not necessarily restricted to English and Celtic. In the case at hand, there are grounds for arguing for *Sprachbund*-type developments with respect to some syntactic features such as the cleft construction that can be best explained within the context of a (north-)west European linguistic area.

The linguistic outcomes of contacts in the modern period, to be discussed in Part II of this volume, provide indirect evidence for Celtic influences in the mediaeval period, as well. This is because the modern contacts entail essentially similar processes of language contact and shift in many parts of the British Isles and Ireland.

Part II

Celtic Influences
in the Modern Age

3 The Historical Background to the Modern Contacts and to Language Shift in Celtic-Speaking Areas

3.1 THE GENERAL NATURE OF THE CELTIC–ENGLISH INTERFACE IN THE MODERN PERIOD

In the modern era, the advance of English into the earlier Celtic-speaking areas has continued in all parts of the British Isles but the pace and outcome of the contacts have varied a great deal from one region to another, depending on many sociohistorical, political and other factors. Areas in Scotland and Wales have been characterised by a relatively slow but steady spread of English at the expense of the indigenous Celtic languages. In Scotland, the wave-like process of the withdrawal of Gaelic has continued towards the west and north-west, and has gradually led to the present-day situation in which all areas, except the far north-west and the islands off the north-west coast of Scotland, are virtually completely English-speaking. Throughout this process, various political measures have been used to promote English and to root out the use of Gaelic. These will be further discussed in section 3.3.

In Wales, too, English has gradually encroached on the positions of Welsh, but the process of language shift has been even slower than in Scotland, despite political efforts similar to those used in Scotland. A special feature of the Welsh situation is the sharp divide between the predominantly Welsh-speaking peasantry and the English-speaking townspeople. Indeed, even as late as the end of the eighteenth century the peasantry had been anglicised only in the eastern parts of Wales, with the mass of the country remaining Welsh-speaking (Thomas 1994: 98). In the nineteenth century, the rapid industrialisation of especially the south-eastern parts of Wales brought about a major change: the heavy demand for labour attracted large numbers of Welsh speakers from the north and west of Wales to the new industrial centres in the south-east, and they were soon followed by increasing numbers of English-speaking immigrants from outside Wales. As a consequence, the social prestige of English rose sharply, while Welsh became more and more restricted to the 'hearth and chapel'. This process was further aggravated by the Education Act of 1870, which proclaimed English the sole medium of instruction in schools and led to an almost complete neglect of Welsh. At present, Welsh retains its strongest positions in some western and north-western areas of Wales, with much smaller pockets holding out in the southern parts. Although Welsh is actively promoted in schools and also used as a medium of instruction, the rest of Wales is predominantly, and in the east, almost completely monolingually English-speaking (see section 3.2 for further discussion).

In comparison with Wales and Scotland, the fortunes of English in Ireland present a very different picture: the near-demise of mediaeval English in Ireland gave Irish only a very short respite, with a new forward thrust of English beginning with the late sixteenth-century plantations of Ulster and parts of Munster. These were soon followed by the large-scale plantations under Cromwell in the mid-seventeenth century. Despite the drastically increased presence of English in formerly predominantly Irish-speaking areas, Irish was able to hold on to most of its positions right up to the end of the eighteenth century. It was the early part of the nineteenth century which then saw the tipping of the scales in favour of English. The process of language shift, once it got under way, proceeded at a pace hardly paralleled in linguistic history, and by the middle of the century English had made inroads into the Irish-speaking communities throughout the country excepting the coastal areas in the west of Ireland and some rather isolated pockets inland. The setting up of National Schools in 1831 with English as the medium of instruction, the choice of English as the main vehicle of the Catholic Emancipation movement, followed by the Great Famine of the 1840s and the subsequent emigration of about one million Irishmen, many of them Irish-speaking, are among the major factors which then led to a 'mass flight' from Irish and to a radical drop in the numbers of especially monoglot speakers of Irish (see, e.g. de Fréine 1977; Hindley 1990). Irish survives today only in some peripheral areas in the west of Ireland and is most probably destined to die out in those areas as a living community language within the next few decades. This despite the fact that Irish has for long been the first official language of the Republic of Ireland and is widely taught in Irish schools. The developments in Ireland will be discussed in greater detail in section 3.4.

The outcome of the English–Celtic interface in the much more confined areas of Cornwall and the Isle of Man has been rather predictable, given the smallness of the indigenous Celtic populations. The decline of Cornish began almost simultaneously with the emergence of Cornish as a separate language at around AD 600, slowly at first, but from the sixteenth century onwards the decline accelerated, and by ca 1800 the Cornish language was no longer used as a means of communication. In the Isle of Man, Manx survived much longer: the (allegedly) last native speaker of Manx died as recently as 1974, though Manx as a living community language had died out by the beginning of the twentieth century.

3.2   WALES

An important landmark in the history of language contact in Wales was the formal annexation of Wales with England, which was carried out with the Acts of Union in 1536 and 1543. Besides administrative reformations, the Acts consolidated the position of English as the only official language of Wales: the Laws in the Wales Act denied the Welsh language and its speakers all official functions in society, thus alienating the monoglot Welsh population from their own legal and administrative offices (Williams 1985: 119–121). In order to avoid their fate, the Welsh gentry had to abandon the Welsh language, and ultimately they did this voluntarily, as being associated with Welsh or Welsh-speakers might have had an adverse effect under the social circumstances of that period. By the eighteenth century there were few Welsh-speaking members of the gentry left in Wales (see also Jones 1993: 541).

In addition to remaining the language of the home, Welsh received an institutional refuge with the translation of the Bible in 1588. The primary aim of the Crown was to convert the Welsh to the Protestant religion, but scholars agree that the Welsh translation of the Bible was of enormous importance for the future of the language (e.g. Williams 1990: 21). At a time when English was about to take over as the language of most high domains, the church was able to remain Welsh. However, as Thomas (1994: 97) points out, granting Welsh a religious role also ensured the Crown a better control of the monoglot Welsh peasantry: isolating the Welsh from their system of government and the politics of the state was convenient for the anglicised ruling classes, and the peasantry, on the other hand, were dis-inclined to make trouble, having retained the use of Welsh in the domains most significant for their everyday lives.

From the late Middle Ages up until the early nineteenth century, Wales can be considered an example of diglossia without bilingualism. The two languages, Welsh and English, had distinctly different roles in society, and the two language communities had little interaction with each other. The advance of English in terms of geography was extremely slow: until the eighteenth century, bilingual communities remained restricted to a narrow belt surrounding the Welsh heartland. This can be seen from Map 3.1 from Pryce (1978: 242).

Even in the eastern borderland villages, where the inhabitants on all levels of society interacted with English speakers, there was little growth of indi-vidual bilingualism. The River Usk formed a boundary between the Welsh and English language communities in Gwent in the late eighteenth century. The Church in Wales Records indicate that in the churches along the transi-tional zone, where services were held in both languages, most of the parish-ioners were still likely to speak either Welsh or English (Pryce 1990: 52, 54). Thomas (1994: 99) concludes that interpreters, typically members of the educated gentry, probably acted as mediators between the two language

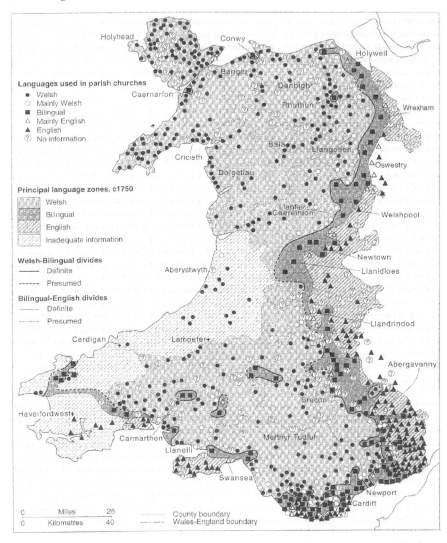

Map 3.1 Language zones in Wales in the mid-eighteenth century (originally from Pryce 1978: 242; revised map (c) W.T.R. Pryce 1999). Reproduced by permission of the author.

communities, as lack of interpreters would have resulted in the creation of a pidgin. Although two or more distinct language communities in close contact often create favourable circumstances for pidginisation, Thomas (*ibid.*) finds nothing in the subsequent linguistic history of Wales to indicate that this would have taken place.

There is, nevertheless, some evidence to suggest that English, as spoken by the inhabitants of the border areas, was influenced by the Welsh language. MacCann and Connolly (1933: 56, cited in Pryce 1990: 50) mention a seventeenth-century gentleman in Abergavenny who sent his son to London "so that he might acquire a sound knowledge of English 'without any corruption from his mother tongue which doth commonly infect men of our countree'". Further input into the south-eastern dialects of English was received from the West Midlands and the southwest of England. The effects of these varieties can be witnessed in certain geographical patterns in contemporary Welsh English (WE) (see Parry 1999 for details).

Whereas the pre-industrial 'old' Wales was rural and Welsh-speaking, with chancery towns being the most important regional centres, the industrial 'new' Wales was urbanised and increasingly English-speaking, with its population and administration concentrated in areas in the south and north-east (Pryce 1978: 229–230). The transition took place over some 150 years, beginning with the first steps of industrialisation taken in the 1770s. The mass migrations of the industrial era, which affected the whole of the western world, also brought about a clash of Welsh and English, a fight for dominance, and ultimately, for survival.

The migrations were triggered by population growth. Between 1770 and 1851 the population of Wales increased from 500,000 (John Davies 1993: 320) to 1,188,914, doubling to 2,442,041 over the next sixty years (Jenkins 1998b: 1, with statistics derived from D. Jones 1998). Davies (1993: 320–323) concludes that the primary catalyst behind the mushroom growth between 1770 and 1851 was the change in the birth and death ratio: people lived longer and had large families. The surplus of labour was forced to migrate in search for work. Emigration was one of the key elements to erode the Irish language (see section 3.4), but the Welsh were more fortunate. Although England and America were common destinations, a large percentage of the people were able to find work in their homeland.

Over the nineteenth century, Wales became one of the leading producers of coal in the world. The booming industry had a dual impact on the Welsh language: it accelerated the anglicisation of South Wales, but without the employment it offered, many more Welsh speakers would have been forced to leave the country. The English language, on the other hand, thrived. Whereas monoglot English speakers constituted some 5 per cent of the population in the late eighteenth century, their proportion rose to 55.4 per cent by 1911. In terms of numbers, the increase was from 30,000 to ca 1,350,000. In 1911, a total of 91.3 per cent of the population were either bilingual or monoglot English, and the numbers of monoglot Welsh speakers were waning rapidly (Jenkins 1998b: 3).

For some time, however, the increase in population figures showed in the numbers of Welsh speakers, too. During the first half of the nineteenth century the industrial valleys still received most of their workforce from Wales. The position of Welsh language and culture was strengthened, and English-speaking immigrant miners found themselves learning Welsh in order to converse with their workmates. The number of Welsh speakers in Wales reached its peak in 1911 at 977,366, but the tide was to turn eventually: in 1881, Welsh migrants were already outnumbered by immigrants from England, Scotland and Ireland, and their share of the workforce was growing (P.N. Jones 1998: 155; see also Williams 1990; Jenkins 1998b).

The anglicisation of the southern industrial valleys was further sped up by the poor prestige of Welsh. The English-speaking gentry had been replaced by English industrialists, but the position of Welsh remained equally low. The only access to social advancement was through English, and most Welsh speakers saw no reason to hang on to the language which held them back. At this stage, the industrialised counties of the south and north-east were the only ones experiencing heavy anglicisation, as these were the regions drawing the majority of the immigrants. The rural heartlands, although gradually becoming bilingual, remained predominantly Welsh-speaking throughout the nineteenth century. Williams (1990: 32) points out that these areas suffered from the opposite problem: emigration, which taxed the economy and social order of the Welsh language communities. English was introduced to the heartland through recent developments such as tourism and newly built roads and railways, but also by returning migratory labour. Seasonal migrations to south-east Wales and to England were financially significant for the working people of the rural south-west (Williams 1985: 145) and probably contributed to the anglicisation of those parts in a way similar to what happened in the Irish *Gaeltacht* areas (see, e.g. Odlin 1997a).

A further, still more effective means of bringing rural Wales into contact with the English language was the educational system. Roberts (1996: 171–172) points out that the trigger for the Education Act of 1870 was the general unease with which the British "culture of progress" of the mid-nineteenth century regarded the distinctive culture and language of Wales. The differences from the English mainstream were fundamental enough to be considered disturbing and even potentially dangerous, and the Welsh problem was eventually tackled by an investigation into the state of education in Wales, carried out by the Commissioners of Inquiry. In their 1847 report, the Commissioners announced that the reason for the vast class differences in Wales and the main obstacle on the nation's path to social progress and material wealth was the Welsh language (Aitchison and Carter 2000: 34). The report was met with a flood of protests but it also resulted in the Welsh beginning to lose confidence in their language, and soon education through the medium of Welsh was perceived as ineffective and useless by both the English promoters and the Welsh themselves (Jones 1993: 548). Education in English was the preferred alternative. From the mid-nineteenth century onwards the number of elementary schools began to rise, and the pupils' proficiency in arithmetic and English was tested regularly. Janet Davies (1993: 48–49) mentions that teachers were active in promoting English in fear of losing a part of the state grant, sometimes forbidding the use of Welsh entirely. This gave rise to the notorious 'Welsh Not' practice, which, however, was less widespread than people today tend to assume.

The Education Act of 1870 made elementary education compulsory, free and thoroughly English, and it was followed by the Intermediate Education Act of 1889 (John Davies 1993: 435–437, 458–459). The financial investments were large and profited the educational system, but the Acts also resulted in even the most persistently Welsh communities gradually becoming bilingual. The proportional decline of Welsh and the advance of English were at their most rapid between 1871 and 1921, when the effects of immigration and the Education Act conjoined (Jones 1993: 549). Despite the adversities, the number of Welsh speakers kept growing throughout the final decades of the nineteenth century, and with the establishment of a Welsh counter-movement the language received renewed support. Jones (1980: 58) observes that one of the major forces which helped Welsh survive was its close connection with Nonconformist religion, which kept up the Welsh language and culture until the 1920s. On a general level, however, the value of Welsh was limited (*op.cit.*, 61), and it became recognised that knowledge of English was socially and economically essential.

The language shift was particularly rapid in the densely populated South Wales coalfield, which is described by Jenkins (1998b: 11) as "a huge, complex, amorphous, even chaotic, sprawl of intensely divergent linguistic communities . . . [where] virtually no community was sheltered from prevailing English influences". Pryce (1978: 5) concludes that communal bilingualism was in many cases transitional, the youngsters already abandoning Welsh in favour of English. Thus, English became the spoken language between 1880 and 1935 in Radnor, Brecon and Monmouth, while in Glamorganshire the language situation still varied from the fully anglicised coastal area to the predominantly Welsh northern parts of the valleys (Williams 1935). The rural counties of South Wales, on the other hand, remained Welsh apart from the towns, where English was becoming more common. The English enclave of South Pembrokeshire had not expanded significantly, either. The vast majority of the South Welsh were, however, concentrated in the counties of Monmouth and Glamorgan, where the anglicisation process was in full spate (*ibid.*).

In 1901, Welsh speakers constituted only 49.9 per cent of the population, and the loss of the majority language status of the language was quite evident by the census of 1911. The following decades put an enormous strain on its survival: the mid-war depression collapsed the Welsh economy, causing such severe unemployment that hundreds of thousands were forced to leave the country in search for work elsewhere. The Welsh language began to seem increasingly worthless: Thomas (1987: 437, cited in Aitchison and Carter 2000: 38) argues that for Welsh, this was the final blow, equivalent to the Irish potato famine.

The English language did not become prevalent in the rural counties of Wales until during the twentieth century, with the speed and mode of the anglicisation process depending on the region. On the whole, the proportion of English speakers and bilinguals grew steadily from the early twentieth century to the 1970s (cf. the map in Pryce 1978: 231). Most of them, however, lived in the towns, where the history of language contact was longer to begin with. Geographically speaking, anglicisation did not concern the majority of the rural west and north until World War II, but gradually the use of English spread from the towns and the urbanised industrial regions to the surrounding countryside. The advance of English into these parts did not lead to a full-fledged language shift but to bilingualism. In the regions where Welsh was traditionally a strong community language, the people found no reason to abandon it completely. English was, nevertheless, an essential means of social and economic progress and there was a practical need to know it, which resulted in the disappearance of the last monoglot Welsh speakers by the time of the 1991 census.

The force currently strongest in anglicising Wales is migration, both in and out of the country. Emigration from the rural areas, motivated by economic factors, has continued throughout the twentieth century and put a strain on the Welsh-speaking communities. The in-migration, on the other hand, has mainly been the result of the counterurbanisation movement of the last decades. In many areas, this last wave of incomers has been critical in tilting the language situation in favour of English. The migrations have changed the constitution of the population in varying ways; on the whole, Aitchison and Carter (2000: 122–123) state that the impact of migration "manifests itself in a pushing back of the frontier between 'Welsh Wales' and Anglicised Wales on the one hand, and in serious disruptions to the integrity of the heartland on the other".

The looming extinction of the Welsh language began to raise concern in the late nineteenth century. Its position was improved gradually through the Welsh Courts Act of 1942, the Welsh Language Act of 1967 and the Welsh Language Act of 1993 (Aitchison and Carter 2000: 46, 136), the last of which finally gave Welsh equal rights with English. Each new step was the result of tenacious campaigning and civic activity. Welsh-medium education, on the primary level at least, was restarted around the turn of the twentieth century, and Welsh radio and TV channels were founded later on to compete with the English mass media. The 1981 census showed that the decline of the language had slowed down considerably, and ten years later the proportion of Welsh speakers had sunk no further (*op.cit.*, 51, 89). The latest census, held in 2001, is historical in being the first one indicating an increase in the number and proportion of Welsh speakers. Aitchison and Carter (2004: 49) state that the 1991 percentage of 18.6 had risen to 20.5; the reported number of speakers was 575,640, with an increase of nearly 68,000 from 1991.[1] The development of the census figures for Welsh from 1901 to 2001 can be seen in Figure 3.1 (the statistics derived from Aitchison and Carter 2000, 2004).

When analysing the 2001 results, Aitchison and Carter (2004) state that the decline had continued in the Welsh heartland, but that the losses had been outweighed by gains in the formerly highly anglicised border regions.

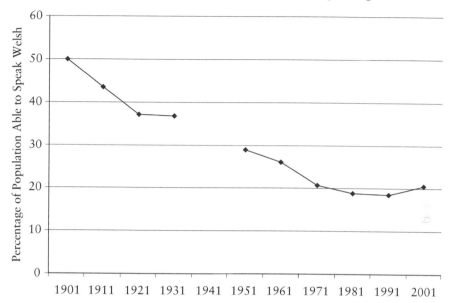

Figure 3.1 Welsh-speaking population census figures in the twentieth century; percentage of Welsh speakers in Wales (based on Aitchison and Carter 2000, 2004).

Although the signs for the future of the language are more positive than before, the writers remain sceptical about the possibilities of Welsh regaining communal significance in the regions where it has traditionally not had any (*op.cit.*, 132). Welsh is cherished today as the national language of Wales, its cultural value probably enhanced by the adversities it has faced. To an extent, its recent resurgence builds upon its prestigious past and distinguished literary history. Its social value, however, has suffered blows from which it has difficulty recovering. The declining numbers of speakers in traditionally strongly Welsh regions such as south-east Carmarthenshire and west Glamorgan are an indication of this (for discussion, see Aitchison and Carter 2004: 130–132). Map 3.2 displays the regional distribution of Welsh speakers in the 2001 census in terms of percentages.

There are geographic, historical and linguistic grounds for perceiving Wales in terms of two culture areas, Inner and Outer Wales (or *Cymru Cymraeg* 'Welsh Wales' and *Cymru-ddi-Gymraeg* 'Wales without Welsh', as, e.g. in Jones 1980). The former comprises, roughly, the rural northern and western heartlands, and the latter is associated with the urbanised south and east. Industrialisation reinforced the divide as the areas became strongly associated with different languages. Pryce (1978: 237–238, summarising Bowen 1959, 1964) observes that while Inner Wales contains—and always has contained—the essence of indigenous Welsh culture, Outer Wales is and has been much more heterogeneous, mixing Welshness with external influences. It is pointed out by Aitchison and Carter (2000: 134–135), however,

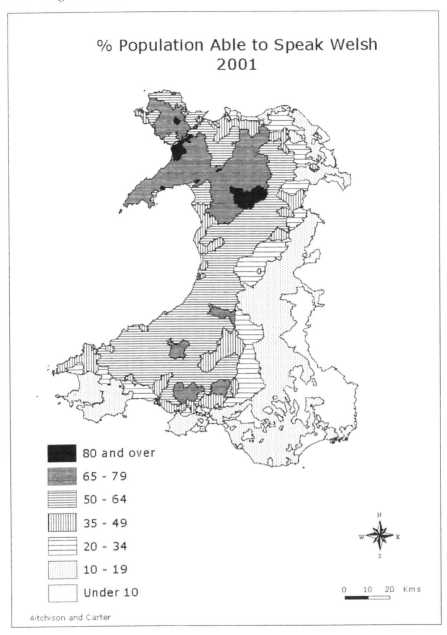

Map 3.2 The percentages of Welsh speakers in Wales in 2001 (from Aitchison and Carter 2004: 52). Reproduced by permission of the authors.

that as the position of Welsh in the heartland is weakened and the numbers of speakers in the cities are on the increase, the traditional geolinguistic divides are gradually crumbling. For example, the definition of *Y Fro Gymraeg*, the heartland, has sunk from the 1901 level of 90 per cent of Welsh speakers down to the present-day level of 50 per cent.

The ideology reflected by the terms 'inner' and 'outer' is in direct reference to the role of the English language and culture in the history of Wales: they are external to the country. The Welsh have had a little over a century to come to terms with English being the majority language, 'a language of Wales', but the adjustment has been an uneasy one. The recent resurgence of Welsh has probably strengthened the link between language and national identity, but concessions towards English have also been made. The present-day Anglo-Welsh writers can be quite nationalistic, being comfortable with defending Wales in English instead of mourning the loss of 'their language'. Plaid Cymru has also moderated its official stand on the language issue. The promotion of Welsh is obviously still high on its list of priorities, but it is no longer stressed quite as forcefully, as the party now strives to gain the support of the whole of Wales.

However, it is not generally recognised that English as spoken in Wales might constitute a variety of its own. There are several reasons for this: the Welsh varieties of English are regionally too varied to be regarded as distinctive of Wales as a whole; most of the grammatical substratum features from Welsh are subsiding, resulting in WE being defined increasingly as an accent rather than a dialect; and finally, the position of Welsh as the national language seems to be too powerful to leave room for a national variety of English. Traditionally, both the English speakers and the Welsh speakers have regarded the dialects or accents of the Anglo-Welsh as somewhat comical and socially inferior, as indicated, e.g. by the popularity of John Edwards's best-selling 'Wenglish' books, *Talk Tidy* (1985) and *More Talk Tidy* (1986). However, the self-denigratory humour of *Talk Tidy* also kindles feelings of sympathy and recognition in the Welsh audience. Whether or not the term 'Welsh English' receives widespread acknowledgement, the Welsh accent nevertheless possesses a level of social and national significance. To the monoglot English Anglo-Welsh, in particular, it is the linguistic surrogate of a national language, as is evidenced by numerous studies (see Giles 1990). Coupland *et al.* (1994), investigating teachers' evaluations of various WE accents, showed that although these accents were often lacking in prestige in comparison with south-east English accents, they received better assessments in terms of pleasantness and dynamism. This concerned especially the regional varieties of Merthyr Tydfil and Carmarthen, the latter of which fared well in terms of prestige, as well. The accents of the anglicised regions were generally less well received.

There are numerous factors affecting the ways in which English is or has been spoken in different parts of Wales, including the speed and stage of the anglicisation process, the mode of language transmission, and the positions of English and Welsh as community languages. Today, the majority of the variation at the level of syntax has been levelled through the widespread availability of Standard English and the effects of modern comprehensive and vocational education. The low significance of WE at the national level has contributed to the process as well. However, as indicated by Paulasto (2006), corpora representing early twentieth-century WE reveal noticeable syntactic variation between south-eastern, northern and south-western dialects. Although the northern and western varieties of English are currently considered to have closer structural ties with the Welsh language than the varieties spoken in the anglicised regions (e.g. Thomas 1984a), Paulasto concludes that the rapidity of the language shift and the largely informal transmission of English in the industrial south-east at the turn of the twentieth century resulted in a regional variety which was structurally highly influenced by the Welsh substratum (see also Ellis 1882 on Merthyr Tydfil 'Welsh English'). Over time, however, with the loss of contemporary Welsh input, the variety gradually shed most of its syntactic substratum features, retaining primarily the Welsh-influenced accent and prosody (see George 1990 for further information on English in the south-eastern valleys).

In the rural parts of North and West Wales, English was mainly learned formally at school, while Welsh kept its position as the primary language of the community. Thus, the effects of Welsh were realised as direct interference from the speakers' first language rather than being reflexes of earlier substratal influence (Paulasto, *op.cit.*). The interference was particularly evident in the speech of the non-mobile, older, rural population, such as the informants interviewed for the *Survey of Anglo-Welsh Dialects*, who had generally received only a minimal education. Paulasto's study (*ibid.*) shows, however, that among her regional corpora, the most nonstandard and Welsh-influenced English of all was spoken in south-east Carmarthenshire, in an area where the cultural and language-historical traits of the rural, Welsh-speaking west and the anglicised, industrialised south-east combined. This regional variety has also felt the impact of standardisation over the course of the twentieth century, but certain syntactic features, such as focus fronting (see Chapter 4, section 4.2), remain fairly widespread in the local English dialect. Thus, although it is likely that WE is evolving towards a collection of regional accents, not all of its syntactic distinctiveness will be levelled out very soon.

3.3   SCOTLAND

In the modern era, English has continued its steady advance into the western and north-western areas of Scotland which were earlier the strongholds of the Gaelic language and culture. This process has over the centuries been sped up by various political and other measures aimed at undermining the position of Gaelic. C. Ó Baoill (1997: 556) refers to MacKinnon's (1991) view, according to which the Acts of the Scottish Parliament in 1496 and 1542 effectively ignored Gaelic at the official level and were aimed at lowering its prestige. The sixteenth-century Reformation and its aftermath in the early seventeenth century also played a significant part in the decline of Gaelic, as C. Ó Baoill (1997: 558) notes: Gaelic was identified with Roman Catholicism and 'incivility', which King James VI wanted to root out from the western parts of Scotland. As part of the same process, in 1609 a number of Highland and Hebridean chiefs were lured into signing the so-called Statutes of Iona, which, among other things, obliged the wealthier Highland people to send their sons to Lowland schools "to speik, reid, and wryte Inglische" (C. Ó Baoill, *op.cit.*, 558–559). While the Statutes themselves did not contain measures explicitly directed against the use of Gaelic, this was not the case with the decision of the Privy Council in 1616, ratifying the said Statutes on the one hand, and ordering, on the other, that

> the vulgar Inglishe toung be universallie plantit, and the Irishe language, whilk is one of the chief and principall causis of the continewance of barbaritie and incivilitie amongis the inhabitantis of the Ilis and the Heylandis, may be abolisheit and removit.

(C. Ó Baoill 1997: 559)

The need to 'abolish' and 'remove' the Gaelic language arose directly from the principal educational objective of the Reformation: to make the Bible available to all Scotsmen in the English language (*ibid.*). As Ó Baoill points out, this implied that Gaelic was not considered a sufficient or proper medium of education, an attitude which has persisted in various forms up to the present day. As an indication of this, he quotes the 1994 report issued by Her Majesty's Inspectors of Schools, according to which it was "neither feasible nor desirable" to introduce Gaelic as the medium of education in secondary schools in Gaelic-speaking areas (C. Ó Baoill 1997: 560).

Map 1.3 in Chapter 1 showed how the borderline between the two languages, Gaelic and Scots/English, developed in the Middle Ages and by the beginning of the modern period. Map 3.3, from Withers (1984), outlines the proportions of Gaelic speakers in the so-called *Gàidhealtachd*, the Scottish Gaelic–speaking areas, in 1705.

Map 3.3 shows that in this period the position of Gaelic was fairly strong throughout the Highlands, excepting some counties in the north-east, east and south-east (the white areas in the north-western Highlands denote parishes for which the relevant information was not available). The next one hundred years or so already witness a considerable thinning-out of the Gaelic-speaking population, as can be seen from Map 3.4 from Withers (1984: 144).

Despite the seemingly simple geographical nature of the retreat of Gaelic, Withers (1984: 97–99) emphasises that the process was much more

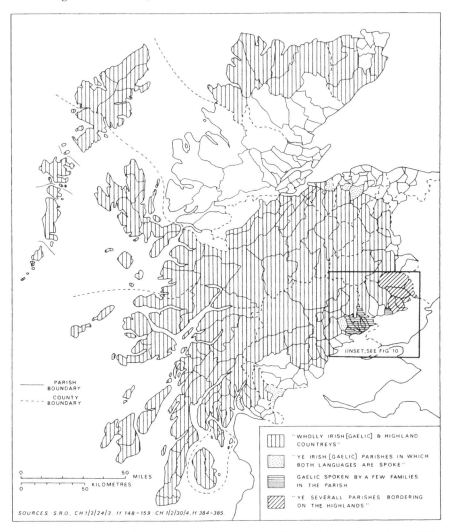

Map 3.3 Proportions of Gaelic speakers in the *Gàidhealtachd*, in 1705 (from Withers 1984: 56). Reproduced by permission of the author.

complicated and took place at varying rates on different levels of society and in different communicative contexts: Gaelic was first replaced in the speech of the upper classes and in the context of trade discourse. In his discussion on the factors which put Gaelic on the decline, Withers first refers to the works by Gregor (1980) and Durkacz (1983), who single out the following principal causes: the disunity of the Scottish people, loss of status of Gaelic, shortage of reading matter in Gaelic, accompanied by lack of instruction in schools, loss of the language in religious life, immigration and emigration, and in recent times, the impact of newspapers,

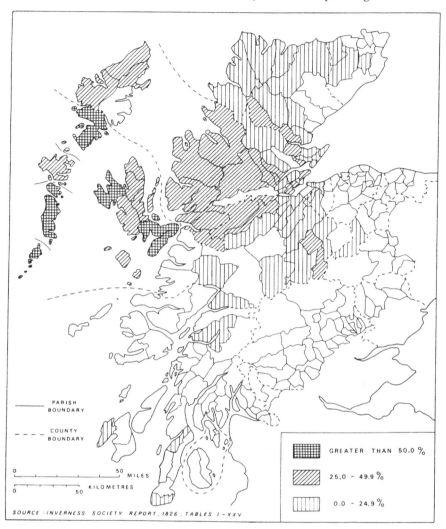

Map 3.4 Estimated percentage of population understanding Gaelic best but unable to read, 1822 (from Withers 1984: 144). Reproduced by permission of the author.

cinema, radio and television. To these Withers adds the "antipathy of the authorities in determining the fortunes of Gaelic" (*op.cit.*, 259). Apart from overtly repressive actions aimed at Gaelic, Withers stresses the role of "less tangible factors", which included changes in the relationship to land within the Highlands, negative attitudes towards the use of Gaelic, and changes relating to the economic, social and political integration of the Gaelic world into the English-speaking one (*op.cit.*, 259). The decline of the traditional Scottish Gaelic cultural forms was yet another factor, as Withers points out (*ibid.*). Thus, the bardic system faded away by the

eighteenth century and deprived the native literary culture of its main sup-
portive structure, making the transmission of Gaelic culture and language
less certain. The effects of this change were further worsened by the low
rates of literacy amongst the Gaelic-speaking population. In sum, the eighteenth century according to Withers (*op.cit.*, 260) was "a period of pro-
scription", aimed at "wearing out the Irish" (i.e., the Gaelic language and
culture).

In the nineteenth century, the decline of Gaelic continued at a steady
pace. A decisive blow for Gaelic was the 1872 Act, which had no provision
for Gaelic at all. The dominance of English in the field of education has led,
as C. Ó Baoill (1997) notes, not only to the geographical reduction of the
Gaelic-speaking area and to an increasing narrowing-down of the domains
in which Gaelic was used formerly, but also to a process of erosion of the
language itself: it has lost some of its former ranges of vocabulary, while its
grammar is absorbing considerable influences from English.

In geographical terms, the position of Gaelic continues to weaken steadily.
This can be seen from Map 3.5, from MacKinnon (1993), which shows the
present-day language situation in Scotland.

The Gaelic language is now holding out in the north-west and in the
islands off the north-west coast of Scotland. All other areas have long been
almost completely English-speaking. Withers (1984: 241) points out some
recent developments which have contributed to the preservation of Gaelic.
Thus, *An Comunn Gaidhealach*, the Gaelic language society, has sought to
improve, with some success, the status of Gaelic in the educational system;
similarly, the *Comhairle nan Eilean*, the Western Isles Council, has tried to
promote a bilingual policy, though only "with variable success", as Withers
remarks (*ibid.*). Yet, the major problem for Gaelic is that it has had a very
minor role in public life in general, even in the *Gàidhealtachd*, the Scottish
Gaelic–speaking areas (*ibid.*). What also makes it harder for Gaelic to find
its way back into everyday life is the virtual disappearance of monoglot
Gaelic speakers by the 1970s or 1980s according to Withers's estimate (*op.
cit.*, 235).

Writing as lately as the 1990s, MacKinnon (1993: 514) deplores the fact
that Gaelic at that time was still not recognised as one of Scotland's national
languages, nor was there any general provision for the language in Scotland's
school system. However, since 1882 it has been possible to take Gaelic as
part of a university degree, and the 1918 Education Act provided for Gaelic
to be taught "in Gaelic-speaking areas". Since 1975, bilingual education has
been provided in the Western Isles and Skye; further steps ahead have been
the introduction of Gaelic as a second language at primary level, introduction of Gaelic-medium primary school units from 1985 and Gaelic-speaking
nursery schools in 1988 (*ibid.*). Finally, in 2005, the Scottish Parliament
passed the Bill for the Gaelic Language (Scotland) Act, which had the purpose of establishing a special body with the name of *Bòrd na Gàidhlig*. The
Act describes this as

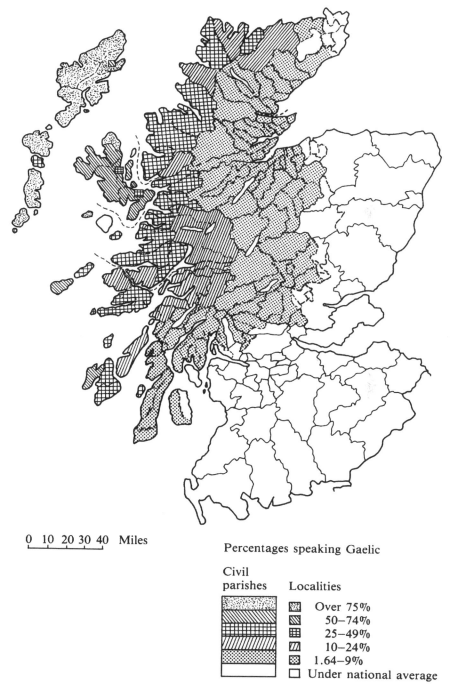

0 10 20 30 40 Miles

Percentages speaking Gaelic

Civil
parishes Localities

Over 75%
50–74%
25–49%
10–24%
1.64–9%
☐ Under national average

Map 3.5 Proportions of local populations speaking Gaelic in 1981 (from MacKinnon 1993: 498). Reproduced by permission of the author.

a body having functions exercisable with a view to securing the status of the Gaelic language as an official language of Scotland commanding equal respect to the English language, including the functions of preparing a national Gaelic language plan, of requiring certain public authorities to prepare and publish Gaelic language plans in connection with the exercise of their functions and to maintain and implement such plans, and of issuing guidance in relation to Gaelic education.

(See http://www.opsi.gov.uk/legislation/scotland/ acts2005/50007--a.htm#1, accessed October 2006)

It remains to be seen to what extent the Bòrd will succeed in its main tasks of promoting and facilitating the use and understanding of the Gaelic language, as well as Gaelic education and culture.

As in Wales and Ireland, the decline of Gaelic has gone hand in hand with the emergence of a distinctive variety, or rather, varieties of English spoken in Scotland. As can be expected, they retain some archaic features from the Anglian dialect of Old English which, as mentioned in Chapter 1, section 1.3, had towards the end of the Middle Ages developed into a full-fledged language in its own right, usually referred to by the term 'Scots'. For a time, Scots occupied the position of a standard literary language in Scotland, but from the sixteenth century onwards it began to absorb more and more influences from southern English, with especially written Scots starting to converge on Standard English. This process eventually led to the formation of Standard Scottish English (SSE), which in many respects represents a compromise between Scots and eighteenth-century English. The name often attached to this process, 'anglicisation' of Scots, is a little misleading, as Macafee and Ó Baoill (1997: 246) point out, because what was being anglicised here was already a form of English. Instead, this term would be better applied to the replacement of Gaelic and the other Celtic languages by English in Scotland and in the other Celtic lands, respectively. Despite the replacement of Scots by SSE in the formal registers of use, the former continues to live in various forms and under different guises in the present-day colloquial variety of SSE, usually termed 'Scottish English', and especially in everyday working-class speech. Yet at the same time attempts are being made by Scots enthusiasts to bring it back to more general use in higher domains of language use, too. Thus, in 2001 Scots achieved recognition by the Council of Europe as one of the minority languages in Europe, and the British government has also recognised Scots as a regional language under the European Charter for Regional or Minority Languages.

Yet another type of English in the complex linguistic set-up of Scotland is the variety which has evolved in the Gaelic-speaking areas of the north-west and the Western Isles: the terms used for this variety, or varieties rather, are 'Highland English' and 'Island English'. The most Gaelic-influenced subvariety of the latter is the one spoken in the Hebrides, known as 'Hebridean

English' (HebE). It is true that Scots and Scottish English, too, contain some traces of influence from Gaelic, but the majority of scholarly opinion considers the Celtic input rather minimal as compared with the Highland and Island Englishes, in which the presence of the Gaelic substratum is much more noticeable, as is shown by the detailed study of HebE by Annette Sabban (see Sabban 1982 and the discussion in Chapter 4).

Yet, the Scots–Gaelic interface has in some of the most recent research emerged as an area which is in clear need of further study. In Chapter 2, section 2.4, we referred to the views expressed by McClure (1986) and Gillies (1994), both of whom argue that Gaelic influence on Scots has probably been greater than has hitherto been accepted. More recently, the issue has been addressed in two very fine articles by Macafee and Ó Baoill (1997) and C. Ó Baoill (1997). Although they argue that Scots in general should not be considered a 'Celtic English', they single out a certain number of phonological and syntactic influences, as well as varying degrees of lexical borrowing, in various dialects of Scots. Apart from the contact-varieties spoken in the Highlands and Islands, in which these influences are greatest, they find considerable lexical and phonological influences in 'peripheral' Scots dialects in areas which were still Gaelic-speaking in the seventeenth century or even later (e.g. Kintyre, Arran and Bute, western Caithness); these dialects may in future research be found to display syntactic influences, too. Another group of dialects preserving traces of Gaelic is formed by dialects spoken in the south-west, the north and especially the north-east; these are all areas in which Gaelic was used until the end of the mediaeval period. Finally, in what these authors call the 'heartland of literary Scots', which means essentially the south-eastern part of Scotland, settled first by the Angles, the influences from Gaelic are minimal even at the lexical level (Macafee and Ó Baoill 1997: 281).

3.4   IRELAND[2]

It was already mentioned in Chapter 1, section 1.3 that there is some controversy amongst scholars about the question of continuity between the mediaeval and modern stages of the English language in Ireland. Contemporary evidence is rather scanty and it can be used to support both positions. Regardless of the exact level of survival of 'Old English' in Ireland, scholars are generally agreed that the plantations of the seventeenth century marked an important turning-point in the linguistic history of Ireland (see, e.g. Kallen 1997a: 14). Already in the latter half of the sixteenth century the counties of Leix and Offaly were planted under Queen Mary. These were to be followed in 1601 by the defeat of the Irish rebels and their Spanish allies at the battle of Kinsale. Subsequently, the failure of various rebellions in Ulster and the so-called Flight of the Earls in 1607 led to an influx of English and Scottish settlers into the northern parts of Ireland. However, the most influential changes were brought about by the Cromwellian Settlement in the 1650s. In Hogan's (1927/1970: 52) eloquent words, this settlement "gave the final blow to the old Irish society, reduced the native race to helotry, and established as the Irish nation an alien upper class". It also gave a strong impulse to the diffusion of the English language. In all provinces except Connacht, the landowners were English-speaking Protestants, and as Bliss (1979: 19) points out, "the great houses formed centres where the English language was spoken: tenants and servants alike had to learn some English in order to communicate with their masters".

It is remarkable that, although the Cromwellian Settlement gave a decisive impetus to 'New English', it did not proceed with any notable speed among the mass of the Irish-speaking population until much later. Thus, Ó Cuív (1951: 18) notes that Irish continued to be spoken even in Dublin throughout the seventeenth century and also during the eighteenth century. As one piece of evidence indicating the tenacity of Irish, Ó Cuív mentions the repeated measures suggested by the authorities for the use of Irish as the most suitable medium of Protestant religious instruction (1951: 18–19). Hindley (1990: 8) writes that the position of Irish stayed so strong throughout the seventeenth century that, apart from the planted parts of Ulster, the descendants of Cromwellian settlers "were commonly monoglot Irish by 1700". As regards the eighteenth century, Ó Cuív (1951) refers to some contemporary estimates of the numbers of Irish speakers, which indicate that in 1731, for example, some two-thirds of the population still used Irish as their everyday means of communication, while as late as 1791 about half of the population were either monoglot Irish or had Irish as their preferred language (Ó Cuív 1951: 19). De Fréine (1977: 73) gives an essentially similar account of the developments in this period. He writes that the language situation at the end of the eighteenth century was not significantly different from that in the year 1700, while Hindley (1990: 8) states that "it is unlikely that Irish began to fall into disuse in native homes before about 1750, except in a handful of towns". On the other hand, there was a clear social division here: as Hindley (*ibid.*) points out, the gentry were anglicised by 1800 throughout the country, and in most eastern and central areas had no knowledge of Irish.

The above accounts are also supported by the statistical analyses carried out by Fitzgerald (1984) on the basis of nineteenth-century censuses and especially the 1881 census. Fitzgerald's study covers the period from ca 1770 to 1870, and by using the data from the age-group tables it seeks to establish the minimum levels of Irish-speaking in successive new generations in different parts of Ireland. His results show that, of those born in the first decade investigated, 1771–1781, more than 90 per cent were Irish-speaking in the (south-)western counties of Kerry, Clare, Galway and Mayo. In Cork, Waterford and Sligo the percentage of Irish speakers was over 80, and the 50 per cent mark was also exceeded by varying degrees in the following counties: Kilkenny (57), Louth (57), Limerick (76), Tipperary (51), Leitrim

(52), Roscommon (74), and Donegal (56) (Fitzgerald 1984: 127). The corresponding figures for the four provinces were of course slightly lower: Leinster 17, Munster 80, Connacht 84, and Ulster 19 per cent, the percentage for all Ireland being 45 (Fitzgerald 1984: 127). As Fitzgerald (1984: 125) notes, the results provide plenty of evidence for the survival of Irish amongst young people "in much the greater part of Ireland". Where Irish turned out to be weakest was the area between Dublin and Wexford, including also parts of the Midlands. Not surprisingly, the level of Irish-speaking was very low in various parts of the north and north-east, and in mid- and south Antrim, Down and north Armagh there was no sign of the survival of Irish (Fitzgerald 1984: 125).

Despite the continued dominance of Irish in the eighteenth century, it is evident that bilingualism spread steadily throughout this period. As Hindley (1990: 11) points out, the "general setting" of eighteenth-century Ireland favoured the adoption of English, but at first only as a second language; it was not until the following century that this policy of bilingualism was abandoned and a large-scale language shift got under way. The numbers of bilinguals in different periods cannot be estimated very exactly, but Hindley (1990), relying on the account given by Dr. Whitley Stokes in 1799, arrives at the figure of 1,600,000 bilinguals at that date out of an estimated population of 5.4 million, i.e. some 30 per cent (Hindley 1990: 15; see also Ó Cuív 1951: 19, who uses the same source but estimates the total population to have been only 4.75 million at this period). According to Stokes's account, the number of monoglot Irish speakers in 1799 was some 800,000, which was about 15 per cent of the total population (Hindley 1990: 15). De Fréine (1977: 80) places the number of the monoglot Irish around 1800 at a considerably higher level, viz. at some two million, while his estimate of the number of bilinguals is 1.5 million.

Leaving the possible inaccuracies in the statistics aside, it is no exaggeration to say that the first half of the nineteenth century tipped the scales in favour of English. This becomes clear, for instance, from the returns of the first official census of 1851. The number of Irish speakers was now estimated at about 1.5 million or 23 per cent of the total population, which by this date had increased by more than a million and amounted to just over 6.5 million (Hindley 1990: 15). A significant change had also taken place in the number of monoglot Irish speakers, which by 1851 had dropped to slightly over 300,000 (or some 5 per cent) from the 800,000 (or two million, as de Fréine writes) in 1799. The 1851 census has been criticised for underrepresenting the numbers of Irish speakers (see, e.g. de Fréine 1977: 80–81; Kallen 1994: 162), but as de Fréine (1977: 81) aptly remarks, "[t]hey [the census data] may not show how far the people had travelled on the road to anglicisation, but they pointed unmistakeably in the direction they were going". The overall trend is perhaps most reliably demonstrated by Fitzgerald's (1984) statistics on the developments from 1771 to 1871. According to them, the Irish-speaking proportion of four decennial cohorts first declined only slightly, dropping from 45 per cent in 1771–1781 to 41 per cent in 1801–1811, but then sank to 28 per cent in 1831–1841 and further down to 13 per cent in 1861–1871. Table 3.1, adapted from Fitzgerald (1984), provides the percentages for each of the four provinces.

There is an extensive literature on the causes of the language shift in Ireland. Some of these are very obvious, like the effect of the Great Famine in the 1840s: about one million people died, while another million were forced to emigrate as a result of the successive failures of the potato crops; those areas where Irish had been strongest were the most badly affected (see, e.g. de Fréine 1977: 85–86). Several writers have pointed out the role of the National School system, launched in 1831, from which Irish was excluded by means of various penalties (see, e.g. O'Rahilly 1932/1976: 12; Wall 1969: 86; Henry 1977: 21). The attitude and policies adopted by the Catholic Church have also been singled out as a factor working against Irish. O'Rahilly (1932/1976: 11–12) emphasises the influence of the foundation of Maynooth College in 1795: though set up for the education of the Catholic priesthood, English was from the outset the primary medium of instruction there, which contributed to the establishment of English as the *de facto* official language of the Church in Ireland (see also Hindley 1990: 13). A further factor was the choice of English as the language of politics and Catholic emancipation even by such leaders as Daniel O'Connell, who was himself a native speaker of Irish (Hindley 1990: 14). As Wall (1969: 82) notes, by 1800 Irish had already had to withdraw from the top of the social scale: from parliament, the courts of law, town and country government, the civil service and the upper levels of commercial life. English now became the symbol for opportunity and success, whereas Irish was increasingly associated with poverty and illiteracy (Wall 1969: 85). This resulted in a mass flight from Irish, a process which de Fréine (1977: 84) has described as "not the product of any law or official regulation, but of a social self-generated

Table 3.1 Percentage of Irish speakers in certain decennial cohorts from 1771 to 1871.

Province	Decades of Birth			
	1771–1781	*1801–1811*	*1831–1841*	*1861–1871*
Leinster	17	11	3	0
Munster	80	77	57	21
Connacht	84	80	63	40
Ulster	19	15	8	4
Ireland	45	41	28	13

Source: Filppula 1999: 9, after Fitzgerald 1984: 127.

movement of collective behaviour among the people themselves". Hindley (1990) explains the same phenomenon in terms of the dialectics of quantitative and qualitative changes:

> The suddenness of Irish language collapse around and after 1800 may be understood in terms of the Marxian model of quantitative changes slowly building up to major qualitative change. The desire for English built up slowly because opportunities for the masses through English built up only slowly. The steady increase in bilingualism was the quantitative change which led around 1800 to qualitative change represented by the mass abandonment of Irish. This is hardly surprising, for a necessary precondition of adjudging Irish unnecessary or 'useless' would be the achievement of very wide-spread near-universal fluency in English. That is to say, universal bilingualism was the essential transitional stage on the way from an Irish-speaking Ireland to an English-speaking Ireland. By 1800 bilingualism was well advanced and the ultimate fate of the native language was near to a final decision.
>
> (Hindley 1990: 12)

Writing some forty years earlier, Ó Cuív (1951) had also recognised the role of widespread bilingualism as a necessary transitional stage, leading first to a situation where Irish was relegated to the status of a secondary language and eventually to one where it fell into disuse and was completely replaced by English. According to Ó Cuív (1951: 27), the stages were thus: Irish only –> Irish and English –> English and Irish –> English only.

In the latter half of the nineteenth century the decline of Irish, already evident from Fitzgerald's (1984) statistics quoted above, continued at a steady pace, and by the census of 1891 the number of Irish speakers had dropped to a little over half a million (Ó Cuív 1969a: 129). What was perhaps even more significant was the dwindling number of Irish-speaking monoglots, which according to one estimate fell from just over 300,000 in 1851 to 38,000 in 1891 (Gregor 1980: 274). As de Fréine (1977: 86) puts it, "by the year 1900 the transformation was almost complete". Statistics on the subsequent developments are not directly comparable with the previous census figures, especially because of the effects of the Gaelic Revival. As Ó Cuív (1951: 27) points out, the continuing decline in the number of Irish speakers in the Irish-speaking *Gaeltacht* areas[3] was offset by increases in the rest of the country. This tendency became particularly prominent following the appointment of the Gaeltacht Commission in 1925, which led to a more positive attitude towards Irish and was reflected in the census returns. These, as Ó Cuív (1951: 28) remarks, "were very often far from showing the true position", and in some cases could yield increases of up to 2,400 per cent in the number of Irish speakers. Ó Cuív's (1951: 31–32) estimate of the number of Irish speakers in the Gaeltacht areas indicates that around 1950 there were only some 35,000 persons using Irish as their daily medium of communication and no more than 3,000 monoglots. The more recent accounts reveal that there are no monoglot speakers, and the number of those who use Irish as their daily medium of communication is most probably less than 50,000 (see, e.g. Ó Danachair 1969: 118; Ó Cuív 1969a: 129–131). Despite the difficulties involved in estimating the real numbers of everyday users of Irish, the situation in the Gaeltacht areas has continued to deteriorate: Ó Murchú (1985: 29) states that "no more than 25,000 of the Gaeltacht population now use Irish consistently in day-to-day communication". Though based on the Census of Ireland as far back as 1961, Map 3.6 shows the principal concentrations of Irish speakers in the various Gaeltacht areas even at the present day.

The official figures provided by the Census of 2002 show that there was a total of 62,157 Irish speakers in all Gaeltacht areas, amounting to 72.6 per cent of the total population in these areas (source: *Census 2002—Irish Language*, Table 7A; available at http://www.cso.ie/census/documents/vol11_entire.pdf, accessed October 2006). The largest concentrations of Irish speakers were found, as before, in Galway County and Galway City (a combined total of 27,179 Irish speakers), followed by Donegal County (16,964). Mayo and Kerry were next with their Irish-speaking populations of 7,050 and 6,243, respectively. The rest were divided between Cork County (2,809), Waterford County (1,006), and Meath County (906) (*Census 2002—Irish Language*, Table 7A). While the overall figure for Irish speakers was slightly up on the 1996 total of 61,035, it does not mean that the actual level of use of the language would have risen. On the contrary, the statistics indicate that the number of those who spoke Irish on a daily basis declined from some 60 per cent in 1996 to slightly under 55 per cent in 2002 (*ibid.*, Table 34A). What is even more alarming is the result of a recent study of Gaeltacht schools, reported in *The Irish Times* (20 June 2005), according to which as many as 10 per cent of their pupils were leaving school with little or no Irish. The same study also found that the main language of conversation among pupils in the Gaeltacht schools was English.

On the other hand, it has to be remembered that Irish is increasingly learnt and used outside the *Gaeltachtaí*. The picture emerging when the whole population of the Republic of Ireland is taken into consideration varies according to the source and method of survey. Thus, on the basis of the 1981 Census of the Population as many as 31.6 per cent of the total population of 3,226,467 were returned as Irish speakers, which was slightly up from the 28.3 per cent of the previous Census in 1971 (Ó Murchú 1985: 30). By the 1996 Census, this figure had further risen to 43.5 per cent out of a total of 3,489,648 persons aged 3 years and over (*Census 1996: Principal Socio-economic Results*, Table 26).[4] The absolute numbers of Irish speakers continued to rise in the census carried out in 2002, although there was a slight drop in their relative share: now the total number of Irish speakers was 1,570,894, which constituted 41.88 per cent of the total population of

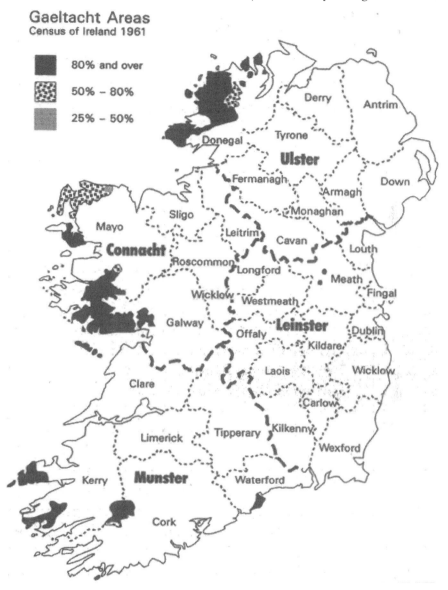

Gaeltacht Areas
Census of Ireland 1961

- 80% and over
- 50% – 80%
- 25% – 50%

Map 3.6 The Gaeltacht areas as scheduled under the Gaeltacht Areas Orders of 1956 and 1967. The different shadings indicating percentages of Irish speakers are based on the returns of the Census of Ireland 1961 (source here: Ó Cuív 1969b).

3,750,995 in the State (*Census 2002—Irish Language*, Table 1). However, as was already pointed out by Ó Murchú in his paper some 20 years ago (1985: 30), the official Census figures cannot be used as direct indicators of the real levels of use. This had become evident from an earlier report issued by the Committee on Language Attitudes in 1976, and quoted in Gregor (1980: 316); the report stated that only 9 per cent of the population of the Republic of Ireland had 'high verbal competence' in Irish. A similar picture emerges from a *Bord na Gaeilge* publication entitled *The Irish Language in a Changing Society* (no date, but evidently published in the 1980s), which surveys the various dimensions of the Irish language use and ability levels. This report concludes that about one-third of the population of the Republic has 'at least moderate bilingual competence', whereas the proportion of those who consider themselves to be 'currently active users of Irish' is only between 5 to 10 per cent, i.e. somewhere between 175,000 and 350,000 persons (*The Irish Language in a Changing Society*, p. 23). By comparison, the 2002 Census puts the figure of those who use Irish daily at 339,641, which is just over one-fifth of the total number of Irish speakers. On the other hand, the numbers of those who use Irish less than once a week or never was 1,044,057, i.e. about two-thirds of the total of Irish speakers (*Census 2002—Irish Language*, Table 31A). Furthermore, if one considers the frequency of use of Irish across age, the situation looks even bleaker from the point of view of the survival of the language: as many as 76.8 per cent of those who used Irish daily were school-children aged 5 to 19 (*Census 2002—Irish Language*, Table 33).

As a counterpoint to the gradual decline of Irish, English has gone on to secure for itself the position of the dominant language in Ireland. Yet, this has not happened without the language shift situation leaving its mark on the type(s) of English now used by the Irish people. The oft-quoted adage about Irish English (IrE) as "a mixture of the language of Shakespeare and the Irish of the Gaelic earls" seeks to capture the general make-up of this variety, which has its main roots in the language of the planters of the sixteenth and seventeenth centuries, mixed with elements brought along by the Irish shifting to English in the course of the following centuries. In his general description of IrE, Bliss (1984: 150) describes the contact-linguistic background of southern IrE (Hiberno-English in Bliss's terminology) as follows:

> In the pronunciation and vocabulary of southern Hiberno-English it is possible to trace the influence both of older strata of the English language and of the Irish language; in grammar, syntax and idiom the peculiarities of southern Hiberno-English depend exclusively on the Irish language. Even in the parts of Ireland where Irish has long been extinct its unconscious influence still controls the usage of speakers of English.

In more recent research, Bliss's account has been found to overemphasise the input from Irish grammar at the expense of other explanatory factors such as preservation of features from earlier English and the possible role of universal features of language acquisition in language-shift situations. Yet, it is hard to deny the Irish origin of a good number of the features of IrE grammar (see, e.g. Filppula 1999 for further discussion). Also, Bliss is right in attributing the Irishness of IrE mainly to the lack of formal instruction in the formative period(s) of IrE. This meant that the principal method of transmission of English was naturalistic:

> One fact is of vital importance for the history of Anglo-Irish dialects: the Irishman learning English had no opportunity of learning it from speakers of standard English. [. . .]
> Irishmen learning English, therefore, had to rely on teachers of their own race, whose own English was very different from standard English, so that there was nothing to check the progressive influence of the Irish language. In each generation the speech of the teachers was already strongly influenced by Irish, the speech of the learners even more so.
>
> (Bliss 1977: 16–17)

This is confirmed by some statistical evidence compiled by Odlin (1997a), which shows that in many rural parts of Ireland much the greater part of the population, though bilingual, were unable to read or write as late as the 1850s (Odlin 1997a: 5–6). Odlin concludes that

> [. . .] there is little support for the claim that in the mid-19th century the acquisition of English by Irish speakers resulted largely from schooling. It is even less probable that schools played a major role before that time. There were fewer schools, and for a considerable period in the 18th century the authorities often tried to enforce legislation against teaching any subject to Irish Catholics. Although the well-known "hedge schools" that arose despite such bans provided education to some Catholics, these opportunities did not affect the majority of schoolchildren.
>
> (Odlin 1997a: 6)

The Irish input to IrE varies from one region to another, depending mainly on various historical reasons. Among these, the most important one is a north–south divide, which goes back to the plantation period. At the turn of the sixteenth and seventeenth centuries, a revolt by the Irish in Ulster was followed by systematic plantation, which introduced a large Scottish population into Ulster and left a significant Scots imprint on the dialects of the northern and especially north-eastern parts of Ireland. Because of the Scots influence, Ulster dialects differ substantially from those of the rest of the country even today. This division is also manifest in the terms used for the

Englishes in the north and south of Ireland. (Southern) 'Irish English' (IrE), 'Hiberno-English' (HE), and 'Anglo-Irish' (AI), depending on the author, are generally the labels used for the southern dialects, which are the least Scots-influenced, but with heavier input from Irish, whereas 'Ulster Scots' (U.Sc.) represents the most Scots-influenced variety, with marginal input from Irish. 'Ulster English' (UE) is then the general term for the various 'transition dialects' between U.Sc. and southern IrE.

3.5   OTHER REGIONS

3.5.1   Cornwall

As George (1993: 410) points out, the Cornish language emerged at around AD 600, after the ancient links between the Celtic (Late British) speaking populations in Cornwall and Wales had been severed, and the south-western dialect of Late British began to develop independently. However, the retreat of the language was evident practically at the same time as Cornish was developing into a separate language. Throughout the Middle Ages, the Cornish language thrived in Cornwall; a flourishing literature in Cornish existed during the Middle Cornish period (1200–1575), with mystery plays in Cornish being performed in a large number of open-air theatres in mid and west Cornwall (George 1993: 413).

The decline of the language began in earnest during the sixteenth century, with the Reformation often identified as a major cause of the relatively rapid process of language death (George 1993: 413). As Soulsby (1986: 75) notes, the existence of monoglot Cornish speakers during the sixteenth century is confirmed by Andrew Boorde, who observed in his *Fyrst Boke of the Introduction of knowledge* (1542) that "[i]n Cornwall is two speches: the one is naughty Englysshe, and the other is Cornysshe speche. And there may be many men and women the whiche cannot speake one worde of Englysshe, but all Cornysshe".

However, already during the sixteenth century bilingualism was widespread even in west Cornwall, as the following report from an ecclesiastical court case at Lelant from 1572 reveals: "the wife of Morrysh David called Agnes Davey 'whore and whore bitch' in English and not in Cornowok".

From the sixteenth century onwards the decline of Cornish was rapid. Soulsby (1986: 75) notes that the performances of the miracle plays ceased during the seventeenth century, and bilingualism was widespread even in the west of Cornwall. In 1662 John Ray observes in his *Itinerary* that "few of the children could speak Cornish, so that the language is like, in a short time, to be quite lost" (Ray 1760: 281). Indeed, it was only a matter of time before the pressure of English became too overwhelming for Cornish to survive. Figure 3.2, drawn on the basis of the information given in George (1993: 415), illustrates the retreat of the Cornish language from the year 1000 onwards (cf. also Map 1.2 in Chapter 1).

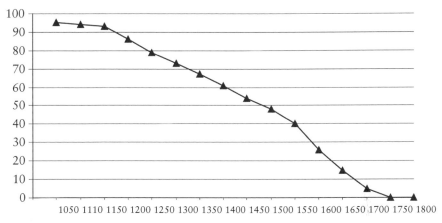

Figure 3.2 Estimated percentage of population speaking Cornish in Cornwall (1050–1800). (Based on the data given in Table 9.1 in George 1993: 415.)

Dolly Pentreath (d. 1777) from the village of Mousehole, is often referred to as the last native speaker of Cornish (cf. Thomas 1984b). In all likelihood, however, the Cornish language survived a little longer. Spriggs (2003) lists a number of contemporary sources that document the gradual demise of Cornish and advance of English in Cornwall from 949 onwards. The last quotation in Spriggs's collection comes from C.S. Gilbert's *An Historical Survey of the County of Cornwall* (1817), where the last speaker of Cornish is identified as William Matthews, who died in the year 1800:

> William Matthews, of Newlyn, near Penzance, who died there about thirty years ago [c.1786], also spoke the Cornish language later and much more fluently than Dolly Pentreath. His son, William Matthews, was also well acquainted with it; he died in the same village about the year 1800.

Although there have been a number of attempts to identify Cornish speakers during the nineteenth century, it is safe to say that by 1800 the Cornish language was no longer used as a means of communication.[5] Soulsby (1986: 76) quotes R. Morton Nance stating that "we must accept 1800 as being about the very latest date at which anyone really spoke Cornish traditionally, as even the remnant of a living language, all traditional Cornish since then having been learned parrot-wise from those of an earlier generation".

However, from the beginning of the twentieth century onwards there have been various attempts to revive Cornish. Though it is as yet mainly used for some ceremonial functions, there are now small communities of enthusiasts in Cornwall who try to promote the teaching and use of 'Revived Cornish' in schools and on all kinds of social occasions.[6] The inclusion of Cornish in the European Charter for Regional or Minority Languages, recognised by the United Kingdom in 2001, has recently given further impetus to the revival of Cornish. The recognition gives Cornish the status of a regional language within the European Union.

The English dialect of Cornwall, Cornish English, is generally considered to show but few traces of the Cornish substratum; these are mainly to be found in its vocabulary. In fact, some scholars argue that the main influence on Cornish English has come from sixteenth- and seventeenth-century Standard English rather than Cornish (see, e.g. Wakelin 1984b: 195), but there are others who would like to see the traditional dialect of the westernmost areas of Cornwall, in particular, as a repository of features going back to the old Cornish substratum (for discussion, see Payton 1997).

3.5.2   The Isle of Man

The nature and outcome of the language contact in Man between the Manx language and English is very similar to that of Cornish and English, although in this case the indigenous Celtic language survived much longer: tradition has it that the last native speaker of Manx, a man by the name of Ned Maddrell, died as late as in 1974, but as Broderick (1997: 123) states, Manx as a living community language did not survive beyond the beginning of the twentieth century.

According to Broderick's (1999) detailed description of the language situation and its history in Man, the process of anglicisation of Man goes back to the late seventeenth century and the aftermath of the collapse of Cromwell's 'Commonwealth'. The appointment of Isaac Barrow as Bishop (1663–1671) marked the beginning of the first systematic efforts to introduce the English language into Man. This took place in the form of a parish school system, which was followed by the setting-up of a grammar school in Castletown in 1676, aimed at those Manx children who wanted to go into higher learning. Though not successful at first, Bishop Barrow's educational programme was resumed at the beginning of the eighteenth century, when penal measures were adopted to force parents to send their children to school to learn English, among other things. Even this scheme failed to reach the objectives set for it, and by 1736 the education system was in a state of bad decline. In fact, Manx was reinstituted as the language of education, first, in a small number of schools, but by 1766, in all but one parish in Man. This was largely due to the efforts of Bishop Mark Hildesley (1755–1772), who was a great supporter of the Manx language. However, after his death the Anglican church withdrew its support for Manx, and the situation changed rapidly in favour of English. By 1782, there were only five schools in the Island which continued to use Manx as their medium of instruction. Although there were some attempts by private religious organisations to continue teaching the Holy Scriptures through Manx, the advance of English gathered momentum in the nineteenth century. Broderick (1999) quotes a number of contemporary sources which give a clear indication of the gradual demise of Manx and dominance of English. The following is a passage from a letter sent by Bishop Murray in 1825, in which he states that "[t]here is no longer any necessity for impressions of the Bible and the Book of Common Prayer in the Manks Tongue; but that in the English Tongue they are much wanted, and sought after with great avidity" (quoted from Broderick 1999: 18).

Another extract quoted by Broderick was written in 1859 by William Gill, editor of an earlier published practical grammar of Manx. Here he expresses, in colourful words, his concern about the decline of Manx:

> The decline of the spoken Manx, within the memory of the present generation, has been marked. The language is no longer heard in our courts of law, either from the bench or the bar, and seldom from the witness-box. [. . .] In the schools throughout the Island the Manx has ceased to be taught; and the introduction of the Government system of education has done much to displace the language. It is rarely now heard in conversation, except among the peasantry. It is a doomed language,—an iceberg floating into southern latitudes.

> (Gill 1859: v; here quoted from Broderick 1999: 26)

The "introduction of the Government system of education" mentioned in the above quotation took place in 1858, but it was not until 1872 that the Manx authorities implemented compulsory schooling for children aged 5 to 13 years. Though not specifically laid down in the English Education Act of 1870, the language of instruction was from that date on to be English (Broderick 1999: 22). Add to this the growing numbers of non–Manx-speaking immigrants and tourists brought to Man by the significant growth of trade and tourism in the latter half of the nineteenth century, and the fate of Manx was sealed. Despite some families who raised their children in Manx as late as the 1870s and 1880s, English was almost universally perceived as a necessary 'means of advancement in life', as Broderick puts it (*op.cit.*, 22). This in turn precipitated the eventual extinction of Manx as a community language around the turn of the century; by the end of the first half of the twentieth century there were only a handful 'terminal' speakers left, with the last reputed speaker of Manx, Ned Maddrell, dying on 27 December 1974 (Broderick 1999: 44).

The official census enumerations from 1871 up to 1971, given in Figure 3.3, also reveal the rapid decrease in the numbers of Manx speakers in the last couple of decades of the nineteenth century and in the early part of the following century. Note that the 1981 Census no longer sought information on the knowledge of the Manx language, because by that time there were no native speakers left.

As in Cornwall, the once-defunct language has been brought back to life through the efforts of Manx enthusiasts. Manx is now being taught

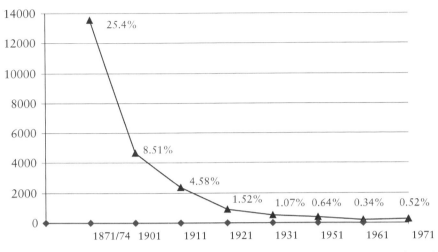

Figure 3.3 Diagram showing the decrease in Manx speakers 1871–1971 (adapted from Broderick 1999: 42).

in schools and evening classes, and it continues to live as a resuscitated medium of communication for a notable number of people in Man. This is also reflected in the most recent census enumerations, which after a break of 20 years again include questions about Manx: thus, the 1991 Census returned a total of 741 persons who can speak and/or read and/or write Manx Gaelic (Broderick 1999: 183). Note, however, that these figures include both those who can be considered fluent speakers and those who have a few phrases only. Also, it has to be borne in mind that for all of them Manx is a language learnt through tuition rather than acquired 'naturally' in the home (Broderick 1999: 185).

Not surprisingly, the traditional dialect of English spoken in Man, called Manx English (MxE) or 'Anglo-Manx' (in some of the early works), exhibits a large amount of features derived from the Manx substratum and is in many ways similar to the Hiberno-English of Ireland (see, e.g. Gill 1934; Barry 1984; Broderick 1997; Preuß 1999). However, as Barry (1984: 167–168) notes, MxE also displays many influences from traditional Lancashire dialect. This is explained by the rise of the tourism and other trade links with Fleetwood and Liverpool in the nineteenth century. Barry refers here to the account of MxE by Ellis (1889), who, however, "may have overstated the similarities with Lancashire dialect and understated the Celtic substratum" (Barry 1984: 168). Essentially similar descriptions are to be found in later studies, which include Wright (1905) and Gill (1934). Barry detects some traces of Manx influence in the spoken language data he collected for *The Survey of English Dialects* in the 1950s and 1960s. These include some phonological and syntactic features, as well as a few hundred lexical borrowings from Manx Gaelic. However, traditional MxE dialect has, all in all, suffered the same fate as Manx Gaelic, having been largely supplanted by the ever-growing influence from the Liverpool area in the latter half of the twentieth century (Barry, *op.cit.*, 168).

Broderick's (1997) description of MxE, based mainly on extensive sound-recorded materials collected by the author in 1989–1992, concurs in the main with that of Barry (1984). Besides phonology, he discusses a number of syntactic features that are evidently modelled on Manx Gaelic, and most of which are also found in IrE. The input from other dialects, especially those spoken in the north and north-west of England as well as Scotland, are also dealt with. Apart from these grammatical influences, Manx Gaelic has left its mark on the vocabulary of traditional MxE.

Preuß (1999) must also be mentioned as one of the very few works on MxE that are based on fieldwork. She adds several syntactic features to the accounts of the earlier authors, many of which underline the similarities between MxE, HebE and IrE, thus providing further evidence of Celtic substratal influence on these varieties.

4 The Linguistic Outcomes of the Modern Contacts

4.1   INTRODUCTION

This chapter will focus mainly on contact effects as they are evidenced in regional varieties of English spoken in present-day or formerly Celtic-speaking areas and in some neighbouring dialects. Although it seems hard to ascertain similar influences in standard or 'mainstream' varieties of English, it is quite possible that certain features of the latter have at least indirectly been influenced or reinforced by their Celtic counterparts—mostly mediated through the millions of speakers of Celtic-influenced varieties who have emigrated to England or further afield to America, Australia and other parts of the world. Some of these features are familiar from the earliest contacts; such are, e.g., the English progressive form and the cleft construction. Both have steadily increased their frequencies of use in most mainstream varieties of the modern period, and they have also greatly expanded their originally rather narrow domains of use (see section 4.2 for further discussion). On the other hand, there are features which were on the verge of demise in mediaeval English, but which have been given a new lease of life in the modern period. Such is, e.g. the so-called medial-object or conclusive perfect (see 4.2). Since all of these are robust features of the various 'Celtic Englishes' (CEs), the possibility of continuing direct or indirect input from the Celtic substrata, or alternatively, *via* the Celtic-influenced varieties of English, will also have to be considered and weighed against other competing hypotheses (see section 4.2 for further discussion).

Phonological contact influences in the modern period appear to be similarly restricted to the regional varieties. While there are no references in the literature to such influences on Standard English (StE), the situation is quite different in studies on the CEs: they abound in phonological and prosodic features which are arguably derived from the corresponding Celtic substrata. These will be discussed in section 4.3. Lexis presents a similar picture: as in the earliest periods of contact, a relatively small number of Celtic items can be shown to have been borrowed into StE, but again, the various CEs and some of their neighbouring regional dialects provide a rich source of words originating in one or the other of the Celtic languages. They will be the topic of discussion in section 4.4.

4.2   GRAMMAR

This section is organised in a rather traditional way around three major headings. The first two subsume features which pertain to the noun phrase and the verb phrase, both understood here in a syntactic rather than morphosyntactic sense. The third subsection looks at features which operate at the levels of the 'simple' and 'complex' sentences, respectively. As in the previous subsections, the emphasis is on the syntactic aspects of these structures. This also applies to prepositional usage, many aspects of which can be argued to have been influenced by the syntax of the Celtic substrata.

4.2.1   The Noun Phrase

Our discussion here concentrates on just two areas of the syntax of the noun phrase in the various CEs and in some dialects of English English (EngE) which on the basis of earlier studies and our own research arguably have a Celtic connection. Note, however, that the possible Celtic influence need not necessarily be of the direct substratal type but may equally be of the reinforcing one; in other words, a structure or a pattern which has parallels in both Celtic and English has been promoted to an even more prominent position in these regional varieties because of the 'double' input in the contact situation. In yet other cases the contacts may have been of the adstratal type, in which case it is impossible to ascertain the direction of the influences or the exact source of the feature in question.

4.2.1.1   *Definite Article Usage*

We will focus here on some usages of the definite article which are shared not only by the CEs but also by some EngE dialects. To begin with, in their survey of dialectal English grammar Edwards and Weltens (1985: 118) list Ireland, Scotland, N. England, S. Wales and S.W. England as dialect areas in which the definite article is used where StE would require a possessive adjective, an indefinite article or no determiner at all. Similar observations have been made in the linguistic literature early on (see, e.g. Wright 1896–1905; Joyce 1910/1988). It is noteworthy that most studies single out Irish English (IrE), Welsh English (WE), Hebridean English (HebE), and Manx English (MxE) as the 'core' of those varieties that make much freer use of the definite article than other regional varieties spoken in the British Isles, not to mention StE (see, esp. Sabban 1982 on HebE; Bliss 1984 and Filppula 1999 on IrE; Parry 1999 on WE; Preuß 1999 on MxE). Contexts in which nonstandard usages of the definite article occur in these varieties include, most notably:[1]

- names of social institutions: *be at the school/in the hospital; go to the church*;
- names of ailments and (unpleasant) physical sensations or states: *have the toothache/the headache*;
- quantifying expressions involving *most/both* (when followed by *of*) or *all*: *the most/both of them; all the day*.
- names of languages: *learn the English/the Gaelic*.

All are strikingly similar to the corresponding Celtic usages, but parallels can, to varying degrees, be found in other dialects of English, especially in Scottish English (ScE) and Scots (see, e.g. Miller 1993), and in some cases, in earlier varieties of 'mainstream' English. The Scottish varieties may, however, have adopted at least part of these usages from Scottish Gaelic, as is suggested, for example, in *The Scottish National Dictionary* (*SND*) with respect to names of languages (*SND* s.v. *the* 5.(3); see also Filppula 1999, section 5.2).

As for earlier English parallels, neither Mustanoja's (1960) nor Jespersen's (MEG VII) thorough accounts mention the use of the definite article with names of languages, physical sensations and states, or the names of social or domestic institutions, which can be taken to mean that the definite article did not occur in these contexts in Middle English (ME). Jespersen does, however, refer to the use of the definite article before some names of diseases, which in earlier English "were regularly used with the definite article, some of them still being so in popular (rather low-class) language, e.g. the flu, the itch, the pip, etc." (Jespersen MEG VII: § 14.47). Yet the fact that variation existed for some names of diseases does not change the overall absence from earlier forms of English of the set of usages described above.

Apart from the usages illustrated above, there are others which have a slightly more restricted geographical distribution. For example, the following have been found to be characteristic of the Irish and Scottish dialects (see the above-mentioned sources), in particular:

- names of feasts, e.g. *over the Christmas*;
- concrete mass and collective nouns, e.g. *I don' know when the coffee came*;
- abstract nouns, e.g. *turn to the drink; starve with the hunger*;
- expressions denoting emotive emphasis, especially eulogy and admiration (or their opposites), e.g. *That's the grand morning; You are the pig!*;
- quantifying expressions involving *half*, e.g. *the half of it*.

Although these do not appear to be used (to the same extent at least) in WE dialects, occasional examples occur in *The Survey of Anglo-Welsh*

Dialects (SAWD) data and in a corpus of speech collected from Llandybie, Carmarthenshire:

(1)   [From milk, you know, the products that you *>can get . . .]
      Oh from *the milk?*<*
      [the thing that you do with milk in the old days?] Cream.
      [What about*>other . . .]
      (In?)<* the top of the milk you mean? (SAWD: Gn 8: 1)

(2)   Well, parents are workin' an' I suppose they just say, you know, have your—go to a fish shop an' have . . . *The life* is totally different. (Wales, Llandybie: E.A.)

A third group of nonstandard usages is formed by patterns which are also found in other varieties of English to varying degrees, but which appear to be particularly characteristic of, and also more frequent in Irish, Scottish, Welsh, and also northern EngE dialects. Examples of these are:

- names of seasons, e.g. *in the summer*;
- units of measurements in a distributive sense, e.g. *twice the week*;
- branches of learning, arts and trades, e.g. *be good at the history*;
- names of diseases, e.g. *the whooping cough, the polio*;
- members of the family, e.g. *. . . the mother was all for the British*;
- parts of the day, e.g. *twelve o'clock in the night*;
- trades or general activities, e.g. *America is a better country in that line of the labouring*;
- expressions denoting body parts, e.g. *. . . and they nearly took the head off him*.

To turn back to the question of Celtic influence on the kinds of usages illustrated above, differing positions can be found in previous research. For the earliest writers like Joyce (1910/1988), the Irish substratum is the self-evident source for the peculiarities of IrE article usage, as can be seen from the following statement:

In Irish there is only one article, *an*, which is equivalent to the English definite article *the*. This article (*an*) is much more freely used in Irish than *the* is in English, a practice which we are inclined to imitate in our Anglo-Irish speech.

(Joyce 1910/1988: 82)

Indeed, a comparison between the uses of the definite article in the mentioned varieties of English and the Celtic languages conducted by Filppula (1999, section 5.2) reveals an almost one-to-one match, which he considers to support the role of Celtic substratum influence. However, others have adopted a more cautious stand. For example, in her description of the English of the Hebrides, Sabban (1982: 381) first notes the tendency for 'contact-English' (i.e. HebE) to insert the definite article in contexts in which it would not be used in StE. She also points out parallel usages in ScE, in some northern EngE dialects and in 'Anglo-Irish' (i.e. IrE). However, as regards the role of the Celtic substratum in the Hebridean context, Sabban hesitates to draw any conclusions one way or the other. Having discussed the use of the definite article before names of languages and having noted the Gaelic and ScE parallels, she states that, in the end, it is not possible to prove Gaelic influence on the HebE usage (Sabban 1982: 397). This statement can be taken to reflect Sabban's general position on the origins of the other HebE usages of the definite article as well.

However, the Celtic substratum hypothesis receives considerable support from the findings of *The Survey of English Dialects (SED)*, which show that, although some of the nonstandard usages illustrated above extend to a number of the northernmost dialects of EngE, they are either not found or are much scarcer in the southern dialects. This is the case, for example, with the geographical distribution of the variants for Item S 5: VIII.5.1 *They go to church*, as presented in Viereck (1991). The responses to this item show that the definite expression *to the church* is used predominantly in the northern counties of Lancashire, Yorkshire, Northumberland, Cumberland and Westmorland. Sabban (1982: 384–385) has calculated that the definite article was recorded in 52 per cent of the responses from these northern areas, while it was virtually nonexistent in the other, more southern, areas. The responses to Item S 6: VIII.6.1: *They go to school* in Viereck (1991) show an almost identical distribution for the variant with definite article. This confirms the mainly northern and western (including Wales, Ireland and Scotland) provenance of these usages and thus lends indirect support to the Celtic substratum hypothesis.

Matters are not, however, so straightforward when the usages of the definite article are considered from a wider, 'global', perspective. Thus, the recent *Handbook of Varieties of English (HVE)* survey found 'irregular use of articles' to be one of the most frequently occurring morphosyntactic features among the World Englishes, being attested in 33 out of the 46 varieties included in the survey (see Kortmann and Szmrecsanyi 2004: 1154–1155). On the other hand, the questionnaire on this point did not focus on the use of the definite article alone but also contained examples with no article or with the indefinite article instead of the definite one. More relevant to the present issue, Sand (2003) is another study to bring to light usages of the definite article that are more or less similar to those in the CEs, e.g. in Indian English, Singapore English, Jamaican English, and in some cases, in American English, too. Her examples from these varieties include the following:

(3)   *The most* of the schools are English medium . . . (India, student essay; cited in Sand 2003: 422)

(4)   Now *the tinnitus* is usually coming because of some disturbance in the middle and the inner part of the ear. (Jamaica, radio phone-in; cited in Sand 2003: 424)

(5)   . . ., she was sentenced for fifteen years in *the jail*. (Singapore; cited in Sand 2003: 425)

The presence of these features in these varieties leads Sand to question the role of Celtic substratal influences in IrE, which is her point of focus in the above-mentioned work. Instead, she seeks to explain the nonstandard usages as a result of one or the other of the following factors: application of universal features of definiteness (such as the so-called Animacy Hierarchy), inherent variation in article use, or the extension of the StE rules. Since these factors could, according to her, explain the IrE usages, there would be no need to have recourse to the Irish substratum (Sand 2003: 430).

The fact that many of the above-mentioned usages are found in 'New Englishes' in widely different settings lends some support to these 'universalist' lines of argumentation, but hardly suffices to eliminate the role of substratal influences in the Irish, Welsh or Scottish varieties. Rather than by the 'overuse' of the definite article as in CEs, the 'New Englishes' mentioned by Sand are characterised by a shift from the definite/indefinite distinction (as in StE) to the specific/nonspecific one, affecting the way articles are used. More specifically, this leads to omission of the indefinite article with non-specific referents and to the use of *one/this/these/that/those/the* with specific ones (see, e.g. Platt, Weber and Ho 1984: 52–59). Writing on the same feature of what she terms 'non-native institutionalised varieties of English' instead of 'New Englishes', Williams (1987: 166–167) approaches the matter from the point of view of general aspects of second-language acquisition. She speaks of the "inherent vulnerability of English" with respect to article usage, and goes on to state that articles are a frequent area of difficulty for second-language learners of English and therefore subject to variability or modification. Relevant as these considerations may be to the case of the CEs as well, it is significant that the kind of tendency observed by Platt *et al.* (1984) is not typical of IrE or the other CEs.

It is also fair to ask that, if, indeed, the CE usages described above are universal in nature, why should they occur in just some varieties and not in others, and even if some of the usages are shared, why should they be clearly more frequent in some as compared with others? What the universalist account also fails to explain is the fact that there is a fairly clearly defined set of nonstandard usages in some, but not all nonstandard varieties of English. In the case of the CEs, this set is closely paralleled by the definite article usages in the relevant Celtic languages. This can hardly be coincidental. It seems clear to us that in each linguistic setting there must have been some factors determining the choice of, or preference for, one or the other variant. In the context of the British Isles and Ireland, it is hard to escape the conclusion that the existence of close parallels in the Celtic substratum languages must have constituted one of the factors promoting the use of the definite article in certain well-defined contexts. This is supported by the geographical distribution of the usages discussed above: it cannot be satisfactorily explained as being only a reflex of some universal properties of definiteness any more than as a result of mere inherent variation in article usage or as extensions of the StE rules. Furthermore, as the discussion in the following sections will show, the CEs share many other syntactic features, not all of which are found in other varieties of English.

4.2.1.2   'Absolute' Uses of the Reflexive Pronouns

The term 'absolute' refers here to those uses of the reflexive pronouns where they occur 'on their own', without the usual anaphoric reference to an antecedent in the same clause or sentence. Syntactically, an absolute reflexive can occur in subject position, object position or as prepositional complement in adverbial prepositional phrases. Some examples from ScE, HebE and IrE are given in (6) to (9). Notice, too, that the reflexive in this function can occur in all persons.

(6)   Is that *yoursel'*, Mr Balfour? (ScE; cited in Macafee and Ó Baoill 1997: 271)

(7)   I used to say to him, "You be careful about that money you've got, I'm sure it's *myself* that will get it after you." (HebE; cited in Filppula 1999: 85)

(8)   And by God, he said, [. .] he'd be the devil, if *himself* wouldn' make him laugh. (IrE; cited in Filppula 1999: 78)

(9)   . . and he thought he'd have a few wrastles [wrestles] with the bull before he'd go to bed. He went in the field, and *himself* and the bull were tuggin' and wrastlin'. (IrE; cited in Filppula 1999: 80)

This feature is commented on in the survey by Edwards and Weltens (1985: 116), who record the use of what they term 'emphatic pronouns' in IrE but not in other dialects. Terminological matters aside, this feature differs from many others discussed in this chapter in that its geographical distribution is, indeed, more restricted: in its 'full-blown' form, it is attested only in Scottish and Irish dialects but not, on the basis of our data, in WE or in conservative EngE dialects. It is true that the recent survey carried out for the HVE found the 'nonreflexive' use of first-person *myself/meself* to be among some of the most widely distributed features in the world's Englishes. However, the survey questionnaire focused on just one type of context, viz. that of conjoined subjects and on the first person, the example sentence being *My/me husband and myself* (see Kortmann and Szmrecsanyi 2004: 1146; 1154–1155). As mentioned above, there is no such constraint on the CE usages, which occur in a wide range of syntactic contexts and are not confined to the first person. What is more, the normal ordering of elements in conjoined subjects with reflexive pronouns is the opposite in these varieties, as is shown by Odlin (1997b) for HebE and by Filppula (1999: 84–85) for both IrE and HebE (witness the example in [9] above).

There is evidence to show that the absolute uses of reflexive pronouns in Irish and Scottish varieties of English have a Celtic background. Besides close parallels in the Celtic languages, the geographical distribution supports the substratum hypothesis. Writing on the origins of absolute reflexives in HebE, Sabban (1982: 378) concludes that their use is modelled on the Scots Gaelic parallel rather than that of earlier English, which also provides at least partial parallels to this feature. Besides the Gaelic parallel and certain kinds of restrictions on the earlier English constructions which distinguish them from the HebE ones, she mentions that 'non-emphatic' uses of reflexives (i.e. absolute reflexives) in subject position were recorded in Uist from very old speakers, whose English was not very good. The Gaelic hypothesis receives further support from Macafee and Ó Baoill (1997: 271), who ascribe similar Scots uses of absolute reflexives to early influence from Gaelic, which is known to have made use of the emphasising forms with *féin* as early as the eighth century.

The substratal background of absolute reflexives is also vindicated by some qualitative features of IrE and HebE reflexives. Thus, Odlin (1997b) notes that reflexives can in these varieties occur on their own in the focus position of clefts in the same way as their Irish and Scottish Gaelic counterparts. He illustrates the parallelism between the HebE and Scottish Gaelic constructions through the following examples (cf. also the HebE example in [7] above):

(10) And it's himself that told me that up in a pub. (SA 1970/105B/
     Tiree: H.K.; cited in Odlin 1997b: 39)

(11) agus 's e   fhéin a   bh'ann.
     and is him self   that was in-it
     'It was himself that was there.' (SA 1970/109/A/Tiree: H.K.; cited
     in Odlin 1997b: 39)

On the basis of the syntactic similarity between the IrE, HebE and the corresponding Celtic constructions, Odlin (1997b) defends the case for substratum influence on both IrE and HebE. Having assessed the possible superstratal origin for the kind of cleft structures in (10) in Lowland Scots and Early Modern English (EModE), and more specifically, in Shakespeare's language, Odlin concludes that the weight of the evidence favours the substratum hypothesis for two main reasons. First, his study of all of Shakespeare's works yielded only two instances of this structure. Secondly, absolute reflexives in both HebE and IrE share some other qualitative features which evidently derive from the Celtic substrata, e.g. the order of conjoined subjects (see the discussion above).

To this it could be added that we found no instances of absolute reflexives in the focus position of clefts in the EModE part of the *Helsinki Corpus*. However, there were sporadic occurrences of other types of absolute reflexives in EModE texts, especially first-person uses (see Filppula 1999: 84–87). This leaves open the possibility of converging adstratal influences between the Celtic languages, earlier 'mainstream' English, and the dialects of English which have evolved in Scotland and Ireland.

4.2.2   The Verb Phrase

The most important features to be discussed under this heading involve the tense-mood-aspect (TMA) systems in one way or another. This comes as no surprise in view of the common observation that TMA systems are particularly prone to contact effects under conditions of long-term language contact or shift. The discussion below will begin with certain distinctive uses of the so-called progressive form of verbs. These will be followed by a discussion of various types of perfects, which also mark off most of the CEs from their neighbouring dialects.

4.2.2.1   *The 'Progressive' Form of Verbs*

A striking feature of Irish, Scottish and Welsh varieties of English is the general use of the 'progressive' or 'expanded' form of verbs (henceforth PF) in contexts where StE and most other mainstream varieties would prefer the simple present tense or past tense form.[2] First of all, the PF can be used with *stative* verbs (or, to be more exact, with verbs used in the stative sense), such as verbs of 'cognition', 'emotion', 'inert perception' and 'stance', as well as 'relational' verbs of 'being' and 'having'. The following examples from IrE, HebE, MxE and WE illustrate these usages:

(12)   There was a lot about fairies long ago [. . .] but I'*m thinkin'* that most of 'em are vanished.
'. . . but I think/believe that most of them have vanished.' (IrE; cited in Filppula 1999: 89)

(13)   I think two of the lads was lost at sea during the War. They *were belonging* to the, them men here. (IrE; cited in Filppula 2003: 162)

(14) No, people don't need the weather like what they did then—they *were depending* on the weather.
'. . . they depended on the weather.' (HebE; cited in Sabban 1982: 276)

(15) And the people then *were having* plenty of potatoes and meal of their own. (HebE; cited in Sabban 1982: 275)

(16) It *was meaning* right the opposite. (MxE; cited in Preuß 1999: 111)

(17) They're *calling* her a jouishag. (MxE; cited in Preuß 1999: 111)

(18) I'm *not thinking* much of it.
'I'm not impressed by it.' (WE; cited in Parry 1999: 111)

Secondly, the PF is commonly used in these varieties with dynamic verbs to express present or past *habitual* activities or states of affairs:

(19) [. . .] but there ,, there's no bogland here now.
[Interviewer: Yeah. = And do people go up there to cut turf?]
They *were going* there long ago but the roads got the . . like everything else . . they got a bit too-o rich and [. . .]. (IrE; cited in Filppula 2003: 162)

(20) I remember my grandfather and old people that lived down the road here, they *be* all *walking* over to the chapel of a Sunday afternoon and they *be going* again at night. (MxE; cited in Preuß 1999: 112)

(21) [Interviewer: How, if you want to know how heavy a thing is, *>you must . . .]
Yes, yes,<* we are—we *are takin'* it to the barn to weigh them. (WE; cited in Paulasto 2006: 219)

Thirdly, the PF frequently combines with the auxiliaries *would/'d/used [to]* to indicate habitual activity. In other regional varieties of the British Isles Englishes, the simple infinitive is clearly preferred in these contexts (see the discussion below). The following are IrE examples of this usage:

(22) So, when the young lads'd *be going* to bathing, like, they'd have to go by his house, and they used to all, he u', he loved children. (IrE; cited in Filppula 2003: 163)

(23) But they, I heard my father and uncle saying they *used be dancing* there long ago, like, you know. (IrE; cited in Filppula 2003: 163)

Fourthly, the PF can, depending on the variety, also be used with other auxiliaries, such as *do/does* and *will/'ll*. The former, exemplified in (24), is restricted to the Irish dialects of English, where it is used to express habitual events or states, while the latter, illustrated in (25), is common in other varieties, too, including StE and other 'mainstream' Englishes. Its main function is to denote some future events or states.

(24)   Yeah, that's, that's the camp. Military camp they call it [. . .]
        They *do be shooting* there couple of times a week or so.
        (Wicklow: D.M.)

(25)   [T]his fellow now, Jack Lynch, that's going to come into power
        now, that he'll, he*'ll be forgetting* the North. (Wicklow: M.K.)

Filppula (2002) finds that there are differences between varieties of British English and IrE in the frequencies of constructions which combine a modal auxiliary with the pattern *be + V-ing*. In Table 4.1 below, data from a WE corpus (Llandybie, Carmarthenshire) have been added to the figures presented in the mentioned work. The figures include instances of the PF occurring after the so-called central modal auxiliaries and the marginal modals *dare/need/ought/used to*.[3]

The main trends emerging from Table 4.1 are clear: the frequencies of the PF after auxiliaries are clearly greater in IrE (north and south) and HebE than in the varieties of EngE investigated here, whether earlier or present-day ones. Needless to say, the EModE corpus is not directly comparable with the spoken corpora, but the figures may still be suggestive of the situation at that stage. The WE corpus appears to fall in between in this respect, although Paulasto (2006) shows that it contains far more frequent use of the simple habitual PF than EngE.

In a more specific vein, Table 4.2 provides the frequencies of the modal auxiliaries *would/'d* or *used (to)* followed by *be V-ing* in the same corpora.

Table 4.1 Frequencies of the pattern *be V-ing* in the Englishes of the British Isles and Ireland.

	N	N/10,000 words
IrE	254	5.3
HebE	103	5.8
WE	12	1.9
EngE	98	1.4
EModE	7	0.1

Table 4.2 Frequencies of the pattern *would/'d*
or *used (to)* followed by *be V-ing* in the
corpora investigated.

	N	N/10,000 words
IrE	148	3.1
HebE	42	3.0
WE	5	0.8
EngE	47	0.7
EModE	7	0.1

As was mentioned above, this combination is commonly used in some varieties to express habitual activities.

The overall pattern emerging from Table 4.2 is very similar to that in Table 4.1, with IrE and HebE displaying higher frequencies than the EngE varieties. The WE figures seem to be close to the EngE ones, but note that there is a certain amount of intradialectal variation in WE here: in interviews from the south-east Welsh Valleys, picked out from the corpus of Ceri George (see George 1990), the use of habitual modals with the PF is very frequent, at 11.0 instances per 10,000 words. Paulasto (2006) therefore concludes that these kinds of constructions are not as characteristic of Welsh heartland English as of varieties of WE where English has been transmitted informally and where the propensity for merging StE and nonstandard means of marking habitual action is therefore higher (see below).

The prominence of the above-mentioned usages in the Irish and some Scottish and Welsh varieties of English naturally raises the question of Celtic substratum influence. Generally speaking, the relevant Celtic languages have grammaticalised what has sometimes been called 'progressive syntax' (see, e.g. Isaac 2003a) to a much greater extent than English, utilising a type of periphrastic construction consisting of the verb 'be' followed by a preposition + verbal noun. However, it should be noted that the Celtic substratum is not completely uniform here. As Isaac (2003a: 62) notes, the Celtic languages differ with respect to their degree of use of 'progressive syntax'. For instance, what Isaac terms 'epistemic' verbs, including *I know, I believe, I think, I feel, I understand,* all use the periphrastic form in Welsh (*Wi'n gwybod, Wi'n credu, Wi'n meddwl, Wi'n teimlo, Wi'n deall*), though not in Irish (*op.cit.,* 62). On the other hand, Scottish Gaelic has grammaticalised the periphrastic form for most of these verbs. Despite these variations, the similarities between the IrE, HebE and WE usages described above and the corresponding Celtic usages are, generally speaking, striking enough to suggest a considerable degree of substratal influence from the Celtic languages upon the CEs.

Besides the slightly differing usages among the Celtic languages, another factor complicating the issue is the general increase in the rates of use of the PF in many 'mainstream' varieties of English, including even StE, from the EModE period onwards. This has been accompanied by the relaxation of some of the semantic constraints on its use (see, e.g. Elsness 1994; Mair and Hundt 1995). In American English (AmE), this tendency appears to be even more pronounced than in British English (see, e.g. Śmiecińska 2002–2003). However, a possible explanation for this may well be the significant input to AmE from the speech of the millions of Irish immigrants and others from the Celtic-speaking regions in Scotland and Wales over the last couple of centuries. In the context of Britain, one should also consider the impetus deriving from the vast numbers of Irish immigrants to Britain in the nineteenth century, in particular (see, e.g. Crépin 1978; Poppe 2003).

Yet another factor to be reckoned with in this matter is the prominent use of the PF in some English-based creoles and various African and Asian varieties of English, as pointed out, e.g. by Williams (1987) and Gachelin (1997). This adds an interesting universalist perspective to the problem at hand. In fact, Gachelin suggests that the high incidence of the PF in all these varieties has turned it semantically into a 'general imperfective', which will probably lead to a further 'devaluation' of the PF, making it less and less sensitive to contextual constraints. Indeed, it is his prediction that the generalisation of the PF will be one of the characteristics of future 'World English' (Gachelin 1997: 43–44). In a similar vein, Mesthrie (2004) notes that the use of the PF with stative verbs is so widespread in the second-language varieties of English in Africa and Asia as to evoke the notion of a universal feature.

A largely similar picture emerges from the results of the *HVE* survey, according to which 'wider range of uses of the Progressive' (primarily meaning the use of the PF with stative verbs) is attested in 8 out of 9 American varieties included in the survey, 8 out of 9 African varieties and 3 out of 4 Asian varieties (see Kortmann and Szmrecsanyi 2004 and the statistics given there). On the other hand, it is interesting to note that this feature was *not* among the top 20 nonstandard features found in the Englishes of the British Isles—the criterion being attestation of a given feature in at least 6 out of the 8 varieties included in the survey (see Kortmann and Szmrecsanyi 2004: 1162–1163). Thus, according to this survey, the wider use of the PF is mainly a feature of the American and the African/Asian second-language varieties; in the British Isles it is restricted to IrE, ScE, northern WE dialects, some northern EngE dialects and the dialects spoken in the Orkney and Shetland Islands (see Kortmann 2004: 1090–1091).[4]

The *HVE* survey findings can be considered to further emphasise the *sui generis* nature of the Irish, Scottish and Welsh varieties of English within the context of the British Isles, which in turn lends additional indirect support to the Celtic hypothesis. Yet another piece of evidence pointing in the same direction comes from a recent study of WE by Paulasto (2006), who found nonstandard uses of the PF to be markedly more frequent in her WE corpora than in conservative EngE dialects, represented by the extensive *SED* tape-recordings. Paulasto's research also indicated that it is the habitual function which most clearly distinguishes the WE usages from those found in the *SED*. In addition, she observed regional differences within the EngE dialects with regard to the stative and habitual functions, the northern and north-western counties displaying the highest frequencies of nonstandard usage. These findings therefore connect the northern dialect region to Lowland Scots, where the PF is likewise employed in a wider range of contexts than in mainstream EngE (e.g. Beal 1997; Miller 2004).

In the context of the British Isles Englishes, then, we believe that the most likely background to the free use of the PF in the Irish, Scottish and Welsh varieties of English is to be found in the corresponding Celtic systems, which favour the so-called verbal noun construction (which is similar, yet more extensive in function than the English -*ing* form) in the same kinds of context. It is interesting to note that one of the first to advocate the Celtic hypothesis is Mossé (1938), who is otherwise very critical towards the idea of Celtic influence on English grammar. Having discarded the Celtic hypothesis with regard to the earliest, mediaeval, forms of the English PF, he states that the abundant use of the PF in the English of Ireland, Scotland and Wales in the modern period probably derives from the parallel tendency in Insular Celtic (Mossé 1938 II: § 106). In more recent research, the same view is defended by Braaten (1967), who has been followed by several writers on one or the other of these varieties. Thus, Filppula (2003) discusses the Irish roots of the IrE usages of the PF. For WE, the Cymric parallels are documented by, e.g. Parry (1999), who suggests that examples like (18) are modelled on the Welsh construction which consists of (*yr* +) BOD 'be' + subject + particle *yn* + verb-noun, e.g. *Y mae ef yn canu pob dydd* 'He sings / is singing every day' (Parry 1999: 111; see also Thomas 1994; Penhallurick 1996; Pitkänen 2003). Heinecke (1999) defines the Welsh verb phrase as the imperfective periphrasis, according to its aspectual role, and Paulasto (2006) confirms that there is a close aspectual and syntactic correspondence between the Welsh construction and nonstandard uses of the PF in WE, particularly in the dialect of the older, bilingual speakers. HebE and its Gaelic heritage in this respect are treated in Sabban (1982) and Macafee and Ó Baoill (1997), while Barry (1984), Broderick (1997) and Preuß (1999) find evidence of reflexes of Manx syntax in the MxE usages of the PF.

4.2.2.2   *Perfect Markers*

Marking of perfect or perfective aspect is another TMA-related domain in which Celtic influences are traceable in many western and northern varieties of the British Isles Englishes. Starting off with the most general one, the use of the present or past tense to denote an event or activity which has been initiated in the past but continues into the present time is extremely common in IrE and HebE, though not in other varieties of ScE or WE. Examples of this feature, which has been rather variably termed 'extended-now perfect' (Harris 1984a; Filppula 1999), 'extended-present perfect' (Kallen 1989), or 'continuative perfect' (Kruisinga 1931) are given in (26)–(29):

(26)   And .. they*'re fighting* out ten years in the North for an all-
Ireland republic. (IrE; cited in Filppula 1999: 90)
'. . . they have been fighting . . .'

(27)   He's working over there, in some building he *is working with a
couple o' weeks*. (IrE; cited in Filppula 1999: 126)
'. . . has been working for a couple of weeks.'

(28)   And they *are* fourteen or fifteen years married now. (HebE; cited
in Sabban 1982: 59)

(29)   I *was smoking* all my life. I *was smoking* since I was—started going to school. (HebE; cited in Sabban 1982: 62)

Besides the existence of direct Celtic parallels to this feature, the likelihood of substratal influence is emphasised by the use of the preposition *with* in a durative temporal meaning in the IrE example in (27). The corresponding Irish preposition *le* has both temporal and instrumental meanings, which explains the frequent use of *with* in this type of context in conservative varieties of IrE.

However, the Celtic background to the use of the present/past tense as perfect markers in IrE and HebE is complicated by the existence of earlier English superstratal parallels. Several studies have established similar use of the present tense to denote perfect aspect in earlier English—which is, indeed, a typical Germanic feature—but there are conflicting views on its frequency of use in the EModE period, which has been considered crucial from the point of view of the development of the Irish, though not the HebE, dialects of English. For instance, Visser (1963–1973: 737) writes that the present was "formerly rather frequently used" alongside the perfect with *have* + past participle. He does not specify what he means by 'formerly', but his examples make it clear that he is mainly referring to the (late) ME and EModE periods. In assessing the possible role of the EModE superstratum in the genesis of HebE, Sabban (1982), relying mainly on the accounts of Fridén (1948) and Jespersen (MEG IV: § 4.7(1)), concludes that although the present (or past) tense was sporadically used in ME and EModE to denote a 'persistent situation', it played there only a marginal role, as the present *have* perfect was already well-established at that stage (Sabban 1982: 110). For these reasons, Sabban considers an explanation in terms of Gaelic influence "sehr wahrscheinlich" ['very likely'] (1982: 111). It is our view that in the Irish context, too, the prominent place of the extended-now perfect in IrE dialects, including even present-day educated speech, is best explained through substratal influence from Irish, although the possible effect of conservatism cannot be ruled out (see Filppula 1999, section 6.2 for detailed discussion).

Besides the extended-now perfect, IrE and HebE share another type of perfect which involves a similar levelling phenomenon, but concerning this time the distinction between the present perfect and the past tense. In these cases, however, the nature of the time reference is different from that of the extended-now contexts: reference is here made to events or states of affairs that take place at some indefinite or unspecified period of time in the past leading up to the present. Harris (1984a: 308), writing on the IrE uses of this type of perfect, calls it the 'indefinite-anterior perfect'. Other terms found in the literature for roughly similar meanings, typically conveyed in StE by the *have* perfect, include 'experiential perfect' (Comrie 1976: 58–59) and 'existential perfect' (McCawley 1971: 104; both quoted here from Brinton 1988: 11). Examples of the indefinite-anterior perfect in IrE and HebE are given in (30)–(34):

(30) [Interviewer: . . . there's so many of them . . at this moment. I think there's more than . . a hundred thousand . . unemployed. It's . . it's becoming a serious problem.]
Yes, but they were there always, and ever, but ye *didn't take* any account of them until now. (IrE; cited in Filppula 1999: 92)

(31) I *went often* looking at television in an . . in another house, you know. Well, when I'd go down to Castlecove for a message there I'd see television. (IrE; cited in Filppula 1999: 94)

(32) Yeah, you *heard* that [i.e. story] before, did you? (IrE; cited in Filppula 1999: 94)

(33) Och! I *was* in Dunvegan Castle, I *was* through èvery room ( ) from top to bottom. (HebE; cited in Sabban 1982: 72)

(34) Well I'm over sixty years a crofter now, I started the croft ( ) at sixteen, and I *saw* a lot of changes. (HebE; cited in Sabban 1982: 72)

As in the case of the extended-now perfect, there are direct parallels to these usages both in Irish and Scottish Gaelic. They have no equivalent of the English *have* perfect, which may explain the rise of the indefinite-anterior perfect with the past tense form in these varieties. As Ó Sé (1992: 55) notes, the Irish preterite is normally used with reference to 'experiences in indefinite past time', i.e. to indefinite-anterior events/states, including also expressions involving universal quantifiers like *riamh* '(n)ever'. The same is true of the corresponding Scottish Gaelic usages. Ó Sé illustrates the Irish usage with the following examples (1992: 55–56):

(35) Ar léigh tú an leabhar sin riamh?
      'Did you ever read that book?'

(36) Níor léigh mé an leabhar sin riamh.
      'I (have) never read that book'.

(37) Chuala mé an t-amhrán sin cúpla uair.
      'I have heard that song a couple of times'.

(38) Is minic a chonaic mé é.
      'I have often seen it'.

The Welsh TMA systems differ from those of Irish and Scottish Gaelic. It comes as no surprise, then, that WE dialects also behave differently in this respect. The *SAWD* indicates that the rural, northern dialects make frequent use of the PF (which is evidently based on the Welsh model), e.g. *I have been using it myself* 'I have used it myself'; *we (have) never been extendin' 'em* 'we have never extended them' (Penhallurick 1996: 327, 328). The same pattern is also found to some extent in the other dialects of WE, but on the other hand, the preterite has found its way into contexts involving *(n)ever*, as in *Were you ever . . .?*[25]

Although it is tempting to conclude that the IrE and HebE indefinite-anterior perfects have their origins in the Celtic substrata, other factors may also be involved. Thus, after a detailed discussion of the earlier English parallels Sabban (1982: 111–112) concludes that the Scottish Gaelic model has indeed promoted the use of the preterite in HebE, but that influences from earlier English cannot be totally excluded. It is a well-known fact that the use of the preterite form for indefinite-anterior time reference was not uncommon in OE and ME and up until the EModE period. For example, Visser (1963–1973: 749–754) writes that the present-day English division of labour between the preterite and the *have* + past participle construction was not established until after Shakespeare's time. Similarly, Jespersen (MEG IV: § 5.1–5.2), in his survey of the usage from EModE onwards, finds continuing variation between the preterite and the perfect in certain types of sentences, depending mainly on the type of time adverbial but also on contextual and pragmatic factors. Among the former, sentences containing the adverbs *always*, *ever*, and *never*, as well as the conjunction *since* and the preposition *until*, are particularly likely to occur with the preterite.

A further dimension to the problem of the historical and also the present-day background is added by the widespread use of the past tense instead of the *have* perfect in modern spoken AmE. Visser (1963–1973: 754), relying mainly on Vanneck (1958), discusses the latter's view according to which the 'colloquial preterite', as Vanneck terms it, is a new development rather than a retention from earlier English. However, Visser is inclined to interpret it as a conservatism, and more specifically, as a survival of what is sometimes called 'Mayflower English' (named after the boat of the first English immigrants to America; see Visser 1963–1973: 754). Sabban (1982: 106–107), commenting on the same AmE tendency, suggests two other possible sources of influence, viz. other immigrants whose native languages did not distinguish between the tense-aspect categories at issue here and 'Anglo-Irish' (i.e. IrE), in which, as she notes, the preterite is used in much the same way as in AmE.

The *HVE* findings shed interesting new light on this problem. The survey data show that the levelling of the difference between the present perfect and the simple past is among the most widely attested features in the varieties spoken in the British Isles but that it is "especially pronounced in ScE, IrE, and the Southwest" (Kortmann 2004: 1090). On a global scale, this feature is also quite prominent, being attested in as many as 34 varieties of English (Kortmann and Szmrecsanyi 2004: 1155). This suggests that the use of the simple past in perfect contexts has become something of a 'vernacular universal' among the world's Englishes. Yet, in the context of the British Isles, the geographical distribution of this feature makes it hard to see it as a mere reflex of the universal tendency; its prominence in IrE and HebE, in particular, seems to call for an additional explanation in terms of substratal reinforcing influences from the relevant Celtic languages displaying the same feature.

Next, we will turn to two other types of perfect, both of which can be characterised as being resultative or, rather, stative-resultative in meaning. The first, rather variably termed 'medial-object perfect' (Filppula 1999), 'accomplishment perfect' (Kallen 1989), or simply 'P II' (Harris 1984a), appears to be restricted to IrE dialects in which, too, it must be considered rather infrequent.[6] In medial-object perfects, the subject is typically understood as being the agent of the action expressed by the verb, which is transitive and in most cases dynamic; the whole construction focuses on the end-point, or result, of the action rather than the action itself. In the literature on IrE, *I have my dinner eaten* has come to be cited as the paradigmatic example illustrating the IrE usage (see, e.g. Kirk and Kallen 2006: 98–100). Further examples of this feature are given in (39) and (40):

(39) When he'd come home, the father [would say to his daughter], 'Mary, I *have your match made*'. (IrE; cited in Filppula 1999: 108)

(40) There's a whole little rhyme about it, and I *have it forgot*. (IrE; cited in Filppula 1999: 108)

Both substratal and superstratal origins have been suggested for the medial-object perfect. The corresponding Irish construction, though slightly different in form, has the same kind of "static interpretation of action" as the IrE medial-object perfect (see Henry 1957: 177 for examples of both Irish and IrE). The virtual absence of this type of perfect from otherwise very similar HebE grammar can be explained by the fact that Scottish Gaelic has no equivalent of the Irish stative-resultative perfect (see Greene 1979: 133).[7] On the other hand, some earlier English parallels to the IrE medial-object perfect can be found, but they seem to have passed out of use by the time English started to spread in Ireland and therefore could hardly have provided the main, or only, model for the Irish usages (see Filppula 1999, section 6.2.3 for discussion).[8] Yet another factor speaking for the Celtic hypothesis is the common use of the medial-object perfect in Newfoundland English (NfldE) (see Clarke 1997).

The other resultative perfect is the so-called *be* perfect. It is the intransitive counterpart of the medial-object perfect and is used with verbs of motion and 'mutative' verbs, such as *go, come, leave, die* and *change*. Though evidently recessive, it is still a fairly common feature of especially the conservative varieties of IrE, and on the basis of the *HVE* survey, also found in ScE, northern dialects of EngE and the Englishes spoken in Orkney and the Shetland Islands (Kortmann 2004: 1090). Examples of this feature are:

(41) This was s'posed to be a Gaeltacht area, but . . all the Irish, they *are* all *gone* out of it, they *are* all *gone*. (IrE; cited in Filppula 1999: 120)

(42) There was a lot about fairies long ago—whether they were right or wrong—but I'm thinkin' that most of 'em *are vanished*. (IrE; cited in Filppula 1999: 117)

The use of *be* as the perfect auxiliary instead of *have* is, of course, an old Germanic feature, and the geographical distribution seems to corroborate the conservative nature of this type of perfect. However, the pervasiveness of the *be* perfect in especially earlier IrE texts, coupled with the existence of a direct Irish parallel, has led some researchers to suggest that the IrE usages are based, or have at least been influenced, by the Irish construction (see, e.g. Bliss 1979: 294). Kallen (1989: 18) also notes the more frequent use of the *be* perfect in IrE as compared with other varieties of English but stops short of taking any stand on the question of possible Irish influence.

Finally, a particularly striking example of a feature which has a clear Celtic background is the type of perfect known as the 'hot news' or *after* perfect, as in (43) recorded from IrE. Besides this variety, it is also attested in HebE in the British Isles context; witness the example in (44). For both of these varieties, the corresponding Celtic parallels offer themselves as the most plausible source.[9] This is also supported by the extreme rarity of this type of perfect in the world's Englishes: for example, the *HVE* survey places the *after* perfect among the bottom 18 morphosyntactic features found in the 46 varieties of English included in the survey. What is more, the only varieties in which it is attested are IrE, NfldE and Cameroon English (CamE) (see Kortmann and Szmrecsanyi 2004: 1151–1152). It is common knowledge that there is a strong historical and linguistic connection between IrE and NfldE, based on the large numbers of Irish immigrants to Newfoundland especially in the first three decades of the nineteenth century (see, e.g. Shorrocks 1997: 334–337). Against this background, it is not surprising to find instances of the *after* perfect in NfldE speech; in fact, research by Clarke (see Clarke 1997) shows that the *after* perfect is no longer restricted to the predominantly Irish-origin part of the population of Newfoundland but is used generally by people with different social backgrounds. A couple of Clarke's examples are given in (45) and (46).

(43) I was in the market, and I *was after buyin'* a load of strawberries.
      '. . . and I had just bought . . .' (Filppula 1999: 99)

(44) He's *after coming* from the Mackenzies.
      'He has just come . . .' (Sabban 1982: 157)

(45) She understands. She's *after havin'* children herself. (NfldE; cited in Clarke 1997: 216)

(46) [Mrs. X] *must be after makin'* all kinds of money. (NfldE; cited in Clarke 1997: 216)

As regards CamE, the Irish connection is perhaps not so well-known, but recent research by Bobda (2006) has shown that Irish missionaries had a strong presence in this part of Africa, in the then British Cameroons, in a period between the end of World War I and 1961 (which marks the year of independence of Cameroon). Bobda discusses several phonological features of CamE that can be attributed to the influence of IrE, mediated mainly through the primary and secondary schools founded by the Irish Catholic missions. Although Bobda's research is limited to phonology, syntactic influences from IrE can also be expected on the basis of his general statement that

> [t]he British settlers migrated from different parts of the United Kingdom, but the Irish clearly dominated. Irish English is, therefore, arguably the native English variety which has exerted the greatest influence on the formation of Cameroon English in the colonial period.

> (Bobda 2006: 219–220)

It is somewhat surprising that there is no *after* perfect in WE, given that Welsh has a close structural parallel for it. However, the aspectual system of Welsh provides a possible explanation for the absence of the *after* perfect from WE syntax. Greene (1979) writes that Welsh has no direct equivalent of the Irish and Scottish Gaelic *tréis/air* constructions which provide the model for the Hiberno-English (HE) and HebE *after* perfects. Instead, Welsh expresses the notion of a recent event by adding *newydd* 'just' (adj. 'new'; cf. Fife 1990: 389–393) to the periphrastic construction. *Newydd* replaces the preposition *wedi* 'after', used (alongside the preterite) for the 'ordinary' present perfect (i.e., with no particular emphasis on the recentness of the event or activity referred to). This leads to a contrast between *yr wyf wedi ei weld ef* 'I have seen him' and *yr wyf newydd ei weld ef* 'I have just seen him' (Greene 1979: 126). Thus, despite the apparent similarity with the Irish and Scottish Gaelic constructions, the Welsh periphrastic perfect requires the presence of the adverb-like operator *newydd* to underline the recentness of the event or activity, much like StE does. This probably explains the fact that WE has no *after* perfect.

4.2.2.3   Habitual Aspect Markers do *and* be

The Irish and Welsh dialects of English are well-known for their use of the auxiliary *do* (in IrE also *do be*) in what could be characterised as a 'habitual' or 'generic/habitual' function (see, e.g. Kallen 1989). In IrE, the auxiliary is normally inflected for person but not always for number, as can be seen from the following examples. IrE is also alone in accepting a variant *do be*, followed either by a noun/adjective phrase or by the *-ing* form of a verb, as in (48) and (49).

> (47)   Two lorries of them [i.e. turf] now in the year we *do burn*. (IrE; cited in Filppula 1999: 130)

> (48)   They *does be* lonesome by night, the priest does, surely. (IrE; cited in Filppula 1999: 130)

> (49)   Yeah, that's, that's the camp. Military camp they call it . . . They *do be shooting* there couple of times a week or so. (IrE; cited in Filppula 1999: 2003: 163)

As yet another variant with a similar function, *be/bees/be's* is used in especially the northern IrE dialects and some ScE dialects. Examples of this usage are the following, drawn from the *Northern Ireland Corpus of Transcribed Speech* (NICTS) (on *be/bees/be's* in especially Ulster Scots, see Montgomery and Gregg 1997: 617):

> (50)   {Where do they [tourists] stay, and what kind of pastimes do they have?}
> Well, they stay, some of them, in the forestry caravan sites. They bring caravans. They *be shooting*, and *fishing* out at the forestry lakes. (NICTS: MC16)

(51) {And who brings you in [to Mass]?}
      We get, Mrs Cullen to leave us in {ahah}. She *be's going*, and she
      leaves us in, too. (NICTS: EM70)

(52) {And what do you do in your play centre? Do you think it's a
      good idea in the holidays?}
      It's better, because you *be's* bored doing nothing {mm} at home.
      (NICTS: KO121)

WE dialects differ from IrE in that the *do*-auxiliary is almost categori-
cally uninflected (Parry 1999: 110–111). The following examples are drawn
from the *SAWD* and from a corpus collected by Ceri George in the Rhondda
valleys in south-east Wales (see George 1990 for more information):

(53) Where you *do 'itch* the 'orse to (SG 1); Lime *do freshen* it (WG
      2); Some *do have* tailboards (P 7; Parry 1999: 110)

(54) But you'd put that, the can of water on top of the fire. And when
      it *do boil* he'd send it down in the carriage to the hitcher down
      the bottom. (Wales, the Rhondda: E.L.)

Another major difference between IrE and WE is the absence of *be/
bees/be's* from the latter. Instead, the northern and western dialects of WE,
in particular, use the PF in a habitual function, whereas the uninflected *do*
is mainly a feature of the south-eastern and some southern WE dialects.[10]
The *SAWD* shows that it is primarily found in the regions where English
has been the spoken language for centuries, i.e. South Pembroke, the Gower
and south-east Wales, with a few instances recorded in Mid-Wales (Parry
1999: 110–111). That these two habitual dialect constructions exist in a
complementary distribution in WE is also confirmed by Thomas (1985),
according to whom 'periphrastic' DO is found primarily in the historically
English-speaking parts, whereas nonstandard uses of the PF are frequent
in the regions that have been anglicised relatively late and, in many cases,
remain bilingual.

Conflicting hypotheses and explanations have been put forward in the
literature concerning the origins of these habitual aspect markers. In the
Welsh setting, the regional differentiation between the northern and western
dialects, on one hand, and the southern and south-eastern dialects, on the
other, can be seen, rather paradoxically, either as an indicator of superstratal
origin or as a vestige of possibly very early substratal influence. As discussed
in Chapter 2, section 2.2.4, there is a strong possibility that a Brythonic substratum entered the English (Anglo-Saxon) language in the early mediaeval
period, resulting in this case in the emergence of DO as an auxiliary and a
habitual aspect marker in the English of the south-west of England (see, esp.
Poussa 1990). Demographic and historical factors support the conclusion

that this south-western English construction was then introduced into dialects of English spoken in Wales during the early anglicisation of the southern and south-eastern regions. From the linguistic point of view, the fact that DO is uninflected for number in both south-western English and in WE dialects strongly suggests historical contacts between the two areas. This is further underlined by the geographical spread of periphrastic DO in present-day conservative varieties of English: the core areas extend from Somerset and Wiltshire north into south-eastern Wales (see, esp. Klemola 1996).

As noted in Chapter 2, section 2.2.4, the early Celtic substratum hypothesis has recently been given a new lease of life through the comparative syntactic studies by scholars such as van der Auwera and Genee (2002) and McWhorter (2006), who have demonstrated that English stands virtually alone among the Germanic languages in having DO-periphrasis. This is a fact which McWhorter (2006), in particular, interprets as evidence of early Celtic influence on OE. Although we agree with McWhorter's account of the early contacts, it is clear that the present-day south-eastern WE usages cannot be explained as a result of recent substratal influence from Welsh, in which the structurally similar periphrastic construction GWNEUD 'do' + verbal noun is essentially perfective in meaning and not found in habitual contexts (Fife 1990: 237, 250–251).[11] As for modern substratal influences, the frequent use of the PF with habitual meaning in the more recently anglicised and bilingual regions is clear testimony to transfer from Welsh, which uses a structurally closely similar periphrastic construction to express habitual aspect (cf. the discussion on the English PF in Chapter 2, section 2.2.5).

The IrE usages present a slightly different case not only because of the formal differences between the WE and IrE constructions but also because of the different historical contact settings. The likelihood of substratal influence from Irish is enhanced by the existence of Irish parallels to both the *do (be)* and the *be/bees/be's* forms. For the latter, a plausible source is the 'consuetudinal' (i.e. habitual) present of the early Modern Irish 'substantive' verb 'be', the 3rd person singular forms of which were *bídh* (the 'independent' form) and *bí* ('dependent' form, used, e.g. after certain particles and conjunctions). It is the existence in the verbal system of a special form reserved for habitual aspect that can then be used to explain why the Irish learners of English should have carried over this feature into their English; the adoption of *be/bees/be's* as a habitual aspect marker would have been further facilitated by the close phonetic resemblance between the Irish and English 'be' words (for an account on these lines, see, e.g. Bliss 1972). The *do (be)* forms, by contrast, are harder to explain, as Irish has (nor had in its earlier stages) no direct formal parallel to them. One could argue that the introduction of the *do (be)* patterns were due to the superstratal model provided by the similar English usages of periphrastic *do* (see, e.g. Harris 1986; Kallen 1986). On the other hand, although these usages were common enough in the early part of the EModE period, they went into a very rapid decline as early as the latter part of the sixteenth century and the first half of the seventeenth century (see, e.g. Ellegård 1953; Rissanen 1991; Nurmi 1996). Another complication is the fact that, unlike IrE, earlier or dialectal EngE never used the auxiliary *do* with *be*. On the other hand, the early Modern Irish verbs had a so-called dependent form ending in *-(e)ann*, which was used for the present indicative of verbs and, as Bliss (1972) argues, had a syntactic distribution very similar to the uses of the auxiliary *do* in English: those contexts which in English required *do* required the dependent ending in early Modern Irish, and *vice versa*, with some minor exceptions. For these reasons, Bliss (1972) is inclined to treat both of the IrE habitual aspect markers as reflexes of the corresponding Irish features. However, Bliss's account has yet to win the support of those who would like to see a greater role for the earlier English superstratum (see, e.g. Harris 1986; Kallen 1994).

Despite the mentioned complications, the likelihood of at least some degree of Celtic influence on both IrE and WE is greatly increased by the returns of the *HVE* survey. All of the habitual markers discussed in this section, i.e. DO-periphrasis in its various realisations and habitual *be/bees/be's*, were found to belong to the list of the 'Worldwide Bottom 18' features (based, as will be remembered, on a survey of 46 varieties of English; see Kortmann and Szmrecsanyi 2004: 1151–1152). *Do* as a tense and aspect marker (including both nonhabitual and habitual uses) is a feature of only a very limited group, consisting of IrE, WE, south-west of England, earlier African American Vernacular English (AAVE), NfldE (habitual uses only), CamE and a few other 'extra-territorial' varieties. As for habitual *be*, it is attested, again, in IrE (but not in WE, as noted above), Gullah, Urban AAVE, NfldE, CamE, Indian South African English and a small number of other 'extra-territorial' varieties (see, *ibid.*). The Irish (and Celtic) connection is obvious for such a large part of these varieties (cf. the discussion on the *after* perfect in CamE in section 4.2.2.2) as to make it unlikely that these features could be explained as 'vernacular universals'.

4.2.3   Clausal and Sentential Structures

4.2.3.1   *Inversion in Indirect Questions*

The use of inverted word order in indirect or embedded questions ('embedded inversion' or 'EI' for short) is yet another feature which in the context of the British Isles and Ireland has been found to be particularly common in the CEs. It has been attested in both southern and northern varieties of IrE (see, e.g. Bliss 1984; Henry 1995; Filppula 1999, 2000), HebE (Sabban 1982), and WE (Parry 1979; Penhallurick 1991; Thomas 1994). Parry's (1999: 119) WE examples are mainly from south-west Wales, but the *SAWD* interviews and other North Welsh data show that it is equally widespread in the north. Besides these varieties, it has been recorded in ScE (Miller 1993) and in some northern dialects of English, especially in Tyneside and what is in the literature termed 'Northumbrian' English (Beal 1993). Examples from each of these varieties are given in (55) to (60), respectively ('SIrE' and 'NIrE' stand for southern Irish English and northern Irish English). EI occurs most often in embedded Yes/No questions, as in (55), (56) and (58), but is also found (with certain restrictions) in embedded WH-questions, as in (57), (59) and (60).

(55) Tyneside: She once asked me *did it interfere* with me. (McDonald 1980: 15; cited in Beal 1993: 204)

(56) ScE: You sort of wonder *is it* better to be blind or deaf. (Miller 1993: 126)

(57) HebE: But he was telling me he didn't know how *did he manage* it. (Sabban 1982: 463)

(58) WE: I wouldn't know *would there be* any there now. (Thomas 1994: 138)

(59) SIrE: They asked when *would you be* back (Bliss 1984: 148)

(60) NIrE: She asked who *had I seen*. (Henry 1995: 106)

The *HVE* survey also contained an item on this feature, but unfortunately, it was exemplified only by the WH-type, which may be reflected in the results. In any case, EI was not among the 'Worldwide Top 15' features (based on 46 varieties), nor even among the 'Top 20 British Isles' features (based on features attested in at least 6 of the 8 relevant varieties) (see Kortmann and Szmrecsanyi 2004: 1154–1155, 1162–1163). However, it was one of the 'Top 20' features of the AmE varieties, being attested in all 9 of them (*op.cit.*, 1166–1167), as well as being listed among the 'Top Australia' and 'Top Asia' features (*op.cit.*, 1173–1175, 1179–1180, respectively).

The geographical distribution of EI in the British Isles and the *HVE* findings give rise to three main hypotheses about the origin of EI: it can be explained as (1) a retention from earlier English, possibly reflecting its formerly robust verb-second ('V2') properties; (2) a 'general vernacular' or 'vernacular universal' feature due to a process of simplification; or (3) a result of substratum influence from the Celtic languages.

To begin with earlier English parallels, language historians give a somewhat vague description of the emergence of EI. For instance, Visser (1963–1973: 780–781) notes that this feature is already found in OE texts but, as he states, "instances do not seem to occur with great frequency before the eighteenth century". Visser's examples include just one from OE, after which comes an example from the end of the fifteenth century (Malory), followed by another dating to the end of the next century (Spenser). The next ones take us as far ahead as the early nineteenth century (Scott), after which he cites several examples from various authors (including James Joyce). Jespersen (MEG III: § 2.4(8)) gives an even later date for the increased use of EI: according to him, it does not become prominent until the mid-nineteenth century.

What complicates the dating here is the often blurred distinction between direct and indirect questions in earlier English texts. Indeed, Visser (1963–1973: 780–781) points out that there was a great deal of variation in the representation of so-called reported questions in the literature up until recent times: in some cases the initial letters could be printed in capitals; in others small letters were used along with various punctuation marks to separate direct questions from reported ones; there was also little consistency in the use of the question mark. However, some of the examples cited by Visser (1963–1973: 780–781) are sufficiently similar to those from the regional dialects cited above so as to make it clear that EI existed in earlier English. The extent of its use is another matter. In Filppula (2000) an attempt was made to find out to what extent indirect questions showed inverted order in the EModE period, which has been argued to be crucial from the point of view of the formation of, e.g. the Irish dialects of English. A quantitative survey was conducted, based on the EModE section of the *Helsinki Corpus*. The search was limited to those four matrix verbs that have been found to be the most common ones in the regional dialects, namely *know, ask, see* and *wonder*. The results confirmed Visser's statement about the relative rarity of EI in pre-eighteenth-century English. In fact, EI turned out to be extremely rare in EModE when one considers the contexts in which it occurred in the *Helsinki Corpus*: of the 17 instances, as many as 15 involved the verb *ask*, while the remaining two were introduced by *see*. There were no tokens with *know*, which on the basis of the data from the regional dialects is the most common matrix verb to trigger inversion in those dialects. The majority of the inverted patterns were found in records of trials, sermons or educational treatises, and most of them, especially the ones occurring in records of trials, raise problems of delimitation.

Although the evidence from written texts is necessarily limited and must be treated with caution, it suffices in this case to show that EI was a very marginal feature of EModE grammar. This casts considerable doubt on the hypothesis according to which its prolific use in the CEs, let alone those American, Australian and Asian varieties in which EI also occurs, could be explained as a retention from earlier English. It is also doubtful whether EI in the mentioned present-day varieties could be interpreted as a reflex of the earlier English, originally Germanic, V2 constraint. The extensive discussion of V2 phenomena in Stockwell (1984) shows that V2 phenomena are largely restricted to root contexts in earlier as well as in present-day StE.

The second hypothesis mentioned above seeks to explain EI as a 'general vernacular' feature, typical of nonstandard or colloquial usage, arising through a process of simplification. Besides the British Isles and other regional varieties mentioned above, it is, according to Jespersen (MEG III:

§ 2.4(8)), common in Modern English colloquial speech. Curme (1931: 247–248) also associates EI with 'colloquial and popular speech' but also mentions its especially common use in 'popular Irish English'. Interestingly, Visser (1963–1973: 780) also notes the commonness of the inverted order in 'Anglo-Irish' but argues that it can hardly be considered a 'trait of Anglo-Irish' or even a case of inverted word order in that dialect. What Visser evidently has in mind here is that EIs are occasional slips from indirect speech into direct speech rather than a grammaticalised feature. EI has furthermore been found to be a feature of AmE colloquial speech, although in the American context, too, it appears to be most common in various regional and nonstandard varieties, such as Appalachian English, Southern White English and AAVE. Besides the strong Scotch–Irish element in Appalachian speech, the latter two may also have been influenced by the language of the Irish settlers (see, e.g. Wolfram and Christian 1976: 127–129; Wolfram and Fasold 1974: 169–170; Martin and Wolfram 1998: 29). Note, however, that EI is not a feature of English-based creoles, which follow StE word order in embedded questions (see, e.g. Holm 1988: 214). This is also confirmed by the *HVE* survey, where EI is among the most frequent vernacular features in first-language and, in particular, second-language varieties of English, but not in pidgins and creoles (Kortmann and Szmrecsanyi 2004: 1185–1193).

In the light of the ubiquity of the evidence, it is hard to deny that EI could, at least partly, be explained as a kind of vernacular universal. This cannot, however, be the only explanation. Among the factors that call for some additional explanation is, firstly, the geographical distribution and rates of usage of EI among traditional dialects of English spoken in the British Isles. As the foregoing discussion has made it clear, EI is a more prominent feature of the varieties spoken in the northern, north-western and western parts of the British Isles than elsewhere. By way of more precise documentation, the frequencies of use of EI in our corpus of southern IrE were clearly higher than those for the *SED* tape-recordings: while the percentage for inverted word order was 30.2 in the IrE corpus, the corresponding figure for the *SED* corpus was only 1.1. The difference was even greater insofar as the rates of occurrence of EI in Yes/No contexts are concerned: there were no such instances in the *SED* corpus, whereas the percentage for IrE was as high as 47.2. This indicates that while there is some truth in saying that EI is a general vernacular feature, there is also compelling evidence to prove that it is clearly more general in some varieties than in some others.

Similar differences emerge when comparing the British Isles varieties with 'extra-territorial' ones. Thus, our investigation of New Zealand English, based on the so-called *Wellington Corpus of Spoken New Zealand English* (totalling 1 million words) yielded only a 2.4 per cent proportion of inversions in embedded contexts. As in the *SED* corpus, the rates of occurrence in the Yes/No contexts were smaller than those in the WH-contexts. By contrast, the Kenyan component of the *ICE—East Africa* returned a relatively high inversion percentage of 34.6, but even there the Yes/No inversions were in a clear minority as compared with the figures for WH-contexts (14.3 vs. 42.1 per cent).

It is quite possible that the differences described above are due to the influence of other languages, which brings us to the third major hypothesis, viz. that based on substrate influences. As regards the English of Ireland, for example, it is a well-known fact that EI has a close parallel in Irish, which has verb-raising in both root and embedded clauses; in other words, the word order of direct questions is retained in indirect questions. This is particularly transparent in the case of Yes/No questions, as can be seen from the following pair of examples cited by Ó Siadhail (1989: 321):

(61) An raibh tú sásta?
'Were you content?'

(62) Chuir sé ceist ort *an raibh tú sásta.*
'He asked you if you were content.'

Example (62) shows that Irish has no equivalent of the English *if/whether*. The Irish counterparts of WH-questions (here referred to by the English term for convenience) are less straightforward, because the Irish questions introduced by an interrogative pronoun normally require a relative clause structure. This is in fact a type of cleft sentence, in which the interrogative word stands independently before the relative clause introduced by the relative particle *a* (see, e.g. Ó Siadhail 1989: 317–319; Mac Eoin 1993: 122–123). Mac Eoin (1993: 122) provides the following illustration of this pattern:

(63) Cé an áit a bhfaca tú é?
'Where did you see it?' [lit. 'where the place that saw you it?']

As can be seen in (64), the same order of elements is preserved in indirect WH-questions despite the rather complex structure:

(64) Chuir sé ceist cé an áit *a bhfaca tú é.*
'He asked where you saw it.'

The same type of structure is found in the other Celtic languages (for Scottish Gaelic, see Gillies 1993: 217; for Welsh, King 1993: 305 and Thomas 1994: 138), which therefore provide direct models for the patterns of inversion found in the mentioned regional varieties. In the case of the Yes/No type the correspondence is complete, whereas in WH-questions it is embedded under an additional layer consisting of the relative clause structure. This may well account for the generally less frequent use of inversion in WH-questions in these varieties and also for the greater degree of variation in usage as compared with Yes/No questions.

Another factor supporting the Celtic hypothesis is the dialectal differentiation between IrE dialects in their frequencies of use of EI. Although IrE as a whole, as was noted above, makes extensive use of EI, it is even more frequent in those dialects which have had the most recent living contacts with the indigenous Irish language (see Filppula 2000: 446–447). In the Scottish context, too, EI appears to be particularly common in HebE, which is a contact vernacular and in many respects strikingly similar to IrE (for a detailed discussion of EI in HebE, see Sabban 1982: 460–483). WE dialects present a slightly different picture. Compared with IrE, embedded inversion is relatively infrequent in WE: of the investigated indirect Yes/No questions, 4.5 per cent were inverted, while for WH-questions the percentage was 21.9. This, despite the fact that the respective structures of indirect questions in Welsh are similar to those in Irish, and the relative particles in Yes/No questions are typically omitted. The reason for this may be the formal transmission of English in most of the bilingual regions, resulting in the acquisition of the StE structures. Yet it should be noted that both Penhallurick (1991: 210) and Thomas (1994: 138) suggest Welsh as a possible source of EI in WE.

To conclude, the role of conservatism in explaining EI in varieties of English spoken in the British Isles is undermined by the marginal status of this kind of feature in earlier English. Similarly, interpreting the EI of the regional dialects as a reflex of the more general V2 properties of earlier English fails to be convincing because of the root nature of the phenomenon in the latter. The general vernacular hypothesis fares much better insofar as the occurrence of EI in different present-day varieties of English all over the world is concerned. What it cannot explain satisfactorily are the obvious quantitative differences in the rates of occurrence in some of these varieties, and in the context of the British Isles, especially between the traditional dialects of EngE and CEs such as IrE. To this should be added the observed pattern of dialectal differentiation among the IrE dialects themselves in their frequencies of use of EI. Hence, while there is evidence to show that EI is to some extent a general vernacular feature, there is also strong evidence to suggest that the CEs have indeed been influenced by the Celtic substrata with respect to the feature at hand.

4.2.3.2   *Focusing Constructions*

Focusing constructions are so called because they serve the purpose of assigning prominence or 'salience' to some element(s) of the sentence or utterance at the expense of the others. Depending on the language, this can happen by means of various kinds of structural devices or through prosodic means. By contrast with StE, which uses both but favours the latter, the CEs show a clear predilection for the use of word order shifts or special syntactic constructions instead of prosodic means. As will be seen below, this is also a well-known characteristic of all the Celtic languages, which use either the so-called copula construction (equivalent to the English cleft construction or 'clefting' for short) or word order arrangements for purposes of thematic prominence.

Word order shifts are a frequently employed focusing device in WE, where the word to be highlighted is placed at the beginning of the clause or sentence, as in (65) from Thomas (1994) and in (66) from Parry (1999):

(65) *Singing* they were.
      'What they were doing was singing'. (WE; cited in Thomas
      1994: 37)

(66) *Coal* they are getting out mostly. (WE; cited in Parry 1999: 120)

Thomas's term for this phenomenon is 'fronting', while Williams (2000) uses the more descriptive term 'predicate fronting'. Other commonly used linguistic terms for the same operation in other CEs are 'topicalisation' or 'focus topicalisation' (see, e.g. Filppula 1986; Kallen 1994). Because of the widely differing meanings attached to the notion of topicalisation in various functional or generative frameworks, Paulasto (2006) adopts the more neutral label 'focus fronting' (FF), which will also be used in this study. Paulasto's WE database provides further examples of FF in present-day WE:

(67) . . . we were sitting up there just the two of us an' the dog was
      lying on the—on the floor by the settee where my husband
      was lying down, and er, *chatting* we were and I said well we'd
      better—might as well go to bed, it's getting late now I said. (WE:
      Llandybie: E.L.; cited in Paulasto 2006: 162)

(68) An' *hens* we had an' eggs and . . . Erm, at Christmas my mother
      would fatten up cockerels and *turkey* she bred,
      [Mm.]
      an' then we used to make our own butter . . . (WE:
      Llanuwchllyn: G.N.; cited in Paulasto 2006: 160)

(69) So you always—er, many people when—whilst buyin' a horse
      with you or somethin' would say: "Does she work either side?"
      "*On the land* she've always worked." And by that you'd know
      that she'd always worked on the left.
      [Yeah.]
      And if they said, oh no, *in the haul* we've always used her, well
      on the right then you would—you would put her. (WE: Camrose
      [SAWD: Dy 13]; cited in Paulasto 2006: 161)

(70) . . . every night there's about forty minutes of items to fill the pro-
      gramme . . . *Various news items* they are, quite funny news items.
      (WE: Llandybie: P.D.; cited in Paulasto 2006: 159)

These examples make it evident that FF in WE does not necessarily follow the contextual or syntactic constraints typical of StE. What is presented as 'new' or otherwise prominent information by the speaker can readily be put in clause- or sentence-initial position, whether it is part of a VP, an object, adverbial or subject complement. This is, indeed, a practice which is characteristic of Welsh—and the other Celtic languages—in which clefting "universally involves fronting of a constituent", as stated by Thomas (1994: 137), and the fronted word order is obligatory in a number of discourse functions (e.g. Watkins 1991). The FFs in WE can thus be said to directly echo the corresponding Welsh structures.

Welsh influence on WE FF is also supported by some of the quantitative findings of Paulasto's study. Her apparent-time comparisons between the usages of different age groups in several localities in Wales show that FF is particularly favoured by the eldest speakers in most of the localities examined. They can be considered to have preserved best features which have a substratal origin (Paulasto 2006: 198–199). Another important factor speaking for Welsh influence on WE FF emerged from Paulasto's comparison between the frequencies of use of FF in WE dialects, on one hand, and in conservative EngE dialects, on the other. The latter were studied on the basis of the *SED* data, which were divided into four broad dialect areas: North, South, East and West. Table 4.3 from Paulasto (2006: 206) shows the distribution of FF by sentence elements in these four areas. The table has been expanded with data elicited from a respective, elderly age group in Llandybie, south-west Wales.

The figures in Table 4.3 give, first, a clear indication of general qualitative and quantitative differences in the use of FF between the WE and EngE dialects: while the former prefers fronting of objects and adverbials (in especially the bilingual areas of Wales, such as Llandybie), in the latter the

Table 4.3 Use of focus fronting in different parts of England in the *SED* corpus and in the speech of elderly informants in Llandybie, Wales.

Region		*Object*		*Adverbial*		*S compl.*		*O compl.*		*VP*		*Total*	
		N	%	N	%	N	%	N	%	N	%	N	N/10,000
SED N	114,500	1	3.2	7	22.6	7	22.6	15	48.4	1	3.2	31	**2.71**
SED E	117,200	8	11.4	15	21.4	22	31.4	23	32.9	2	2.9	70	**5.97**
SED S	144,000	18	17.8	14	13.8	38	37.6	25	24.8	6	5.9	101	**7.01**
SED W	103,000	16	21.3	21	28.0	22	29.3	14	18.7	2	2.7	75	**7.27**
SED	478,700	43	18.9	57	20.6	89	32.1	77	27.8	11	4.0	277	**5.79**
Wales	52,000	15	24.6	25	41.0	13	21.3	8	13.1	0	0.0	61	**11.73**

fronted constituents are more typically either subject or object complements than objects or adverbials. The elderly informants in Llandybie also use this construction considerably more frequently than the *SED* informants. Another interesting result is the more frequent use of FF in the western dialect areas than anywhere else; there the proportions of fronted objects and adverbials are also higher than in the other three areas. It is conceivable that Welsh influence (mediated either through WE dialects or, less plausibly, through Welsh itself) is felt the most in those areas which have historically been closest to Welsh-speaking Wales. A somewhat similar pattern emerged in Filppula's (1986) study of FFs in four different dialect areas in Ireland: FFs and cleftings, in particular, were in this study found to be more common in the speech of the (south-)western areas of Kerry and Clare where Irish retains the strongest positions.

By contrast with WE, in IrE as well as in HebE dialects, the preferred means of emphasis is clefting, although FF is also used to some extent. The difference between the two devices is, in fact, rather minimal: in the cleft construction, too, the item to be highlighted is the first stressed element in the sentence; the introductory *it is* or *it's* never receives stress. The examples in (71)–(76), drawn from earlier written and present-day spoken IrE and HebE, illustrate the uses of clefting in these two varieties. Note, especially, the syntactic freedom of IrE clefts which distinguishes them from those used in StE and most other varieties of English, for that matter; thus, a part of a VP, an adverb of manner or a reflexive pronoun can occur in the focus position of clefts in IrE and HebE.

(71) Dear Catolicks, you shee here de cause dat is after bringing you to dis plaace: 'tis *come bourying* you are de corp, de cadaver, of a verie good woman, . . . (John Dunton, *Report of a Sermon*, 1698; quoted here from Bliss 1979: 133)

(72) Don't blame me for Robert's not going out lastyear [last year] It was *himself* that would not go and the reason he gave was . . . (*The Oldham Papers*, No. 8, 1854; Trinity College MS 10,435/8; cited in Filppula 1999: 256)

(73) 'Tis *joking* you are, I suppose. (IrE; cited in Ó hÚrdail 1997: 190)

(74) 'Tis *well* you looked. (IrE; cited in Ó hÚrdail 1997: 190)

(75) And this day I happened to be doing something, I think it was *painting* I was. (HebE; cited in Odlin 1997b: 40)

(76) Och, it's *myself* that's glad to see you [. . .] (HebE; cited in Sabban 1982: 374)

Although there is a clear preference for clefting in both HE and HebE speech, frontings also occur in contexts which are very similar to those observed in WE. Again, many of these would be contextually unusual or odd, if not ungrammatical as such, in EngE. Consider, for example, (77)–(78) recorded from IrE and HebE, respectively:

(77)   My brother that's over in England, . . . when he was young, *a story* now he told me, when he was young. (HE; cited in Filppula 1997: 194)

(78)   [Interviewer: And there would be no care for people like that at this time?]
Aye, there was. *Very, very little* they were getting but they were cared for all the same. (HebE; cited in Filppula 1997: 194)

Although both clefting and especially fronting have long been part of StE grammar, their uses are functionally and syntactically more restricted than those of their Celtic counterparts.[12] Therefore, the prominent use and the syntactic and functional liberties of these focusing devices in the CEs can hardly be a coincidence but must be attributed to Celtic substratum influence (see Filppula 1997 and 1999 for further discussion). The evidence is especially clear in the case of clefting, but fronting, too, owes a lot to substratal influence, as is shown by the WE evidence, in particular. It seems reasonable to argue that WE provides here indirect support to the claim that frontings in IrE and HebE have also been influenced by the Celtic substratum. This is not to deny the possibility of earlier English superstratal input in the Irish context, in particular, because of the existence of parallels for most structural types of clefting and fronting in earlier forms of English. The safest conclusion here is that the contact influences on the two constructions in the varieties at issue have been of two types: both reinforcing (i.e. consolidating already existing structural parallels in varieties of English) and direct (coming exclusively from the substrate languages, as in certain types of clefting). As a further piece of evidence pointing to the same conclusion one could mention the case of *c'est*-clefting in Breton French. German (2003) has established that it is more prominent there than in standard French both in terms of its frequency of use and syntactic properties. This German attributes to influence from the corresponding features of Breton (German 2003: 400–402).

4.2.3.3   *Prepositional Usage*

Prepositional usage is a domain of grammar which is known to give rise to transfer phenomena in language contact situations, and the CEs appear to be no exception to this. However, one has to keep in mind that a great deal of variation in the use of prepositions exists among other varieties of English in the British Isles and elsewhere, as is shown, for instance, by the discussion in Edwards and Weltens (1985). This makes it hard to draw straightforward conclusions about the possible Celtic origins of some of the CE usages. Furthermore, as with many other grammatical features, the distribution of distinctive usages varies from one CE variety to another; some have a wider distribution, while others are limited to one or the other variety. The prepositions which seem to be the most susceptible to contact effects are *at*, *in*, *on*, *of* and *with*.

Expressions denoting *possession* of some object or thing and related notions offer a good example of prepositional usages that are shared by most of the CEs. The preposition used for this purpose varies from one variety to another, though. Thus, in MxE and HebE it can be *at* or *in*, whereas IrE and WE prefer *with* in this function. Consider the following examples:

(79) There's a nice car *at him*.
'He has a nice car.' (MxE; cited in Preuß 1999: 63)

(80) The money was *in the family* of these Campbells.
'These Campbells had plenty of money.' (HebE; cited in Filppula 1999: 237)

(81) The money is *with them*.
'They have plenty of money.' (IrE; cited in Henry 1957: 141)

(82) There's no luck *with the rich*.
'The rich have no luck.' (WE; cited in Thomas 1994: 139)

In present-day WE colloquial usage, the preposition *with* seems to have extended its domain to cover a somewhat wider semantic field than possession as defined above. The following examples recorded from speakers in Llandybie, Carmarthenshire, illustrate this tendency:

(83) Well the boys are grown up *with her* now, you see? (Llandybie: L.Z.)
'Her boys have grown up.'

(84) It's an utility room *with the people* that's there now (Llandybie: A.M.)
'The people . . . have/keep it as a utility room.'

Despite obvious variation in the prepositions used, all the examples cited above are similar in that the 'possessor' is indicated by means of a prepositional phrase placed at the end of the clause or sentence rather than by placing it in the subject position, which is generally the case in other varieties of English, including StE. The CE usages are in all likelihood based on the corresponding Celtic patterns. A special feature of the Celtic languages is that they have no equivalent of the verb *have*; possession and other related notions must therefore be expressed by means of the verb 'be' followed by the thing or property 'possessed' in subject position and, finally, the 'possessor' cast in the form of a prepositional phrase just as in the CE examples above. Examples (85)–(87) from Irish, Manx, and Welsh, respectively, illustrate the typical Celtic constructions:

(85) Tá airgead agam
'Money is at-me'
'I have money'. (Henry 1957: 132)

(86) Ta gleashtan mie echey.
Is nice car at-him
'He has a nice car.' (Preuß 1999: 63)

(87) Mae car gyda ni.
Is [a] car with us.
'We have a car.' (Parry 1999: 117)[13]

Possession of *inherent mental or physical properties* is another area where the CEs display similar usages. The following are examples of this feature, which is also known as 'inalienable possession'. Prepositions typically used for this purpose are *in*, *on* and *with* (the last-mentioned especially in WE):

(88) . . . ah, if it's in a dog he'll train himself, if the goodness is *in 'im*.
'. . . if he's good.' (IrE; cited in Filppula 1999: 229)

(89) All the cattle had the horns *on them* that time. (IrE; cited in Filppula 1999: 221)

(90) And he . . . there was a big whiskers *on him*, they were telling my father. (HebE; cited in Filppula 1999: 225)

(91) There's no horns *with the sheep* about this way. (WE; cited in Parry 1999: 117)

Names of persons, animals or other things can also be mentioned in this connection as a subcategory of inalienable possession, mostly expressed by means of *on*:

(92) There was another old lad used to clean windows. But I can't think the name that was *on him*. (IrE; cited in Filppula 1999: 221)

Parry (1979: 161) comments on a similar use of *on* in WE dialects, pointing out the Welsh parallel:

> In Welsh, AR 'on' corresponds to English OF in expressions such as <u>The name of the farm</u> (<u>Yr enw ar y fferm</u>), and this construction is paralleled in SWW [southwestern WE] in phrases such as the following that are recorded in IM [Incidental Material]: <u>the name on it</u> D[yfed]/Cdg [Cardiganshire] 2; <u>another name on that</u> D/Cdg 4; <u>There's no name on them</u> D/Pem[broke] 9; <u>I don't think there is a name on it</u> D/Cth [Carmarthenshire] 4; <u>There's no name on that</u> D/Cth 5; <u>No special name on it</u> D/Cth 6; <u>You didn't have no other name on them</u> D/Cth 11.

A third major area of prepositional usage distinctive of the CEs is formed by expressions denoting *physical states* or *sensations*, mostly unpleasant ones:

(93) . . . sheep are so daring when the hunger is *on them*.
  '. . . when they are hungry.' (HebE; cited in Sabban 1982: 448)

(94) The health isn't great *with her*.
  'Her health . . .' (IrE; cited in Moylan 1996: 352)

A fourth category consists of usages that have traditionally been treated under the heading of *dativus incommodi* or 'dative of disadvantage' (see, e.g. Hayden and Hartog 1909: 939; Bliss 1984: 149). These are expressions which imply a disadvantage of some kind or another from the point of view of the referent of the pronoun acting as the complement of the preposition. In the following extract from our IrE database the informant and his wife describe how a fox managed to deprive them of half of their flock of hens:

(95) Mrs. F: We heard the hens rushing. You know, the . . when they sound there, rushed across the yard. And we went out, err, it was just there. Oh, it was just there.
  JF: Oh dear, so they are terrible.
  Mrs. F: One year then he took the half of them *on me*. (IrE; cited in Filppula 1999: 219)

Sabban (1982) has recorded similar examples in the English of the Isle of Skye in the Inner Hebrides:

(96) The plants would die *on me*. (P&P, Skye; cited in Sabban 1982: 451)

(97) The little boy disappeared *on her*. (No. 38, P&P; cited in Sabban 1982: 452)

It is interesting to note that *EDD* records *on* in the sense 'to the disadvantage of; against' only in Scotland and Ireland (*EDD*, s.v. *on* 13.). This suggests that the dativus incommodi is confined to the Celtic-influenced varieties of English and has its roots in the corresponding Celtic system. The same holds, incidentally, for the use of *on* to express physical or mental states or sensations and the various types of possession described above: *EDD* does not recognise these usages at all, which lends further support to the Celtic hypothesis.

Besides expressions of possession, the CEs share a fair number of other prepositional idioms, which are discussed in some detail in the works mentioned above. Though clearly recessive in most of the varieties at issue, these usages provide compelling evidence of the direct syntactic input from the Celtic substrata to the earliest, 'basilectal', forms of the CEs, in particular.

4.3   PHONOLOGY

In this section we discuss some phonological features that are shared by the CEs, thus raising the question of Celtic substratal influences. We begin our discussion with those features that are found in all or most of the CEs, and in some cases, in especially the northern dialects of EngE and Scots, too. This is followed by a survey of some of the most salient examples of divergent development, caused by differences in the Celtic substrata and/or different sociohistorical circumstances surrounding the language contact and shift situations.

4.3.1   Shared Phonological Features and Their Origins

Perhaps the most striking phonological feature shared by the CEs is the retention of syllable-final /r/ in all positions, including (in many CE varieties) word-final position (as in *car*) where Received Pronunciation (RP) has a 'silent' /r/. The CEs thus belong to 'rhotic' or 'r-pronouncing' dialects, although the articulation of /r/ varies from one CE variety to another. Hickey (2004: 87) characterises the /r/ of 'traditional' southern IrE as a velarised alveolar continuant, as opposed to the Scottish-style retroflex /r/, which is the predominant realisation in northern IrE dialects and Ulster Scots. Writing on the south-western and northern WE dialects, Thomas (1994: 128) states that the occurrence of post-vocalic /r/ in words like *part* and *cord* "is clearly a feature of pronunciation which is carried over from the phonetic and phonological schema of the Welsh language". To turn back to IrE dialects, a similar substratal account has been proposed, e.g., by D.P. Ó Baoill (1997). However, despite the existence of a parallel feature in the Celtic languages, it is debatable whether this feature can be ascribed to Celtic influence alone, as it is also found in some dialects of EngE and universally in earlier stages of English. Thus, writing on the origins of postvocalic /r/

in IrE, Lass (1990: 145–146) points out that "no orthoepists before the mid-eighteenth century describe /r/-loss as a general feature of the southern [EngE] standard". His conclusion is that, instead of looking to the Celtic languages as a source of this feature, rhotic dialects such as IrE retain it from seventeenth-century (and earlier) "Mainland English" (Lass 1990: 146). Yet, putting the matter in the wider CE perspective, it should be borne in mind that there are dialects of English spoken in the Celtic areas which have not evolved until relatively recent times, and consequently, they cannot be expected to display reflexes of seventeenth-century English. Even in the Irish setting, where English has had a strong presence since the beginning of the early modern period, the phonological system of Irish must have exercised at least reinforcing influence upon that of the emerging new variety of English (cf. Hickey 2004: 81).

Another striking consonantal feature shared by IrE and most other CEs is word-final 'clear' [l], which is a robust feature of IrE (Bliss 1984; D.P. Ó Baoill 1997: 83) and Highland and Island English (Shuken 1984). There is again a close counterpart in the substrate languages, Irish and Scottish Gaelic. It is noteworthy that, on the question of the origin of this feature in IrE, Lass too is willing to accept the role of the Irish substratum (Lass 1990: 139). Hickey (2004: 81) also ascribes the IrE use of what he terms 'alveolar /l/' to the model of the nonvelar, nonpalatal /l/ of Irish. In WE, the situation is slightly more complex. The use of clear [l] in all phonetic environments and word positions is one of the distinctive characteristics of southern WE. Parry (1999: 39) reports that this feature is particularly common in Dyfed and most of Powys—Radnorshire excepted—but in the long-standing English regions of South Wales, clear and dark /l/ are mainly distributed as in RP. Outside these areas, on the other hand, the distribution varies in ways distinct from either of the above patterns. In the northern varieties of WE there is a tendency towards the dark realisations of /l/ in all positions. Furthermore, as Penhallurick (1993: 36–37) notes, in many northern Welsh varieties, both in the Welsh and English languages, the dark [ɫ] is accompanied by strong pharyngalisation. The geographical distribution of the clear and dark /l/ in WE—clear in the southern varieties, dark in the northern—is parallel with the situation in Welsh. Jones (1984: 48–49) reports that southern Welsh varieties have a clear /l/, while in northern Welsh "the nonfricative lateral has a marked dark quality, [ɫ], which may be due to pharyngalization". The similarity of the geographical distribution clearly suggests that the distribution of the clear and dark /l/ in WE is due to substratal influence from Welsh.

Turning to vowels, perhaps the most striking commonality between IrE and other CEs is the use of monophthongs /oː/ and /eː/ in words that belong to the GOAT and FACE lexical sets (see, e.g. Bliss 1984, Harris 1984b and Hickey 2004 on IrE; Shuken 1984 on Highland and Island English; Thomas 1994, Parry 1999 and Penhallurick 2004 on WE). There are some variations based on spelling, though (see, e.g. Thomas 1994: 117–118 on WE in this respect). Although parallels to the CE usages exist in the Celtic languages, similar pronunciations are typical of the northern dialects of EngE and of earlier English, which complicates the issue of the origins. As in the case of rhoticity, the timing of the diphthongisation of these two vowels in EngE dialects is rather late, which Lass (1990: 144–145) takes to be proof of their archaic rather than substratal nature in IrE. In a similar vein, Bliss (1984: 139) assigns IrE /eː/ to the class of seventeenth-century survivals in IrE. In this case, then, any influence from the Celtic languages on the varieties in question must have been of the reinforcing rather than direct type.

Insertion of an epenthetic vowel between certain pairs of consonants is yet another characteristic shared by most CE varieties, with the notable exception of WE. Thus, a word like *film* is pronounced as [fɪləm], [fɪlɪm] or [fɪlʌm], depending on the variety. As for IrE, D.P. Ó Baoill (1997: 84) states that the epenthetic vowel "has been borrowed from Irish where it is obligatory". Hickey (2004: 81) gives an essentially similar account, describing epenthesis in syllable codas as an "areal feature" shared by Irish and English in Ireland. Shuken (1984: 160) records this feature for "some speakers" in Highland and Island English (with some phonetic variations in the unstressed vowel). Macafee and Ó Baoill (1997: 266) note the same phenomenon in Scots and, relying on Wright (1905: § 234), in most of the counties of England, but also point out the widespread use of this type of epenthesis in Scottish Gaelic, Irish and Manx. However, they leave open the question of the influence of Gaelic on Scots.

Prosody is another potentially interesting area where similarities between the CEs may exist, but little research has so far been done to document them. Thomas (1994: 122) draws attention to the WE tendency for the final, unstressed syllable(s) to involve considerable pitch movement, inducing a prominence equal to, or even greater than, that of a preceding stressed syllable. This he considers to be a result of transfer from the Welsh system of intonation, which may explain the 'high-pitch' impression of WE, as Thomas, following Pilch (1983–1984), points out. Shuken (1984: 164) observes a somewhat similar phenomenon in some varieties of Highland and Island English, and it is also known to be characteristic of some dialects of IrE, though no systematic investigations are available. However, Hickey (2004: 74–75) makes a special mention of the "considerable intonational range" typical of some southern and western IrE dialects, and most especially, of the English of Cork City. According to him, the stressed syllables in this variety characteristically display a drop in pitch, a feature which is also found in the Irish of the same region.

To sum up so far, there are a number of obvious commonalities between the CEs with respect to phonological features, but there are many differences as well. The absence of the epenthetic vowel from WE is but one example; other phonological dissimilarities will be discussed in the next section. Some of these are explained by the differences between the Celtic languages themselves and especially by their internal historical division into so-called Q-Celtic (Irish, Scottish Gaelic and Manx) and P-Celtic varieties (Welsh and Cornish). For others, explanations have to be sought in independent linguistic developments or in extra-linguistic factors such as the differing conditions of emergence of the varieties at issue and differing amounts of input from other, 'superstratal' varieties of English.

4.3.2   Divergent Developments

Just as one can point out linguistic similarities between the CEs, there are several clear differences between them. As was mentioned above, some of these can be plausibly explained by differences in the Celtic substrata, while others reflect genuinely divergent developments due to, for example, historical contacts with different dialects of English or to different sociolinguistic and historical circumstances surrounding the language contact and shift situations. These can lead to different linguistic outcomes, as has been shown by cross-linguistic evidence from other contact situations. In the following, we exemplify some of the most salient cases of divergent phonological development in CEs.

Anyone with even scant knowledge of IrE is bound to be struck by the absence of the voiceless and voiced interdental fricatives /θ/ and /ð/ from most varieties of especially southern IrE, where they are replaced by the dental stops /t̪/ and /d̪/, respectively. For example, the words *thin* and *then* are pronounced as [t̪ɪn] and [d̪en]. In some varieties of IrE, the distinction between dental and alveolar stops is lost, which means that words like *thin* and *tin* sound alike (see Bliss 1984: 138; D.P. Ó Baoill 1997: 80–81). However, the dental realisation of the interdental fricatives is not a feature of WE or HebE, or even of the northern varieties of IrE, except in certain consonant clusters and in areas of County Donegal where Irish is still in living contact with English (Harris 1984b; Hickey 2004). As regards WE, the nonoccurrence of dental stops is easily explained by the Welsh consonant system, which contains both /θ/ and /ð/, unlike Irish, in which these consonants changed to /h/ and /ɣ/ in the course of the twelfth and thirteenth centuries (see Thurneysen 1946: 76–77). In HebE and northern IrE varieties, the situation is not so simple: dental stops do occur in both in clusters like /tr/ and /dr/ just as in southern varieties of IrE, though not in lieu of interdental fricatives generally, as in southern IrE (Shuken 1984: 156; Harris 1984b: 130). This latter feature of the northern IrE varieties can be explained by the strong historical influence from ScE (D.P. Ó Baoill 1997: 82). The same explanation probably accounts for the nonoccurrence of dental stops outside the mentioned clusters in HebE, too.

Strong aspiration of plosives is often presented in the literature as one of the trademark features of the WE accent, beginning from the speech of Fluellen, the famously Welsh character in Shakespeare's *Henry V*. Fluellen is known for aspirating his voiced stops as well, resulting in literary representations such as *a most prave pattle* and *St Tavy's day*. Thomas (1994: 122–124) confirms the existence of this feature in WE, but it is a fair assumption that in most present-day varieties the aspiration of voiced stops is no longer discernible. Based on the *SAWD* data, Parry (1999: 37–38) concludes that strong aspiration of the voiceless stops /p, t, k/ is normal in WE in stressed initial positions, and often word-finally, but there is no mention of aspiration in the context of the voiced stops. Penhallurick (2004: 108–109) is even more careful in his assessment of this feature, restricting the "exceptionally prominent" aspiration of /p, t, k/ mainly to northern WE. Our own WE corpora support Penhallurick's view; strong aspiration of initial voiceless stops clearly appears to be a feature of northern rather than south-western WE. Of the other Celtic varieties, strong aspiration of /t, k/ in initial (and medial) position is found (at least) in MxE (Barry 1984: 173–174).

Finally, we turn to prosodic features, some of which were already touched on in the previous section. In the absence of systematic studies enabling comparison between the various CEs and other dialects, we are content to mention here just one feature, viz. the so-called Welsh lilt, which is one of the most distinctive elements of southern WE. The lilting effect is produced by two suprasegmental factors: stress and intonation. The stress in Welsh polysyllabic words is placed on the penultima. In WE, as in Welsh, there can be considerable pitch movement on the final, unstressed syllable, while the stressed syllable is distinguished by its prominent utterance. Morris-Jones (1913: 47) concludes that the word accent in Modern Welsh is primarily based on stress rather than intonation. In RP, on the other hand, stress is generally indicated by a higher pitch level. Southern WE reflects the Welsh stress pattern so faithfully that an RP speaker may have difficulty identifying the position of the stress: final unstressed syllables are not reduced, as in RP, but they may even be lengthened (Thomas 1984a: 183). The intonation on the final syllable may also begin higher or rise from the stressed one. Walters (2003: 238) finds that this, in particular, is a feature of WE prosody which contributes to its distinctive melody. He also notes (*op.cit.*, 233) that similar rising intonation on the post-stressed syllable occurs in other varieties of English which are presumably influenced by Celtic languages, such as those spoken in Western Scotland and Northern Ireland. Walters includes the Liverpool accent in the set as well.

Prosody, just as other aspects of phonology, is obviously subject to regional, individual and situational variation, which makes it a rather elusive object of study. Nevertheless, one can fairly safely conclude that the English accents of North Wales and of the highly anglicised regions are much less distinctive in their rhythm and intonation than those of the South Welsh 'core' of WE, i.e. the industrial valleys and the rural south-west. To what extent similar generalisations can be made concerning the other CE varieties remains a subject for future studies.

4.4   LEXIS

Accounts of the impact of Celtic languages on the English word-stock generally focus on the early contacts between the two language groups and/or
Celtic loanwords in more or less StE usage. As pointed out by Stalmaszczyk
(1997: 80), this approach neglects the role of Celtic-originated lexicon in
regional varieties of English. In Wales and Ireland, for example, the indigenous languages have had a majority status up until the modern period,
thus maintaining a mutually influential contact relationship with English.
Numerous Celtic loans survive even in Scots and Cornish English.

Transfer of lexicon from a substratum language to the target language
is rather different in nature from transfer of phonological or syntactic features. In language shift situations, the lexicon of the target language is generally acquired with little interference from the learners' native language
because of its significance for the smooth communication between the shifting group and the target-language speakers. Lexical items may nevertheless
be transferred through borrowing, retention or code-switching. The mode
of transmission influences the outcome, too: the native language is unlikely
to have a permanent effect on the lexis of the target-language when the
latter is learnt through formal instruction, as was the case in most of rural
Wales in the late nineteenth and early twentieth centuries. Ireland, by contrast, turned essentially bilingual or English-speaking by the mid-nineteenth
century, and it was much more common there that English was acquired
through informal transmission (see, e.g. Odlin 1997a: 6). According to Kallen (1996: 106), this contributed to the adoption of large numbers of Irish
loanwords into IrE. Yet, even there the substratal influences remain less per-
vasive than in syntax or phonology.

Lexis also differs from phonology and grammar because of its high
salience for the speakers: they constantly make conscious choices on the lexical items they use, and any variation of usage is noticeable to all those who
know the language (Trudgill 1986: 25; Hickey 2000: 58). Dialect vocabulary is thus easily influenced by stigma, on one hand, and covert prestige, on
the other. Loanwords from the indigenous Celtic languages remain in use
in dialect communities only if the regional idiosyncrasies are regarded posi-
tively, or at least neutrally. In most cases their use has grown independently
of lexical transfer from the substratum language, but in WE, for example,
bilingualism continues to matter: although the number of Welsh words is
quite limited in the English spoken by the monoglot Anglo-Welsh, bilingual
Welsh speakers are likely to use the occasional Welsh word. In IrE, too, the
line between loanwords and code-switching can be difficult to draw.

4.4.1   Welsh Loanwords in Welsh English

The main reasons for the relatively small number of Welsh lexical items in
WE are the nature of the language contact situation, widespread availability

of, and exposure to, standard English, and the low prestige of Welsh during the most intensive periods of anglicisation. Over the past decades, the final geographical and socioeconomic barriers in the path of standardisation have been removed, and the less commonly used Welsh words have gradually disappeared from WE.

However, there is evidence pointing to more frequent use of loanwords during the earlier stages of anglicisation. Ellis (1882: 207) makes observations both on the presence of Welsh words in the contemporary varieties of WE, as well as—perhaps a little rashly—on their ultimate fate, stating that "[t]here is very little of real mixture; but naturally Welshmen use Welsh idioms at times and even Welsh words. Their children do not, and the transition is complete" (Ellis 1882: 207).

At least in the conservative Welsh dialects covered by the *SAWD*, Welsh loanwords are still numerous. They are used for items and phenomena in specialised lexical categories, such as farming implements, some plants and animals and matters specific of the Welsh cultural experience. Penhallurick (1993: 39) points out that, in many cases, the English word was simply not known to the informants taking part in the survey. Welsh words were thus used to fill lexical gaps in the English vocabulary. Parry (1999: 128–201) contains a detailed glossary of the dialect lexicon which emerged from the survey, including responses elicited by the questionnaire as well as incidental material. Although Welsh loanwords remain in the minority in the glossary, they constitute an element in the investigated variety of WE which distinguishes it from EngE dialects.

Most of the Welsh-originated words in the *SAWD* have not undergone phonological anglicisation but remain in their original form, suggesting that their users are typically first-language Welsh speakers. Yet many of these words appear in anglicised regions, too, such as Radnorshire. Williams (1935) finds them particularly indicative of the language contact history of the region:

> The English speech of Radnorshire people is evidently akin to that of the border counties of Shropshire and Hereford, and even to-day the every-day use of words of Welsh origin in an English form, such as *caib*–hoe, *pentan*–hob, *mochyn*–pig, seems to suggest the superimposition of a foreign tongue upon an indigenous Welsh-speaking community.

> (Williams 1935: 245)

The loanwords tend to have a regional flavour, arising from the local dialects of Welsh. Words which recur in a number of localities of the *SAWD* include *bargod* 'the eaves of a haystack', *beudy* 'cow-house', *cawl* 'mixed vegetable soup', *col, cola* 'bristles of barley, awns', *gambo* usually 'farm wagon or cart, with or without sides', *mamgu* 'grandmother', *moel > moiled, moiling* of cows or sheep, 'hornless' (Eng. *moil(ed)* < Ir. *maol*, Welsh *moel* 'bald'), *mwnci* 'hames' (lit. 'monkey'), *nain* 'grandmother' (> Eng. *nan, nana*), *pentans* 'hobs of a grate', *pistyll* 'water welling from a hill or rock-face', *swch* > *sock*, *suck* 'sole of a plough', 'plough-share', *tadcu/taid* 'grandfather', *twp* 'foolish, stupid', *twrch ddaear* 'mole', (lit. 'ground boar'), *tŷ bach* 'outside lavatory, toilet' (lit. 'little house'), and *winci/wincin* 'weasel' (Parry 1999: 128–201).

Of the above, at least *cawl, gambo, mamgu, nain, taid, twp* and *tŷ bach* are words that still have some currency in WE, even among the Anglo-Welsh population. *Gambo, moil(ed), nan(a)* and *sock* are used in certain EngE and/or AmE dialects, as well (*OED* Online, Dec 2005).

Celtic loanwords in WE can also be historically layered or etymologically complex. In the long-standing English regions there are dialect words which have been borrowed into English from the Celtic languages during the OE or ME periods, and which they thus share with the traditional English dialects (see section 2.4). Another case is dialect words which appear in Welsh as well as in WE, although their origins are not in the Welsh language. The clearest example of this kind is *cwtsh*, a Welsh dialect word which has crept into WE:

> *cwtsh* n. 'pantry', 'potato-clamp', 'storage place, e.g. under the stairs', 'hiding place'; ME *couch* < (O)F *couche*; Welsh *cwtsh* n. 'recess', 'kennel', 'cuddle'
> *cwtsh (down)* v. 'to squat down', 'to hide', 'to cuddle up'; (O)F *coucher* v.; Welsh *cwtsio* 'to cuddle'

> (Parry 1999: 147)

Thomas (1984a: 193; 1994: 143) lists a number of Welsh dialect words with restricted regional use in WE. These include *dôl* 'meadow' in North Powys; *gwas* > *wuss* 'form of address to a male' and *pentan* 'hob' in southeast Wales; *clennig* '(New Year's gift), an allowance of money' (*calennig*), *dreven* 'untidiness' (*trefn*), *glaster* 'a drink made with milk and water' (*glasdwr*), and *wackey* 'unwell' (*gwachul*) in Buckely, Clwyd (see Parry 1972 and Griffiths 1969, cited by Thomas 1994). Lewis (1990: 110–111) lists Welsh words in Glamorganshire English, e.g. *cariad* 'darling', *crachach* 'élite', *didorath* 'shiftless' (*didoreth*), *mochyn* 'pig', a term of abuse, *bopa* 'auntie', *cam* 'step, pace', *shwmai* 'hello' (*sut mae*) and *teishen lap* 'fruit cake' (*teisen lap*). Lewis points out that Welsh loanwords are often "confined to fairly consciously picturesque speaking", thus being overt rather than covert Welshisms and not fully integrated into English. There are exceptions, too. It is possible that because of the relatively informal transmission of English in the industrial valleys, the number of Welsh loanwords in the local dialect of English is greater than in WE on average. Even so, the more 'picturesque' and old-fashioned ones are probably falling out of use.

Exclamations and terms of endearment represent pragmatic lexical items which may be dropped into English language conversation independently of the general topic of discussion. These may be in restricted use among the Anglo-Welsh as well, but characteristically they occur in the English of bilingual (and elderly) Welsh speakers. They include *ach-y-fi!* exclamation of disgust, 'yuck, ugh', *Duw!* exclamation, lit. 'God' (*Duw, duw* 'Dear, dear, Good God'), *champion* 'great, marvellous', *na fo* exclamation 'That's right', 'you've got it' (from Welsh *dyna fo* 'there it is'), *del, bach, fach* 'dear, little one', and *bachgen* 'boy'. The Welsh toast *iechyd da* 'good health' is certainly well-known enough among the non-Welsh speakers, too.

Thomas (1994: 142–143) specifies the uses of many of the above words and adds a few to the list with the observation that loanwords with general currency in WE are "less than a handful" and primarily cultural. In spite of the present-day situation, the above sources indicate that during the language shift process, approximately a century ago, lexical transfer was quite common. The subsequent dissociation of WE from Welsh concerns both lexis and grammar.

4.4.2   Irish Loanwords in Irish English

As mentioned above, the history of language contact in Ireland is rather different from that in Wales, Irish having made a significant impact on the grammar of IrE and also contributed to the lexicon of IrE to a greater extent than Welsh to WE. One of the reasons for this is the long history of English in Ireland as compared to Wales, be it that the majority of Irish loanwords have only entered IrE during the modern period when the language contact has been at its most intense. The unevenness of the anglicisation process has resulted in plenty of regional variation, too, affecting the meanings of many of the words mentioned below (see Kallen 1996: 119–125). Ulster is a special case: because of its strong historical links with Scotland, the Ulster dialects preserve many words that originate in Lowland Scots, and a few of these go back to Scots Gaelic (see, esp. Macafee 1996).

Bliss (1984) divides the nonstandard element in IrE vocabulary into two main classes: first, words which are not part of StE lexis at all, and secondly, words which are used in IrE in senses not found in StE (Bliss 1984: 140). Both groups can have two possible sources, as Bliss continues: on the one hand, IrE retains a number of words which have fallen out of use in StE or have only been used in dialectal English in the first place; on the other hand, there are a number of words in IrE that are direct loans from Irish, or they are English words used in senses which derive from Irish. Thus, the influence from Irish has here, as in syntax, been either direct or—in the majority of cases—indirect (for further discussion and examples of each class, see Bliss 1984: 140 ff.). According to Bliss, the number of direct Irish loans in IrE is small, even in the rural dialects, and they are mainly negative terms of abuse or restricted to rural life, such as *ommadhawn* 'fool' (< Ir. *amadán*), *oanshagh* '(female) fool' (< Ir. *óinseach*), *bosthoon* 'clown' (< Ir. *bastún*), *soogawn* 'hay rope' (< Ir. *súgán*), *gowlogue* 'forked stick' (< Ir. *gabhlóg*), and *kish* 'basket' (< Ir. *cis*) (Bliss 1984: 141–142).

More recent research has revealed that the number of Irish loanwords may be larger than what Bliss (1984) had assumed. However, Kallen (1994: 183, 1997b: 145) cautions that the categorisation of Irish and English words in IrE is not always straightforward, as their etymologies may involve cognate words and word-internal code-switching. Yet, dozens of Irish loanwords can be found in English language documents written in Ireland as early as from the mediaeval period onwards. Kallen (1994: 167) refers to Irwin's (1935: 205–330) survey of 200 early IrE dialect words, a quarter of which originate from Irish. These include, e.g. legal, technical and agricultural terminology, such as *collop* 'unit of cattle for levying taxes, etc.' and *garran* 'gelding'. Lexical items related to law and society constitute a major category of loanwords in early IrE, as well as in Scots, as a result of the distinctive Celtic systems of government. Kallen (1994: 167–169, 1997b: 141) mentions the archaic dialect of Forth and Bargy in County Wexford as a significant source of information. It is descended from the dialect of the early colonists who borrowed Irish vocabulary quite freely, and it still preserved many early Irish loanwords during the time of the late eighteenth- and nineteenth-century investigations. As examples, Kallen cites, e.g. *booraan* 'a drum' (Ir. *bodhrán*), *muskawn* 'a large heap or lump' (Ir. *meascán*) and *chi* 'a small quantity'. The dialect vocabulary of Forth and Bargy is best illustrated in the nineteenth-century glossary compiled by Jacob Poole (see Dolan and Ó Muirithe 1979/1996).

Early IrE also contains dialectal vocabulary from OE and ME and Scandinavian sources, as well as words of other, obscure origin. Kallen (1994: 174) observes, however, that lexical items entering IrE in the sixteenth to eighteenth centuries arise mainly from Irish. These include, e.g. words related to soldiering, such as *kerne, rapparee* and *galloglass*. To these can be added *bonagh* 'permanent soldier', *Feinne* 'soldiers of the Irish militia' and *stokaghe* 'attendant on a *kerne* / an Irish foot-soldier', all cited here from the *OED* Online (Dec 2005).

Borrowing and retention of Irish words continue throughout the Modern English period. A survey of the *OED* shows that another significant category of loanwords is that of words related to nature, farming and housekeeping, e.g. *bilders* (*biolar*), *boneen* 'young pig' (*bainbhín*), *bonny-clabber* 'clotted, sour milk' (*bainne* + *claba*), *booly* 'temporary fold for cattle' (*buaile*), *cleave* 'basket' (*cliabh*), *corcass* 'salt marshes along river banks' (*corcach*), *fiorin* 'a species of grass' (*fiorthán*), *frawn* 'bilberry' (*fraochan*), *gibbon* 'sand eel' (*goibín*), *loy* 'an Irish spade' (*laighe*), *malahane* 'cheese curds' (*mulchán*), etc. Another field is that of supernatural or mythical phenomena: *banshee* (*bean sídhe*), *cluricaune* 'a type of elf' (*clúracán*), *merrow* 'mermaid or merman' (*muruach*), *pishogue* 'witchcraft or superstitious belief' (*píseog*), *pooka, phooka* 'hobgoblin' (*púca*), *sheogue* 'fairy' (*sióg*), *Sidhe* 'hills of the fairies', *Tir-na-nog* 'a fabled land of perpetual youth'. Irish words are also used as terms of abuse or endearment, perhaps reflecting the precedence of the native language under emotional circumstances (see Van Ryckeghem 1997: 171). The former are exemplified, in addition to the words mentioned by Bliss (1984) above, by *carrow* 'gambler' (*cerrbach*), *gelt* 'lunatic' (*geilt*), *omadhaun* 'mentally slow person, fool' (*amadán*), *stalko* 'idler' (*stócach*), *streel* 'untidy or disreputable woman' (*straoill(e)*), *unchaghe* 'foolish or wanton woman' (*óinseach*). The OED also presents a variety of interjections which originate from Irish, e.g. *nabocklish* 'never mind!, leave it alone!' (*ná bac leis*) and *wisha*, an exclamation indicating dismay, emphasis, or surprise (*mhuise*). These more pragmatic expressions also include the Irish toast, *sláinte* '(good) health', and the ironic tag *mar dhea*, roughly meaning 'supposedly' (see Kallen 1997b: 152).

Irish cultural loans in the OED include *bandle* 'an Irish measure (ca 2 ft)' (*bannlamh*), *barmbrack/barnbrack* 'currant-bun' (*bairigen breac*), *caoine/ keen* 'an Irish funeral song', *caubeen* 'an Irish hat' (*caipín*), *fine* 'an old Irish family or sept', and *glib* 'thick mass of matted hair on the forehead and over the eyes, formerly worn by the Irish'. However, Kallen (1996: 115–116) points out that, unlike in Australian or African Englishes, cultural borrowings constitute a small part of the Irish lexicon in IrE, while the vast majority of Irish words in IrE belong to its core vocabulary, enabling what Kallen—following Myers-Scotton (1993)—describes as 'unmarked code-switching' from English to Irish. Kallen (1996: 114–118) finds that for IrE speakers, this strategy is a "vehicle for vernacularisation", giving the regional variety an expressive power that is not found in formal English. Using Irish-derived lexical items need not signify an overt identification with the Irish language subculture.

The OED is here a useful source as it gives an indication of the degree to which words have been adopted into international English usage. As a guide to the regional lexicon of IrE it is less useful. Van Ryckeghem (1997) offers an overview of word lists containing general or regional IrE lexicon. In these lists, the earliest of which were mostly compiled by amateurs interested in their local dialects of English, Irish-originated lexical items can be found in large numbers. Some are more sophisticated; for example, Ó hAnnracháin (1964) presents a list of 500 dialect words, together with phonetic transcriptions, from County Kerry, including many words which have become obsolete in present-day vernacular Irish or in standard literary language (see Kallen 1994: 185; van Ryckeghem 1997: 181–182). The most recent scholarly compilations are the dictionaries by Dolan (1998 and later editions), giving a comprehensive account of the distinctive elements in the IrE lexicon, and Ó Muirithe (2000), focusing on lexicon originating from Irish. In addition to regional variation, Kallen (1996, 1997b: 148, 154) draws attention to the range of social and stylistic variation within IrE lexical usage: these are factors which affect the use of Irish loans as well as the larger set of characteristically Irish vocabulary.

As has been noted above, the exact extent of the Irish element in IrE vocabulary has been a matter of some debate, and the situation has varied from one period and region to another. Yet, some of the most recent works such as Dolan (1998/2004) make it clear that, in present-day usage, the number of Irish-derived words is on a decline. In his Introduction to the second edition of his *Dictionary of Hiberno-English*, Dolan puts this down to the diminishing numbers of speakers who could "move easily between Irish and English, not so much in their ability to speak fluently in both languages, as in their comfortable use of words, phrases, proverbs, and grammar from the Irish language in their daily use of English" (Dolan 1998/2004: xix).

4.4.3   Scots Gaelic Loanwords in Scots/Scottish English

The standard assumption is that the number of Scots Gaelic loans in Scots is minimal (cf. Gillies 1994: 164). However, McClure (1986) argues that, especially in the regional dialects, Gaelic loans are much more numerous than is often assumed:

> . . . at a level closer to the grass roots of the language—in the spoken dialects, especially those of outlying areas—hundreds of Gaelic-derived words have been, and in many cases still are, in use, albeit largely un-noticed and unrecorded. The debt of Scots to Gaelic is not small, but very great: even if we must wait until all things are made known to appreciate it in its entirety.

> (McClure 1986: 97)

Gillies (1994) argues that there are more Gaelic words even in 'general' Scots usage than is generally assumed:

> We may also observe that a good number of Gaelic words, more than are customarily acknowledged, did win their way through to 'general' Scots usage—against the odds, as it were. When these occur in diction-aries they tend to be given the tag 'etymology unknown', or to appear decked out with elaborate but unnecessary Romance or Germanic derivations.

> (Gillies 1994: 165)

Although even the known Gaelic loans are counted in their hundreds, they may seem relatively few as a percentage of the total of Scots lexicon (cf. Macafee 1997: 190). Nevertheless, it seems strange that the role of Gaelic in Scots should be dismissed, e.g. on the grounds that many of these words are archaic, known today to a wider community (only) through the works of classical authors such as Burns and Scott, or that they are restricted to regional dialects (see Görlach 2002: 126). These arguments fail to appreciate the historical and regional impact of Gaelic on Scots and ScE; though not great in extent, Gaelic-derived words are "firmly established at the core or heart of the language", as described by McClure (1986: 89).

English and Scots share a centuries-long coexistence with Gaelic. C. Ó Baoill (1997: 552) states that the intimacy of the contact situation and the societal and individual bilingualism involved created a fertile environment for lexical borrowing in both directions. A number of Gaelic loans entered Scots as early as in the OE period. McClure (1994: 58–59) files them under the categories of topography (e.g. *ben* 'mountain', *corrie* 'a hollow in a mountainside', *drum* 'ridge' and *strath* 'river valley'), societal and legal terminology (e.g. *kenkynolle*, from *cenn cineoil* 'head of the kindred', *duniwassal* from *duin-uasal* 'nobleman', *couthal* from *comhdhail* 'court of justice' and *breive* from *brithem* 'judge'), cultural loans (e.g. *bard* 'poet' and *clarschach* 'harp') and other, common words (*bladdoch* 'buttermilk', *clachan* 'village', *cranreuch* 'frost' and *ingle* 'hearth'; see also McClure 1986; Macafee 1997; C. Ó Baoill 1997: 552–554). Some of the early vocabulary has survived in general or restricted use until this day.

The regional dialects of Modern Scots also contain some Gaelic loanwords, most of them adopted in Modern times (see Shuken 1984 for Highland and Island English). Tulloch (1997: 384–387) gives detailed descriptions of the history of several Gaelic borrowings in Scots (and ScE), including *Gaelic* (*Gàidhlig*), the Highlanders' own name for their language. Among the recent, regional loans are *shangan* 'ant', *smiach* 'a slight sound, a whisper', and *cuttag* 'middle-sized, sturdy woman'.

The decline of the traditional dialects which has taken place over the last century in Wales and Ireland has also taxed the inventory of traditional dialectal expressions in the Scottish varieties of English. McClure (1986) nevertheless finds that a large part of the Gaelic loans still belong to the core vocabulary of Lowland culture. Others are terms related to Highland culture—the culture by which Scotland is known throughout the world— and a third group are Gaelic terms used in historical and anthropological contexts, not integrated into everyday Scots. He points out (1994: 86) that many Gaelic loanwords have regained popularity as indicators of Scottish cultural phenomena of the 'travel-brochure' type. These include, e.g. *philibeg* 'kilt' (*fillebeg*), *sporran* 'ornamental purse worn in front of the kilt', *claymore* 'basket-hilted sword' and *ceilidh* 'entertainment with traditional Gaelic music'. The last one is also a well-known term in Ireland. The similarities between Irish and Scots Gaelic and the historical connections between the two regions cause difficulty in distinguishing the source language in some cases, but as observed by Tulloch (1997: 388–389), there are also loanwords in regional varieties of Scots whose origins have been identified as Irish. These include the Galloway terms *callan* 'girl', from Ir. *cailin*, and *spalpean* 'naughty child' from Ir. *spailpín*.

4.4.4   Cornish Loanwords in Cornwall

In Cornwall, too, the Cornish language was carried on in the form of loanwords in spite of having disappeared as a community language for a few centuries. Wakelin lists in his *Language and History in Cornwall* (1975) 18 loans from Cornish, the majority of which are not included in the second edition of the *OED*:

> *bannel* 'broom', *bucca* 'scarecrow', *clunk* 'to swallow', *clunker* 'windpipe', *dram* 'swath', *flam-new* 'brand-new', *fuggan* 'pastry dinner-cake', *gook* 'bonnet', *griglans* 'heather', *gurgoe* 'warren', *hoggan* 'pastry cake', *kewny* 'rancid' *muryans* 'ants', *muryan-bank* 'ant-hill', *pig's-crow* 'pigsty', *scaw (-tree)* 'elder tree', *stank* 'to walk, trample, step (on, in)', *tidden* 'tender', *(piggy-)whidden* 'weakling' (of a litter of pigs).
>
> (Wakelin 1975: 180–201)

If Wakelin's list seems shorter than one might expect, it must be pointed out that it is based on the *SED* materials only and, as Wakelin himself points out, the *SED* survey conducted in the 1950s was not specifically designed to elicit loanwords in any variety of English but was rather geared towards finding items that are widespread in dialects. In a footnote Wakelin refers to Jenner (1905), who has identified a considerably larger number of Cornish loans in use in Cornwall:

> Cf. H. Jenner, 'Cornwall a Celtic Nation' *The Celtic Review*, I (1905), 234–46). In this paper, read before the Pan-Celtic Congress at Carnarvon, Jenner states that a considerable number of words—perhaps a hundred or more, mostly names of things—were still in use among the Cornish working-classes (p. 241).
>
> (Wakelin 1975: 180)

Similar conclusions can be drawn from Berresford Ellis (1998: 20), who cites Jago's (1887) observation that "the Cornish dialect is to this day full of Celtic Cornish words", however reliable this assessment can be considered. The instances mentioned here nevertheless represent a rather small population: Wakelin (1991: 203) concludes that overwhelmingly greater numbers of words have been borrowed from English into Cornish than *vice versa*. On the other hand, Stalmaszczyk (2000: 34) argues that, because of the lengthy absence of living contact with the Cornish language, the Cornish words which survive in present-day Cornish English can be considered well established. He lists some lexical items based on Phillipps (1993), including *bravish* 'moderately well' (*breyf* 'fine, well' + *-ish*), *clicky* 'left-handed' (*cledhyas*), *peeth* 'a well' (*pyth* 'pit, shaft, well'), *quilkin* 'a frog' (*gwylskyn*) and *wrasse* 'old woman, witch' (*gwrach*). The *OED* Online (Dec 2005), too, gives a number words for which a Cornish origin is suggested, e.g. *bowssen* 'immerse' (*beuzi*), *fogou* 'a Cornish souterrain or earth-house' (*fogo/fougo* 'a cave'), *grig* 'common heath or heather' (*grig*, Welsh *grug*) and *guary* 'a miracle play' (*guare*). There are also many Cornish words related to the mining trade.

4.4.5   Manx Loanwords in Manx English

As observed in Chapter 3, section 3.5.2, Manx as a living community language did not survive beyond the beginning of the twentieth century. In MxE, however, the number of Manx Gaelic loanwords has been considerable. Moore, Morrison and Goodwin (1924) recorded more than 750 Manx Gaelic words in nineteenth-century MxE literature, and Gill, in his collection of Manx dialects words and phrases, presents an extensive collection of "words brought over from the Manx language with or without changes in their form" (Gill 1934: 9). Barry (1984: 175) observes that he managed to record 126 lexical borrowings from Manx Gaelic during his fieldwork for the *SED* in the 1950s. The majority of the words recorded by Barry related to farming and farm animals (*saie* 'paddock', *collagh* 'stallion', *groabey* 'drain'), sailing and fishing (*becks* 'seats' (in a rowing boat), *aley* 'a rough spot in sea where there is likely to be fish'), human beings, behaviour etc. (*ayr* 'father', *graney* 'feeling unwell') and the house (*chiollagh* 'hearth', *jeush* 'pair of scissors'). Barry (1984: 176) concludes, however, that "clearly the use of Gaelic expressions is likely to be reduced much further".

4.4.6   Institutions and Organisations

It is an indication of the present national significance of the Celtic languages in their home countries that certain organisations and cultural institutions are best known by their Celtic rather than English names; they are identified through the language that is an integral part of their ideology. In Ireland, most public institutions have Irish names. The official Irish titles are generally modern coinages, but many of them have gained precedence over the English ones. Some examples are *Garda*, the police force, the nationalist party *Sinn Féin* (lit. 'we ourselves'), the *Oireachtas*, the National Parliament of the Republic of Ireland (and also the title of an annual cultural festival), *Dáil Éireann*, the House of Representatives, *the Ceann Comhairle*, chairman of the Dáil Éireann, *Taoiseach*, Prime Minister, *Tánaiste*, Deputy Prime Minister. In Wales, these titles have sprung from the Welsh language community and they include *Eisteddfod*, a Welsh festival of arts, *Plaid Cymru*, the Party of Wales, and *Cymdeithas yr Iaith (Gymraeg)*, the Welsh Language Society. These Welsh titles also appear in English language contexts (e.g., "The National Eisteddfod of Wales", "Join Plaid Cymru now!", and "the

Cymdeithas yr Iaith policy on rural schools"). The national connotation of the Welsh titles is illustrated by Lindsay's (1993) example of the vans of the Water Board:

> The inscription on one side reads *Mae Dŵr Cymru gymaint yn fwy na Welsh Water*, whereas the other side reads *Dŵr Cymru means so much more than Welsh Water*. The two versions of the slogan are identical in meaning, but in each case the organization's Welsh title is celebrated as being more significant than its synonymous English title.

> (Lindsay 1993: 16–17)

The title of the Cornish Language Board, *Kesva an Tavas Kernewek*, is not quite as institutionalised as that of *Cymdeithas yr Iaith*, and it is usually accompanied by the English translation. *Gorsedd (Kernow)*, on the other hand, an organisation promoting Celtic culture in Cornwall, is solely referred to by its Cornish title.

4.5   CONCLUSION

The foregoing discussion has shown that the linguistic effects of the English–Celtic contacts in the modern period are best in evidence, as can be expected, in some regional varieties of English spoken in, or close to, the present-day or earlier Celtic-speaking areas in Wales, Ireland and Scotland. The same can be said for the traditional dialects of English in Man and Cornwall, but there the nature of the evidence is rather scattered and partly anecdotal, too, because of the lack of records and small numbers of traditional dialect speakers. By contrast to the mediaeval period, contact influences in the more standard varieties of English remain limited. Yet, there are grounds for arguing that some syntactic features of the latter have been influenced or at least reinforced by the robustness of these features in the CE varieties. The most likely examples are, as was discussed above, certain types of perfects, the PF of verbs and the cleft construction, all of which have not only increased their frequencies of use in most mainstream varieties of the modern period but also expanded their originally rather narrow syntactic or functional domains of use. Thus, the CEs may well have provided a springboard for the spread of these features into other varieties of English, mediated through generations of emigrants to Britain, America and other parts of the world from Wales, Scotland, and especially Ireland.

Phonological contact influences in the modern period appear to be exclusive to regional varieties. As can be expected on the basis of general contact-linguistic theory, the language shift situation in the formerly Celtic-speaking areas has led to the adoption of several phonological and prosodic features in the English of these areas that can be traced back to corresponding features in the Celtic substrata. As was seen, however, the existence of earlier English parallels to some of the putative contact effects makes it hard to exclude the possibility of conservatism or multiple causation. Finally, lexis largely replicates the same general scenario as that in the mediaeval periods of contact: relatively few Celtic words have found their way into mainstream Englishes, including StE. By contrast, the CEs and even some of their neighbouring English or ScE regional dialects retain a fair number of words originating in one or the other of the Celtic languages. They have in all likelihood been much more common in the most intense periods of language shift in the past centuries than in the present-day varieties.

As mentioned in the Conclusion to Chapter 2, the linguistic outcomes of the contacts in the modern period are also important from the point of view of ascertaining Celtic influences in the mediaeval period, as well. This is because the contact settings in both cases are essentially similar and, more particularly, involve prolonged and intense periods of contact between speakers of Celtic and English, leading eventually to language shift on the part of the former. Although the linguistic systems of the two groups of languages are by no means directly comparable between the two periods for obvious reasons, the similarities are such that we can consider the modern contact effects to provide significant indirect evidence of rather similar effects in the mediaeval period.

Epilogue

The Extent of Celtic Influences in English

5 The Debates on the Extent of Celtic Influences in English[1]

It is widely accepted today that the Celtic languages have played a significant role in the development of the so-called Celtic Englishes. Many of the characteristic features of especially the syntax and phonology of Irish English or Welsh English, for example, can best be explained by assuming a Celtic substratum in these contact varieties of English. When we turn to the history of the English language in England, however, the situation is very different. The traditional 'Received View' holds that the influence of the Celtic languages upon the early forms of English is almost negligible and is restricted to some place-names, river-names and just a handful of loanwords.

In this chapter, we provide a brief historical survey of the research and debates on the nature and extent of the linguistic contacts between English and the Celtic languages. Although most of the views to be surveyed below have already been referred to in one or another of the previous chapters, we believe that it is important to try and capture the broad line of development of studies in this area. As will be seen in the discussion below, this area of research is now undergoing rapid expansion and something that could even be called a 'paradigm shift'. Essentially, this shift entails changing attitudes towards the Celtic hypothesis, which is now being taken much more seriously than it was in most of the earlier works on the English–Celtic contacts. We begin with a short account of the Received View on the linguistic outcomes of the early contacts, which we trace back to the statements made by some eminent early twentieth-century historians of the English language and subsequently reiterated by even some of the most recent textbooks on the subject. This will be followed by a discussion of the 'dissident' voices in the philological and linguistic scholarship, starting with some early and mid-twentieth-century scholars and proceeding thence to the most recent studies, all of which have in some way or other called in question the basic tenets of the Received View.

5.1   THE RECEIVED VIEW

Textbooks on the history of the English language provide a good illustration of the prevailing view in philological research on English–Celtic contacts.

Briefly, this view holds that the Celtic languages have played only a minimal role in the development of English. In the following are some quotations from textbooks on the history of English, spanning almost a century of scholarship from Jespersen (1905) to Fennell (2001). Jespersen, whose authoritative statement can be said to have laid the basis for almost all of the subsequent treatments of this subject, characterises the role of the Celtic languages in the development of English in the following terms:

> We now see why so few Celtic words were taken over into English. There was nothing to induce the ruling classes to learn the language of the inferior natives; it could never be fashionable for them to show an acquaintance with that despised tongue by using now and then a Celtic word. On the other hand the Celt would have to learn the language of his masters, and learn it well; he could not think of addressing his superiors in his own unintelligible gibberish, and if the first generation did not learn good English, the second or third would, while the influence they themselves exercised on English would be infinitesimal.

> (Jespersen 1905: 39)

Variants of Jespersen's basic line of argumentation appear again and again in widely used textbooks. Thus, Baugh and Cable (1993: 85) state that "outside of place-names the influence of Celtic upon the English language is almost negligible", while Pyles and Algeo (1993: 292) conclude that "we should not expect to find many [Celtic loanwords in English], for the British Celts were a subject people, and a conquering people are unlikely to adopt many words from those whom they have supplanted". An essentially similar account is given by Strang (1970) in her influential book on the history of English. According to her, "the extensive influence of Celtic can only be traced in place-names" (1970: 391). In another context, she notes that "[t]he poverty of the Celtic contribution to English vocabulary even in this area, and at a time when Celtic cultural influence was enormous, is very remarkable" (1970: 374).

In a recent textbook, *A History of English: A Sociolinguistic Approach*, Barbara Fennell describes the early English–Celtic contacts in a way which closely echoes Jespersen's account from almost a hundred years ago:

> By contrast with Latin, fewer than twelve Celtic words are thought to have been in English before the twelfth century. [. . .] It has been suggested that the limited influence of Celtic on the language stems from the fact that the Celts were a submerged race in the Old English period. Once again, it appears that they were neither sufficiently well organized or centralized, nor militarily or culturally superior, so that their influence was extremely limited.

In these instances we can talk about prestige borrowing vis-à-vis Latin and casual or superficial contact between the languages (Celtic), which resulted in only minor lexical borrowings and no influence on language structure. This would accord with stage 1 on Thomason and Kaufman's borrowing scale.

(Fennell 2001: 89–90)

The basic tenor of the textbook accounts of the linguistic outcomes of the early English–Celtic contacts has thus scarcely altered during the past one hundred years or so of scholarship: only a handful of Celtic words were borrowed into English, and this is only to be expected given the relative status of the speakers of these languages in the given historical circumstances. Furthermore, the limited number of Celtic loanwords is often taken as definitive proof against the possibility of Celtic influence on English on other levels of language, especially syntax and phonology.

The same line of reasoning also characterises a large part of the specialised linguistic studies. Thus, as was seen in the chapter on the rise of the English progressive form (see Chapter 2, section 2.2.5), works such as Mossé (1938) dismiss the possibility of Celtic influence on the grounds that, although parallels exist between English and Celtic with regard to this feature, they can be explained as a mere coincidence. Since there are no traces of Celtic influence in the extant Old English (OE) texts, no influences from Celtic need be assumed. And the lack of such influences is, not surprisingly, explained by Mossé by the socially inferior status of the British Celts. To mention another, more recent, example, van der Wurff (1995: 404–409) rejects the possibility of Celtic influence on English periphrastic DO because of the paucity of Celtic loanwords in English. However, there are those, too, who seriously consider the possibility of Celtic influences but remain 'noncommittal' for some reason or other. This position is represented by, e.g. Denison (1993). Having surveyed the existing accounts of the rise of the English progressive form, including those advocating Celtic origin, he stops short of committing himself to any conclusive judgment on the issue of Celtic influence, apart from stating that much of the evidence for Celtic contact effects is "largely circumstantial" and the argument remains "speculative" (Denison 1993: 402).

5.2   DISSIDENT VOICES IN THE EARLIER LINGUISTIC SCHOLARSHIP

The Received View described above has come under increasing criticism in recent years. Yet, it is important to remember that there are numerous early works which have called in question one or another aspect of the prevailing canon in linguistic or philological research on English–Celtic contacts and produced various kinds of evidence to show that the extent of Celtic influence on English is considerably larger than the proponents of the traditional account have accepted. The ideas of these early 'dissidents' are regularly referred to even in present-day scholarship, and therefore deserve to be explained in this connection, too.

One of the earliest and most influential supporters of the Celtic hypothesis is Wolfgang Keller (1925), who has inspired a series of other studies, especially by Walther Preusler (see, e.g. Preusler 1956), Ingerid Dal (1952), Gerard J. Visser (1955), and Bjørn Braaten (1967). Heinrich Wagner (see esp. Wagner 1959) is yet another scholar, seemingly independent from the aforementioned, who is sympathetic to the idea of a Celtic substratum in English. Likewise, J.R.R. Tolkien raises the possibility of early Celtic (Welsh) influences on English phonology, syntax and lexis in one of his articles (see Tolkien 1963). In the following, we will present a brief summary of the views and most important findings of these and a few other scholars.

Keller, whose work was in turn inspired by A.G. van Hamel's (1912) paper on 'Anglo-Irish', is perhaps the first to highlight the role of syntax rather than lexicon as the main area where Celtic contact effects can be expected. He argues that the OE distinction between the (reconstructed) *es- and *bheu-forms of the 'substantive' verb 'be' is of Celtic origin. This distinction corresponds exactly to the Cymric one and has no parallels in the other Germanic languages. According to Keller (1925: 60), it was introduced into English by the English-speaking Britons; this is a view which sounds very plausible in the light of what contact linguistics today has to say about the mechanism of transfer in situations of language shift.

The English gerund or 'verbal noun' construction is another feature of the English verb system discussed by Keller. In fact, his views on the rise of the English gerund are much better known and more often quoted in later research than those on the OE distinction between the *es- and *bheu-forms. According to Keller, the use of the verbal noun as the predicate of the verb 'be' gradually gave rise to the so-called progressive form. This, as Keller argues, has a close parallel in the Cymric construction consisting of the substantive verb 'be' + preposition *yn* + verbal noun (e.g. *mae yn dysgu* '[he] is learning'). Keller further notes that the English progressive form *to be (a) doing* is not found in the other Germanic languages, except for the Low German dialect of Westfalish and also Dutch folk-speech, which, however, involve the infinitive instead of the verbal noun. As regards the vexed question of the date of emergence of these features in English and the timing of the contact influences, Keller accepts without further comment the oft-mentioned difference in the dating of the OE *is/bið* distinction and of the verbal noun construction: while the former is already found in OE literary sources, the verbal noun does not become established in English until the fourteenth century (Keller 1925: 60, 64).

Writing both before and after World War II, Walther Preusler (our source here Preusler 1956) is the next to hoist the Celtic flag in the field of the history of English. Generally speaking, he concurs with Keller's account and also puts forward some new arguments concerning, e.g., the origin of the English gerund: he notes the early attestation of the verbal noun construction in northern English and Scottish dialects and also draws attention to the strong preservation of this construction in Scottish English even today. This he considers evidence speaking against the rival explanations based on either independent development (the stand adopted, e.g. in Curme 1912), French influence (Einenkel 1914), or Latin/Greek influence (Mossé 1938).

Preusler is also often quoted for other features of English which he ascribes to Celtic models: these include especially the so-called DO-periphrasis; clefting; the 'contact-clause' (or 'zero-relative' clause); 'stranding prepositions' with the relative *that*; and place-names of the type *County Antrim, Market Drayton, Mount Everest*. The last-mentioned are, as Preusler points out, particularly frequent in northern England, Scotland, Wales and Ireland. According to him, there can be no doubt that they reflect the Celtic patterns, in which the genitive is placed after the governing word (here *Antrim*, etc.), with the head of the phrase (here *County*, etc.) preceding the attribute (Preusler 1956: 341).

The general reception of Preusler's work among Anglicists has been rather critical. Objections have been raised, among other things, in relation to the timing of the Celtic influences and the late emergence of most of the features discussed by Preusler in ME texts. Another object of criticism has been Preusler's account of periphrastic DO. It involves an assumption about early Celtic influence on the parallel construction in some southern German dialects which also exhibit periphrasis with the verb *tun* 'do' (see, e.g. Mossé 1938; Visser 1963–1973; Denison 1993). On the other hand, a substantial number of the features identified by Preusler as being of Celtic origin have continued to intrigue scholars even at the present day, and it is therefore reasonable to expect that at least some of his findings will be vindicated by the ongoing research.

Dal (1952), G. Visser (1955), Wagner (1959), and Braaten (1967) are perhaps the most vocal exponents of the Celtic hypothesis in the post-war decades. To these could be added Lewy (1956, 1966), who discusses a number of Celtic (Irish) loanwords in English (see below). Dal—who unfortunately wrote her important article on the rise of the English progressive form in German—provides a plausible explanation for the relative lack of Celtic loanwords in OE, very much in line with Keller's earlier account and with some of the recent general models of contact-induced change (especially that advocated by Thomason and Kaufman 1988):

Es ist aber die einseitige Betrachtung des *Wortmaterials*, die zu dieser Ansicht geführt hat; die neuere etymologische Forschung hat die Zahl der keltischen Lehnwörter im Englischen auf eine sehr geringe reduziert,

vgl. Luick Hist. Gramm. d. engl. Spr. § 45. Jedoch man muß sich klar ma-
chen, daß die Einwirkung der Sprache eines unterdrückten Volkes auf die
des Herrenvolks viel eher in der Syntax als im Wortmaterial zu erwarten
ist. Das besiegte Volk hat die Sprache der Eroberer lernen müssen, hat
jedoch, wie oben erwähnt, wahrscheinlich seine syntaktischen Gewohn-
heiten beibehalten und in der neuen Sprache auszudrücken gesucht.[2]

(Dal 1952: 114–115)

Dal also seeks to explain why, for example, the progressive form does not
surface any earlier in OE and early ME texts. She attributes this to the influence of the conservative Anglo-Saxon literary tradition, which regarded the
use of the verbal noun constructions as vulgar language and as something
which should be avoided:

Das Hauptargument für unsere Auffassung der Sache ist aber, daß wir
wegen der historischen und sozialen Verhältnisse keine reiche Verwen-
dung von syntaktischen Keltizismen in der altengl. Literatur erwarten
können. Die Kelten waren das unterdrückte Volk, ihre Syntax, soweit
sie in englischer Sprache zum Ausdruck kam, trug das Gepräge von Vul-
garismus, der von der gepflegten Literatursprache vermieden werden
mußte. Es is gewiß keine Seltenheit, daß Konstruktionen der vulgären
und alltäglischen Sprache Jahrhunderte lang leben können, ohne in der
Schriftsprache zu erscheinen.[3]

(Dal 1952: 113)

Finally, Dal disputes the old wisdom, according to which the Celts were
exterminated from the areas conquered by the Germanic tribes. On the contrary, she argues, the circumstances favoured the influence of the Celtic substratum on English, especially in the domain of syntax.

G. Visser's 1955 article on Celtic influence in English draws its main
inspiration from the earlier work by van Hamel, Keller and Preusler. While
he concurs with these authors on most points, he also expresses some criti-
cisms especially against Preusler's view on the origins of periphrastic DO,
which, as he states, is "based on very insecure foundations" (1955: 279).
Visser's own contribution consists of a number of syntactic features which
he adds to the list of those English constructions which can be considered
to derive from Celtic (and Welsh, in particular). His principal focus is on
constructions involving a prepositional object followed by an infinitive (as
in *It is good for you to walk/It would be nonsense for you to say that*) and
on the use of the verb *go* as a copula with the meaning 'to become' (as in *to
go mad*). For both, he offers an explanation based on Welsh parallels.

Also writing in the 1950s, Wagner (1959) must be mentioned as a forerunner of especially the notion of linguistic area or *Sprachbund* in the context of

the British Isles. In his thought-provoking study, which can now be said to have been very much ahead of its time, Wagner argues for what he calls the 'North European linguistic area', embracing the Celtic languages, Germanic, and even the Baltic Finnic languages. According to Wagner, the languages of this area display striking similarities especially in the development and placement of word stress; these are best explained in terms of a linguistic area and 'adstratal influences' (although he does not use this term) rather than in those of genetic relatedness. Linguistic areas and adstratal relationships have attracted new interest in some of the most recent studies in this field, as we will shortly see.

Tolkien (1963), whose paper originates in a seemingly little-known O'Donnell lecture entitled "English and Welsh", discusses several features of English against the background of possible contact influences from Welsh. These include, most notably, the *b*-forms of the OE substantive verb 'be'—the very feature dealt with earlier by Keller (whose work, incidentally, is not mentioned in Tolkien's paper). Tolkien considers the possibility that the peculiarity of OE in this respect is simply a retention of a feature lost from the other Germanic dialects but emphasises the fact that "this preservation occurred in Britain and in a point in which the usage of the native language [Welsh] agreed" (1963: 31–32). Tolkien notes another peculiarity of the OE *b*-forms, viz. the Northumbrian plural forms *biðun/bioðun*. Of these, he says that they "must be an innovation developed on British soil" and that their similarity with the Welsh form *byddant* "is obvious" (1963: 32). In phonology, Tolkien mentions the preservation in English of the consonants *þ* and *w*; again, as he points out, no other Germanic dialect has preserved them both, Icelandic being the only dialect apart from English which has *þ*. Tolkien formulates his conclusion in very cautious terms:

> It may at least be noted that Welsh also makes abundant use of these two sounds. It is a natural question to ask: how did these two languages, the long-settled British and the new-come English, affect one another, if at all; and what at any rate were their relations?
>
> (Tolkien 1963: 20)

In answer to his own question, Tolkien suggests that, despite many differences in their 'linguistic heritage', English, Welsh, and indeed, the languages of the north-west of Europe, form 'a single philological province' (Tolkien 1963: 33). This is clearly a notion which entails contact influences and on its part vindicates the relevance of the classic concept of *Sprachbund* in the context of the British Isles.

Finally, before moving on to more recent research, Braaten (1967) represents yet another effort to vindicate the Celtic hypothesis with respect to the rise of the English progressive. Braaten builds on the arguments put forward in the previous research and especially in that by Dal. He presents the following summary of the factors which according to him show that the English 'continuous tense' system (as he terms it) could not have developed out of the OE structure *beon/wesan* + *-ende* participle:

(i) Modern English continuous tenses are clearly durative, while the Old English phrase could be used to replace either a durative or a perfective verb—probably for a dramatic effect.

(ii) The Modern English *-ing* participle (originally a verbal abstract) is different in nature from the Old English *-ende* participle.

(iii) In other Germanic languages, the construction *be + present participle* never developed into anything like continuous tense.

(iv) The similarity between Modern English continuous tenses and corresponding constructions in Cymric is too striking to be purely coincidental.

(v) Continuous tenses tend to be used more in bilingual or formerly Celtic-speaking areas than in other parts of the country. (Braaten 1967: 180)

Braaten's conclusion is that some degree of Celtic influence is a prerequisite to an explanation of the Modern English continuous tense system.

5.3   NEW PERSPECTIVES ON CELTIC INFLUENCE ON ENGLISH

After a relatively quiet period in the 1970s and 1980s, the 'Celtic front' in the research on historical syntax and phonology was put back in the news by the ideas propounded by Patricia Poussa (see, especially, Poussa 1990). In this paper she advances some rather far-reaching theories concerning early Celtic influences on English, especially with regard to the rise of periphrastic DO. She traces its origins to the early Celtic–English interface in the southwest of England, from where it spread to other areas. As a significant piece of evidence supporting her account she mentions the fact that periphrastic DO is first found in western texts in the thirteenth century, whereas it is not until about a century later that this feature appears in eastern texts. What according to her provides the crucial link between the parallel Celtic constructions and the resulting English usages is a kind of a creolisation process which has in many contact situations been known to give rise to the development of auxiliaries such as periphrastic DO. She also proposes that periphrastic DO might originally have had a habitual meaning, based on the corresponding feature of the Celtic periphrastic constructions. This is also supported by the preservation of habitual periphrastic DO in the traditional south-western dialects even today. However, as in the case of Keller's and Preusler's studies, Poussa's account has been considered by many historians of English to be 'speculative' or based on merely 'circumstantial', not textual, evidence especially in early ME; furthermore, attention has been drawn to the rather late emergence of DO in English texts (see, e.g. Denison 1993: 282–283, 401–402).

Despite the rather unenthusiastic response to Poussa's views among 'mainstream' Anglicist scholarship, the south-west of England has continued to preoccupy later writers, and the possibility of contact effects arising from that direction has by no means been ruled out. For example, Klemola (1996) discusses the possibility of Celtic (especially Cornish) substratum influence on periphrastic DO in the traditional south-western dialects. He expresses a couple of reservations in this regard, though. One has to do with the standard nature of the English introduced into Cornwall in the fifteenth and sixteenth centuries, i.e. in those periods which witnessed the rise of periphrastic DO even in standardised varieties of English. The possibility thus remains that the prominence of periphrastic DO in the English of Cornwall could be a retention from that period. The other problem for the Celtic hypothesis stems from the curious paucity of periphrastic DO in the traditional English dialect of Devon, which is thus left in the middle of 'DO–rich' areas in Cornwall in the west and Somerset and Dorset in the east. Klemola seeks to explain this by recourse to geographical factors which could have formed 'natural' obstacles to the spread of this feature into Devon from the east.

Periphrastic DO is also in the focus of a recent work by van der Auwera and Genee (2002), who adopt a sympathetic approach to the possibility of Celtic substratum influence. First of all, they point out that, from an areal perspective, periphrastic DO is strongest in the westernmost Germanic language, i.e. English, and in Brythonic (Welsh), i.e. the Celtic language that has had the longest history of direct contacts with English. Like Poussa, they also stress the importance of the first attestation of this feature in the south-western dialects of ME, i.e. in areas close to the Celtic languages. The continued existence of non-emphatic affirmative DO in present-day south-western dialects is yet another fact which according to these authors is hard to explain as a coincidence (*op.cit.*, 299). Although they acknowledge the lack of direct proof of Celtic influence, van der Auwera and Genee consider the Celtic hypothesis plausible and something that is backed up by "good circumstantial evidence" (*op.cit.*, 302). At the same time, they deplore the fact that accounts based on the Celtic substratum influence "thrive best on non-English soil", i.e. are defended by scholars of other than English extraction. This they take to imply that even the nationality or ethnic background of researchers may play a certain, hardly justifiable, role (*ibid.*).

While van der Auwera and Genee stop short of concluding that periphrastic DO is due to Celtic influence, a more determined stand on this issue is propounded by John McWhorter in a paper he read at the DELS Conference in Manchester in April 2006. In sharp contrast with his earlier account, which looked to Scandinavian influence as the main factor behind the simplification processes English underwent in the earliest periods (see McWhorter

2002), McWhorter now argues that contacts with Cornish must have been another factor distancing English from what he calls the "Proto-Germanic template". Like van der Auwera and Genee, he focuses on the emergence of periphrastic DO, which he considers most likely to be of Celtic origin on the basis of comparative facts. Interestingly, he also now holds that the lack of evidence of purported contact effects in OE texts does not suffice to reject the Celtic hypothesis; on the contrary, he argues that "the sociolinguistic realities of written language are such that it would be peculiar if this had NOT been the case".

Tristram (1999a) is yet another work suggesting contact influences which may have had the south-west of England as their base. She mentions retroflex *r* and the sonorisation of initial spirants in the south-western dialects as features which might be due to early substratal influences (see Tristram 1999a: 36 for further discussion). White (2002) describes the south-west as a historically 'Brittonic zone', where the indigenous Celtic-speaking population was largely left in place after the Anglo-Saxon conquest and gradually learnt the language of their new masters as a second language. This, as could be expected, led to contact effects in both the grammar and phonology of the English dialects spoken in these parts. According to him, periphrastic DO is one such feature, along with what he terms 'gerundial progressive', i.e. the (earlier and modern) progressive form which can function as both a gerund and a participle.

On a more general level, the debate on Celtic syntactic and phonological influences has been carried on by scholars like Raymond Hickey (e.g. Hickey 1995) and by Hildegard L.C. Tristram (see, especially, Tristram 1999a, 1999b, 2002a and 2002b). Both Hickey and Tristram underline the nature and importance of the early Celtic-English contact situation for the kind of typological shift—or 'typological disruption', as Tristram puts it—which the Celtic languages and English have experienced through the centuries. Both language groups have gradually moved from predominantly synthetic constructions to analytic ones, including various kinds of periphrastic constructions characteristic of these languages today. A central argument in favour of a Celtic origin for this trend is its earlier attestation in Brythonic than in English; in Welsh especially, the analytic trend is by now more advanced than in English, particularly in the declension of nouns (though not in its verbal morphology). Therefore, as these authors argue, contacts with the Celtic languages must have been instrumental in triggering the shift towards analytical structures in early English. In Tristram's words,

> the very vital contribution of the speakers of the Brythonic languages to the creation of the English language lay in triggering the (initial) typological change from a predominantly synthetic language to a predominantly analytical language.

(Tristram 1999a: 30)

Tristram (1999a) lists a number of analytic typological features which are shared by Welsh and English (and most of which, interestingly, already appeared in Preusler's list of Celtic-derived features): the periphrastic progressive construction, clefting, a predilection for analytically formed prepositional and phrasal verbs, relative clauses with 'stranded' (or 'hanging', as Tristram calls them) prepositions, 'zero' relatives, reflexivisation, the 'internal possessor' construction, the group genitive, and 'DO support'. She provides a more detailed discussion of some of these in Tristram (1999b, 2002a, 2002b). Writing also on the typological change in early English, Hickey emphasises the 'low-level' (especially phonological and prosodic) influences from the Celtic languages, which eventually led to a profound restructuring of the grammatical system of English, unparalleled in the other Germanic languages (Hickey 1995: 115; see also German 2000: 370–373).

Typological considerations, coupled with simplification processes typical of second-language acquisition, also feature prominently in David L. White's work on Celtic influences in ME (see White 2002). White endeavours to show that, for example, the loss of case and grammatical gender in ME can be explained as a result of a process of simplification which was triggered by the combined and converging influences from Norse in the northern parts of Britain and from Brittonic both in the northern and (south-)western areas. A similar process accounts, as he argues, for the loss of concordial variation in the definite article and adjectives.

Apart from the typological and second-language acquisition perspectives, new evidence for Celtic influence has emerged from the hitherto little-researched regional dialects of English. For example, Klemola (2000) uses data collected from English dialects by the *Survey of English Dialects* (*SED*) fieldworkers to explain the phenomenon known as the Northern Subject Rule (NSR) as a possible reflex of early Brythonic (Cumbric) influence. By this rule, the verb takes the suffix *-s* in all persons, singular and plural, unless it is immediately preceded by a personal pronoun subject. Thus there is no ending in a sentence like *They **peel** them*, whereas *-s* appears in *Birds **sings*** and *They peel them and **boils** them* (where the subject is not adjacent to the verb *boils*) (Klemola 2000: 330). Originating in northern ME and Middle Scots, this feature persists in traditional northern dialects of English, as Klemola shows on the basis of the *SED* data. He goes on to note a close typological parallel to the NSR in the Brythonic languages—Welsh, Cornish and Breton—and, following an earlier suggestion by Hamp (1975–1976), concludes that substratum influence from Brythonic on northern dialects of English is a strong possibility (Klemola 2000: 345–346).

Klemola's work on the distinctive usages of personal pronouns in the south-western and West Midlands dialects of English, including especially the phenomenon known as Pronoun Exchange, also sheds light on the possible role of the Celtic (Welsh) substratum in the development of these dialects (see Klemola 2003 and Chapter 2, section 2.2.8). The term 'Pronoun Exchange' refers to the use of the subjective form of personal pronouns in non-subject positions (as in *X come to we*) and to the use of the objective form in subject position (as in *Him comed up this way*). Apart from Pronoun Exchange, the mentioned dialects share a couple of other features of pronoun morphosyntax, neither of which occurs, as Klemola points out, in the other regional dialects of English. By contrast, all of these features have parallels in Brythonic languages, which raises the question of contact-induced change in the south-western English dialects.

Another important recent study of the Northern Subject Rule is Vennemann (2001), who mainly relies on the arguments put forward by Klemola (2000) and Hamp (1975–1976) insofar as Celtic influence on English and some of its dialects is concerned. Concurring with the views expressed by these authors, Vennemann expands the scope of discussion by drawing attention to the Semitic parallels to what he describes as "these [cross-linguistically] strange and rare agreement rules". His conclusion is that the Northern Subject Rule is indeed a substratum feature, which is ultimately based on the prehistoric Semitic substratum in Insular Celtic. From the latter, it has then been carried over into English where it survives in some traditional dialects spoken in the north of England and Scotland.

In the same paper, Vennemann discusses two other syntactic features of English which according to him share the same 'Atlantic' background. These are the verbal noun (or the *-ing* form of verbs) and the 'internal possessor construction', both of which were discussed at length in Chapter 2. Another scholar focusing on these two features is Tristram (1999a, 1999b). In Vennemann's view, the exact formal and functional correspondence between the English verbal noun/progressive construction and the parallel Welsh constructions provides clear evidence for Celtic substratum influence on the former. It is most manifest in the way in which the Anglo-Saxon present participle construction (suffix *-inde/-ande*) was supplanted by the 'Celtic-motivated' verbal noun construction (suffix *-ung/-ing*). Drawing on earlier work by Pokorny (1927–1930; 1959), Vennemann notes that Insular Celtic, which relies heavily on verbal noun constructions, is in this respect 'non-Indo-European' and shares this feature with Basque and Egyptian. In a similar vein, Vennemann argues for a Celtic (and ultimately Semitic) source for the 'internal possessor construction', which denotes the use of the possessive genitive for affected possessors as in *The queen cut off **the king's** head*, as opposed to the non-genitival 'external possessor construction', which is exemplified by the German *Die Königin schlug **dem König** den Kopf ab*. The latter type, also termed 'sympathetic dative' by Vennemann (in accordance with grammatical tradition), was possible in OE, but did not survive into Modern English except in some residual expressions like *He looked her in the eyes, She stared him in the face*. Vennemann cites Haspelmath (1998) and König and Haspelmath (1998), who have established that, among the languages of Europe, English and Celtic are the only language groups which lack the external possessor constructions (Lezgian and Turkish can be added to this list according to the same authors, as Vennemann notes). Vennemann adduces examples from Middle and Modern Welsh and Old and Middle Irish to show that, despite some variations especially in Modern Irish, the Celtic languages predominantly use the internal possessor constructions. They therefore provide the most plausible explanation for the loss of the earlier external constructions in English. What in Vennemann's view also strongly suggests Celtic contact influence is the fact that loss of external possessors cannot be considered a 'natural' or 'predictable' development in a cross-linguistic perspective. On the contrary, as Vennemann shows on the basis of the work by Payne and Barshi (1999), external possessor constructions are found in all parts of the world and can thus be regarded as a linguistically natural phenomenon.

Yet another researcher to use evidence from regional dialects of English is Filppula, who tackles the problem of the origins of the English progressive in Filppula (2001) and (2003). In these articles, he discusses the nonstandard usages of the progressive form in Irish and in other 'Celtic Englishes' and also examines their geographical distribution in traditional English English dialects on the basis of the *SED* data. The concentration of the nonstandard features in the western and north-western regions of the British Isles, with the Celtic Englishes forming the 'core' area, provides clear evidence for some degree of Celtic influence on the modern varieties of English;[4] as regards the earliest periods of Celtic–English contacts, this type of evidence can only provide indirect support for the substratum hypothesis. However, as we have seen above, Braaten (1967) mentions the prolific use of the progressive form in bilingual or formerly Celtic-speaking areas as one of the factors suggesting even earlier contact effects, and a similar research strategy is advocated by Vennemann (2000), who states that

> whenever a variety of English spoken in a Celtic country deviates substantially from standard varieties, a good deal of the differences can be traced to similar properties of the regional Celtic, and that whenever English deviates from the other Germanic languages, chances are that the differences (or at least a goodly portion of the differences) can be traced to similar properties of Insular Celtic.

(Vennemann 2000: 406)

On the Celticist and Indo-Europeanist side, there have been only sporadic forays into Celtic–English contacts over the years. Of course, there is a lot more literature written by Celticists on the earlier, mainly continental, contacts between Celtic and Germanic but these are not our primary concern in this connection (see, e.g. Dillon 1943 and Hickey 1995 for discussion of some of the main issues and controversies in that area). Among those works which have particular relevance to the Celtic–English contacts, we have already mentioned Wagner's (1959) ideas concerning linguistic areas and commonalities in the verbal systems of Irish and English and, indeed, of many other genetically unrelated languages in the west and north of Europe. As noted above, his insights into the 'areal-linguistic' dimensions of these problems have only recently been given the attention they deserve—mainly outside the field of Celtic studies, though (see, e.g. Hickey 1999; Tristram 1999a). Among Celticists, Wagner's contribution in this respect has received positive appraisal, e.g. from David Greene (Greene 1966), who, interestingly, considers Tolkien's essentially similar idea of the British Isles as a single philological province to be "sound doctrine" (*ibid.*, 136). The Celticist and Indo-Europeanist Wolfgang Meid is another scholar who takes a favourable attitude towards Wagner's areal approach (see, e.g. Meid 1990).

In this connection, one should also mention an earlier paper by Wagner (see Wagner 1958), in which he offers a contact-based explanation for the vexed question of the origins of the English third-person pronoun *she*: he points out that the Old Irish and Manx forms for this pronoun were phonetically identical with the Modern English form (written *sí* in OIr.), and since the English pronoun with palatal *s* was first found in the northern ME dialects, the Norwegian settlers in these areas could have acted as intermediaries in spreading southwards the new form which eventually supplanted the OE forms *hēo*, *hīo*. Wagner relies here on a suggestion by Eugen Dieth, who assumes that the palatalisation of the initial consonant first arose in the speech of the Norwegian conquerors in the northern counties.

Another Celticist (and Indo-Europeanist) looking at the linguistic outcomes of the Celtic–English interface, and far beyond, in fact, is Julius Pokorny (see, especially, Pokorny 1927–1930), who discusses, among other things, the Celtic and, ultimately, non-Indo-European substratum in the English internal possessor constructions (a topic later taken up by Vennemann and Tristram; see the discussion above). Yet another Celtic scholar to 'trespass' the language boundary is Eric P. Hamp, who suggests that certain aspects of the English relative clauses, especially the deletion of the relative element in so-called zero-relatives or contact-clauses, are the result of "the diffusional penetration of English by grammatical rules of the neighbouring British Celtic" (Hamp 1975: 297). He draws attention to the difference between English and German in that the latter cannot delete the relative pronoun; also, he points out that important changes took place in the English deletion rules towards the end of the ME period and that these changes "may be put in strikingly direct relation with certain configurations of Medieval Welsh surface structure" (*op.cit.*, 299). Hamp's observations add a new perspective on the earlier discussions of the English contact-clause and its possible Celtic origin by Preusler (1956) and Tristram (1999a), among others.

The series of colloquia on the 'Celtic Englishes', organised by Hildegard L.C. Tristram in Potsdam from 1995 onwards, has been instrumental in provoking new interest among Celticists in a more systematic study of the linguistic contacts between Celtic languages and English. This is particularly evident in recent advances in the research on syntactic and other parallels between the two language groups, which in turn have made it possible to document contact effects with greater certainty than before. We would like to mention, first, Ingo Mittendorf's and Erich Poppe's (see Mittendorf and Poppe 2000) research on the Celtic parallels to the English progressive. Through a painstaking comparison of the Middle Welsh and ME periphrastic verbal noun and progressive constructions, Mittendorf and Poppe are able to demonstrate a high degree of syntactic and functional similarity between them, which is yet another factor speaking for Celtic contact influence on the English progressive. In his most recent works, Poppe (see Poppe 2002, 2003) has extended his survey of the parallel constructions to Middle Irish and to the other historical and present-day dialects of Germanic as well as other languages. The earliest strata of the Celtic periphrastic constructions are also examined in Patricia Ronan's (see Ronan 2003) study of Old Irish texts and of the functions of the verbal noun constructions in these. Taken together, these studies confirm the chronological precedence of the Celtic constructions vis-à-vis their English counterparts.

Persuasive as the evidence for Celtic influence on the English progressive is, there remain problems which have to do with the existence of at least partial parallels in some Germanic dialects (see Poppe 2003) and with the possibility of two-way, adstratal, influences between Celtic and English. It is also true that not all scholars find the argumentation based on syntactic and functional parallelisms sufficient to prove that contact influence has indeed taken place in this case (see, especially, Isaac 2003a). Nonetheless, there is an increasing body of work being carried out by Celticists which promises to discover new areas of possible contact effects. As yet another example, we would like to mention Anders Ahlqvist's cross-linguistic survey of the cleft constructions, which form a central element in the syntax of the Celtic languages and have possibly provided the model not only for the English clefts but even for those of such continental languages as French (see Ahlqvist 2002; cf. also Ahlqvist 1977). The possible connection between French and English clefting is also discussed by Gary German (see German 2003), who brings up an interesting point of comparison, viz. Breton French. In this variety, as German shows, clefting is even more prominent than in standard French, which can most plausibly be explained by Breton substratal influence.

In comparison with syntax, there appear to be few traces of Celtic influence in English phonology—or at least mainstream scholarship has been rather reluctant to accept that possibility. As Laker (2002) points out, this is largely due to the lack of English sound-changes which could be plausibly traced back to Celtic. This does not mean that inquiries probing into that direction would not have been made; recall Tolkien's (1963) suggestion concerning the preservation in English of *þ* and *w*, a development which sets English apart from most other Germanic languages and could be of Celtic (Welsh) origin. Tolkien also mentions OE *i*-mutation or *Umlaut* as a possible reflex of the corresponding phonological changes in Welsh. Although

Tolkien acknowledges "differences in detail and in chronology in the two languages", he points out that the English changes are "closely paralleled by the changes which in Welsh grammar are usually called 'affection' " (1963: 32). This idea has not, to the best of our knowledge, been followed up in later research, possibly because of the problems of dating (acknowledged by Tolkien himself, as noted above), and also because of the cross-linguistic generality of this type of changes. However, the latter argument can hardly be wielded against the case of the English interdental fricatives, which remain rare and are, by any standards, 'marked' among the languages of Europe. Interestingly, this feature of English and its parallels in Welsh have received fresh attention in a recent paper by Tristram (see Tristram 2002b), who notes that the preservation of the interdental fricatives in English and Welsh is "remarkable" from a typological point of view and raises the question of contact influence.

As further areas of possible substratal transfer in phonology, we have already mentioned 'low-level' influences as discussed by Hickey (1995) and Tristram's observations on retroflex *r* and the sonorisation of initial spirants in the south-western dialects. The term 'low-level' refers here to such non-distinctive sound phenomena as allophonic realisations, phonetic reductions and mergers. In British Celtic, as Hickey notes, these phenomena entailed, most notably, the weakening or 'lenition' of consonants in voiced and inter-vocalic environments and vowel reduction in unstressed syllables. He suggests that contacts between the British Celts and the Anglo-Saxons may well have at least accelerated (possibly already existing) similar tendencies in the allophony of OE and thus contributed to the phonetic weakening and even-tual loss of unstressed syllables in that language, too. Though not part of the conventional wisdom in Anglicist scholarship, the scenario put forward by Hickey receives indirect support from some studies of the early continental contacts between Celtic and its neighbouring languages: Hickey refers here to Martinet's (1952) suggestion that the lenition found in Western Romance is due to influence from continental Celtic, which exhibited the same feature (Hickey 1995: 111).

It remains to be seen how the scholarly community will respond to Hick-ey's and Tristram's findings and suggestions. In any case, they manage to raise questions which have for too long been neglected and clearly need to be addressed in future research. Writing on another hitherto unnoticed area of phonological contacts, Laker (2002) adduces interesting evidence for a British Celtic substratum in the northern varieties of OE, which exhibit the changes from *kw-*, *hw-* to *χw-*. His results are telling proof of the gaps in our existing knowledge about the extent of linguistic contacts between Celtic and English.

Next, to put things in an even wider areal and contact-linguistic perspec-tive, mention must be made of Peter Schrijver's work on Coastal Dutch and the possible British Celtic substratum in its vowel system; this, as the author argues, links the early medieval Coastal Dutch dialect with the other North

Sea Germanic languages (English and Frisian) rather than with the other Dutch dialects (see Schrijver 1999). In a more recent work (see Schrijver 2002), he examines the complex relationships between British Latin, Brittonic and OE, an area which, apart from the same writer's 1995 monograph on the historical phonology of British Celtic, has received little attention in previous research. The same can be said for Vennemann's efforts to demonstrate a connection between features of Celtic and English, on one hand, and those of the Hamito-Semitic languages, on the other. Following suggestions put forward by Morris-Jones (1900) and Pokorny (1927–1930), he defends in several papers the idea of an early Semitic substratum in Celtic, some aspects of which have subsequently been transferred to English, thus setting it apart from the other Germanic languages (see, e.g. Vennemann 2000, 2001, 2002a).

Finally, before moving on to discuss new perspectives on lexical influences, we should mention the textual and rhetorical approach to the Celtic–English contacts represented by Wolfgang Kühlwein (see Kühlwein 1998). His work on the possible Celtic influence on OE rhetoric opens up a wholly new perspective on the matter at hand, transcending as it does the usual syntactic or lexical boundaries. His study of the textual and rhetorical features found in OE texts reveals a much greater affinity between OE and Celtic texts than between OE and the other early Germanic texts, such as High German and North Germanic poetry. More specifically, he claims that Celtic influence manifests itself in the prominent use of rhetorical devices which, though also used in Germanic poetry to some extent, "enjoyed special highlighting in Celtic rhetoric" (1998: 234). These include the interweaving of natural and supernatural and of human and non-human elements; strong emphasis on colour and on iconicity; and certain ways of expressing personal emotion and involvement (for further discussion, see *op.cit.*, 230–231). Besides rhetoric, Kühlwein considers the Celtic tradition to have also left its imprint in Anglo-Saxon art, especially metalwork and book illumination (*op.cit.*, 235–241).

Although scholarly opinion now seems ready to accept the idea that most of the Celtic influences must in fact have affected the syntax and (to less extent) phonology of earlier English rather than its lexicon, it is interesting to note some of the recent discoveries in the area of lexical studies. As we know from textbooks on the history of English, lexicon is the primary domain in which historians of English have (somewhat grudgingly, though) admitted the possibility of Celtic influences in the OE and ME periods. However, the extent of this influence has been considered minimal, especially with regard to common nouns. Breeze summarises the prevailing view as follows:

> [T]here is an academic orthodoxy, often repeated since the 1920s (when Max Förster carried out the last major study of the problem), that Old English borrowings from Celtic are few. Alistair Campbell accepted fourteen such loans (eight from Brittonic, six from Irish); Loyn gives

a 'miserably thin' twelve (*ass, bannock, binn, bratt, brock, carr, cumb, hog, luh, toroc, torr*, and *funta* 'spring', with *dun, mattock, beck* 'hoe' and *gavelock* among the doubtfuls); Barbara Strang, stating that 'the numbers are extremely small', lists *bannoc* 'bit', *dunn* 'dark', *brocc* 'badger' *gafeluc* 'spear', *bratt* 'cloak', *carr* 'rock' and *luh* 'lake'; while James Campbell declares there are 'almost no British words in the English language'.

(Breeze 1997: 1)

While the views mentioned in the above quotation still provide the main database for textbooks on the history of English, there have been occasional attempts by some scholars to add to the lists compiled by Förster and his followers. Thus, Lewy (1956, 1966) discusses a number of English words which possibly are of Irish origin. Such is *bother*, for which the *OED* states "etym. dub.; first in Irish writers, Swift, Sterne, etc.". Lewy points out a probable Irish source in the verb *bodhraim* 'I make deaf, I stun, I confuse'; *ná bodhair mé* 'don't annoy me'; *ná bhí am' bodhradh* 'don't bother me'. Other examples are *fond* (cf. Ir. *fonn* 'longing desire, fancy, liking pleasure, delight'); *merry* (cf. Ir. *meadhrach* 'merry, glad, joyful'); *jilt* 'be faithless to sb.; (of a woman) cast off lover after giving him encouragement' (cf. Ir. *diúltaim* 'I deny, oppose, renounce, abandon . . .'). Finally, Lewy (1956) suggests the possibility of borrowing in the case of E. *dear* (cf. Ir. *daor*). Lewy (1966) adds to this list *cant*, which *The Concise Oxford Dictionary* describes as 'peculiar language of class, profession, jargon; words used for fashion without being meant, unreal use of words implying piety, hypocrisy; earlier of musical sound, of intonation, & of beggars' whining, *perh*. f. singing of religious mendicants; prob. f. L. *cantus*'. This is paralleled by Ir. *cainnt* 'talk, speech, conversation, style; idiom; a proverbial saying' (Lewy 1966).

Of the words discussed by Lewy, *jilt* is also confirmed as a probable Irish or Scottish Gaelic loan by Ahlqvist (see Ahlqvist 1988), who traces its roots as far back as Common Celtic. Another English word for which Ahlqvist suggests a Celtic origin is *twig* 'look at, perceive, understand'. As in the case of the Irish ancestor of *jilt*, the Modern Irish and also Scottish Gaelic form *tuig* 'understand, know meaning of, comprehend, etc.' is, and has long been, part of the core lexicon and, to quote Ahlqvist, offers "excellent correspondence between Irish *tuig* and English *twig*" (Ahlqvist 1988: 72). In conclusion, Ahlqvist notes that, although these two etymologies have long been known to Celticists, they are not as yet acknowledged by English etymologists (*ibid.*).

Celtic loans in OE and ME have in recent years been investigated by Andrew Breeze, whose numerous etymologies for words not hitherto recognised as borrowings from Celtic languages have called in question the prevailing view about the dearth of Celtic loans in English. Apart from trying to confirm some of the findings of earlier works, Breeze has discovered a host of new words—many more in fact than in any of the lists offered so far—from both the OE and ME periods for which he proposes Celtic origins. In most cases these are words whose origins have for long been unclear or in dispute. They include items like OE *deor* 'brave', *trum* 'strong', *truma* 'host', *cursung* 'curse', *gafeluc* 'javelin', *stær* 'history', *syrce* 'coat of mail'; ME *clog(ge)* 'block, wooden shoe', *cokkunge* 'striving', *tirven* 'to flay', *warroke* 'hunchback', and many more (see, e.g. Breeze 1993a, 1993b, 1997). In a summarising article (see Breeze 2002), Breeze discusses and exemplifies the Celtic loanwords in English under seven different headings: (1) Brittonic words in OE; (2) Irish words in OE; (3) Welsh words in ME; (4) Irish words in ME; (5) Welsh words in Early Modern English; (6) Irish words in the same; (7) Scottish Gaelic words in the same. It is quite evident that Breeze's findings mark only the beginning of new discoveries. Breeze himself states that "Celtic loans in Old English (not all of them from the early period) are commoner than has been supposed. More such loans certainly await identification in Old English and Middle English alike" (Breeze 1997: 1–2).

Stalmaszczyk (1997, 2000) is yet another writer who has explored hitherto unknown or otherwise neglected survivals of Celtic loanwords. He discusses a significant number of words which, though not recorded in standard varieties in the past or present, nevertheless survive, or survived until lately, in many regional varieties of English, including those spoken in Cornwall, Wales, Isle of Man, Scotland and Ireland. While many of these do not date back to the earliest contact period, there may well be some which have a long pedigree in these varieties. In any case, the regional English aspect has been largely overlooked in the previous research, although general remarks on such survivals had been expressed, e.g. by Meid (1990). While Meid concurs with Förster's view of the small number of Celtic loanwords in Standard English, he considers it quite plausible that many more are preserved in regional dialects (1990: 113–114).

Place-names, river-names and personal names are generally agreed to be a much richer source for Celtic loans than common nouns. As Tristram (1999a: 6–7) notes, the foundations for the study of these were laid in the monumental works by Max Förster (Förster 1921, 1941) and Kenneth Jackson (Jackson 1953). In recent years the study of Celtic place-names has received a new impetus through the work by Richard Coates and Andrew Breeze. Their research has focused on place-names for which no satisfactory source has been found in English or any other Germanic language. In his introduction to their jointly produced volume (Coates and Breeze 2000), which brings together a large number of their publications in this field, Coates states as their methodological starting-point that

> names which are problematic for philological analysis are at least as likely to be of Brittonic as of English origin, and that nowhere in the country should one reject *a priori* the possibility of a Brittonic survival. [. . .] The present default assumption, that problematic names are likely

to be English or Scandinavian in most counties, can only be eroded by showing that for a substantial body of them a Brittonic solution is (a) credible and (b) at least as likely as competing Germanic solutions.

(Coates 2000a: 7)

The authors base their arguments on linguistic as well as historical and archaeological research, and in Coates and Breeze (2000) manage to build a convincing case for Celtic origins of 68 previously unresolved place-names in different parts of England, including even names found in the eastern parts of England. This volume also includes, for the first time in one place, a gazetteer which provides a comprehensive list, location and etymology for all 'reasonably-claimed' examples of Brittonic and Goidelic names in England. The gazetteer is supplemented by distribution maps, which also indicate the degree of certainty of the etymologies.

On the basis of this survey of research, it seems safe to conclude that the last decade or so has introduced a new phase in the history of research on the early Celtic–English contacts: a substantial amount of new research has been undertaken, or is under way, on a wide range of problems covering the general historical and archaeological background to these contacts and the linguistic outcomes in all domains of language. Compared with the studies of the early pioneers, we are now better equipped both theoretically and methodologically, and can avail ourselves of the recent advances in contact linguistics, areal linguistics and typology. Already at this stage it can be said that, despite an obvious need for further research in many areas, the time is ripe for a critical reassessment of the 'textbook' views on the nature and outcome of the Celtic–English contacts. As Hildegard Tristram writes,

the history books and encyclopaedias of the English language should be rewritten in line with these findings and [. . .] they should pay tribute to the very important contribution of Brythonic/Welsh to the creation of Present Day English.

(Tristram 1999a: 31)

Tristram also underlines the continuity of contacts between Brythonic/ Welsh and English by pointing out that, besides the "initial rapid shift from Brythonic to English", contacts between these two languages continued in the following centuries and, indeed, extend up to the present day. In a sense, then, one can speak of a 'double contact situation' in Britain, as compared, e.g. with the circumstances under which the Romance languages have developed and where the source languages have disappeared. This situation, as Tristram argues, must have involved continued interaction between the two ethnic groups, probably assuming the form of 'loose-knit network ties' familiar from the modern sociolinguistic theory, which considers them

essential avenues for linguistic change (Tristram 1999a: 29). These considerations, too, emphasise the need for a more balanced approach to the Celtic–
English contacts and their linguistic outcomes than has hitherto been the
case. This, indeed, will be the topic of the next chapter where we will try to
pull together the various strands of evidence for both the earlier contacts
and those which have taken place in the modern period.

6   A Reassessment of the Evidence for Celtic Influences

The discussion in the previous chapter and, indeed, throughout this book has brought to light a wealth of evidence, partly fresh, partly known of old, which clearly calls for a reassessment of the extent of Celtic influence on English. It is our aim in this chapter to build a synthesis of all the available evidence and present our view of the nature and extent of both the earlier contacts between English and Celtic and of those which have taken place in the modern period. Our approach will be holistic, that is, we believe that it is of utmost importance to consider the widest possible range of both linguistic and 'extra-linguistic' evidence speaking for or against contact influences and that neither of these two types of evidence is sufficient on its own to ascertain these influences. The holistic approach also applies to individual syntactic or phonological features. Like Thomason and Kaufman (1988), we adhere to a view which sees language as a system, the parts or 'subsystems' of which depend on each other. In language contact situations this means that if one subsystem or part of a subsystem is affected by a contact-induced change, it is more than likely that other parts are also affected by such changes. This is often forgotten in works concentrating on just one or two syntactic or phonological features.

We begin by returning once more to the extra-linguistic demographic and other historical evidence which, as has been seen, has been at the heart of the differences of opinion concerning the very possibility of Celtic influence upon English in the early centuries of the contacts. This will pave the way for a discussion of three major kinds of linguistic evidence. The first of these rests upon language-internal developments, which are often seen to provide the primary motivation for changes but will here be set against contact influences as an alternative explanatory factor. Next, we will consider the evidence and generalisations obtainable from recent research on other language contact situations and their linguistic outcomes in widely different settings all over the world. Finally, we turn to some areal and typological considerations which in our view provide crucial support for the Celtic hypothesis.

6.1   DEMOGRAPHIC AND HISTORICAL EVIDENCE

The main points we will argue for in this section are the following. First, the demographic and sociohistorical circumstances surrounding the *adventus Saxonum* in the early mediaeval period were such that linguistic contact influences were not just possible but inevitable. The principal source of the Celtic substratal influences were the Britons who, after a period of extensive bilingualism, shifted to English and were gradually assimilated to the Anglo-Saxon population in the course of the first two or three centuries following the *adventus*. Secondly, the same type of language shift process, with largely similar linguistic outcomes, has taken place in the modern period in those areas of the British Isles and Ireland where English has gradually replaced the indigenous Celtic language as the dominant language. Both are characterised by periods of extensive bilingualism as an intermediate stage towards eventual abandonment of the Celtic language in favour of English. Demographically, too, the modern contact and shift situations resemble the mediaeval ones in that the modern contacts have also involved large-scale movements of populations away from, or into, the formerly Celtic-speaking areas. Obvious examples are the large-scale plantations of Ulster and other provinces of Ireland in the sixteenth and seventeenth centuries, extensive emigration from Ireland, Scotland and Wales in the eighteenth and nineteenth centuries, and the influx of immigrant industrial workforce from England, Scotland and Ireland into the southern and south-eastern parts of Wales in the nineteenth century.

The first point takes us back to the much-debated question of the relative numbers of the Anglo-Saxon settlers vis-à-vis the British population. In Chapter 1, section 1.2, significant new historical and archaeological evidence was discussed which shows that the numbers of the Anglo-Saxon settlers in the initial stages of the Anglo-Saxon invasions were significantly smaller and the relationships between the two populations more peaceful than has hitherto been the standard wisdom among historians. However, although there is now considerable consensus about this, it is important to keep in mind some of the potential pitfalls when trying to use archaeological and historical evidence to back up one's arguments about the linguistic situation at the time. To what extent can we use the former to say something definite about the latter, or about the dominance of one or the other language, and hence, population, at a given point of time? Or, even more importantly: is there a risk of circularity here, and to what extent are the systems of language and material culture independent of each other? These are questions posed and finely dealt with by John Hines in his article "Philology, Archaeology and the *adventus Saxonum vel Anglorum*" (Hines 1990).

Hines starts off by tackling an argument put forward by Welch (1985), who seeks to refute the view that the fifth- and sixth-century archaeological finds could provide a reliable guide to estimating the numbers of the

Anglo-Saxon settlers vis-à-vis the indigenous population. More specifically, Welch argues that they do not suffice to vindicate what he terms the 'minimalist view of Anglo-Saxon settlement':

> [T]here are great dangers for those who accept the minimalist view of Anglo-Saxon settlement, for this flies in the face of the combined available evidence from linguistic, historical and archaeological sources. The fact that modern English is a Germanic language derived ultimately from the Old English spoken by Anglo-Saxons cannot be lightly dismissed. England's landscape is littered with place-names and field-names recognisably derived from Old English place-names. [. . .] The contrast with the impact of the Norman settlement is instructive, for the Normans, together with their northern French and Flemish allies, did arrive as a conquering aristocratic elite. Yet despite the presence of some Norman-French elements in modern English, we speak English not French . . . If there were so few Anglo-Saxon settlers why did not British Celtic triumph? The obvious implication is that considerable numbers of Anglo-Saxons settled in southern and eastern England . . .

> (Welch 1985: 13–14; cited in Hines 1990: 17–18)

Hines's counterargument to this is that, instead of putting so much emphasis on language as Welch does, language and material culture should be seen as integrated processes, which in this case have worked towards minimising the linguistic diversity which must have existed in early mediaeval Britain and which is best evidenced by the archaeological record. As Hines points out, linguistic data from AD 400 to 600 do not match the material remains either in terms of survival or its reliability, given the risks of distortion involved in the transmission of such data to the present. Archaeology is therefore in a better position to give us a detailed account of the settlement history at this period (Hines 1990: 18–19).

Hines's own description of this history is, some minor details notwithstanding, in line with the accounts by Laing and Laing (1990), Higham (1992) and Härke (2003), discussed in Chapter 1. Thus, when tracing the sequence from Roman Britain to Anglo-Saxon England, Hines prefers to speak of the 'beginning of the Anglo-Saxon Period' rather than of *adventus Saxonum*; in other words, this period marks the start of the "connected series of Germanic contexts, features and artefacts in Britain" (Hines 1990: 20). The dating of these 'contexts' is, however, bound to be approximate and relative. As Hines points out, there is evidence of the probable presence of Germanic men serving in official capacities as early as late Roman Britain, but he places the earliest Germanic 'contexts' of the Anglo-Saxon period in the first half of the fifth century. The settled areas were then expanded in the later fifth and sixth centuries. Hines dates the common 'Anglo-Saxondom' of material and social culture to the late sixth century, while a sense of common English identity in linguistic terms takes longer, emerging by the time of Bede and his *lingua Anglorum*, which for Bede was the collective term for the varieties of the English language (*op.cit.*, 32; fn. 43).

Like Hines and the others mentioned above, we believe that archaeological and other historical evidence should be in a central position in efforts to trace the patterns of settlement in early mediaeval Britain. Yet, it can be usefully supplemented with linguistic evidence, especially that arising from some of the most recent research on place-names and their background. As noted in Chapter 2, section 2.4, of particular importance here is the work reported in Coates and Breeze (2000), who provide detailed information on the survival of Celtic place-names in various parts of England. According to their findings, most survivals of Celtic place-names are, as can be expected, concentrated in the south-western, western and north-western parts of England. However, scattered Celtic names are also found in the south and east, which testifies to a certain degree of coexistence of, and social interaction between the Britons and the Anglo-Saxons even in these areas (see Coates and Breeze 2000 for detailed cartographic illustrations).

Unlike the early mediaeval period, population movements and the other sociohistorical circumstances surrounding the English–Celtic interface in the modern period are relatively well documented. This is of special significance for the whole history of the English–Celtic contacts and their linguistic outcomes, as the developments in the Celtic-speaking areas give a strong indication of the type of contact effects that probably arose from the English–Celtic interface in the earliest periods, too. This is a powerful argument speaking for the Celtic hypothesis, and it has been used by some scholars, as was noted in the previous chapter.

As said above, the modern contact and shift situations have, like the mediaeval ones, involved large-scale movements of populations away from, or into, the formerly Celtic-speaking areas. These have then had a clear impact on the linguistic set-up of the areas most affected by demographic changes, leading mostly to a gradual erosion of the status and position of the indigenous Celtic language and, eventually, to language shift in most parts of Ireland and Scotland. The same has happened in Wales, too, although Welsh has managed to hold out slightly better against the pressure from English than its Celtic sisters.

It should be noted, however, that the migration patterns in the modern period have not affected the linguistic situations in the Celtic lands alone but have also had far-reaching linguistic effects on present-day nonstandard varieties of English spoken in other parts of the British Isles. Particularly influential have been the nineteenth-century migrations of Irish people to urban areas in England and Scotland, with London, Liverpool, Glasgow, Manchester, Dundee and Edinburgh being the cities that received the greatest numbers of Irish-born citizens on the basis of the 1851 Census (see Davis 1991: 176). As a result, Irish English features are especially prominent in the local vernacular speech of Liverpool and Glasgow (see also Beal 1993 on Tyneside English). Finally, one should not forget the traditional seasonal migrations in the past centuries from Ireland to Scotland, the Scottish Isles to mainland Scotland, Ireland to Wales and from Wales to England. All these have in the course of time contributed to the spread of many originally substratal features from one regional variety to another.

6.2   LANGUAGE-INTERNAL DEVELOPMENTS VS. CONTINUING CONTACT INFLUENCES

The discussion of both the early and modern contacts in Parts I and II has demonstrated the primacy of language-internal factors over contact effects in traditional accounts of the English–Celtic interface and its linguistic outcomes. Recall, for example, the debates on the emergence of periphrastic DO or on the origins of the English 'progressive' (or 'expanded') form, discussed in Chapter 2, sections 2.2.4 and 2.2.5, respectively: for many earlier writers, in particular, contact influences from Celtic (or from any other language, for that matter) do not present themselves as a plausible or viable alternative at all, or even if they do, they are at best considered to merely reinforce already existing trends in English or Germanic.

The same is true of historical linguistic studies in general. Though challenged by many today, contact-induced change in all domains of language except perhaps the lexicon has up until quite recent times been regarded as something of a 'last resort'; it enters the picture only if explanations in terms of language-internal factors fail to yield satisfactory results. Gerritsen and Stein (1992: 5–6) have put this approach down to the structuralist credo, according to which language is a system *où tout se tient*, with only system-internal factors playing a role in language change. McMahon (1994: 210), writing on the same kind of approach, refers to the old argument that contact influences are not evoked "so long as there is a case somewhere of the same change being internally motivated". This underlying assumption has characterised various generativist schools of thought, as well. Although there have been exceptions such as Weinreich's classic book on language contacts, written in the early 1950s (Weinreich 1953), it was not until the last two or three decades that language-external factors, including contacts between speakers of different languages, began to receive serious attention.

Despite the increasing interest in external considerations, much of the literature on contact-induced change still reflects the old ideas about the primacy of language-internal factors. Thus, Hock (1984), writing on the possibility of early contact influences between Indo-Aryan and Dravidian, lays down extremely stringent criteria for contact-induced change:

> ... any case made for a specific scenario of early contact—and for specific consequence of that contact—must needs be circumstantial.

Circumstantial cases of this sort, however, should be established in the same manner as circumstantial cases in a court of justice. They ought to be established *beyond a reasonable doubt*. That is, in each case it ought to be established that the nature of the evidence is such that it precludes any interpretation other than the one advocated.

(Hock 1984: 90)

Although the goal of ascertaining contact effects "beyond a reasonable doubt" is a *desideratum* in all historical research, it is something that can hardly ever be achieved: what we have to be content with in most cases are *likelihoods*, which are greater or smaller depending on the nature of the available evidence. On the other hand, the same can be said of most arguments based on language-internal factors such as analogy or various kinds of functional considerations: explanations based on these factors are also *post facto*, and therefore not essentially different from those based on contact influences. And as the discussions in the previous chapters have shown, the available evidence is very often such that it leaves room for the possibility of *multiple causation*.

A slightly different approach to the problem at hand is propounded by Lass (1990: 148), who emphasises the more 'parsimonious', i.e. economical nature of explanations relying on non-contact-induced change. For instance, writing on the possible substratal influence of Irish phonology on Hiberno-English, he argues that whenever a feature of Hiberno-English has a parallel in English English, there is no need to consider the substratal source, even if there is a parallel to that feature in Irish. In situations like this, endogeny provides a more parsimonious account of the facts and is therefore to be preferred to language contact. Lass formulates this in terms of a general methodological principle as follows:

Therefore, in the absence of evidence [for either endogeny or contact], an endogenous change *must* occur in any case, whereas borrowing is never necessary. If the (informal) probability weightings of both source-types converge for a given character, then the choice goes to endogeny.

(Lass 1997: 209; for a more detailed discussion of the same methodological principle, see Lass and Wright 1986).

Lass's principle must be seen against the background of his critique of scholars whom he describes as 'contact romantics'. These are scholars who according to Lass seek to derive "the maximal number of characters in a given language from contact sources" (Lass 1997: 201). While it is true that such 'contact-romantic' accounts can be found in especially the earlier literature on Hiberno-English, for example, we wish to argue that historical linguists should first and foremost aim at the *best* explanations, whether more or less parsimonious (see also Filppula 2003). Hock's (1991) discussion of the applicability of Occam's razor to the reconstruction of the inflectional paradigms of Old Latin offers a good point of reference here. What according to him provides the most economical explanation may not necessarily be the best:

> Given two alternative analyses, we will prefer the one which provides *greater explanation or motivation* for the postulated changes, as well as for the attested synchronic facts. Such explanations often refer to issues of over-all linguistic structure.
>
> (Hock 1991: 536; emphasis added)

In much the same vein, Thomason and Kaufman (1988: 58) emphasise the importance of 'complete' explanations. They also caution against rejecting a contact-based explanation simply because a similar change has been observed to have taken place in some other setting:

> The flaw in this type of argument is its assumption that a given change that arises through internal motivation in one language can and should automatically be ascribed to the same sort of cause when it occurs in another language. Since even the most natural changes often fail to occur, it is always appropriate to ask why a particular change happened when it did.
>
> (Thomason and Kaufman 1988: 59)

How can we then decide between language-internal and contact-induced changes in each given case? *Chronological priority*, if that can be established, is one obvious criterion, and has been applied, for example, by Macafee (1996) to the case of lexical borrowing between English and Scots, on one hand, and Irish, on the other. As editor of the *Concise Ulster Dictionary*, she adopts a rather strict editorial policy with regard to putative Irish borrowings in the *CUD*. In her editor's introduction to the *CUD*, she writes:

> Because the dialects we are dealing with in this dictionary are essentially English or Scots, we make the presumption that if a word, form, sense, compound, or phrase has a prior history in English or Scots then that is the source of the Ulster item.
>
> (Macafee 1996: xxxiii)

She adds, however, that

[t]here may nevertheless be support or reinforcement from Irish, which shares a large vocabulary with English/Scots both through their common membership of the Indo-European language family, and through borrowing in both directions.

(Macafee 1996: xxxiii)

McMahon (1994: 210) introduces another useful criterion, arising from Thomason and Kaufman's (1988) discussion on language contacts and the way in which their typical outcomes are distributed across the different subsystems of languages: external causation can be invoked only in those cases in which the allegedly borrowing language has undergone changes in more than one subsystem. McMahon also refers here to Thomason and Kaufman's observation that there are no known cases of structural borrowing that would have affected a single subsystem of a language. Based on this, McMahon tentatively puts forward the following guiding principle, which, however, "requires further testing and refinement" (*op.cit.*, 210): "[F]or feature x in the phonology of language A to be from language B, there must also be some feature y in another subsystem, say the morphology, which is also demonstrably from B" (McMahon 1994: 210).

We may now assess the English–Celtic contacts in the light of these two criteria or principles. To begin with chronological priority, many of the putatively Celtic-derived features examined above are attested in one or the other of the Celtic languages prior to their first attestations in English. Such are, for example, the absolute uses of the reflexive pronouns, periphrastic DO, the cleft construction, and arguably, the progressive form of verbs. The other criterion, requiring contact effects on more than one subsystem of a language, is also borne out by the facts: though not so striking as in syntax, both the phonology and even lexicon of the English language bear witness to early influences from Celtic, and the same kind of influences are even more prominent (and certainly, easier to document) in the so-called Celtic Englishes in the modern period.

Useful as the criteria discussed so far are, they need to be complemented by others to provide the best or most complete explanations. At the most general level, Thomason and Kaufman (1988) set the following methodological prerequisites for demonstrating what they call 'interference through shift', i.e. substratum influence in our terminology:

[. . .] we must be able to identify a substratum language or language group (some of) whose speakers shifted to the target language at the relevant time period; we must have information about its structure; and we must have information about the structure of the target language before the shift.

(Thomason and Kaufman 1988: 111)

Identifying the relevant substratum language or languages hardly poses a problem for the English–Celtic contact situation, and despite the lack of records from the earliest periods and from the formative periods of the Celtic Englishes, we have reasonable amounts of information about the structural properties of the languages or varieties involved in these situations. In most cases there is also sufficient evidence of the full syntactic, semantic and functional range of the features at issue, which helps to tell apart contact effects from endogenous developments. As is well known, superficial similarity, i.e. the existence of mere formal parallels, does not suffice to prove contact influences. Besides, as was seen in the discussion on the progressive form of verbs and the cleft construction above, formal parallels are often only partial, which further highlights the need to consider other supporting evidence.

6.3   CONTACT-LINGUISTIC PERSPECTIVES

Recent advances in language-contact studies and accumulation of evidence from a wide variety of contact situations worldwide have made it possible to develop new theories and models of language contacts and their linguistic outcomes. Particularly influential and of particular relevance to the English–Celtic contacts is the model of contact-induced change proposed by Thomason and Kaufman (1988). Their model endeavours to capture the interplay between language-internal and language-external factors by incorporating both types of factors in a comprehensive and predictive model of contact-induced change. A central element in this model is a distinction between two basic types of language-contact situations: *language maintenance* and *language shift*. This distinction rests on sociohistorical, i.e. language-external, factors. The linguistic outcomes in each case are vastly different, as Thomason and Kaufman demonstrate. They discuss a wealth of evidence from contact situations all over the world which shows that, in conditions of language contact and shift, language-external factors are capable of overriding the language-internal ones (for further discussion, see Thomason and Kaufman 1988: 35). They also argue that a weak internal motivation for a change is less convincing than a strong external one, but at the same time they emphasise the (often very likely) interplay of both external and internal factors (Thomason and Kaufman 1988: 61).

Of particular importance for the case at hand is Thomason and Kaufman's generalisation that, in conditions of large-scale language shift like the ones that have taken place in the formerly Celtic-speaking parts of the British Isles, syntactic and phonological influences clearly prevail over lexical influences. In fact, their model predicts very little lexical transfer in circumstances in which the shifting population is large and the learning process 'imperfect' in the sense that very few speakers can avail themselves of formal instruction in the target language. This, as we know, was the situation in many parts of Britain in the earliest stages of the Anglo-Saxon–Brythonic contacts when the vast majority of the population had no access to formal education. The same was true of the modern-age language shift situation in nineteenth-century Ireland, where schooling was still rare and illiteracy very common up until the latter part of the nineteenth century (see, e.g. Odlin 1997a for some statistical evidence). This then explains the rather heavy substratal input in the Irish dialects of English, which owe a great deal to the rapid advance of language shift especially in the first half of the nineteenth century.

It is interesting to note that the minor role of lexical evidence vis-à-vis syntactic and phonological evidence is now becoming widely accepted even by scholars who had previously taken a sceptical stand on the extent of Celtic influence on English. McWhorter (2006) is one of the latest to acknowledge this. As one good example of a contact situation where grammatical influence is accompanied by very few loanwords, he mentions Uralic and Russian: despite uncontroversial Uralic influence on Russian, the latter has only a very marginal number of Uralic loanwords. Another similar case is that of Dravidian and Indo-Aryan. Again, Dravidian grammatical influence on Indo-Aryan is indisputable, yet the latter has borrowed almost no loanwords over the last one thousand years.

Evidence from other contact situations is also relevant to the problem of 'delayed contact effects' discussed above, e.g., in connection with periphrastic DO as well as the progressive form of verbs. As will be remembered, the relatively late emergence of these features in English has always been one of the main arguments advanced against Celtic influences in English. It has been repeated in the literature despite the efforts of scholars such as Dal (1952), who has convincingly argued that the social stigma attached to the Celtic-influenced English of the Britons shifting to English effectively prevented it from appearing in the refined literary language of the Anglo-Saxon period. Dal's view has received support from more recent work by, for example, Hickey (1995), Vennemann (2002a), and McWhorter (2006). The last-mentioned adduces evidence from a variety of contact situations to show that delayed effects are not only possible, but even likely in certain types of conditions. Thus, Old Persian was rich in inflections, whereas Middle Persian had shed most of these inflections; yet these changes did not become visible until after a three-century documentational gap. Other cases discussed by McWhorter include Standard Finnish vs. 'Universal Colloquial Finnish', Ecuadoran Spanish and Moroccan Arabic, all of which display similar delays in making the already existing changes manifest in the written language. This leads him to postulate that "[i]f there were attestations of Celticized English **any less than several centuries** after its emergence, then this would be quite unexpected—so very much so that it **would itself demand explanation**" (McWhorter 2006; original emphasis). Again, this is a nice illustration of the relevance of cross-linguistic evidence to the proper understanding of the English–Celtic interface and its linguistic outcomes.

Although the linguistic outcomes of both the earliest contacts and those which took place in the modern period can largely be explained by the special type of language shift situations among the formerly Celtic-speaking populations, it should be noted that the other major type of language contact, viz. language maintenance, has been—and to some extent still is—the prevailing situation in many parts of the British Isles and Ireland. For these, Thomason and Kaufman's model predicts very different linguistic consequences: maintenance of the two (or more) languages usually leads to heavy lexical borrowing, especially in situations in which there is prolonged, intensive contact and much bilingualism among the borrowing-language speakers. Syntactic and phonological borrowing also occurs, but it does not occupy such a central role as in the type of language shift situations described above. Our knowledge of the earliest contacts is too limited to enable us to say with any certainty to what extent and how long Brythonic was maintained in any given area or locality and to what extent this coexistence affected the local or regional varieties of the two languages. However, the number of those early Celtic loanwords that have since become obsolete in mainstream English (discussed in Chapter 2, section 2.4) gives support to the view that in some parts of the British Isles at least the two languages survived side by side for a considerable period of time. In the modern period, the linguistic effects of the maintenance situation are more clearly to be seen in the bilingual areas of Wales, Ireland and Scotland: depending on the particular history of the contact setting in each area, the regional varieties exhibit varying degrees of linguistic influences in both directions.

Two-way influences raise the question of possible *areal* features, i.e. features which are shared by languages or varieties spoken in more or less closely contiguous geographical areas, often called 'linguistic areas' or *Sprachbund* developments. In this type of situation the languages involved exercise, or have exercised, mutual influence on each other in such a way that it is usually not possible to establish the direction of influence. They are therefore said to stand in an 'adstratal' relationship to each other (see, e.g. Lehiste 1988: 61). Perhaps the best-known example is the so-called Balkan *Sprachbund*. Note further that the languages in question need not be genetically related, which adds another, typological, dimension to the issue of areal features. Both will be the topic of the next section.

6.4   AREAL AND TYPOLOGICAL CONSIDERATIONS

In the context of the British Isles and the neighbouring continental areas, the notion of 'linguistic areas' has been brought up in several works, both earlier and more recent ones. It is implicitly present, e.g., in the work of the Celticist Heinrich Wagner (see Wagner 1959), who observes major similarities in the tense, aspect and mood systems of the languages spoken in the British Isles and Ireland. On the Anglicist side, Tolkien (1963) writes on what clearly suggests *Sprachbund* type developments in the same general area:

> The north-west of Europe, in spite of its underlying differences of lin-
> guistic heritage—Goidelic, Brittonic, Gallic; its varieties of Germanic;
> and the powerful intrusion of spoken Latin—is as it were a single philo-
> logical province, a region so interconnected in race, culture, history, and
> linguistic fusions that its departmental philologies cannot flourish in
> isolation. I have cited the processes of *i*-mutation/*i*-affection as a strik-
> ing example of this fact. And we who live in this island may reflect that
> it was on this same soil that both were accomplished.
>
> (Tolkien 1963: 33)

These ideas have since been followed up by various scholars on both sides. In his 1975 paper entitled "On the Disappearing English Relative Particle", Eric P. Hamp argues for

> diffusional penetration of English by grammatical rules of the neigh-
> bouring British Celtic in a way typical of the seepage of grammar
> and surface structure over time within an area commonly termed a
> Sprachbund.
>
> (Hamp 1975: 297)

Hamp's example here is omission of relative pronouns or the so-called contact-clause (see Chapter 2, section 2.2.7). According to him, this con-struction was influenced by Welsh, in which the relative particle is often reduced to a mere lenition phenomenon. This of course has never had any counterpart in English and was therefore replaced by the contact-clause structure in the speech of bilingual Welsh-English speakers in the border areas (1975: 300). Hamp further elaborates on what he considers to have been a long-standing adstratal situation as follows:

> Of course, not all the inhabitants of the island of Britain were bilingual
> many centuries after the Anglo-Saxon conquest, let alone by the 14th
> century. But apart from the fact that British Celtic surely did not die out
> in England immediately, there was throughout the Middle Ages for a
> long time a substantial border of bilingualism and language contact in
> the history of English tends regularly to be overlooked or minimized.
> Surely that cultural contact must account for a fair part of the diver-
> gence of English from its sister West Germanic languages.
>
> (Hamp 1975: 300–301)

In recent research, the notion of a British Isles *Sprachbund* has been revived by the German Anglicist and Celticist Hildegard L.C. Tristram (see, especially, Tristram 1999a), who proposes a linguistic area consisting mainly of Britain and Ireland, but extending even to the Continent with respect to some phonological features such as the presence of retroflex *r* and initial sonorisation of consonants (Tristram 1999a: 36). The German-based Anglicist Raymond Hickey is another writer who has been concerned with areal phenomena, although his work focuses mainly on the island of Ireland as a linguistic area (see Hickey 1999). And in section 6.2 above, we referred to Macafee's (1996) work on lexical borrowing between Scots and/or English, on one side, and Irish, on the other; again, there is evidence that suggests two-way lexical influences, i.e. borrowing in both directions.

In our own research reported in Parts I and II, the possibility of *Sprachbund*-type developments has come to the fore with regard to several syntactic constructions, including especially the internal possessor construction, periphrastic DO, the progressive and the cleft construction. Although the linguistic areas at issue seem to vary somewhat in geographical detail from one feature to another, one thing is shared by all: English distinguishes itself from most of the other Germanic languages, and significantly, lines up with the Celtic languages with respect to these features. We now have to bear in mind that, in order to come into existence at all, linguistic areas must have involved more or less close historical contacts between the speakers of the participating languages at some stage or other. This is clearly the case in the classic example of a *Sprachbund*, viz. that existing between several languages spoken in the Balkans. In the context of the British Isles and Ireland, too, it is possible to ascertain the existence of such contacts, which have to varying degrees extended to speakers of the neighbouring continental languages. Taken together, these facts provide yet another argument speaking for Celtic contact influences upon English, be they substratal or adstratal in nature.

Finally, linguistic areas and the observed distinctiveness of English among the Germanic languages lead us to consider typological factors, and more specifically, to ask whether it is possible, or likely even, that the English–Celtic interface could have shaped English typologically into the direction of the Celtic languages. The very features listed above as plausible candidates for areal-linguistic ones (i.e., the internal possessor construction, periphrastic DO, the progressive and the cleft construction) are also un-Germanic in a typological perspective, especially when compared to modern and earlier German. They are therefore hard to explain as language-internal developments or as merely coincidental in English. A much more likely explanation for their emergence in English is, indeed, contacts with the neighbouring Celtic languages and the kind of 'typological disruption' described by Tristram (1999a).

The line of argumentation described above receives significant support from the case studies on English periphrastic DO conducted by van der

Auwera and Genee (2002) and by McWhorter (2006). The former pay attention to the facts that, within Germanic, this type of construction is strongest in the westernmost West Germanic language, that is, English, while on the Celtic side the same kind of construction is strongest in Brythonic, that is, the Celtic language with the longest contacts with English. Whether this is a coincidence is left open by these writers, but their discussion makes it clear that they consider Celtic influence on English periphrastic DO quite likely.

McWhorter, then, puts the case of periphrastic DO in an even wider typological perspective. The central issue for him is why English has such a "starkly peculiar" (as he puts it) usage of its DO-verb, which according to him is "alien" to the Indo-European family and is also cross-linguistically "bizarre". McWhorter acknowledges the existence of various DO-type constructions in other Germanic languages but also points out that these have syntactic or semantic constraints which make them different from English periphrastic DO. The fact that in English, DO has developed into a semantically empty auxiliary that can be used with almost all verbs underlines its cross-linguistically special nature not only among the Germanic group, but worldwide. As McWhorter points out, the Celtic languages are among the very few languages of the world that exhibit this feature. Having considered and discarded a few other potential objections to the Celtic hypothesis, including the possibility of internal development, the late attestation of periphrastic DO and the paucity of Celtic loanwords in English, McWhorter concludes that English was impacted by transfer from Brythonic-speaking Celts alongside the influences brought about by the Scandinavian invasions.

While it is sometimes hard to distinguish between the areal and typological aspects of linguistic phenomena, the fact remains that together they constitute forceful evidence for contact effects. What is also important from the point of view of the case at hand is that these effects are not in all likelihood limited to just one individual syntactic feature but comprise several features at the very core of the grammar of English. Their number may well increase when research into the question of Celtic influences advances. Besides syntax, one should recall some of the phonological and morphological changes of English, discussed by Tolkien (1963), Kastovsky (1994), Hickey (1995), and Tristram (1997a), which also mark off English typologically from its Germanic sister languages and may well have been set in motion by contacts with Celtic.

7 Conclusion

What we have in this book called the 'Celtic hypothesis' forms a most interesting chapter in the history of diachronic studies of English and also in a wider cross-linguistic context. Torpedoed at its birth by some of the most eminent scholars of the late nineteenth and early twentieth centuries, such as Otto Jespersen and Max Förster, it has simply refused to die, surfacing over the following century here and there in the writings of scholars who have probably even put their academic careers at risk in challenging the prevailing doctrine by re-raising the possibility of substratum transfer from Celtic. To what extent the 'anti-Celtic' stand in historical-linguistic scholarship has been a matter of an ideological, more or less hidden, agenda is difficult to tell, but certainly the wordings used by Jespersen, for example, closely echo the general tenets of nineteenth-century Anglo-Saxonist historians. That these views have then come to be repeated in even some of the most recent textbooks on the history of English can be explained by the general trend in scholarship in any discipline: once a theory or view becomes widely accepted, it is very hard for subsequent research to break free from the existing 'paradigm' in the Kuhnian sense of the word. As has become evident from the foregoing chapters, this is no longer the situation in the research into the contacts between English and the Celtic languages: new voices have joined those of the early pioneers of the Celtic hypothesis, and it now seems that the balance of opinion is in the process of shifting towards a more favourable stand on the issue of Celtic influences.

What we have sought to do in this book is to give additional momentum to this development: first, by exposing some of the inherent weaknesses of the accounts based on the Received View on the extent of Celtic influence on English, and secondly, by adducing new evidence and fresh ways of interpreting the 'old' evidence that pertains to this matter. As said at the beginning of Chapter 6, our approach has been holistic in the sense that we have endeavoured to bring together all kinds of both extra-linguistic and linguistic evidence that has bearing on the issue of the linguistic outcomes of the English–Celtic interface. It also follows from this approach that we have not been content to discuss a limited number of grammatical or other features, but have made an effort to provide a comprehensive picture across the whole system or systems of language, difficult as it is. In this we have been guided by the general language contact theory, which shows that contact effects scarcely ever occur in just one subsystem of a language. We have similarly considered it important to cover the whole history of the contacts between English and Celtic, as it is evident that the kinds of contact effects that have taken place in the modern period in the so-called Celtic Englishes are very similar in nature to those that have been argued to have occurred in the earliest stages. The modern contacts therefore provide an important window into the past and lend further indirect support to the Celtic hypothesis.

In our reassessment of the extent of Celtic influence on English, demographic and historical evidence has occupied a central position. We have, indeed, considered it a prerequisite for ascertaining linguistic contact influences. For contact effects to occur, the demographic and historical circumstances must be such that they bring about (more or less) extensive bilingualism among the populations involved in a contact situation. There is now enough evidence to prove that this was the situation in early mediaeval Britain. Instead of being swept away, the Celtic-speaking part of the population largely remained in their earlier places of residence and were gradually assimilated to their new Germanic neighbours both linguistically and culturally.

Turning next to the linguistic factors, there is again no principled reason to exclude the possibility of contact influences. On the contrary, the existence of close Celtic parallels to several features of English, together with the established chronological precedence of many of the Celtic features, suggests that English has adopted them from Celtic, or at least the two languages or language groups have influenced each other, that is, formed an adstratal relationship. This line of argumentation is further supported by the commonly observed tendency for contact effects to manifest themselves in more than one subsystem of a language. The general theory of language contacts is also helpful in determining which domains of language are the most susceptible to contact influences in any given type of language contact situation. In the early stages of the Celtic–English interface, which was characterised by language shift affecting large numbers of the British-speaking population, the phonology and syntax of the emerging new contact variety, rather than its lexicon, were the areas that were the most likely to absorb influences from the declining Celtic languages. Too much of the previous research has been based on the ill-informed view which interprets the paucity of Celtic loanwords in English as proof of a more general lack of Celtic contact effects in English.

Finally, our discussion has relied on some of the recent work on areal and typological linguistics, which has, on one hand, highlighted the special nature of English as compared with its closest Germanic sisters and, on the other, brought to light some clear affinities between English and its neighbouring Celtic languages. Combining this type of evidence with those discussed above further underlines the need to take the Celtic hypothesis more seriously than has hitherto been the case in English historical scholarship. All in all, the 'case' of the Celtic–English contacts serves to highlight the methodological perils of the classic type of argument known as *argumentum ex silentio*, which stipulates that no argument can be put forward if there is no evidence, or does not appear to be any evidence, to support it. This is exactly what those subscribing to the Received View have done: from the small number of Celtic loanwords they have hastened to draw the conclusion that Celtic had virtually no influence on English or that it is at best negligible, but in so doing have missed the other kinds of evidence that lead to a very different conclusion. We make no claim of having been able to provide a definitive account of the nature and extent of Celtic influence on English, but we do not hesitate to argue that the history of the English language should be rewritten so as to pay proper attention to this influence.

Notes

NOTES TO CHAPTER ONE

1. Nick Higham (personal communication) points out that Hunter Blair's account does not tally with the archaeological evidence; there is a relatively clear break between the collapse of Roman Britain and the first appearance of Anglo-Saxon materials in the region around fifty years later.
2. *Thames* is, in fact, pre-Brittonic, either non-Indo-European, as Jackson (1955: 154) believes, or Indo-European, but pre-Celtic, as Kitson (1996: 90) has argued, cf. Coates (1998: 218).
3. For Anglo-Saxonism in the context of nineteenth-century philology and attitudes towards the possibility of a Celtic substratum in English, see especially German (2000); MacDougall (1982) and Frantzen and Niles (1997) provide more general discussions of Anglo-Saxonism. For a wider perspective on the history of originary myths in Europe, cf. also Poliakov (1974).
4. Härke (2003: 24), in a postscript to his article on the population history of Britain, refers to the study of Weale *et al.* (2002) and to the evidence that this study provides for Anglo-Saxon mass migration.
5. Spriggs's map is a revised version of an earlier, so-called Holmes-George map, published in George (1986). For a discussion, see Spriggs (2003: 232 ff.).

NOTES TO CHAPTER TWO

1. Mitchell also refers to Visser (1963–1973: § 351), who discusses these phenomena under the heading of "Type: 'he wæs me freond'" (referred to in Mitchell 1985: § 308). Visser wants to draw a semantic distinction between constructions with the possessive (pro)noun and those with the (pro)noun in the dative. Thus sentences like *þa sticode **him** mon þa eagan ut* and *þa sticode man **his** eagan ut* differ in the same way as present-day English *she kissed **me** on the cheek* and *she kissed **my** cheek*. This analysis is not, however, accepted by Mitchell (1985: § 310). Visser also considers in this context the pattern with the preposition *to*, e.g. *Ich **am** to criste vend* (§ 354).
2. Dutch, however, is not a particularly good example here because, although it preserves the external possessor type as a relic feature in certain kinds of contexts, it has otherwise shifted to the internal possessor construction. See also the discussion below.
3. 'I do not therefore doubt that the English usage derives from the Celtic substratum, which in turn has in this case been influenced by pre-Indo-European.' (Our translation.)

4. 'The Old English forms and functions of the root *bheu, which are alien to the other Germanic dialects, arose in the mouths and thinking of the English-speaking Britons.' (Our translation.)
5. In a forthcoming article, Angelika Lutz discusses this feature and also draws attention to the reluctance of Anglicists to consider the Celtic connection. In the same context she mentions Krahe and Meid's (1969) book, in which they argue that the preservation of the old Indo-European dual paradigm of the verb 'be' in Old English may be due to Celtic influence (see Lutz, forthcoming).
6. This construction type is also discussed in Börjars and Chapman (1998), Murray (1873: 211–213), Wright (1905: 296) on Modern British English; McCafferty (2003) on Northern Irish English; McCafferty (2004) on Southern British English; Bailey, Maynor and Cukor-Avila (1989) on early Modern English; Benskin and Laing (1981: 93–94), McIntosh (1989), Murray (1873: 211–213), Mustanoja (1960: 481–482) on Middle English; King (1997: 175–177), Montgomery (1994) on Older Scots; Montgomery (1989), Poplack and Tagliamonte (1989), Tagliamonte and Poplack (1993) on varieties of American English. Other names used to describe the phenomenon include 'the personal pronoun rule' (McIntosh 1989), 'Northern Present Tense Rule' (Montgomery 1994), 'Subject-Type Constraint' (Montgomery 1989), 'NP/pro Constraint', and 'Proximity Constraint'. In the following we will continue to use Ihalainen's term 'Northern Subject Rule' for this type of subject–verb agreement.
7. As pointed out by Theo Vennemann (2002b), the close parallels between Insular Celtic and Hamito-Semitic languages were already noticed by Morris-Jones (1900), who discusses a number of striking syntactic parallels—including agreement—between Welsh and the Hamitic languages of North Africa, such as Coptic and Berber. These parallels raise the possibility that we may be dealing with an even earlier, Atlantic substratum influence here (cf. Vennemann 2002b).
8. We use SMALL CAPITALS to refer to the lexeme DO to distinguish it from the grammatical forms *do, does, did, done*.
9. For recent discussions on the question of the origins of DO, see Denison (1993: 255–291), Garrett (1998), van der Auwera and Genee (2002).
10. Our discussion of the geographical distribution of periphrastic DO in affirmative declarative clauses in the following is largely based on Klemola (1996).
11. See Klemola (1996: 21–74) for further details.
12. For a more detailed discussion of the geographical distribution of DO on the basis of Ellis (1889), see Klemola (1996: 22–27).
13. Ellis (1889: 4–5) describes Hallam's method of selecting his informants as follows:

> On arriving at a station he would inquire where he could find old and if possible illiterate peasants, whom he would "interview", gaining their confidence, and then noting their peculiarities of pron. in his note books (now more than lxx. in number, a goodly Septuagint), using palaeotype, which he wrote most accurately. In the same books he entered all passing pron. which he heard, forming the "words noted" [. . .], which are so frequently referred to hereafter, reduced to the form of my cwl [classified word list]. Also, making acquaintance with native dialect speakers, he obtained numerous cs. [comparative specimens] and dt. [dialect tests], most of which are given below, and thus enabled me to illustrate dialectal pron. in a most unexpectedly accurate manner over about 22 counties.

(Ellis 1889: 4–5)

14. For more detailed discussions of the apparent time method, see Chambers and Trudgill (1998: 149–165) and Labov (1994: 43–72).
15. For a more detailed discussion of the backwards projection of the geographical distribution of periphrastic DO, see Klemola (1996: 155–175).
16. The term that Ellegård (1953: 29) uses is 'permutation'.
17. Van der Auwera and Genee (2002: 300) list the following scholars as proponents of some type of Celtic hypothesis for the origin of DO: Preusler (1938, 1940, 1956), Dal (1952), Wagner (1959), Haarmann (1976), Vincent (1986), Molyneux (1987), Meid (1990), Poussa (1990), Tristram (1997a), and German (2000).
18. For a recent and thorough survey of constructions with 'do' and a verbal noun in Celtic languages, see also van der Auwera and Genee (2002: 288–291).
19. The particle *yn* is historically a locative preposition, which in Modern Welsh functions as a marker of imperfective aspect (for discussions on the origins and role of aspectual *yn* in Welsh periphrastic constructions, see, e.g. Watkins 1957, 1960, 1962; Fife 1990; Isaac 1994; Heinecke 1999).
20. 'All these turns of expression can be explained very well in terms of the English language, without a need to resort to a hypothesis based on an external influence. The analogy between the Celtic and English expressions is therefore, in our opinion, a simple coincidence.' (Our translation.)
21. 'However, the main argument for our view on the matter is that because of the historical and social circumstances we cannot expect any extensive use of syntactic Celticisms in OE literature. The Celts were a submerged people, hence their syntax, insofar as it manifested itself in the English language, bore the label of vulgarism which had to be avoided in the educated language of literature. It is by no means rare that vulgar and everyday language can live for centuries without appearing in the written language.' (Our translation.)
22. This is also confirmed by Roibeard Ó Maolalaigh (personal communication), although he points out that omission of the copula is possible in present-day Gaelic when the focus constituent is a pronoun.
23. See also Gillies (1993: 211) and Lamb (2001: 90) for the same phenomenon in Scottish Gaelic.
24. 'Should a stressed word stand at the beginning of a sentence because of emphasis, a **relative inversion** is used: the word to be emphasized becomes the predicate of the (often unexpressed) copula and the antecedent of a relative sentence, which contains the actual proposition.' (Our translation.)
25. She also informs us (communication by e-mail 11/09/04) that clefts occur in the even earlier *Gododdin*, dating from the sixth or seventh century AD.
26. 'The issue is not, however, whether a construction occurs in a language or not, but to what extent it has developed as a grammatical category and what syntactic range this category (if it is alive) possesses.' (Our translation.)
27. 'The question has arisen whether the French pattern is due to a Celtic substrate: until now no Gaulish text has provided evidence for that.' (Our translation.)
28. See, however, Lambert (1987), who has questioned Koch's interpretation of some of the crucial forms in the Chamalières tablet.
29. As Evans (1990: 171) points out, Welsh later undergoes a shift, possibly cyclical, to subject-prominence.
30. One should, however, note that the system of concord was different in earlier English: as Ball (1991: 150) points out, the copula (i.e. the verb *be*) agreed in number with the focused NP until the mid-fifteenth century.
31. 'a bretonism which one can often hear in the speech of Bretons speaking French; this is because French has no equivalent for it.' (Our translation.)

32. The only instance in which the focus is the object is according to Ball a 'predicational cleft' and not directly comparable with the rest of her examples (see Ball 1991: 300 for discussion).

33. There are different terms for resumptive pronouns in the literature on Welsh. Thus, Watkins (1993: 341) prefers to speak of 'anaphoric' pronouns in his description of Modern Welsh. His examples include sentences like *hwn yw'r dyn y gyrraist ei gar* (lit. this is-the man that drove-you his car) 'this is the man whose car you drove' and *hwn yw'r dyn y siaradaist amdano* (lit. this is-the man that talked-you about-him) 'this is the man whom you talked about' (*ibid.*).

34. 'The Cymric relative clauses often have [. . .] no relative marker, but are marked by special verb forms. In the mouths of English-speaking Britons this could easily adapt itself into the so-called contact-clause, which is popular in present-day English [. . .]' (Our translation.)

35. One has to note, however, that Scottish Gaelic also retains the 'pied-piping' construction, dominant in Old Irish, where the preposition stands before the relative particle *an: am fear ris an robh mi a' bruidhinn* 'the man to whom I was speaking' (Gillies 1993: 219; see also Isaac 2003b: 77; Poppe 2006: 202–203).

36. This does not mean that resumptive pronouns are not found in other British English dialects. This is shown, e.g. by the *SED* data, although the questionnaire contains only one item that is relevant to the issue at hand. This is Item IX.9.6 WHOSE UNCLE WAS DROWNED, which focuses on the use of the possessive form *whose* in the sentence frame *That man's uncle was drowned last week. In other words, you might say, that's the chap. . . .* The responses collected, for instance, from the six northernmost counties included forms such as *at/as/that his uncle was drowned*, although the majority favoured the standard form *whose uncle was drowned* (Orton *et al.* 1962–1971: 1085). Of the three variant forms involving the resumptive pronoun *his*, the forms *at his* and *that his* were mainly limited to the northern dialects, including the Isle of Man (9 and 8 responses in all, respectively). *As his uncle was drowned*, by contrast, turned out to be more widespread (56 responses), and was recorded especially in the southern, midland, and north-western dialects. Pending quantitative comparisons between varieties in different parts of the British Isles, it is impossible to say anything about possible differences between them in their rates of use of resumptive pronouns.

37. In a footnote to his 2003a paper, Isaac acknowledges the existence of examples like (14) in Irish English and considers them 'genuine' symptoms of contact. However, he does not accept their value as indirect evidence for similar contact effects in the past (Isaac 2003a: 48, fn. 6). Interestingly, in another footnote he mentions that the ModE-style preposition stranding is gradually making its way into present-day informal Welsh, producing sentences as *Be ti lan i?* (what are-you up to) 'What are you up to?' (Isaac 2003a: 49, fn. 8). He explains this as a case of "the grammar of a minority language being distorted by contact with the majority language of political hegemony" (*ibid.*). This may well be so but another, less sentimental, way to look at it is to acknowledge that the relative structures of English and Welsh are similar enough to be susceptible to contact effects in both directions—which, once more, strengthens the case for similar effects in the past.

38. An interesting parallel case of borrowing of a comparative particle is offered by Campbell (1987). Campbell presents evidence to show that the American Indian language Pipil has borrowed the Spanish comparative particle *que*, which has replaced the original Pipil comparative particle.

39. Barry (1969) contains an exhaustive bibliography of articles dealing with sheep-scoring numerals.

40. Scattered, relatively late, examples of these numerals have also been reported from an area that spreads through Yorkshire and Lincolnshire to East Anglia and the South-East, but as Barry (1969: 76) notes, these "can most probably be explained by the numerals being carried further afield by natives travelling away from the original districts of England". These numerals have also been reported in the United States, where the earliest reported example of 1717 in fact predates the earliest recorded example in Britain (Barry 1969: 82). Barry (1969: 77) believes that the explanation for the American occurrences is that "some of the early colonists came from northern England and brought the scores with them".

41. Unless otherwise indicated, all the examples quoted in this section come from the corpus of *SED* tape-recordings; see Klemola and Jones (1999).

42. Map 2.5 is based on the answers to the following 15 *SED Basic Material Questionnaire* items: VI.5.8; VI.14.14; VIII:1.11; VIII.9.5.1; VIII.9.5.3; IX.6.4; IX.7.2.1; IX.7.2.2; IX.7.2.3; IX.7.7.2; IX.7.7.3; IX.7.9.1; IX.7.10.2; IX.8.2; IX.8.4.

43. Map 2.6 is drawn on the basis of the answers to the following *SED Basic Material Questionnaire* items: VI.5.8; VI.14.14; VIII.9.5.1; VIII.9.5.3; IX.6.4; IX.7.2.1; IX.7.2.2; Ix.7.2.3; IX.7.7.2; IX.7.7.3; IX.7.9.1; IX.7.10.2.

44. Map 2.7 is drawn on the basis of the answers to the following *SED Basic Material Questionnaire* items: VIII.1.11; IX.8.2; IX.8.4.

45. The exact details of the rules governing the use of *en, it, him*, and *her* in south-western dialects are rather complex and need not concern us here. For further details, see Elworthy (1877) and Ihalainen (1985).

46. See Elworthy (1877) and Paddock (1988) for details. For a recent, very interesting discussion of pronominal gender in English dialects from a typological perspective, see Siemund (2007).

47. There is a possibility that the changes in the gender systems of the Brythonic languages and the adjacent south-western dialects of English could represent a convergent adstratal development (cf. Tristram 1999a: 21 on gender in present-day Standard English and present-day Welsh).

48. As Raymond Hickey (personal communication) notes, /θ/ is also preserved in Faroese, and /ð/ is found in Danish, but as a later development.

49. This is confirmed by John Harris (personal communication).

50. For details of '*i*-affection' in Welsh singular nouns, see Evans (1964: § 30, p. 30); see also Morris-Jones (1913: 210–212).

51. John Harris (personal communication) points out that *i*-mutation is problematic as a contact feature because of its predictability on the basis of universal constraints; only two types or 'settings' are possible for this parameter.

52. On lenition in Celtic languages, see Oftedal (1985), who discusses the origins of Celtic mutations and parallels in, e.g. Scandinavian languages. He also draws comparisons with the Old High German sound shift and surveys initial consonant alternations in other languages of the world, including West African languages, Modern Greek, Old High German, French and Italian.

53. Schrijver (2002), however, modifies the conclusions of Schrijver (1999) significantly. In the more recent article Schrijver argues that by the fifth century AD most of Lowland Britain was Latin rather than Brittonic speaking. Thus, he argues, the Brittonic substratum features in Old English phonology must have been transmitted via British Latin: "a Brittonic substratum in British Latin and a British Latin substratum in prehistoric Old English transmitted features of the Brittonic sound system to Old English" (Schrijver 2002: 105).

54. The head-attribute ordering of place-names is also discussed by Jackson (1953: 225–227), who further points out that Ekwall has shown that such names are found in Cumberland, Northumberland, Lancashire, Shropshire, Herefordshire, Worcestershire, Gloucestershire and Devon. Preusler (1956: 341) is probably also referring to this head-attribute ordering of place-names when he draws attention to place-names of the type *County Antrim* or *Market Drayton*. The last-mentioned are, as Preusler points out, particularly frequent in northern England, Scotland, Wales and Ireland. According to him, there can be no doubt that they reflect the Celtic patterns, in which the genitive is placed after the governing word (here *Antrim*, etc.), with the head of the phrase (here *County*, etc.) preceding the attribute (Preusler 1956: 341).

55. "Sehr stark ist das keltische Sprachgut vertreten unter den englischen Familiennamen, in alter wie in neuer Zeit" (Förster 1921: 177).

56. Thomason and Kaufman point out the fallacy of this type of argumentation in the following terms:

> Perhaps the most common error made by historical linguists in weighing the evidence of language contact is to assume that (as we observed in chap. 2) a lack of numerous loanwords critically weakens the case for any structural interference. One such argument is the frequently-made claim that, since there are few early Dravidian loanwords in Indic, there is little likelihood of early contact between Dravidian and Indic. This conclusion is not justified, however. The lack of numerous loanwords means only that if there was sufficient early contact for Dravidian features to be diffused into Indic, that contact must have involved shift of Dravidian speakers to Indic, not borrowing by Indic from Dravidian.
>
> (Thomason and Kaufman 1988: 42–43, emphasis in the original)

57. It should be noted, however, that McWhorter has since modified his views on the question of the role of loanwords. In McWhorter (forthcoming), his position on the loanword issue is essentially similar to the position we argue for here.

58. A search of the electronic version of the MED produced the following list of words whose etymology is given as Celtic (Bret.; Celt.; Celtic, Corn.; Gael.; Ir.; MIr.; Mn Sc.Gael.; MWel.; Sc.Gael.; Wel.): *amobre, bannok, bat, bauded, bavein, birling, bog, bonaghtie, brag, bragot, brat, brok, cāder, cammed, candred(e), car(e), coigne, commorth, commŏut, corī, cork, corrīn, cosh, crag, crannok, creag, crŏud, currok, dŏn, drī, durdan, fawe, flānen, gaine, garie, genou, glen, glāveren, glōrien, gog(e)len, gulle, hagh, hōne, hog(ge), irk(e), kaire, keineth, keis, kenning, ketherin, kid, kēlim, kērne, laggen, lavei, lābī, lenew(e), lough, lŏupe, mailen, mallok(e), mart, mīles, mover, mŏunthe, obilas, oghane, pēte, phither, piln, porthien-keis, poullok, raglōre, raglotīe, ringildīe, ringild-ship, ron, russīn, scailen, skēne, suwing, tor, tunk, warrok, wolc, wratbihe.*

59. "Es gibt Anzeichen dafür, daß sie zunächst versuchten, den Angelsachsen gegenüber ihre höhere römische Lebensweise hervorzukehren. Sicher spielte sich auch der sprachliche Verkehr teilweise, wenn nicht überwiegend, auf Latein ab. Von diesen bereits sprachlich in hohem Maße romanisierten Briten konnte daher nicht viel altes britisches Wortgut in das Englische—hier in den sächsischen Dialekt—eingehen. Weiter nach Norden und Westen war die Situation anders; dort übernommenes Wortgut konnte sich aber—wenn überhaupt—nur in den lokalen Mundarten erhalten." (Meid 1990: 114)

60. The work of Davies was first brought to our attention by Stalmaszczyk (1997). For other recent discussions of Davies, see also Viereck (2000: 397) and Stalmaszczyk (2005: 32–33).

61. Davies's abbreviation S. stands for Salop, which is the older, Norman-derived name for the county of Shropshire.

NOTES TO CHAPTER THREE

1. These figures include respondents able to speak Welsh. The total figure including everyone with one or more skills in the Welsh language is 797,717 (Aitchison and Carter 2004: 38).
2. This section is a revised and updated version of Section 2.2 in Filppula (1999).
3. These are areas officially designated as Irish-speaking. According to *The Gaeltacht*, an information booklet on the present-day Irish-speaking areas, the Gaeltacht comprises some coastal areas in the counties of Kerry, Galway, Mayo and Donegal; it also includes the Aran Islands, the island of Aranmore and Clear Island. Furthermore, small pockets of Irish-speaking are found in the mountain area of West Cork, on the Waterford coast and as far east as Co. Meath. The total area covers some 4,800 square kilometres.
4. The Census figures are not directly comparable, because a new wording on the ability to speak Irish and the frequency of speaking it was introduced in the 1996 census. However, it remained the same in the 2002 census.
5. Soulsby (1986: 76) identifies John Davey, who died in 1891, as perhaps the last speaker of traditional Cornish, "reputed to have been able to recite traditional rhymes and verses".
6. For a discussion of Revived Cornish, see George and Broderick (1993).

NOTES TO CHAPTER FOUR

1. It should be noted that the use of the definite article in these contexts is not categorical; both inter- and intra-individual variation occurs, depending on factors which are often hard to pin down.
2. As in Chapter 2, section 2.2.5, we use here the familiar term 'progressive' form. However, as is shown by our discussion, the progressive form is not restricted to the expression of progressivity in these varieties.
3. The normalised frequencies given in Tables 4.1 and 4.2 must be considered approximative, as the word counts of the corpora include questions or comments by the interviewers as well as other metatextual material. However, since the same applies to all of the corpora, this was not deemed too harmful for the present purposes. The IrE figures are based on a combined corpus of southern IrE (totalling ca 221,000 words; see Filppula 1999) and northern IrE (the NICTS Corpus, totalling ca 254,300 words). The corresponding total for HebE is ca 177,400 words, for WE ca 63,600 words, for EngE ca 714,500 and for EModE ca 566,800.
4. Some researchers have sought to explain the recent spread of the progressive form as a language-internal phenomenon. Thus, Mair and Hundt (1995) suggest that the increase of the PF in written English may result from a stylistic shift by which formal language is becoming more informal:

> [t]he increase in the use of the progressive could be regarded as a symptom of the "colloquialisation" of written English.

> (Mair and Hundt 1995: 118)

5. We owe this piece of information to the late Professor Alan Thomas.

6. In Filppula's corpus, consisting of 158,000 words of recorded speech, there were 40 instances of the medial-object perfect. By comparison, the *International Corpus of English* (ICE)—Ireland corpus, which has a total of one million words representing Irish Standard English, their number was 34 (see Kirk and Kallen 2006: 98).

7. Note, however, that the *HVE* survey lists ScE as a variety in which the medial-object perfect is attested (Kortmann 2004: 1090).

8. What complicates the issue is the fact that, after the near-demise of the 'medial-object' perfect by the end of the ME period, it has become more frequent again from especially the nineteenth century onwards even in StE. Thus, e.g. Visser (1963–1973: 2190) notes that constructions such as *I have him beaten, he had him trapped, I have her cornered* are found in present-day StE "with increasing frequency, especially in popular diction". He also finds them to be common in Anglo-Irish and AmE.

9. It has to be pointed out that not all Celticists agree on the availability of the substratal constructions at an early enough date and with the type of meanings associated with the IrE *after* perfect. However, the thorough discussion of the history of the Irish 'after' perfect and similar constructions in Scottish Gaelic in Ó Sé (2004) suffices to show that the IrE *after* perfect has its most likely source in the late Middle Irish and Early Modern Irish constructions involving the verbal noun preceded by *iar* 'after' and a few other similar prepositions.

10. The *SED* data from Monmouthshire indicate that periphrastic DO is, or has been, very common in the conservative rural dialect of south-east Wales. Apart from some estimates (e.g. Connolly 1990; Lewis 1990), there are no surveys on its present-day frequencies of use. However, in the interviews conducted by Ceri George in the Rhondda, the instances of periphrastic DO are far outnumbered by those of habitual PF, indicating that in this respect, the Welsh substratum has had a greater impact on the dialects of the industrial valleys than the English superstratum (Paulasto 2006).

11. Note, however, that there are other sentence types in Welsh where inserting the GWNEUD auxiliary is obligatory, i.e. the mixed or cleft sentence and the Middle Welsh abnormal sentence: when the verb-noun is fronted, GWNEUD takes the position of the predicate (cf. Fife 1988, Mac Cana 1991; see also van der Auwera and Genee 2002). These constructions are capable of indicating habituality, as well:

(1) Cyfansoddi dan   orfodaeth a   wnawn . . . (Watkins 1991: 343)
    compose.VN under pressure   RPR °do.IMPF.1SG
    '(It was) compose under pressure (that) I used to do . . .', i.e. 'What I used to do was . . .'

12. As mentioned in Chapter 2, section 2.2.6, clefting seems to have been rather rare even as late as the late ME and EModE periods. It was only after then that cleft constructions have become more frequent and both functionally and syntactically more versatile (see, esp. Ball 1991: 509 ff.).

13. Parry (1999: 117), indeed, ascribes this usage to the Welsh possessive construction *bod* 'be' + object + *gyda* 'with' + possessor; e.g. *mae car gyda ni* 'there is a car with us' or 'we have a car'.

NOTES TO CHAPTER FIVE

1. This chapter is an abridged and updated version of the authors' introduction to the edited volume entitled *The Celtic Roots of English* (Filppula *et al.* 2002).

2. 'But it is the one-sided consideration of the lexical material that has led to this view; the more recent etymological research has reduced the number of Celtic loanwords in English to a minimum, cf. Luick Hist. Gramm. d. engl. Spr. § 45. One must, however, make it clear to oneself that the influence of the language of a submerged people upon that of the conquerors is to be expected much more in syntax than in lexicon. The conquered nation has had to learn the language of the conquerors; however, as mentioned above, in doing so it has preserved its own syntactic characteristics and sought to express them in the new language.' (Our translation.)

3. 'The main argument supporting our account of this matter is, however, that because of the historical and social circumstances one could not *expect* any significant use of syntactic Celticisms in Old English literature. The Celts were a submerged race; their syntax, insofar as it became manifest in the English language, carried the label of being vulgar, something which had to be avoided in the refined literary language. It is by no means rare that constructions belonging to vulgar and everyday language could live on for centuries without surfacing in the written language.' (Our translation.)

4. It is interesting to note that this is also accepted by Mossé (1938 II: 59–66), who does not otherwise endorse the Celtic hypothesis, but considers the parallelisms between Celtic and English as merely coincidental.

Bibliography

Ahlgren, A. (1946) *On the Use of the Definite Article with 'Nouns of Possession' in English*, Uppsala: Appelbergs Boktryckeriaktiebolag.

Ahlqvist, A. (1977) 'Typological notes on Irish word-order', in P.J. Hopper (ed.) *Studies in Descriptive and Historical Linguistics. Festschrift for Winfred P. Lehmann*, Amsterdam and Philadelphia: John Benjamins, 267–281.

——— (1988) 'Of unknown (?) origin', *Studia Anglica Posnaniensia*, 21: 69–73.

——— (2002) 'Cleft sentences in Irish and other languages', in M. Filppula, J. Klemola and H. Pitkänen (eds), 271–281.

Aitchison, J. and Carter, H. (2000) *Language, Economy and Society: The Changing Fortunes of the Welsh Language in the Twentieth Century*, Cardiff: University of Wales Press.

——— (2004) *Spreading the Word: The Welsh Language 2001*, Talybont: Y Lolfa.

Bailey, G., Maynor, N. and Cukor-Avila, P. (1989) 'Variation in subject-verb concord in Early Modern English', *Language Variation and Change*, 1: 285–300.

Ball, C.N. (1990) 'Word order and frequency of clefts: cross-linguistic and diachronic data', Paper presented at the Penn Linguistics Colloquium, February 9–10, University of Pennsylvania.

——— (1991) *The Historical Development of the it-cleft*, University of Pennsylvania Dissertation in Linguistics, Ann Arbor, MI: University Microfilms International.

Ball, M.J. (ed.) (1993) *The Celtic Languages*, London: Routledge.

Bammesberger, A. and Wollmann, A. (eds) (1990) *Britain 400–600: Language and History*, Heidelberg: Universitätsverlag C. Winter.

Barnes, W. (1886) *A Glossary of the Dorset Dialect with a Grammar of Its Word Shapening and Wording*, London: Trübner & Co. [Reprinted 1970, Guernsey: Steven Cox, The Toucan Press]

Barry, M.V. (1967) 'Yorkshire sheep-scoring numerals', *Transactions of the Yorkshire Dialect Society*, XII.LXVII: 21–31.

——— (1969) 'Traditional enumeration in the North Country', *Folk Life*, VII: 75–91.

——— (1984) 'Manx English', in P. Trudgill (ed.), 167–177.

Baugh, A.C. and Cable, T. (1993) *A History of the English Language*, London: Routledge.

Beal, J. (1993) 'The grammar of Tyneside and Northumbrian English', in J. Milroy and L. Milroy (eds), 187–213.

——— (1997) 'Syntax and morphology', in C. Jones (ed.), 335–377.

Beckman, N. (1934) 'Västeuropeisk syntax. Några nybildningar i nordiska och andra västeuropeiska språk', *Göteborgs Högskolas Årsskrift*, 40: 3–44.

Benskin, M. and Laing, M. (1981) 'Translations and "Mischsprachen" in Middle English Manuscripts', in M. Benskin and M.L. Samuels (eds) *So Meny People*

Longages and Tonges: Philological Essays in Scots and Medieval English. Presented to Angus McIntosh, Edinburgh: Benskin & Samuels, 55–106.

Berresford Ellis, P. (1998) *The Story of the Cornish Language*, 3rd edn, Redruth: Tor Mark Press.

Bever, T.G. and Langendoen, D.T. (1972) 'The interaction of speech perception and grammatical structure in the evolution of language', Ch. 3 in R.P. Stockwell and R.K.S. Macaulay (eds) *Linguistic Change and Generative Theory*, Bloomington/London: Indiana University Press, 32–95.

Blake, N. (ed.) (1992) *The Cambridge History of the English Language, Vol. 2: 1066–1476*, Cambridge: Cambridge University Press.

Bliss, A.J. (1972) 'Languages in contact: some problems of Hiberno-English', *Proceedings of the Royal Irish Academy 72*, Section C, 63–82.

——— (1977) 'The emergence of modern English dialects in Ireland', in D. Ó Muirithe (ed.), 7–19.

——— (1979) *Spoken English in Ireland 1600–1740*, Dublin: The Dolmen Press.

——— (1984) 'English in the south of Ireland', in P. Trudgill (ed.), 135–151.

Bobda, A.S. (2006) 'Irish presence in colonial Cameroon and its linguistic legacy', in H.L.C. Tristram (ed.), 217–233.

Börjars, K. and Chapman, C. (1998) 'Agreement and pro-drop in some dialects of English', *Linguistics*, 36: 71–98.

Bowen, E.G. (1959) 'Le Pays de Galles', *Transactions of the Institute of British Geographers*, 26: 1–23.

——— (1964) *Daearyddiaeth Cymru fel cefndir i'w hanes*, London: BBC (Radio lecture).

Braaten, B. (1967) 'Notes on continuous tenses in English', *Norsk Tidsskrift for Sprogvidenskap*, XXI: 167–180.

Breeze, A. (1993a) 'Old English *trum* 'strong', *truma* 'host': Welsh *trwm* 'heavy'', *Notes and Queries*, 40:1 (238), 16–19.

——— (1993b) 'Celtic etymologies for Old English *cursung* 'curse', *gafeluc* 'javelin', *stær* 'history', *syrce* 'coat of mail', and Middle English *clog(ge)* 'block, wooden shoe', *cokkunge* 'striving', *tirven* 'to flay', *warroke* 'hunchback'', *Notes and Queries*, 40:3 (238), 287–297.

——— (1994) 'Celtic etymologies for Middle English *brag* 'boast', *gird* 'strike', and *lethe* 'soften'', *Journal of Celtic Linguistics*, 3: 135–148.

——— (1997) 'A Celtic etymology for Old English *deor* 'brave'', in J. Roberts and J.L. Nelson, with M. Godden (eds) *Alfred the Wise: Studies in Honour of Janet Bately on the Occasion of Her Sixty-Fifth Birthday*, Cambridge: D.S. Brewer, 1–4.

——— (2002) 'Seven types of Celtic loanword', in M. Filppula, J. Klemola and H. Pitkänen (eds), 175–181.

Brinton, L.J. (1988) *The Development of English Aspectual Systems*, Cambridge: Cambridge University Press.

Britton, D. (1994) 'The etymology of Modern Dialect *'en*, 'him'', *Notes and Queries*, 41(1): 16–18.

Broderick, G. (1997) 'Manx English: an overview', in H.L.C. Tristram (ed.), 123–134.

——— (1999) *Language Death in the Isle of Man: An Investigation into the Decline and Extinction of Manx Gaelic as a Community Language in the Isle of Man*, Tübingen: Max Niemeyer Verlag.

Burchfield, R. (ed.) (1994) *The Cambridge History of the English Language, Vol. 5: English in Britain and Overseas. Origins and Development*, Cambridge: Cambridge University Press.

Burnley, D. (1992) 'Lexis and semantics', in N. Blake (ed.), 409–499.

Bybee, J.L. (1985) *Morphology: A Study on the Relation between Meaning and Form* (Typological Studies in Language 9), Amsterdam and Philadelphia: John Benjamins.

Campbell, A. (1959) *Old English Grammar*, Oxford: Clarendon Press.

Campbell, L. (1987) 'Syntactic change in Pipil', *International Journal of American Linguistics*, 53(3): 253–280.

Capelli, C. Redhead, N., Abernethy, J.K., Gratrix, F., Wilson, J.F., Moen, T., Hervig, T., Richards, M., Stumpf, M.P.H., Underhill, P.A., Bradshaw, P., Shaha, A., Thomas, M.G., Bradman, N. and Goldstein, D.G. (2003) 'A Y chromosome consensus of the British Isles', *Current Biology*, 13: 979–984.

Chadwick, N.K. (1963) 'The British or Celtic part in the population of England', in *Angles and Britons* (O'Donnell Lectures), Cardiff: University of Wales Press, 111–147.

Chambers, J.K. and Trudgill P. (1998) *Dialectology*, 2nd edn, Cambridge: Cambridge University Press.

Clark, C. (1992) 'Onomastics', in R.M. Hogg (ed.), 452–489.

Clarke, S. (1997) 'The role of Irish English in the formation of New World Englishes: the case from Newfoundland', in J.L. Kallen (ed.), 207–225.

Coates, R. (1998) 'A new explanation of the name of London', *Transactions of the Philological Society*, 96:2, 203–229.

—— (2000a) 'Introduction', in R. Coates and A. Breeze, 1–14.

—— (2000b) 'Evidence for the persistence of Brittonic in Wiltshire', in R. Coates and A. Breeze, 112–116.

—— (2002) 'The significances of Celtic place-names in England', in M. Filppula, J. Klemola and H. Pitkänen (eds), 47–85.

—— (2004) 'Invisible Britons: the view from linguistics', Paper presented at the conference "Britons in Anglo-Saxon England", Manchester, 14–16 April, 2004.

—— (2007) 'Invisible Britons, the view from linguistics', in N. Higham (ed.) *Britons in Anglo-Saxon England* (Publications of the Manchester Centre for Anglo-Saxon Studies 7), Cambridge: Boydell & Brewer, 172–191.

Coates, R. and Breeze, A., with D. Horovitz (2000) *Celtic Voices, English Places: Studies on the Celtic Impact on Place-Names in England*, Stamford: Shaun Tyas.

Comrie, B. (1976) *Aspect: An Introduction to the Study of Verbal Aspect and Related Problems*. Cambridge: Cambridge University Press.

Connolly, J. H. (1990) 'Port Talbot English', in N. Coupland, 121–129.

Coupland, N. (ed., in association with A.R. Thomas) (1990) *English in Wales: Diversity, Conflict and Change*, Clevedon: Multilingual Matters.

Coupland, N. and Thomas, A.R. (1990) 'Social and linguistic perspectives on English in Wales', Introduction to N. Coupland (ed.), 1–18.

Coupland, N., Williams, A. and Garrett, P. (1994) 'The social meanings of Welsh English: teachers' stereotyped judgements', *Journal of Multicultural and Multilingual Development*, 15(6): 471–489.

Craigie, W.A., Aitken, A.J., *et al.* (1931–) *A Dictionary of the Older Scottish Tongue* (*DOST*), Oxford: Oxford University Press.

Crépin, A. (1978) *Grammaire historique de l'anglais*, Paris.

Crystal, D. (2004) *The Stories of English*, London: Penguin.

Curme, G.O. (1912) 'History of the English gerund', *Englische Studien*, 45: 349–380.

—— (1931) *A Grammar of the English Language, Vol. 2: Syntax*, Boston: Heath.

Dal, I. (1952) 'Zur Entstehung des englischen Participium Praesentis auf -*ing*', *Norsk Tidsskrift for Sprogvidenskap*, 16: 5–116.

Davies, Janet (1993) *The Welsh Language*, Cardiff: University of Wales Press.

Davies, John (1882–1883) 'The Celtic element in the Lancashire dialect', *Archaeologia Cambrensis*, Fourth Series, vol. XIII, no. LII, 243–264; vol. XIV, no. LIII, 1–13, vol. XIV, no. LIV, 89–108.

——— (1884) 'The Celtic element in the dialects of the counties adjoining Lancashire', *Archaeologia Cambrensis*, Fifth Series, vol. I, no. I, 1–31; 105–128.

——— (1885) 'The Celtic element in the dialectic words of the counties of Northampton and Leicester', *Archaeologia Cambrensis*, Fifth Series, vol. II, no. V, 1–32; no. VI, 81–96; no. VII, 161–182.

Davies, John (1993) *A History of Wales*, London: Penguin.

Davies, R.R. (1997) 'Presidential address: the peoples of Britain and Ireland, 1100–1400: IV Language and historical mythology', in *Transactions of the Royal Historical Society*, Sixth Series, VII, Cambridge: Cambridge University Press, 1–24.

Davis, G. (1991) *The Irish in Britain 1815–1914*, Dublin: Gill and Macmillan.

de Fréine, S. (1977) 'The dominance of the English language in the 19th century', in D. Ó Muirithe (ed.), 71–87.

Dekeyser, X. (1986) 'English contact clauses revisited: A diachronic approach', *Folia Linguistica Historica*, 7.1: 107–120.

Denison, D. (1985) 'The origins of periphrastic *do*: Ellegård and Visser reconsidered', in R. Eaton, O. Fisher, W. Koopman and F. Van der Leek (eds) *Papers from the Fourth International Conference on English Historical Linguistics. Amsterdam 10–13 April 1985*, Amsterdam and Philadelphia: John Benjamins, 45–60.

——— (1993) *English Historical Syntax: Verbal Constructions*, London: Longman.

Dietz, K. (1989) 'Die historische Schichtung phonologischer Isoglossen in den englischen Dialekten: II. Mittelenglische Isoglossen', in A. Fischer (ed.) *The History and the Dialects of English. Festschrift for Eduard Kolb*, Heidelberg: Universitätsverlag C. Winter, 133–175.

Dillon, M. (1943) 'Germanic and Celtic', *The Journal of English and Germanic Philology*, 42: 492–498.

Dolan, T. P. (1998) *A Dictionary of Hiberno-English: The Irish Use of English*, Dublin: Gill & Macmillan.

Dolan, T.P. and Ó Muirithe, D. (1979/1996) *The Dialect of Forth and Bargy, Co. Wexford, Ireland*, Dublin: Four Courts Press.

DOST. See Craigie, W.A., *et al.* (1931–).

Downes, W. (1984) *Language and Society*, London: Fontana.

Durkacz, V.E. (1983) *The Decline of the Celtic Languages*, Edinburgh: John Donald Publishers.

Ebert, R.P. (1978) *Historische Syntax des Deutschen*, Stuttgart.

EDD. See Wright, J. (1896–1905).

Edwards, J. (1985) *Talk Tidy: The Art of Speaking Wenglish*, Cowbridge.

——— (1986) *More Talk Tidy*, Cowbridge.

Edwards, V. and Weltens, B. (1985) 'Research on non-standard dialects of British English: progress and prospects (1)', in W. Viereck (ed.), 97–139.

Edwards, V.K. (1993) 'The grammar of southern British English', in J. Milroy and L. Milroy (eds), 214–242.

Edwards, W.F. (1844/2000) *Recherches sur les langues celtiques*, Paris. [Reprinted 2000, London and New York: Routledge (*Celtic Linguistics 1700–1850*, 8)]

Einenkel, E. (1914) 'Die Entwickelung des englischen Gerundiums', *Anglia*, 38: 1–76.

Ellegård, A. (1953) *The Auxiliary Do: The Establishment and Regulation of Its Use in English* (Gothenburg Studies in English II), Stockholm: Almqvist & Wiksell.

Ellis, A.J. (1879) 'The Anglo-Cymric score', *Transactions of the Philological Society*, 1877–1879: 316–372.

—— (1882) 'On the delimitation of the English and Welsh languages', *Y Cymmrodor*, 4: 173–208.

—— (1889) *On Early English Pronunciation. Part V: The Existing Phonology of English Dialects Compared with that of West Saxon Speech*, London: Asher & Co. for the Early English Text Society and the Chaucer Society, Trübner & Co. for the Philological Society.

Elsness, J. (1994) 'On the progression of the progressive in early Modern English', *ICAME Journal*, 18: 5–25.

Elworthy, F.T. (1877) *An Outline of the Grammar of the Dialect of West Somerset. Illustrated by Examples of the Common Phrases and Modes of Speech Now in Use among the People* (English Dialect Society, 19), London: Trübner & Co.

Eroms, H.-W. (1998) 'Periphrastic *tun* in present-day Bavarian and other Germanic dialects', in I. Tieken-Boon van Ostade, *et al.* (eds), 139–157.

Evans, D.E. (1990) 'Insular Celtic and the emergence of the Welsh Language', in A. Bammesberger and A. Wollmann (eds), 149–177.

Evans, D.S. (1964) *A Grammar of Middle Welsh*, Dublin: Dublin Institute for Advanced Studies.

—— (1971) 'Concord in Middle Welsh', *Studia Celtica*, VI: 42–56.

Fennell, B.A. (2001) *A History of English: A Sociolinguistic Approach*, Oxford: Blackwell.

Fife, J. (1988) *Functional Syntax: A Case Study in Middle Welsh*, Lublin: Katolicki Uniwersytet Lubelski.

—— (1990) *The Semantics of the Welsh Verb: A Cognitive Approach*, Cardiff: University of Wales Press.

Fife, J. and Poppe, E. (eds) (1991) *Studies in Brythonic Word Order*, Amsterdam and Philadelphia: John Benjamins.

Filppula, M. (1986) *Some Aspects of Hiberno-English in a Functional Sentence Perspective* (Publications in the Humanities 7), Joensuu: University of Joensuu.

—— (1997) 'Grammatical parallels in 'Celtic Englishes'', in A.R. Thomas (ed.) *Issues and Methods in Dialectology*, Bangor: The Department of Linguistics, University of Wales Bangor, 192–199.

—— (1999) *The Grammar of Irish English. Language in Hibernian Style*, London: Routledge.

—— (2000) 'Inversion in embedded questions in some regional varieties of English', in R. Bermúdez-Otero, D. Denison, R.M. Hogg and C.B. McCully (eds) *Generative Theory and Corpus Studies: A Dialogue from 10ICEHL*, Berlin: Mouton de Gruyter, 439–453.

—— (2001) 'Irish influence in Hiberno-English: some problems of argumentation', in J.M. Kirk and D.P. Ó Baoill (eds), *Language Links: The Languages of Scotland and Ireland*, Belfast: Cló Ollscoil na Banríona, 23–42.

—— (2002) 'The English progressive on the move', Paper presented at the Twelfth International Conference on English Historical Linguistics, Glasgow 22–26 August 2002.

—— (2003) 'More on the English progressive and the Celtic connection', in H.L.C. Tristram (ed.), 150–168.

Filppula M., Klemola J. and Pitkänen H. (eds) (2002) *The Celtic Roots of English* (Studies in Languages 37), Joensuu: University of Joensuu.

Filppula, M., Klemola, J. and Pitkänen H. (2004) 'What's Celtic and what's English in the British Isles Englishes', Paper presented at the Fourth Colloquium on the Celtic Englishes, Potsdam, 23–26 September, 2004.

Fischer, O. (1992) 'Syntax', in N. Blake (ed.), 207–408.

Fitzgerald, G. (1984) 'Estimates for baronies of minimum level of Irish-speaking amongst successive decennial cohorts: 1771–1871', *Proceedings of the Royal Irish Academy*, Section C 84, 117–155.

Förster, M. (1921) *Keltisches Wortgut im Englischen* (Texte und Forschungen zur englischen Kulturgeschichte. Festgabe für Felix Liebermann zum 20. Juli 1921), Halle: Verlag von Max Niemeyer.

—— (1941) *Der Flußname Themse und seine Sippe. Studien zur Anglisierung keltischer Eigennamen und zur Lautchronologie des Altbritischen*, München: Verlag der Bayerischen Akademie der Wissenschaften.

Frantzen A.J. and Niles, J.D. (1997) 'Introduction: Anglo-Saxonism and Medievalism', in A.J. Frantzen and J.D. Niles (eds) *Anglo-Saxonism and the Construction of Social Identity*, Gainesville: University of Florida Press, 1–14.

Freeman, E.A. (1870) *The History of the Norman Conquest of England, Its Causes and Its Results*, Vol. 1, Oxford.

Fridén, G. (1948) *Studies on the Tenses of the English Verb from Chaucer to Shakespeare with Special Reference to the Late Sixteenth Century* (Essays and Studies on English Language and Literature 2), Uppsala: Almqvist & Wisell.

Gachelin, J.-M. (1997) 'The progressive and habitual aspects in non-standard Englishes', in E.W. Schneider (ed.), 33–46.

Gaeltacht, The (n.d.) The Irish Environmental Library Series 27, Dublin: Folens.

Garrett, A. (1998) 'On the origin of auxiliary *do*', *English Language and Linguistics*, 2.2: 283–330.

Gärtner, K. (1981) 'Asyndetische Relativsätze in der Geschichte der Deutschen', *Zeitschrift für Germanistische Linguistik*, 9: 152–163.

Gelling, M. (1992) *The West Midlands in the Early Middle Ages*, Leicester: Leicester University Press.

George, C. (1990) *Community and Coal: An Investigation of the English-Language Dialect of the Rhondda Valleys, Mid Glamorgan*, unpublished PhD thesis, Swansea: University College Swansea.

George, K. (1986) 'How many people spoke Cornish traditionally?', *Cornish Studies*, 14: 67–70.

—— (1993) 'Cornish', in M.J. Ball (ed.), 410–468.

George, K. and Broderick, G. (1993) 'The revived languages: Modern Cornish and Modern Manx', in M.J. Ball (ed.), 644–663.

Gericke, B. and Greul, W. (1934) *Das Personalpronomen der 3. Person in spätags. und frühmittelenglischen Texten. Ein Beitrag zur altenglischen Dialektgeographie*, Palaestra 193, Leipzig: Mayer & Müller.

German, G.D. (2000) 'Britons, Anglo-Saxons and scholars: 19th century attitudes towards the survival of Britons in Anglo-Saxon England', in H.L.C. Tristram (ed.), 347–374.

—— (2003) 'The French of Western Brittany in light of the Celtic Englishes', in H.L.C. Tristram (ed.), 390–412.

Gerritsen, M. and Stein, D. (eds) (1992) *Internal and External Factors in Syntactic Change*, Berlin/New York: Mouton de Gruyter.

Gilbert, C.S. (1817) *An Historical Survey of the County of Cornwall*, London.

Giles, H. (1990) 'Social meanings of Welsh English', in N. Coupland (ed.), 258–282.

Gill, W. (ed.) (1859) *John Kelly. A practical grammar of the Antient Gaelic, or language of the Isle of Man, usually called Manks*, Douglas: Manx Soc. II, First published in 1804.

Gill, W.W. (1934) *Manx Dialect Words and Phrases*, London and Bristol: Arrowsmith.

Gillies, W. (1993) 'Scottish Gaelic', in M.J. Ball (ed.), 145–227.

—— (1994) 'Discussion: languages in contact', in M. Laing and K. Williamson (eds) *Speaking in our Tongues: Proceedings of a Colloquium on Medieval Dialectology and Related Disciplines*, Cambridge: D.S. Brewer, 159–168.

Görlach, M. (1991) *Introduction to Early Modern English*, Cambridge: Cambridge University Press.

—— (2002) *A Textual History of Scots*, Heidelberg: Universitätsverlag C. Winter.

Greene, D. (1966) 'The making of Insular Celtic', in *Proceedings of the Second International Congress of Celtic Studies, held in Cardiff 6–13 July, 1963*, Cardiff: University of Wales Press, 123–136.

—— (1971) 'Linguistic considerations in the dating of early Welsh verse', *Studia Celtica*, VI: 1–11.

—— (1979) 'Perfects and perfectives in Modern Irish', *Ériu*, 30: 122–141.

Gregor D.B. (1980) *Celtic: A Comparative Study*, New York: The Oleander Press.

Griffiths, D. (1969) *Talk of my Town*, Buckley: Young People's Cultural Association.

Haarmann, H. (1976) *Aspekte des Arealtypologie. Die Problematik der europäischen Sprachbünde*, Tübingen: Narr.

Hamp, E. (1973) 'Inordinate clauses in Celtic', in C. Corum, S.T. Smith and A. Weiser (eds) *You Take the High Node and I'll Take the Low Node: Papers from the Comparative Syntax Festival*, Chicago, 229–251.

—— (1975) 'On the disappearing English relative particle', in G. Drachman (ed.) *Akten der Salzburger Frühlingstagung für Linguistik, Salzburg vom 24. bis 25. Mai 1974*, Tübingen: Gunter Narr, 297–301.

—— (1975–76) 'Miscellanea Celtica I, II, III, IV', *Studia Celtica*, X/XI: 54–73.

Härke, H. (2003) 'Population replacement or acculturation? An archaeological perspective on population and migration in post-Roman Britain', in H.L.C. Tristram (ed.), 13–28.

Harris, J. (1984a) 'Syntactic variation and dialect divergence', *Journal of Linguistics* 20, 303–327.

—— (1984b) 'English in the north of Ireland', in P. Trudgill (ed.), 115–134.

—— (1986) 'Expanding the superstrate: habitual aspect markers in Atlantic Englishes', *English World-Wide*, 7: 171–199.

Harris, J., Little, D. and Singleton, D. (eds) (1986) *Perspectives on the English Language in Ireland*, Dublin: Trinity College Dublin, Centre for Language and Communication Studies.

Harris, M.B. (1967) *The Phonology and Grammar of the Dialect of South Zeal, Devonshire*, unpublished PhD thesis, University of London.

Haspelmath, M. (1998) 'How young is Standard Average European?' *Language Sciences*, 20: 271–287.

—— (1999) 'External possession in a European areal perspective', in D.L. Payne and I. Barshi (eds) *External Possession*, Amsterdam and Philadelphia: John Benjamins, 109–135.

Hatcher, A.G. (1948) 'From *Ce suis je* to *C'est moi* (the ego as subject and as predicative in Old French)', *PMLA*, 63.4: 1053–1100.

Havers, W. (1911) *Untersuchungen zur Kasussyntax der indogermanischen Sprachen*, Straßburg: Karl J. Trübner.

Hayden, M. and Hartog, M. (1909) 'The Irish Dialect of English: its origin and vocabulary', *Fortnightly Review*, 85: 775–85; 933–947.

Heinecke, J. (1999) *Temporal Deixis in Welsh and Breton*, Heidelberg: Universitätsverlag C. Winter.

Henry, A. (1995) *Belfast English and Standard English: Dialect Variation and Parameter Setting*, New York and Oxford: Oxford University Press.

Henry, P. L. (1957) *An Anglo-Irish Dialect of North Roscommon*, Dublin: University College.

—— (1977) 'Anglo-Irish and its Irish background', in D. Ó Muirithe (ed.), 20–36.

Hickey, R. (1995) 'Early contact and parallels between English and Celtic', *Vienna English Working Papers*, 4: 87–119.

—— (1999) 'Ireland as a linguistic area', *Ulster Folklife*, 45: 36–53.

―――― (2000) 'Salience, stigma and standard', in L. Wright (ed.) *The Development of Standard English 1300–1800: Theories, Descriptions, Conflicts*, Cambridge: Cambridge Universiry Press, 57–72.

―――― (2004) 'Irish English: phonology', in E.W. Schneider *et al.* (eds), 68–97.

Higham, N.J. (1992) *Rome, Britain and the Anglo-Saxons*, London: Seaby.

―――― (1994) *The English Conquest: Gildas and Britain in the Fifth Century*, Manchester: Manchester University Press.

Hindley, R. (1990) *The Death of the Irish Language*, London: Routledge.

Hines, J. (1990) 'Philology, archaeology and the adventus Saxonum vel Anglorum', in A. Bammesberger and A. Wollman (eds), 17–36.

Hock, H.H. (1984) '(Pre-)Rig-Vedic convergence of Indo-Aryan with Dravidian? Another look at the evidence', *Studies in the Linguistic Sciences*, 14(1): 89–107.

―――― (1991) *Principles of Historical Linguistics*, Berlin: Mouton de Gruyter.

Hogan, J.J. (1927/1970) *The English Language in Ireland*, College Park, MD: McGrath Publishing Company.

Hogg, R.M. (ed.) (1992) *The Cambridge History of the English Language, Vol. 1: The Beginnings to 1066*, Cambridge: Cambridge University Press.

Holm, J. (1988) *Pidgins and Creoles*, Vol. 1, Cambridge: Cambridge University Press.

Holthausen, F. (1913) 'Negation statt Vergleichungspartikel beim Komparativ', *Indogermanische Forschungen*, XXXII: 339–340.

Hunter Blair, P. (1947) 'The origins of Northumbria', *Archaeologia Aeliana*, Fourth Series, xxv: 1–51.

Ihalainen, O. (1985) '"He took the bottle and put 'n in his pocket": the object pronoun *it* in present-day Somerset', in W. Viereck (ed.), 153–161.

―――― (1994) 'The dialects of England since 1776', in R. Burchfield (ed.), 197–274.

The Irish Language in a Changing Society: Shaping the Future (no date), Baile Átha Cliath: Bord na Gaeilge.

Irwin, P.J. (1935) *A Study of the English Dialects of Ireland, 1172–1800*, unpublished PhD thesis, University of London.

Isaac, G.R. (1994) 'The progressive aspect marker: W *yn* / OIr. *oc*', *Journal of Celtic Linguistics* 3, 33–39.

―――― (2003a) 'Diagnosing the symptoms of contact: some Celtic-English case histories', in H.L.C. Tristram (ed.), 46–64.

―――― (2003b) 'The structure and typology of prepositional relative clauses in Early Welsh', in P. Russell (ed.) *Yr Hen Iaith. Studies in Early Welsh*, Aberystwyth: Celtic Studies Publications, 75–93.

Jackson, K.H. (1953) *Language and History in Early Britain*, Edinburgh: Edinburgh University Press.

―――― (1955) 'The Britons in southern Scotland', *Antiquity*, 29: 77–88.

―――― (1963) 'Angles and Britons in Northumbria and Cumbria', in *Angles and Britons* (O'Donnell Lectures), Cardiff: University of Wales Press, 60–84.

―――― (1973–74) 'Some question in dispute about Early Welsh literature and language', *Studia Celtica*, VIII–IX: 1–32.

Jago, F. (1882) *The Ancient Language and the Dialect of Cornwall*, Truro: Netherton and Worth.

―――― (1887) *An English-Cornish Dictionary*. [Reprinted 1980, London: Simpkin Marshall]

Jamieson, J. (1808) *An Etymological Dictionary of the Scottish Language*, Edinburgh: Creech.

Jenkins, G.H. (ed.) (1998a) *A Social History of the Welsh Language: Language and Community in the Nineteenth Century*, Cardiff: University of Wales Press.

―――― (1998b) Introduction to G.H. Jenkins (1998a) (ed.), 1–20.

Jenner, H. (1904) *A Handbook of the Cornish Language*. London.

────── (1905) 'Cornwall a Celtic nation', *The Celtic Review*, I: 234–246.

Jenni, E. (1981) *Lehrbuch der hebräischen Sprache des Alten Testaments*, Basel: Helbing & Lichtenhahn.

Jespersen, O. (1905) *Growth and Structure of the English Language*, Leipzig: B.G. Teubner.

────── (1909–1949) *A Modern English Grammar on Historical Principles*, 7 vols, Copenhagen: Ejnar Munksgaard. [Reprinted 1961, 1965, 1970, 1974, London: George Allen & Unwin]

────── (1937) *Analytic Syntax*, London: George Allen & Unwin.

Joly, A. (1967) *Negation and the Comparative Particle in English* (Cahiers de Psychomécanique du Langage, 9), Québec: Les Presses de l'Université Laval.

Jones, C. (ed.) (1997) *The Edinburgh History of the Scots Language*, Edinburgh: Edinburgh University Press.

Jones, D. (1998) *Statistical Evidence Relating to the Welsh Language 1801–1911/ Tystiolaeth Ystadegol yn ymwneud â'r Iaith Gymraeg 1801–1911*, Cardiff: University of Wales Press.

Jones, G.E. (1984) 'The distinctive vowels and consonants of Welsh', in M.J. Ball and G.E. Jones (eds) *Welsh Phonology: Selected Readings*, Cardiff: University of Wales Press, 40–64.

Jones, I.G. (1980) 'Language and community in nineteenth century Wales', in D. Smith (ed.) *A People and a Proletariat: Essays on the History of Wales 1780–1980*, London: Pluto Press in association with Llafur, the Society for the Study of Welsh Labour History, 47–71.

Jones, P.N. (1998) 'The Welsh Language in the Valleys of Glamorgan c. 1800–1914', in G. H. Jenkins (1998a), 147–180.

Jones, R.O. (1993) 'The sociolinguistics of Welsh', in M.J. Ball (ed.), 536–605.

Jost, K.H. (1909) Bēon *und* wesan, *eine syntaktische untersuchung* (Anglistische Forschungen, XXVI), Heidelberg: Universitätsverlag C. Winter.

Joyce, P.W. (1910/1988) *English as We Speak It in Ireland*, Rept. Dublin: Wolfhound Press.

Kallen, J.L. (1986) 'The co-occurrence of *do* and *be* in Hiberno-English', in J. Harris *et al.* (eds), 133–147.

────── (1989) 'Tense and aspect categories in Irish English', *English World-Wide* 10, 1–39.

────── (1994) 'English in Ireland', in Burchfield, R. (ed.), 148–196.

────── (1996) 'Entering lexical fields in Irish English', in J. Klemola, M. Kytö and M. Rissanen (eds), 101–129.

────── (1997a) 'Irish English: context and contacts', in J.L. Kallen (ed.), 1–33.

────── (1997b) 'Irish English and World English: lexical perspectives', in E.W. Schneider (ed.), 139–158.

────── (ed.) (1997c) *Focus on Ireland*, Amsterdam and Philadelphia: John Benjamins.

Kastovsky, D. (1992) 'Semantics and vocabulary', in R.M. Hogg (ed.), 290–408.

────── (1994) 'Typological differences between English and German morphology and their causes', in T. Swan, E. Mørck and O.J. Westvik (eds) *Language Change and Language Structure: Older Germanic Languages in a Comparative Perspective*, Berlin/New York: Mouton de Gruyter, 135–157.

Keenan, E.L. (1996) 'Creating Anaphors: An Historical Study of the English Reflexive Pronouns', unpublished manuscript, University of California–Los Angeles.

Keller, W. (1925) 'Keltisches im englischen Verbum', *Anglica: Untersuchungen zur englischen Philologie*, Bd. 1: *Sprache und Kulturgeschichte* (Palaestra 147), Leipzig: Mayer & Müller, 55–66.

Kellner, L. (1892/1905) *Historical Outlines of English Syntax*, New York: Macmillan.

King, A. (1997) 'The inflectional morphology of Older Scots', in C. Jones (ed.), 156–181.

King, G. (1993) *Modern Welsh: A Comprehensive Grammar*, London.

Kirk, J. and Kallen, J.L. (2006) 'Irish Standard English: How Celticised? How Standardised?', in H.L.C. Tristram (ed.), 88–113.

Kitson, P.R. (1996) 'British and European river names', in *Transactions of the Philological Society*, 94: 73–118.

Klaeber, Fr. (1929) 'Eine germanisch-englischer Formel: ein stilistisch-syntaktischer Streifzug', in *Britannica. Max Förster Festschrift*, Leipzig, 1–22.

Klemola, J. (1994) 'Periphrastic *do* in South-Western dialects of British English: a reassessment', *Dialectologia et Geolinguistica*, 2: 33–51.

—— (1996) *Non-standard Periphrastic* do: *a Study in Variation and Change*, unpublished PhD thesis, University of Essex.

—— (2000) 'The origins of the northern subject rule: a case of early contact?', in H.L.C. Tristram (ed.), 329–346.

—— (2002) 'Periphrastic DO: dialectal distribution and origins', in M. Filppula, J. Klemola and H. Pitkänen (eds), 199–210.

—— (2003) 'Personal pronouns in the traditional dialects of the South West of England', in H.L.C. Tristram (ed.), 260–275.

Klemola, J. and Jones, M.J. (1999) 'The Leeds Corpus of English Dialects project', in C. Upton and K. Wales (eds) *Dialectal Variation in English: Proceedings of the Harold Orton Centenary Conference 1998*, Leeds: Leeds Studies in English, N.S. XXX, 17–30.

Klemola, J., Kytö, M. and Rissanen, M. (eds) (1996) *Speech Past and Present. Studies in English Dialectology in Memory of Ossi Ihalainen* (University of Bamberg Studies in English Linguistics, Vol. 38), Frankfurt am Main: Peter Lang.

Koch, J.T. (1985) 'Movement and emphasis in the Gaulish sentence', *The Bulletin of the Board of Celtic Studies* XXXII, 1–37.

König, E. and Haspelmath M. (1998) 'Les constructions à possesseur externe dans les langues d'Europe', in J. Feuillet (ed.) *Actance et Valence dans les Langues de l'Europe*, Berlin and New York: Mouton de Gruyter, 525–606.

König, E. and Siemund, P. (2000) 'The development of complex reflexives and intensifiers in English', *Diachronica*, 17: 39–84.

Kortmann, B. (2004) 'Synopsis: Morphological and syntactic variation in the British Isles', in B. Kortmann *et al.* (eds), 1089–1103.

Kortmann, B., Burridge, K., Mesthrie, R., Schneider, E. and Upton, C. (eds) (2004) *A Handbook of Varieties of English, Vol. 2: Morphology and Syntax*, Berlin and New York: Mouton de Gruyter.

Kortmann, B. and Szmrecsanyi, B. (2004) 'Global synopsis: morphological and syntactic variation in English', in B. Kortmann *et al.* (eds), 1142–1202.

Krahe, H. and Meid, W. (1969) *Germanische Sprachwissenschaft II: Formenlehre*, Sammlung Göschen 780b, 7th edn, Berlin: Walter de Gruyter.

Kruisinga, E. (1931) *A Handbook of Present-Day English, Part II: English Accidence and Syntax*, Vol. 1, 5th edn, Groningen: P. Nordhoff.

Kühlwein, W. (1998) 'Celtic influence on Old English rhetoric—a case study of the interface between diachronic contrastive rhetoric and history of art', *Studia Anglica Posnaniensia*, XXXIII: 213–243.

Labov, W. (1994) *Principles of Linguistic Change, Vol. 1: Internal Factors*, Oxford: Blackwell.

Laing, L. and Laing, J. (1990) *Celtic Britain and Ireland, AD 200–800: The Myth of the Dark Ages*, Dublin: Irish Academic Press.

Laker, S. (2002) 'An explanation for the changes kw-, hw- > χw- in the English dialects', in M. Filppula, J. Klemola and H. Pitkänen (eds), 183–199.

———— (n.d.) 'Zur Herkunft der negativen Vergleichspartikel im Englischen', unpublished manuscript, University of Munich.

———— (forthcoming) 'The English negative comparative particle', *Transactions of the Philological Society*.

LALME (*A Linguistic Atlas of Late Mediaeval English*). See McIntosh et al. (1986).

Lamb, W. (2001) *Scottish Gaelic*, München: LINCOM EUROPA.

Lambert, P.-Y. (1987) 'A restatement on the Gaulish tablet from Chamalières', *The Bulletin of the Board of Celtic Studies* XXXIV, 10–17. (Cardiff: University of Wales Press.)

———— (1994) *La langue gauloise. Description linguistique, commentaire d'inscriptions choisiesI*, Paris: Editions Errance.

Lass, R. (1990) 'Early mainland residues in southern Hiberno-English', *Irish University Review*, 20: 137–148.

———— (1992) 'Phonology and morphology', in N. Blake (ed.), 23–155.

———— (1997) *Historical Linguistics and Language Change*, Cambridge: Cambridge University Press.

Lass, R. and Wright, S. (1986) 'Endogeny vs. contact: 'Afrikaans influence' on South African English', *English World-Wide*, 7(2): 201–223.

Lehiste, I. (1988) *Lectures on Language Contact*, Cambridge, MA: MIT Press.

Lewis H. and Pedersen H. (1961) *A Concise Comparative Celtic Grammar*, Göttingen.

Lewis, J. W. (1990) 'Syntax and lexis in Glamorgan English', in N. Coupland (ed.), 109–120.

Lewy, E. (1956) 'Zu den Irisch-Englischen Beziehungen', *Neuphilologische Mitteilungen LVII*, 7–8: 315–318.

———— (1966) 'Einige englische und irische Worte', in *Münchener Studien zur Sprachwissenschaft*, Im Auftrage des Münchener Sprachwissenschaftlichen Studienkreises herausgegeben von Karl Hoffmann und Johannes Bechert zusammen mit Bernhard Forssman und Johanna Narten, Heft 19, München: In Kommission bei J. Kitzinger, 59.

Lindsay, C. F. (1993) 'Welsh and English in the city of Bangor: a study in functional differentiation', *Language in Society*, 22: 1–17.

Lipiński, E. (1997) *Semitic Languages: Outline of a Comparative Grammar*, Leuwen: Peeters.

Löfstedt, B. (1966) 'Die Konstruktion *c'est lui qui l'a fait* im Lateinischen', *Indogermanische Forschungen*, 71: 253–277.

Löfstedt E. (1928–1933) *Syntactica: Studien und Beiträge zur historischen Syntax des Lateins, voll. 1 Über einigen Grundfragen der lateinischen Nominalsyntax 1928, voll. 2 Syntactisch-stilistische Gesichtspunkte und Probleme 1933*. (Skrifter utgivna av Humanistiska vetenskapsamfundet i Lund 10), Lund: Gleerup.

Lutz, A. (1988) 'The history of English /h/ and Old Norse influence', in W.U. Dressler, et al. (eds) *Wiener Linguistische Gazette*, Supplement 6 (= *Sixth International Phonology Meeting and Third International Phonology Meeting July 1–7, 1988, Krems, Austria: Discussion Papers, Vol. 1: Phonology*), Vienna, 49–51.

———— (forthcoming) 'Why is West-Saxon English different from Old Saxon?', to appear in H. Sauer and J. Story (eds) *Anglo-Saxon and the Continent*.

Macafee, C.I. (1992–1993) 'A short grammar of Older Scots', *Scottish Language*, 11/12: 10–36.

———— (1996) 'Introduction', in C. Macafee (ed.) *A Concise Ulster Dictionary*, Oxford: Oxford University Press.

———— (1997) 'Older Scots Lexis', in C. Jones (ed.), 182–212.

Macafee, C.I. and Ó Baoill, C. (1997) 'Why Scots is not a Celtic English', in H.L.C. Tristram (ed.), 245–286.

McCafferty, K. (2003) 'The Northern Subject Rule in Ulster: How Scots, how English?', *Language Variation and Change*, 15: 105–139.

—— (2004) ' "Thunder storms is verry dangese in this countrey they come in less than a minnits notice . . .": The Northern Subject Rule in Southern Irish English', *English World-Wide*, 25: 51–79.

Mac Cana, P. (1991) 'Further notes on constituent order in Welsh', in J. Fife and E. Poppe (eds), 45–80.

MacCann, J. and Connolly, H. (1933) *Memorials of Father Augustine Baker and Other Documents Relating to the English Benedictines*, Catholic Record Society Publications, Vol. 33.

McCawley, J.D. (1971) 'Tense and time reference in English', in C.J. Fillmore and D.T. Langendoen (eds) *Studies in Linguistic Semantics*, New York: Holt, Rinehart and Winston, 97–113.

McClure, J.D. (1986) 'What Scots owes to Gaelic', *Scottish Language*, 5: 85–98.

—— (1994) 'English in Scotland', in R. Burchfield (ed.), 23–93.

MacDougall, H. (1982) *Racial Myth in English History. Trojans, Teutons, and Anglo-Saxons*, Montreal: Harvest House.

McDonald, C. (1980) 'Some contrasts in teachers' and pupils' language and aspects of their relevance in the classroom', Graduate Certificate of Education Dissertation, University of Newcastle.

Mac Eoin, G. (1993) 'Irish', in M.J. Ball (ed.), 101–144.

McIntosh, A. (1989) 'Present indicative plural forms in the later Middle English of the North Midlands', in A. McIntosh, M.L. Samuels and M. Laing (eds) *Middle English Dialectology: Essays on Some Principles and Problems*, Aberdeen, 116–122.

McIntosh, A., Samuels, M.L. and Benskin, M. (1986) *A Linguistic Atlas of Late Mediaeval English*, 4 vols, with the assistance of M. Laing and K. Williamson, Aberdeen: Aberdeen University Press. [*LALME*]

MacKinnon, K. (1991) *Gaelic: A Past & Future Prospect*, Edinburgh: Saltire Society.

—— (1993) 'Scottish Gaelic today: Social history and contemporary status', in M.J. Ball (ed.), 491–535.

McMahon, A. (1994) *Understanding Language Change*, Cambridge: Cambridge University Press.

McWhorter, J.H. (2002) 'What happened to English?' *Diachronica*, 19: 217–272.

—— (2006) 'What else happened to English?', Paper read at the Directions in English Language Studies Conference (DELS), Manchester, 6–8 April 2006.

—— (forthcoming) 'What else happened to English? A brief for the Celtic Hypothesis'.

Mair, C. and M. Hundt (1995) 'Why is the progressive becoming more frequent in English?', *Zeitschrift für Anglistik und Amerikanistik*, XLIII: 111–122.

Martin, S. and Wolfram, W. (1998) 'The Sentence in African-American Vernacular English', in S. Mufwene, J. Rickford, G. Bailey and J. Baugh (eds) *African-American English: Structure, History and Use*, New York: Routledge, 11–36.

Martinet, A. (1952) 'Celtic lenition and Western Romance consonants', *Language*, 28: 192–217.

Meid, W. (1990) 'Englisch und sein britischer Hintergrund', in A. Bammesberger and A. Wollmann (eds), 97–119.

Mesthrie, R. (2004) 'Synopsis: morphological and syntactic variation in Africa, South and Southeast Asia', in B. Kortmann *et al.* (eds), 1132–1141.

Meurman-Solin, A. (1993) 'Periphrastic *do* in sixteenth- and seventeenth-century Scots', in M. Rissanen, M. Kytö and M. Palander-Collin (eds), *Early English in the Computer Age: Explorations through the Helsinki Corpus* (Topics in English Linguistics 11), Berlin: Mouton de Gruyter, 235–251.

Miller, J. (1993) 'The grammar of Scottish English', in J. Milroy and L. Milroy (eds), 99–138.

———— (2004) 'Scottish English: morphology and syntax', in B. Kortmann *et al.* (eds), 47–72.

Milroy, J. and Milroy, L. (eds) (1993) *Real English: The Grammar of English Dialects in the British Isles*, London: Longman.

Mitchell, B. (1985) *Old English Syntax*, Vol. 1, Oxford: Clarendon Press.

Mittendorf, I. and Poppe, E. (2000) 'Celtic contacts of the English progressive?', in H.L.C. Tristram (ed.), 117–145.

Molyneux, C. (1987) 'Some ideas on English-British Celtic language contact', *Grazer Linguistische Studien*, 28: 81–89.

Montgomery, M. (1989) 'Exploring the roots of Appalachian English', *English World-Wide*, 10: 227–278.

———— (1994) 'The evolution of verb second in Scots', in A. Fenton and D.A. MacDonald (eds) *Studies in Scots and Gaelic: Proceedings of the Third International Conference on the Languages of Scotland*, Edinburgh: Canongate Academic and the Linguistic Survey of Scotland, School of Scottish Studies, University of Edinburgh, 81–95.

Montgomery, M. and Gregg R.J. (1997) 'The Scots Language in Ulster', in C. Jones (ed.), 569–622.

Moore, A.W., Morrison S. and Goodwin E. (1924) *Vocabulary of the Anglo-Manx Dialect*, London: Humphrey Milford.

Morris-Jones, J. (1900) 'Pre-Aryan syntax in Insular Celtic', in J. Rhys and D. Brynmor-Jones (eds) *The Welsh People: Chapters on their Origin, History, Laws, Language, Literature and Characteristics*, London, 617–641.

———— (1913) *A Welsh Grammar: Historical and Comparative. Phonology and Accidence*. Oxford: The Clarendon Press.

———— (1931) *Welsh Syntax: An Unfinished Draft*, Cardiff: The University of Wales Press Board.

Mossé, F. (1938) *Histoire de la Forme Périphrastique* Être + *Participe Présent en Germanique. Deuxième Partie: Moyen-Anglais et Anglais Moderne*, Paris: Librairie C. Klincksieck.

Moylan, S. (1996) *The Language of Kilkenny: Lexicon, Semantics, Structures*, Dublin: Geography Publications.

Murray, J.A.H. (1873) *The Dialect of the Southern Counties of Scotland: Its Pronunciation, Grammar, and Historical Relations*, London.

Mustanoja, T. (1960) *A Middle English Syntax, Part I: Parts of Speech*, Helsinki: Société Néophilologique.

Myers-Scotton, C. (1993) *Duelling Languages: Grammatical Structure in Code-Switching*, Oxford: Clarendon Press.

Myres, J.N.L. (1986) *The English Settlements* (Oxford History of England, 1B), Oxford: Oxford University Press.

Nickel, G. (1966) *Die expanded Form im Altenglischen: Vorkommen, Funktion und Herkunft der Umschreibung* 'beon/wesan' + *Partizip präsens*, Neumünster: Karl Wachholtz Verlag.

Nurmi, A. (1996) 'Periphrastic *do* and *be* + *ing*: Interconnected developments?', in T. Nevalainen and H. Raumolin-Brunberg (eds) *Sociolinguistics and Language History. Studies Based on The Corpus of Early English Correspondence* (Language and Computers 15), Amsterdam and Atlanta: Rodopi, 151–165.

Ó Baoill, C. (1997) 'The Scots-Gaelic Interface', in C. Jones (ed.), 551–568.

Ó Baoill, D. P. (1997) 'The emerging Irish phonological substratum in Irish English', in J.L. Kallen (ed.), 73–87.

Ó Cuív, B. (1951) *Irish Dialects and Irish-Speaking Districts*, Dublin: Dublin Institute for Advanced Studies.

―――― (1969a) 'Irish in the modern world', in B. Ó Cuív (ed.), 122–132.

―――― (ed.) (1969b) *A View of the Irish Language*, Dublin: Stationery Office.

Ó Danachair, C. (1969) 'The Gaeltacht', in B. Ó Cuív (ed.), 112–121.

Odlin, T. (1997a) *Hiberno-English: Pidgin, Creole, or Neither?* (CLCS Occasional Paper 49), Dublin: Trinity College, Centre for Language and Communication Studies.

―――― (1997b) 'Bilingualism and substrate influence: a look at clefts and reflexives', in J.L. Kallen (ed.), 35–50.

Oftedal, M. (1985) *Lenition in Celtic and Insular Spanish: The Secondary Voicing of Stops in Gran Canaria*, Oslo-Bergen-Stavanger-Tromsø: Universitetsforlaget AS.

Ó hAnnracháin, S. (1964) *Caint an Bhaile Dhuibh*, Dublin: An Clóchomhar Tta.

Ó hÚrdail, R. (1997) 'Hiberno-English: historical background and synchronic features and variation', in H.L.C. Tristram (ed.), 180–200.

Ó Murchú, M. (1985) *The Irish Language*, Dublin: Department of Foreign Affairs and Bord na Gaeilge.

Ó Muirithe, D. (ed.) (1977) *The English Language in Ireland*, Dublin: The Mercier Press.

―――― (2000) *A Dictionary of Anglo-Irish: Words and Phrases from Gaelic in the English of Ireland*, Dublin: Four Courts Press.

O'Rahilly, T.F. (1932/1976) *Irish Dialects Past and Present with Chapters on Scottish and Manx*, Dublin: Dublin Institute for Advanced Studies.

Orton, H., Barry, M.V., Halliday, W.J., Tilling, P.M. and Wakelin, M.F. (1962–1971) *Survey of English Dialects. (B): The Basic Material*, 4 vols, Leeds: E.J. Arnold.

Orton, H., Sanderson, S. and Widdowson, J. (eds) (1978) *The Linguistic Atlas of England*. London: Croom Helm.

Ó Sé, D. (1992) 'The perfect in Modern English', *Ériu*, 43: 39–67.

―――― (2004) 'The 'after' perfect and related constructions in Gaelic dialects', *Ériu*, LIV: 179–248.

Ó Searcaigh, S. (1950) 'Some uses and omissions of the article in Irish', *The Journal of Celtic Studies*, 1: 239–248.

Ó Siadhail, M. (1989) *Modern Irish: Grammatical Structure and Dialectal Variation*. Cambridge: Cambridge University Press.

Paddock, H.J. (1988) 'The actuation problem for gender change in Wessex versus Newfoundland', in J. Fisiak (ed.) *Historical Dialectology: Regional and Social*, (Trends in Linguistics. Studies and Monographs 37), Berlin: Mouton de Gruyter, 377–395.

Parry, D. (1972) 'Anglo-Welsh dialects in south-east Wales', in M.F. Wakelin (ed.), *Patterns in the Folk Speech of the British Isles*, London: Athlone Press, 140–163.

―――― (1979) *The Survey of Anglo-Welsh Dialects, Vol. 2: The South-West*, Swansea: David Parry, University College.

―――― (1990) 'The conservative English dialects of north Carmarthenshire', in N. Coupland (ed.), 142–150.

―――― (1999) *A Grammar and Glossary of Conservative Anglo-Welsh Dialects of Rural Wales*, NATCECT, Occasional Publications, No. 8, University of Sheffield.

Paulasto, H. (2006) *Welsh English Syntax: Contact and Variation* (Publications in the Humanities 43), Joensuu: Joensuu University Press.

Payne, D.L. and Barshi, I. (1999) 'External possession: what, where, how, and why', in D.L. Payne and I. Barshi (eds) *External Possession* (Typological Studies in Language 39), Amsterdam and Philadelphia: John Benjamins, 3–29.

Payton, P. (1997) 'Identity, ideology and language in modern Cornwall', in H.L.C. Tristram (ed.), 100–122.

Pedersen, H. (1913) *Vergleichende Grammatik der keltischen Sprachen*, Göttingen: Vandenhoeck und Ruprecht, Zweiter Band.

Penhallurick, R. (1991) *The Anglo-Welsh Dialects of North Wales* (University of Bamberg Studies in English Linguistics, Vol. 27) Frankfurt am Main: Peter Lang.

—— (1993) 'Welsh English: a national language?', *Dialectologia et Geolinguistica*, 1: 28–46.

—— (1994) *Gowerland and Its Language*, (University of Bamberg Studies in English Linguistics, Vol. 36), Frankfurt am Main: Peter Lang.

—— (1996) 'The grammar of northern Welsh English: progressive verb phrases', in J. Klemola, M. Kytö and M. Rissanen (eds), 308–342.

—— (2004) 'Welsh English: phonology', in E.W. Schneider *et al.* (eds), 98–112.

Phillipps, K. C. (1993) *A Glossary of the Cornish Dialect*, Padstow: Tabb House.

Pilch, H. (1983–1984) 'The structure of Welsh tonality', *Studia Celtica*, 18/19: 234–252.

Pitkänen, H. (2003) 'Non-standard uses of the progressive form in Welsh English: an apparent time study', in H.L.C. Tristram (ed.), 111–128.

Platt, J., Weber, H. and Ho, M.L. (1984) *The New Englishes*, London, Boston, Melbourne and Henley: Routledge and Kegan Paul.

Pödör, D. (1995–1996) 'The phonology of Scottish Gaelic loanwords in Lowland Scots', *Scottish Language*, 14/15: 174–189.

Pokorny, J. (1927–1930) 'Das nicht-indogermanische Substrat im Irischen', *Zeitschrift für celtische Philologie* 16: 95–144, 231–266; 17: 373–388; 18: 233–248.

—— (1959) 'Keltische Urgeschichte und Sprachwissenschaft', *Die Sprache*, 5: 152–164.

Poliakov, L. (1974) *The Aryan Myth. A History of Racist and Nationalist Ideas in Europe*, London: Chatto Heinemann for Sussex University Press.

Poplack, S. and Tagliamonte, S. (1989) 'There's no tense like the present: verbal *-s* inflection in Early Black English', *Language Variation and Change*, 1: 47–84.

Poppe, E. (2002) 'The 'expanded form' in Insular Celtic and English: Some historical and comparative considerations, with special emphasis on Middle Irish', in M. Filppula, J. Klemola and H. Pitkänen (eds), 237–270.

—— (2003) 'Progress on the progressive? A report', in H.L.C. Tristram (ed.), 65–84.

—— (2006) 'Celtic influence on English relative clauses', in H.L.C. Tristram (ed.), 191–211.

Potts, W.T.W. (1976) 'History and blood groups in the British Isles', in P.H. Sawyer (ed.) *Medieval Settlement. Continuity and Change*, London: Edward Arnold, 236–253.

Poussa, P. (1990) 'A contact-universals origin for periphrastic *do*, with special consideration of OE-Celtic contact', in S.M. Adamson, V.A. Law, N. Vincent and S. Wright (eds) *Papers from the Fifth International Conference on English Historical Linguistics, Cambridge, 6–9 April 1987*, Amsterdam and Philadelphia: John Benjamins, 407–434.

Preusler, W. (1938) 'Keltischer Einfluss im Englischen', *Indogermanische Forschungen*, 56: 178–191.

—— (1940) 'Zu: Keltischer Einfluss im Englischen', *Indogermanische Forschungen*, 57: 178–191.

—— (1956) 'Keltischer Einfluss im Englischen', *Revue des Langages Vivantes*, 22: 322–350.

Preuß, M. (1999) *Remaining Lexical and Syntactic Borrowings from Manx Gaelic in Present Day Manx English*, Master of Philosophy Thesis, University of Liverpool, Liverpool.

Price, G. (1984) *The Languages of Britain*, London: Arnold.

—— (2000) 'Cumbric', in G. Price (ed.) *Languages in Britain and Ireland*, Oxford: Blackwell, 120–126.

Pryce, W.T.R. (1978) 'Wales as a culture region: patterns of change 1750–1971', *Transactions of the Honourable Society of Cymmrodorion*, 229–261.

—— (1990) 'Language shift in Gwent, c. 1770–1981', in N. Coupland (ed.), 48–83.

Pyles, T. and Algeo, J. (1993) *The Origins and Development of the English Language*, 4th edn, Fort Worth/Philadelphia/San Diego: Harcourt Brace Jovanovich.

Ray, J. (1760) *Selected Remains of the Learned John Ray . . . with his Life by the Late William Derham*, London.

Renfrew, C. (2001) 'Commentary: from molecular genetics to archaeogenetics', *Proceedings of the National Academy of Sciences of the United States of America (PNAS)*, 98.9: 4830–4832.

Renfrew, C. and Boyle, K. (eds) (2000) *Archaeogenetics: DNA and the Population Prehistory of Europe*, Cambridge: McDonald Institute.

Rissanen, M. (1991) 'Spoken language and the history of *do*-periphrasis', in D. Kastovsky (ed.) *Historical English Syntax*, Berlin: Mouton de Gruyter, 321–342.

Roberts, G.T. (1996) '"Under the hatches": English Parliamentary Commissioners' views of the people and language of mid-nineteenth-century Wales', in B. Schwarz (ed.) *The Expansion of England: Race, Ethnicity and Cultural History*, London/New York: Routledge, 171–197.

Robertson, J.D. (1890) *A Glossary of Dialect and Archaic Words Used in the County of Gloucester* (English Dialect Society 61), London: Kegan Paul, Trench, Trübner & Co.

Rogers, N. (1979) *Wessex Dialect*, Bradford on Avon: Moonraker Press.

Ronan, P. (2003) 'Periphrastic progressives in Old Irish', in H.L.C. Tristram (ed.), 129–149.

Rowland, T. (1876) *A Grammar of the Welsh Language, Based on the Most Approved Systems, with Copious Examples from Some of the Most Correct Welsh Writers*, 4th edn, Wrexham: Hughes & Son.

Sabban, A. (1982) *Gälisch-Englischer Sprachkontakt*, Heidelberg: Julius Groos.

Salmons, J.C. (1984) *Accentual Change and Language Contact. Comparative Survey and a Case Study of Early Northern Europe*, Stanford: University Press.

Sand, A. (2003) 'The definite article in Irish English and other contact varieties of English', in H.L.C. Tristram (ed.), 413–430.

Schrijver, P. (1999) 'The Celtic contribution to the development of the North Sea Germanic vowel system, with special reference to Coastal Dutch', *Nowele*, 35: 3–47.

—— (2002) 'The rise and fall of British Latin: evidence from English and Brittonic', in M. Filppula, J. Klemola and H. Pitkänen (eds), 88–110.

Schneider, E.W. (ed.) (1997) *Englishes Around the World, Vol. 1: General Studies, British Isles, North America*, Amsterdam and Philadelphia: John Benjamins.

Schneider, E.W., Burridge, K., Kortmann, B., Mesthrie, R. and Upton, C. (eds) (2004) *A Handbook of Varieties of English, Vol. 1: Phonology*, Berlin/New York: Mouton de Gruyter.

Sebba, M. (1997) *Contact Languages: Pidgins and Creoles*, Houndmills: Macmillan.

Shorrocks, G. (1992) 'Response: case assignment in simple and coordinate constructions in Present-Day English', *American Speech*, 67: 432–444.

—— (1997) 'Celtic influence on the English of Newfoundland and Labrador', in H.L.C. Tristram (ed.), 320–361.

Shuken, C.R. (1984) 'Highland and Island English', in P. Trudgill (ed.), 152–166.

Siegel, J. (1999) 'Transfer constraints and substrate influence in Melanesian Pidgin', *Journal of Pidgin and Creole Languages*, 14(1): 1–44.

Siemund, P. (2007) *Pronominal Gender in English: A Study of English Varieties from a Cross-Linguistic Perspective*, London: Routledge.

Sims-Williams, P. (1983) 'Gildas and the Anglo-Saxons', *Cambridge Medieval Celtic Studies*, 6: 1–30.

Skeat, W.W. (1881–1900) *Ælfric's Lives of Saints*, EETS 76, 82, 94, 119, London: Trübner & Co.

Small, G.W. (1924) *The Comparison of Inequality. The Semantics and Syntax of the Comparative Particle in English*, Baltimore, Md.: The Johns Hopkins University

Śmiecińska, J. (2002–2003) 'Stative verbs and the progressive aspect in English', *Poznań Studies in Contemporary Linguistics*, 38: 187–195.

Soulsby, I. (1986) *A History of Cornwall*, Chichester: Phillimore.

Spriggs, M. (2003) 'Where Cornish was spoken and when: a provisional synthesis', *Cornish Studies* (Second Series), 11: 228–269.

Stalmaszczyk, P. (1997) 'Celtic elements in English vocabulary. A critical reassessment', *Studia Anglica Posnaniensia* 32: 77–87.

—— (2000) 'The Cornish language and Cornish elements in English', *Studia Indogermanica Lodziensia*, III, Łódź, 27–36.

—— (2005) *Celtic Presence. Studies in Celtic Languages and Literatures: Irish, Scottish Gaelic and Cornish*, Łódź: Łódź University Press.

Stenton, Sir F. (1943) *Anglo-Saxon England* (Oxford History of England, 2), Oxford: Oxford University Press.

Stockwell, R.P. (1984) 'On the history of the verb-second rule in English', in J. Fisiak (ed.) *Historical Syntax*, Berlin: Mouton de Gruyter, 575–592.

Stokes, W. (1799) *Project for Re-establishing the Internal Peace and Tranquillity of Ireland*, Dublin: Moore.

Strachan, J. (1909). *An Introduction to Early Welsh*. Manchester: The University Press.

Strang, B.M.H. (1970) *A History of English*, London: Methuen.

Stubbs, W. (1870) *Select Charters*. 9th edn 1913–1969, revised H.W.C. Davies, Oxford.

Sykes, B. (2006) *Blood of the Isles: Exploring the Genetic Roots of our Tribal History*, London: Bantam Press.

Tagliamonte, S. and Poplack, S. (1993) 'The zero-marked verb: testing the creole hypothesis', *Journal of Pidgin and Creole Languages*, 8(2): 171–206.

Thomas, A. (1984a) 'Welsh English', in P. Trudgill (ed.), 178–194.

—— (1984b) 'Cornish', in P. Trudgill (ed.), 278–288.

—— (1985) 'Welsh English: a grammatical conspectus', in W. Viereck (ed.), 213–221.

—— (1994) 'English in Wales', in R. Burchfield (ed.), 94–147.

Thomas, B. (1987) 'A cauldron of rebirth: population and the Welsh language in the nineteenth century', *The Welsh History Review*, 17: 418–437.

Thomason, S.G. and Kaufman, T. (1988) *Language Contact, Creolization, and Genetic Linguistics*, Los Angeles: University of California Press.

Thurneysen, R. (1946) *A Grammar of Old Irish*, Dublin: The Dublin Institute for Advanced Studies.

Tieken-Boon van Ostade, I., van der Wal, M. and van Leuvensteijn, A. (eds) (1998) *Do in English, Dutch and German: History and Present-Day Variation* (Uitgaven Stichting Neerlandistiek VU; 24), Münster: Nodus Publikationer.

Tolkien, J.R.R. (1963) 'English and Welsh', in *Angles and Britons* (O'Donnell Lectures), Cardiff: University of Wales Press, 1–41.

Traugott, E.C. (1972) *The History of English Syntax*, New York: Holt, Rinehart and Winston.

—— (1992) 'Syntax', in R.M. Hogg (ed.), 168–289.

Trépos, P. (1980) *Grammaire bretonne*, Rennes: Simon.

Tristram, H.L.C. (1997a) 'DO-periphrasis in contact?', in H. Ramisch and K. Wynne (eds) *Language in Time and Space: Studies in Honour of Wolfgang Viereck on the Occasion of his 60th Birthday*, Stuttgart: Franz Steiner Verlag, 401–417.

—— (ed.) (1997b) *The Celtic Englishes*, Heidelberg: Universitätsverlag C. Winter.

—— (1999a) *How Celtic Is Standard English?* ([Publications of the] Institut lingvisticeskich issledovanij, Rossijskoj akademii nauk), St. Petersburg: Nauka.

—— (1999b) ''The Celtic Englishes'—Zwei grammatische Beispiele zum Problem des Sprachkontaktes zwischen dem Englischen und den keltischen Sprachen', in S. Zimmer, R. Ködderitzsch and A. Wigger (hrsg.) *Akten des zweiten Deutschen Keltologen-Symposiums (Bonn 2.-4. April 1997)*, Tübingen: Max Niemayer Verlag, 254–276.

—— (ed.) (2000) *The Celtic Englishes II*, Heidelberg: Universitätsverlag C. Winter.

—— (2002a) 'Attrition of inflections in English and Welsh', in M. Filppula, J. Klemola and H. Pitkänen (eds), 111–149.

—— (2002b) 'The politics of language: Links between Modern Welsh and English', in K. Lenz and R. Möhlig (eds) *Of dyuersitie & chaunge of langage. Essays Presented to Manfred Görlach on the Occasion of his 65th Birthday*, Heidelberg: Universitätsverlag C. Winter, 257–275.

—— (ed.) (2003) *The Celtic Englishes III*, Heidelberg: Universitätsverlag C. Winter.

—— (ed.) (2006) *The Celtic Englishes IV*, Potsdam: Potsdam University Press.

Trudgill, P. (ed.) (1984) *Language in the British Isles*, Cambridge: Cambridge University Press.

—— (1986) *Dialects in Contact*, Oxford: Blackwell.

Tulloch, G. (1997) 'Lexis', in C. Jones (ed.), 278–432.

van der Auwera, J. and Genee, I. (2002) 'English *do*: on the convergence of languages and linguists', *English Language and Linguistics* 6.2: 283–307.

van der Horst, J.M. (1998) '*Doen* in Old and Early Middle Dutch: A comparative approach', in I. Tieken-Boon van Ostade *et al.* (eds), 53–64.

van der Wurff, W. (1995) 'Language contact and syntactic change: Some formal linguistic diagnostics', in J. Fisiak (ed.) *Linguistic Change under Contact Conditions*, (Trends in Linguistics, Studies and Monographs 81), Berlin: Mouton de Gruyter, 383–420.

van Gelderen, E. (2000) *A History of English Reflexive Pronouns: Person, Self, and Interpretability*, (Linguistics Today 39), Amsterdam and Philadelphia: John Benjamins.

van Hamel, A.G. (1912) 'On Anglo-Irish syntax', *Englische Studien*, 45: 272–292.

Vanneck, G. (1958) 'The colloquial preterite in Modern American English', *Word* 14, 237–242.

van Ryckeghem, B. (1997) 'The lexicon of Hiberno-English', in J.L. Kallen (ed.), 171–188.

Vennemann, T. (2000) 'English as a 'Celtic' language: Atlantic influences from above and from below', in H.L.C. Tristram (ed.), 399–406.

—— (2001) 'Atlantis Semitica: Structural contact features in Celtic and English', in L. Brinton (ed.) *Historical Linguistics 1999: Selected Papers from the Fourteenth International Conference on Historical Linguistics* (Current Issues in Linguistic Theory 215), Amsterdam and Philadelphia: John Benjamins, 351–369.

—— (2002a) 'On the rise of 'Celtic' syntax in Middle English', in P.J. Lucas and A.M. Lucas (eds) *Middle English from Tongue to Text: Selected Papers from the Third International Conference on Middle English: Language and Text, held at Dublin, Ireland, 1–4 July 1999* (Studies in English Medieval Language and Literature 4), Bern: Peter Lang, 203–234.

—————— (2002b) 'Semitic → Celtic → English: The transitivity of language contact', in M. Filppula, J. Klemola and H. Pitkänen (eds), 295–330.

Vezzosi, L. (2005a) 'The development of *himself* in Middle English: a 'Celtic' hypothesis', in N. Ritt and H. Schendl (eds) *Rethinking Middle English. Linguistic and Literary Approaches*, Frankfurt am Main/Berlin/Bern/Bruxelles/New York/Oxford/Wien: Peter Lang, 228–243.

—————— (2005b) 'Areality and grammaticalization: how to solve a puzzling case in the English grammar', *Archivio Glottologico Italiano*, Vol. XC, Fasc. II: 174–209.

Viereck, W. (ed.) (1985) *Focus on: England and Wales* (Varieties of English Around the World 4), Amsterdam and Philadelphia: John Benjamins.

—————— (2000) 'Celtic and English—an intricate relationship', in H.L.C. Tristram (ed.), 375–398.

Vincent, M.E. (1986) 'English interrogation, inversion and *do*-support', in J. Harris *et al.* (eds), 161–171.

Visser, F. Th. (1963–1973) *An Historical Syntax of the English Language*, 4 vols, Leiden: E.J. Brill.

Visser, G.J. (1955) 'Celtic influence in English', *Neophilologus*, 39: 276–293.

Wagner, H. (1958) 'Keltisches-Germanisches', in H.-E. Keller (ed.) *Etymologica: Walther von Wartburg zum siebzigsten Geburtstag 18. Mai 1958*, Tübingen: Max Niemayer, 835–841.

—————— (1959) *Das Verbum in den Sprachen der Britischen Inseln: ein Beitrag zur geographischen Typologie des Verbums*, Tübingen: Max Niemeyer.

Wakelin, M.F. (1975) *Language and History in Cornwall*, Leicester: Leicester University Press.

—————— (1977) *English Dialects: An Introduction*, Revised edition, London.

—————— (1983) 'The stability of English dialect boundaries', *English World-Wide*, IV.1: 1–15.

—————— (1984a) 'Rural dialects in England', in P. Trudgill (ed.), 70–93.

—————— (1984b) 'Cornish English', in P. Trudgill (ed.) 195–198.

—————— (1991) 'The Cornishness of Cornwall's English', in P.S. Ureland and G. Broderick (eds) *Language Contact in the British Isles*, Tübingen: Max Niemeyer Verlag, 199–225.

Wall, M. (1969) 'The decline of the Irish language', in B. Ó Cuív (ed.), 81–90.

Walters, J.R. (2003) 'A study of the prosody of a South East Wales "Valleys Accent"', in H.L.C. Tristram (ed.), 224–239.

Watkins, T.A. (1957) 'Yr arddodiad HG *(h)i, in* : CC. *y* (= yn), *yn*', *Bulletin of the Board of Celtic Studies*, 17: 137–158.

—————— (1960) 'CC. *y/yn* berfenwol', *Bulletin of the Board of Celtic Studies*, 18: 362–372.

—————— (1962) 'Ffurfiant a chystrawen y geirynnau adferfol/traethiadol mewn Cymraeg, Cernyweg a Llydaweg', *Bulletin of the Board of Celtic Studies*, 19: 295–315 (section on Breton by J.R.F. Piette, 304–305).

—————— (1991) 'The function of cleft and non-cleft constituent orders in Modern Welsh', in J. Fife and E. Poppe, 329–351.

—————— (1993) 'Welsh', in M.J. Ball (ed.), 289–348.

Weale, M.E., Weiss, D.A., Jager, R.F., Bradman, N. and Thomas, M.G. (2002) 'Y chromosome evidence for Anglo-Saxon mass migration', *Molecular Biology and Evolution*, 19.7: 1008–1021.

Wehr, B. (2001) 'Ein westlich-atlantischer Sprachbund: Irisch, Französisch, Portugiesisch', in H. Eichner, P.-A. Mumm, O. Panagl, and E. Winkler (eds) *Fremd und Eigen. Untersuchungen zu Grammatik und Wortschatz des Uralischen und Indogremanischen in memoriam Hartmut Katz*, Wien: Edition Praesens, 253–278.

Weinreich, U. (1953) *Languages in Contact: Findings and Problems*, Paris: Mouton de Gruyter.

Welch, M.G. (1985) 'Rural settlement patterns in the Early and Middle Anglo-Saxon periods', *Landscape History*, 7: 13–25.

White, D.L. (2002) 'Explaining the innovations of Middle English: what, where, and why', in M. Filppula, J. Klemola and H. Pitkänen (eds), 153–174.

Whitelock, D. (ed.) (1930) *Anglo-Saxon Wills*, Cambridge: Cambridge University Press.

Williams, C.H. (1990) 'The Anglicisation of Wales', in N. Coupland, 19–47.

Williams, D.T. (1935) 'Linguistic divides in South Wales; a historico-geographical study', *Archaeologia Cambrensis*, 90: 239–266.

——— (1936) 'Linguistic divides in North Wales; a study in historical geography', *Archaeologia Cambrensis*, 91: 194–209.

Williams, G.A. (1985) *When Was Wales? A History of the Welsh*, London: Penguin.

Williams, J. (1987) 'Non-native varieties of English: a special case of language acquisition', *English World-Wide*, 8(2): 161–199.

Williams, M. (2000) 'The pragmatics of predicate fronting in Welsh English', in H.L.C. Tristram (ed.), 210–230.

Winterbottom, M. (1978) *Gildas: The Ruin of Britain and other works*, London: Phillimore.

Withers, C.W.J. (1979) 'The language geography of Scottish Gaelic', *Scottish Literary Journal*, Supplement 9, 41–53.

——— (1984) *Gaelic in Scotland 1698–1981*, Edinburgh: John Donald Publishers.

Witty, J.R. (1927) 'Sheep and sheep-scoring', *Transactions of the Yorkshire Dialect Society*, XXVIII.4: 41–49.

Wolfram, W. and Christian, D. (1976) *Appalachian Speech*, Arlington, Virginia: Center for Applied Linguistics.

Wolfram, W. and Fasold, R.W. (1974) *The Study of Social Dialects in American English*, Englewood Cliffs, New Jersey: Prentice-Hall.

Wright, J. (ed.) (1896–1905) *English Dialect Dictionary (EDD)*, 6 vols. [Reprinted 1961, Oxford: Oxford University Press.]

——— (1905) *The English Dialect Grammar*, Oxford: Henry Frowde.

Name Index

Subject Index